Psychological Science

FOURTH EDITION

Michael S. Gazzaniga • Todd F. Heatherton •
Diane F. Halpern

D1605262

STUDY GUIDE

Psychological Science

FOURTH EDITION

Michael S. Gazzaniga • *Todd F. Heatherton* •
Diane F. Halpern

David K. Payne
WALLACE COMMUNITY COLLEGE

with contributions by
Brett L. Beck
BLOOMSBURG UNIVERSITY

Eileen Astor-Stetson
BLOOMSBURG UNIVERSITY

Jennifer Adrienne Johnson
BLOOMSBURG UNIVERSITY

 W • W • NORTON & COMPANY • NEW YORK • LONDON

W. W. Norton & Company has been independent since its founding in 1923, when William Warder Norton and Mary D. Herter Norton first published lectures delivered at the People's Institute, the adult education division of New York City's Cooper Union. The firm soon expanded its program beyond the Institute, publishing books by celebrated academics from America and abroad. By midcentury, the two major pillars of Norton's publishing program—trade books and college texts—were firmly established. In the 1950s, the Norton family transferred control of the company to its employees, and today—with a staff of four hundred and a comparable number of trade, college, and professional titles published each year—W. W. Norton & Company stands as the largest and oldest publishing house owned wholly by its employees.

Associate editors, ancillaries: Matthew A. Freeman and Callinda Taylor
Production manager: Sean Mintus
Developmental editor: Kurt Wildermuth
Composition by Westchester Book Group
Manufacturing by Sheridan

ISBN 978-0-393-91306-4

W. W. Norton & Company, Inc.
500 Fifth Avenue, New York, N.Y. 10110-0017

wwnorton.com

W. W. Norton & Company Ltd.
Castle House, 75/76 Wells Street, London W1T 3QT

1 2 3 4 5 6 7 8 9 0

CONTENTS

HOW TO USE THIS STUDY GUIDE

Dear Student:

Welcome to Psychological Science!

As I wrote this Study Guide, I revisited my experience taking an introductory psychology course. Although it's been many years, I still remember the sense of excitement I felt as I discovered explanations for my behavior and the behavior of other people in my life. I'm excited for you as you begin this journey, and I'm sure that, like most people, you will finish this course with information that will help you to understand yourself and others better as well as information that will improve the quality of your life.

HOW TO USE THIS STUDY GUIDE

What's the best way to study? This may have become a more important question for you since you've been in college. It has been an important question for psychologists for many years, and through research psychologists have discovered techniques that make it easier to learn and retain information.

This Study Guide is based on three assumptions about learning that are derived from psychological and educational research:

1. Learners who make repeated attempts at learning increase their knowledge.

2. Effective learners become specific about what they know and what they need to know.

3. Multiple assessments help learners master new information.

This guide will reinforce these three ideas. Let's visit them in greater detail.

Tying your shoe, parallel parking, and successfully playing your favorite video game all have something in common: they are all things you learned, but they are also things you probably did not successfully complete the first time you tried. As with these examples, learning most things takes more than one attempt. So the exercises in this Study Guide are built around the idea that repeated attempts at learning will increase your learning. How does this change how you approach this textbook (and maybe all of the rest of your courses)? Rather than reading through the textbook one time and *hoping* that you got all of the information, you will need to expose yourself to (read) the information in small chunks and review it several times.

Another key to learning is to be specific. Do you need to read the *entire* chapter over and over again? No; besides being boring, that method is ineffective and time-consuming. Using this Study Guide (and SmartWork, if your professor has set up an account for your class), you can become increasingly precise in your studying. As you study, continually ask yourself, "What do I already know and what do I need to know?"

So, how do you know what you do know and what you don't know? This Study Guide will offer you repeated opportunities to assess your knowledge, which will help you answer that question at each stage of your learning. You will, of course, not know much of the material at the beginning, but if you follow the sequence, check to see what you don't know, and go back to the text to check your knowledge, by the end of the sequence you will know much of the information.

SO, WHAT DO I DO?

Each chapter is divided into sections. We suggest that you read one section at a time, following this study sequence as directed in each chapter of this Study Guide:

1. Look at the introductory paragraph below each section heading in this Study Guide. This will help prepare you for what you're going to read by directing your attention to specific questions and topics.

2. Read the Guiding Questions before you read the chapter section. These questions cover the major points you will want to learn as a result of reading this section.

3. Read the section of the chapter. As you find the answers to the Guiding Questions you might want to underline them or attach a sticky note.

4. Go back to the Guiding Questions and see if, based upon your reading, you can answer the questions. Rather than looking at a question and saying to yourself, "Yes, I know the answer to that," try speaking aloud as if you were explaining the topic to a friend.

5. If you can't answer a question, go back to the chapter and find the answer. Then see if you can again "teach" the concept to someone else.

6. After you can answer all of the Guiding Questions, see if you can answer the multiple-choice questions about that section. Check to see which questions you missed and then go back to the chapter to review that material again.

7. For a final check on each section, see if you can answer the questions under the "Another Opportunity to Review" section without using your book. The questions you can't answer can be listed under the "What do I Need to Know?" section as information you'll want to continue to review even as you go on to the next section.

8. Repeat this sequence for each section of the chapter. At the end of the Study Guide chapter, you will find short answer questions that you can use as part of your preparation for your class exam and as a way to continue to check on your learning. You'll also find a summary of the main points in the chapter that you will probably find helpful in reviewing for your class exams.

If you practice these techniques, you will learn information more rapidly and retain it more easily. Then you'll have more time for other activities.

WHAT ARE THE "TRY IT" BOXES?

Psychology is not just about learning facts. It is about understanding how people function intellectually, emotionally, and academically, among other areas. Psychologists know that if people perform their best in each of these areas, it is easier to learn. So, this Study Guide will not only help improve your study skills but also expose you to ways in which psychology has provided practical information designed to better people's lives. Throughout the chapters of the Study Guide you'll see a number of "Try It" boxes, which contain skills to help you improve your sense of well-being and lower your level of stress. We encourage you to try these and see if they work for you. If they do, they're yours for life.

Sincerely,
David K. Payne

STUDY GUIDE

Psychological Science

FOURTH EDITION

Michael S. Gazzaniga • *Todd F. Heatherton* •
Diane F. Halpern

CHAPTER 1 | The Science of Psychology

CHAPTER OVERVIEW

Take a trip to your favorite bookstore, and you'll find that the psychology or self-help section is usually one of the largest nonfiction sections in the store. Figuring out why we think and act the way we do and how we can change the way we think or act is of interest to most people. These are the questions that psychology asks and answers. Through the development of the field, several different theoretical approaches to psychology have emerged to answer important questions about how human thought, emotion, and behavior develop.

▉▉ Why Study Psychology?

Psychological science has developed over time to help in answering important questions about why humans act in the way they do. Psychological science is practical and explores different aspects of human functioning. Although there are a variety of techniques that psychologists use in their investigation, one of their primary tools is critical thinking, which involves looking at information in an objective manner.

At the beginning of each section in the Study Guide, there will be guiding questions. Before you read the chapter in your textbook, read through these questions and maybe even attempt to answer them based on either what you've already read or what you think the answer should be. Then as you study the chapter, you can use them to help guide your reading.

1.1 Guiding Questions

To guide your reading of the text, review the following questions. Then, as you read the chapter, look for the answers to these questions. You may want to note in your textbook where you find these answers.

1. What are the goals of psychological science?
2. What different aspects of psychological functioning interest psychologists?
3. How is psychology is relevant to real-life situations?
4. What is critical thinking, and why do psychologists think this is important?

NOW READ Section 1.1 "Why Study Psychology?" keeping these questions in mind.

REVIEW: Now that you've read this section, go back to the 1.1 Guiding Questions and see if you can answer them based on what you've read. This is a check on your reading. If you can't answer a question, you need to go back to the text to reread that section.

VISUAL SUMMARY: Below is a summary of the major concepts in this section. To check your comprehension of the chapter, read the summary and ask yourself if you understand the concepts. If the concepts seem unfamiliar to you, you may want to go back to the book and reread those sections. This text is taken from the Visual Summaries on StudySpace at wwnorton.com/studyspace.

    I. Psychology Is about *You* and about *Us*
       A. Psychology is:
          i. one of the most popular majors at most universities.
          ii. easy to see as personally relevant.
    II. Psychologists Explain Human Behaviors in Real-Life Contexts
       A. Psychological science is the study of:

i. the mind (mental activity = perceptions, thoughts, memories, and feelings).

ii. the brain (mental activity results from biological processes within the brain).

iii. behavior (observable actions).

III. Psychological Knowledge Is Used in Many Professions
   A. Careers for people with graduate degrees in psychology are expected to grow by 12 percent in the next decade.
   B. An undergraduate degree in psychology provides knowledge useful in many occupations.

IV. Psychological Science Teaches Critical Thinking
   A. Psychologists critically evaluate information to reach reasonable conclusions.
   B. Critical thinking skills are applicable to other courses and everyday life.

REINFORCE: Are you ready to check your knowledge of this section? Answer the following multiple-choice questions with your textbook closed.

1. Janice is interested in studying mental activity. Therefore, the aspect of psychological science that she is most clearly focusing on is the:
   a. mind
   b. brain
   c. behavior
   d. nonconscious

2. Psychological science is based on critical thinking. This means that psychological scientists:
   a. evaluate information before they accept it
   b. do not believe anything that they did not discover themselves
   c. do not have any kind of faith
   d. accept without question any information that is given to them by an authority

3. Dr. Clark just read a study indicating that a new surgical technique might significantly help some kinds of depression. Dr. Clark thinks this is very interesting, but she would like to see more evidence that the technique works. Dr. Clark's attitude exemplifies:
   a. the Mozart effect
   b. amiable skepticism
   c. structuralist support
   d. functionalism

4. Who of the following would be least likely to use psychological science in his or her professional activities?
   a. a physician treating an elderly patient who is showing early symptoms of dementia
   b. a teacher working with children with autism

c. a lawyer who is selecting individuals to serve on a jury
   d. an accountant who is monitoring the business expenses of his clients

5. Which of the following is an example of using scientific reasoning?
   a. believing that sugar causes ADHD because you feel hyper after eating a candy bar
   b. concluding that listening to Mozart improves cognition in children after reading a popular magazine article
   c. using a personal example to show how a psychological principle must be wrong
   d. conducting research to investigate the effectiveness of left brain/right brain games in improving memory

6. Which of the following best describes psychological science?
   a. Psychological science is really just common sense.
   b. Psychological science is applying common sense.
   c. Psychological science principles are highly applicable to everyday life.
   d. Psychological principles are too scientific to apply to everyday life.

7. Tom is interested in the impact of stress on the production of chemicals in the brain. Which aspect of psychological science does his interest reflect?
   a. mind
   b. brain
   c. behavior
   d. nonconscious

WHAT DID YOU MISS? Check your answers against the Answer Key at the end of this chapter of the Study Guide. The Answer Key also lists the page(s) in your text where each question is explained. If you missed any questions, go to the pages indicated in the Answer Key, reread those sections, go back to the questions, and see if you can answer them correctly this time.

ANOTHER OPPORTUNITY TO REVIEW: Answer these questions without your textbook. As a rule of thumb, if you can write only a few words about these questions, you probably need to go back and review.

1. What are the goals of psychological science? _____

_____

_____

2. What different aspects of psychological functioning interest psychologists? _____

_____

_____

3. How is psychology relevant to real-life situations? _____

_____

_____

4. What is critical thinking, and why do psychologists think this is important? _____

_____

_____

WHAT DO I NEED TO KNOW? Based on what you've discovered above, what are the areas where you need to focus your studying? Which objectives do you need to spend more time mastering? Write this information down in your own words.

1. _____
2. _____
3. _____
4. _____
5. _____
6. _____

1.2 What Are the Scientific Foundations of Psychology?

In this section, you will read a brief history of psychology and psychological science. Throughout the history of psychology, questions about the importance of environment, the importance of genetics, and whether the mind and body are separate have been answered in different ways by the various schools of psychological thought. As you read, see which school of thought best fits your view of human psychology.

1.2 Guiding Questions

To guide your reading of the text, review the following questions. Then, as you read the chapter, look for the answers to these questions. You may want to note in your textbook where you find these answers.

1. How has psychology developed from 1879 until the present?

2. What is the nature/nurture debate in psychology?

3. What is the mind/body problem in psychology?

4. What major schools of thought have characterized the history of psychology?

TRY IT

Three Blessings

Psychology has continued to evolve as a field. One of the newest areas of interest in psychology is "positive psychology," which focuses on how people flourish and become the best they can be. Through the use of research, this field has developed a number of techniques designed to enhance well-being. The following technique is called "Three Blessings."

Each night before you go to bed, take a moment to reflect back on the day and think of three events that happened and turned out well for you. Write them down and then also write down WHY each event happened.

For instance:

My friend brought me a cup of coffee. This happened because she values my friendship.

According to research in positive psychology, people find it easier to explain why bad events happen than to explain why good events happen. Maybe, however, if we focus on WHY good events happen we can make them happen more frequently. Researchers in positive psychology have also found that this technique helps to counteract depression and anxiety. Why not start off the semester with this exercise and see if it helps your sense of well-being through the semester?

NOW READ Section 1.2 "What Are the Scientific Foundations of Psychology?" keeping these questions in mind.

REVIEW: Now that you've read this section, go back to the 1.2 Guiding Questions and see if you can answer them based on what you've read. This is a check on your reading. If you can't answer a question, you need to go back to the text to reread that section.

VISUAL SUMMARY: Below is a summary of the major concepts in this section. To check your comprehension of the chapter, read the summary and ask yourself if you understand the concepts. If the concepts seem unfamiliar to you, you may want to go back to the book and reread those sections. This text is taken from the Visual Summaries on StudySpace at wwnorton.com/studyspace.

    V. What Are the Scientific Foundations of Psychology?
      A. Psychology:
        i. originated in philosophical ideas found in Eastern and Western cultures.
        ii. developed as a discipline in nineteenth-century Europe.
    VI. The Nature/Nurture Debate Has a Long History
      A. Nature/nurture debate:
        i. began with ancient Greek philosophers.

ii. consists of this question: Are psychological characteristics innate (nature) or acquired through experience (nurture)?

VII. The Mind/Body Problem Also Has Ancient Roots
A. The mind/body problem:
i. consists of this question: Are mind and body separate, or is the mind the physical brain's subjective experience?
ii. for Descartes, this question is answered by dualism (mind and body are separate but intertwined).

VIII. Experimental Psychology Began with Introspection
A. Wilhelm Wundt established the first psychology laboratory (in Germany, in 1879).
B. Introspection is the systematic examination of subjective mental experiences.

IX. Introspection and Other Methods Led to Structuralism
A. Structuralism is based on the concept that conscious experience can be broken down into basic components.

X. Functionalism Addressed the Purpose of Behavior
A. Stream of consciousness is each person's continuous series of ever-changing thoughts.
B. Functionalism is concerned with how the brain or mind helps humans function or adapt.
C. Evolutionary theory (natural selection, adaptive value of mental activity and behavior) was a major influence on functionalism.
D. Adaptation is the evolutionary process through which organisms become better able to live in their environment.

XI. Gestalt Psychology Emphasized Patterns and Context in Learning
A. Gestalt psychology:
i. arose in opposition to structuralism.
ii. says the whole of personal experience is more than the sum of perceptions (constituent elements).
iii. influenced many areas of psychology, including vision and personality.

XII. Women Have Helped Shape the Field
A. Despite sexism and other barriers, women have contributed substantially to all areas of psychology.

XIII. Freud Emphasized the Power of the Unconscious
A. Sigmund Freud:
i. was a neurologist and found that patients had physical symptoms caused by psychological factors.

ii. proposed that much of human behavior is determined by unconscious mental processes.
iii. developed psychoanalysis, an early psychotherapy.

XIV. Behaviorism Studied Environmental Forces
A. Behaviorism:
i. emphasizes environmental forces in producing behavior.
ii. was pioneered by John B. Watson and further developed by B. F. Skinner.
iii. focuses on changing and modifying behaviors.

XV. Cognitive Approaches Emphasized Mental Activity
A. Cognitive psychology focuses on how thoughts influence behavior.
B. Cognitive neuroscience studies neural mechanisms underlying thought, learning, and memory.

XVI. Social Psychology Studies How Situations Shape Behavior
A. Social psychology focuses on situations and how interactions shape people.

XVII. Science Informs Psychological Therapy
A. Treatment of psychological disorders is influenced by advances in psychological theory and science.
B. Disorders are now seen as the result of both nature and nurture.

REINFORCE: Are you ready to check your knowledge of this section? Answer the following multiple-choice questions with your textbook closed.

1. Sy believes that if people are bad it is because they were born that way. June disagrees: She feels that poor treatment by others makes people turn out bad. Their disagreement reflects:
a. James's ideas on stream of consciousness
b. different levels of extroversion
c. differences in their abilities to introspect
d. the nature/nurture debate

2. Renee believes that although the mind and body are linked, they have separate distinct functions. Her view reflects:
a. monism
b. dualism
c. the nature/nurture debate
d. the limitations of adaptation

3. The nature in the nature/nurture debate refers to:
a. biological factors affecting the brain, mind, and behavior

b. environmental factors affecting the brain, mind, and behavior

c. the interaction between biological or environmental factors that affect the brain/mind and behavior

d. behaviors learned in the natural environment but not learned in a formal setting

4. Stuart believes that each person has a soul that is distinct from the person's body. He wonders, however, about the relationship between soul and body. Stuart's interests reflect:
   a. the neuroscience-cognition debate
   b. the mind/body problem
   c. the application of Darwin's theory to psychology
   d. the basic question of behaviorism

5. Which researcher is credited with opening the first psychological laboratory?
   a. Wundt
   b. James
   c. Freud
   d. Cattel

6. If you believe that the mind is not made of discrete elements but rather is flowing, changing, and continuous, your beliefs are most similar to those of:
   a. Wundt
   b. Titchner
   c. James
   d. Watson

7. For most of human history, Western scholars believed that the mind and body were separate and that humans were unique because:
   a. they possessed a soul
   b. they controlled other animals
   c. they were mortal
   d. the mind and body interacted for a divine purpose

8. Of the following, who is most closely associated with the school of functionalism?
   a. Sigmund Freud
   b. B. F. Skinner
   c. Wilhelm Wundt
   d. William James

9. If you were to asked to report on the content of your thoughts while looking at an apple, the technique used would be:
   a. inspection
   b. conscription
   c. abstraction
   d. introspection

10. Dualism is the idea that:
    a. the mind and the brain are separate but intertwined
    b. the mind and the brain are the same entity

c. there is no brain, just the mind
d. there is no mind, just the brain

11. The approach to psychology that emphasizes the adaptive value of the mind is:
    a. social psychology
    b. structuralism
    c. introspection
    d. functionalism

12. The _____ perspective views the whole of personal experience as different from the sum of its parts.
    a. Gestalt
    b. psychoanalytic
    c. structuralist
    d. introspectionist

13. Annie's therapist believes that Annie's problems are caused by unconscious conflicts. To uncover these problems, the therapist analyzes Annie's dreams. The approach Annie's therapist is taking is:
    a. psychoanalysis
    b. structuralism
    c. behaviorism
    d. cognitivism

14. Dr. Cohen believes that the study of psychology should be limited to stimuli that can be measured and responses that can be observed. This approach is:
    a. psychoanalysis
    b. structuralism
    c. behaviorism
    d. cognitivism

15. The theories of Sigmund Freud and his followers:
    a. are based on the idea that much of human behavior is determined by mental processes operating below the level of conscious awareness
    b. emphasize the functions served by the mind
    c. emphasize the concept that the whole is different than the sum of its parts
    d. state that behavior can be altered by the application of reinforcement and punishment

16. Dr. Johnson studies the ways in which specific types of memory are tied to activity in specific parts of the brain. Dr. Johnson's research exemplifies:
    a. cognitive neuroscience
    b. structuralism
    c. Gestalt analysis
    d. behaviorism

17. A researcher presented an individual with a musical tone. The individual was asked to describe the tone in detail: was it pleasant, was it clear, how long was it, and so on. The technique the researcher used exemplified:
    a. genomics
    b. introspection

  c. brain imaging
  d. psychoanalysis

18. The cognitive revolution focused research in psychology on things such as:
   a. how consequences influence rats' behaviors
   b. thinking and decision making
   c. neuroanatomical structures
   d. the building blocks of thought

WHAT DID YOU MISS? Check your answers against the Answer Key at the end of this chapter of the Study Guide. The Answer Key also lists the page(s) in your text where each question is explained. If you missed any questions, go to the pages indicated in the Answer Key, reread those sections, go back to the questions, and see if you can answer them correctly this time.

ANOTHER OPPORTUNITY TO REVIEW: Answer these questions without your textbook. As a rule of thumb, if you can write only a few words about these questions, you probably need to go back and review.

1. How has psychology developed from 1879 until the present? _____

   _____

   _____

2. What is the nature/nurture debate in psychology? _____

   _____

3. What is the mind/body problem in psychology? _____

   _____

4. What major schools of thought have characterized the history of psychology?

   _____

   _____

   _____

   _____

   _____

WHAT DO I NEED TO KNOW? Based on what you've discovered above, what are the areas where you need to focus your studying? Which objectives do you need to spend more time mastering? Write this information down in your own words.

1. _____

2. _____

3. _____

4. _____

5. _____

6. _____

1.3 What Are the Latest Developments in Psychology?

As psychology has developed, information from other scientific disciplines has added to the understanding of human functioning. More-current knowledge of biology and genetics has enhanced the knowledge of the mechanisms underlying human behavior. Evolutionary theory has helped to demonstrate how human behavior is helpful in survival and how behaviors continue to evolve. Additionally, the awareness that different cultures have different attitudes about human functioning has broadened the understanding of the differences among people. Finally, psychology has evolved into a field with a broad scope of research and practical interests.

1.3 Guiding Questions

To guide your reading of the text, review the following questions. Then, as you read the chapter, look for the answers to these questions. You may want to note in your textbook where you find these answers.

1. How have recent findings in biology influenced psychological science?

2. How have recent findings in genetics influenced psychological science?

3. How have recent findings in evolutionary theory influenced psychological science?

4. How have recent findings in culture influenced psychological science?

5. What are the subfields of psychology?

NOW READ Section 1.3 "What Are the Latest Developments in Psychology" keeping these questions in mind.

REVIEW: Now that you've read this section, go back to the 1.3 Guiding Questions and see if you can answer them based on what you've read. This is a check on your reading. If you can't answer a question, you need to go back to the text to reread that section.

VISUAL SUMMARY: Below is a summary of the major concepts in this section. To check your comprehension of the chapter, read the summary and ask yourself if you understand the concepts. If the concepts seem unfamiliar to you, you may want to go back to the book and reread those sections. This text is taken from the Visual Summaries on StudySpace at wwnorton.com/studyspace.

XVIII. Biology Is Increasingly Important
    A. Understanding of human behavior has been influenced by research on:
        i. brain chemistry, brain functioning, and neural functioning.
        ii. genetics.

XIX. Evolution Is Increasingly Important
    A. Evolutionary theory determines whether behaviors and physical mechanisms are adaptive.
    B. Adaptive behavior makes sense in terms of the challenges faced by our early ancestors.

XX. Culture Provides Adaptive Solutions
    A. Culture:
        i. evolves more rapidly than genetics.
        ii. plays a role in how we view and reason about the world.
    B. Cultural neuroscience studies how cultural variables affect the brain, the mind, genes, and behavior.

XXI. Psychological Science Now Crosses Levels of Analysis
    A. Biological level: how the physical body (brain) contributes to mind and behavior.
    B. Individual level: how differences in personality and in mental processes affect perception.
    C. Social level: how group contexts affect both interactions and people's influences on each other.
    D. Cultural level: how people's thoughts, feelings, and actions differ across cultures.
    E. Psychologists:
        i. focus on predicting behavior or understanding mental life.
        ii. may take a neuroscientific/biological approach.
        iii. may take a cognitive approach.
        iv. may take an experimental approach.
        v. may take a developmental approach (people's changes across the life span).
        vi. may study personality (people's enduring characteristics).
        vii. may take a social approach (how people are affected by others).
        viii. may take a cultural approach (how people are influenced by societal and cultural rules).
        ix. may take a clinical approach (causes and treatment of psychological disorders).
        x. may offer counseling about everyday life concerns.
        xi. may work in schools (studying academic progress, designing curricula and tests).
        xii. may specialize in industrial and organizational psychology (job placement, workplace training and morale).

REINFORCE: Are you ready to check your knowledge of this section? Answer the following multiple-choice questions with your textbook closed.

1. Which statement best summarizes the role of culture in shaping behaviors?
    a. Culture has a minor role that is far secondary to biology.
    b. Culture plays a foundational role in shaping how people view and reason about the world.
    c. Cultural experiences allow us to break down complex ideas.
    d. Culture affects only social behaviors and not the way we think.

2. Which of the following is NOT considered one of the three developments in the biological revolution that helped guide psychological science?
    a. developments in the understanding of brain chemistry
    b. the Human Genome Project
    c. evolutionary evidence that proves that the mind developed from the brain
    d. brain scan methods that allow scientists to watch a working brain

3. The Human Genome Project refers to:
    a. the project attempting to map the basic human genetic code
    b. the project attempting to alter the basic human genetic code
    c. the project attempting to alter behavior using humanistic approaches
    d. the project investigating the role of the environment in behavior

4. Which of the following is NOT an example of questions scientists might ask regarding evolutionary adaptations in humans?
    a. Why do people like sweets and food high in fat?
    b. Why do young children develop a fear of heights, as shown in visual cliff studies?
    c. How has walking upright increased human survival?
    d. Can you learn to adapt your note-taking style from lecture to small group discussion classes?

5. According to research conducted by Richard Nisbett, Eastern cultures tend to be _____ in their thinking.
    a. individualistic
    b. holistic

c. idiosyncratic
d. analytic

6. According to research conducted by Richard Nisbett, Western cultures tend to be _____ in their thinking.
   a. analytic
   b. holistic
   c. idiosyncratic
   d. collectivist

7. What is the best definition of the interdisciplinary approach to psychological science?
   a. working on multiple questions in the same scientific area
   b. working on the same question across scientific fields
   c. working on the same questions at different points in time
   d. working on a question by applying disciplined guidelines to the course of the inquiry

8. Which of the following would be an example of the biological level of analysis?
   a. examining how the death of a spouse results in changes in serotonin in the brain
   b. examining whether a person's personality is enduring or changing across the life span
   c. examining how being in a group changes whether a person will engage in illegal behavior
   d. examining how different cultures define mental illness

9. Who of the following is studying psychological science from a cultural level? The researcher who:
   a. studies how memory influences mathematical problem solving
   b. studies differences in dopamine levels in individuals suffering from depression and individuals not suffering from depression
   c. observes the behaviors of two colonies of rats during mating
   d. observes how American parents teach their children to behave in restaurants

10. How are clinical and counseling psychologists different?
    a. Clinical psychologists focus on treating brain problems, whereas counseling psychologists focus on social problems.
    b. Counseling psychologists focus on helping people go through difficult situations, whereas clinical psychologists help people who have mental disorders.
    c. Clinical psychologists have an M.D., whereas counseling psychologists have a Ph.D.
    d. Counseling psychologists cannot prescribe medication, whereas clinical psychologists can prescribe medication.

11. One outgrowth of humans living together in complex groups is the development of:
    a. anterior socialization
    b. monism
    c. culture
    d. Gestaltism

WHAT DID YOU MISS? Check your answers against the Answer Key at the end of this chapter of the Study Guide. The Answer Key also lists the page(s) in your text where each question is explained. If you missed any questions, go to the pages indicated in the Answer Key, reread those sections, go back to the questions, and see if you can answer them correctly this time.

ANOTHER OPPORTUNITY TO REVIEW: Answer these questions without your textbook. As a rule of thumb, if you can write only a few words about these questions, you probably need to go back and review.

1. How have recent findings in biology influenced psychological science? _____

2. How have recent findings in genetics influenced psychological science? _____

3. How have recent findings in evolutionary theory influenced psychological science? _____

4. How have recent findings in culture influenced psychological science? _____

5. What are the subfields of psychology? _____

WHAT DO I NEED TO KNOW? Based on what you've discovered above, what are the areas where you need to focus your studying? Which objectives do you need to spend more time mastering? Write this information down in your own words.

1. _____

2. _____

3. _____

4. _____

5. _____

6. _____

TRY IT

What Matters to Me

It may not surprise you to know that if information is personally relevant to you, if it means something to you, you are more likely to remember it. Psychologists have found that people find it easier to remember information if they have given it personal significance. This effect can occur in a variety of ways. If you read information that reminds you of something or somebody familiar to you, it is often easier to remember. Sometimes, if you simply ask yourself how you feel about a particular topic—if you agree, disagree, like it, or dislike it—you may find it easier to remember. You will find a lot of information in this textbook that has the potential to enhance the quality of your life. In each chapter of this Study Guide, there is a place for you to note the facts in the book that are personally meaningful to you. You can also use this technique as a study tool. When you are studying, ask yourself, "How do I feel about this?" You may find it easier to remember the information later.

WHAT MATTERS TO ME: What facts in this chapter are personally relevant to you?

_____

_____

_____

_____

CHAPTER SUMMARY

1.1 Why Study Psychology?

- *Psychology Is about You and about Us:* Psychology can help us better understand ourselves and others, and it can help us improve the quality of our lives. The field has broad applications to all areas of life.
- *Psychologists Explain Human Behaviors in Real-Life Contexts:* Psychological science is the study of the mind, the brain, and behavior. Although psychological science explains behavior in real-life contexts, the results of psychological research are often surprising and run counter to common beliefs.
- *Psychological Knowledge Is Used in Many Professions:* Because psychology focuses on human behavior, it is of interest to many students and professionals and is used in virtually every profession.
- *Psychological Science Teaches Critical Thinking:* The use of critical thinking skills improves how we think. Skepticism, an important element of science, requires a careful examination of how well evidence supports a conclusion. Using critical thinking skills and understanding the methods of psychological science are important for evaluating research reported in the popular media.

1.2 What Are the Scientific Foundations of Psychology?

- *The Nature/Nurture Debate Has a Long History:* Nature and nurture depend on each other. Their influences cannot be separated.
- *The Mind/Body Problem Also Has Ancient Roots:* Older dualist notions about the separation of the brain and mind have been replaced with the idea that the (physical) brain enables the mind. Brain and mind cannot be separated.
- *Experimental Psychology Began with Introspection:* Psychology's intellectual history dates back thousands of years. As a formal discipline, psychology began in 1879, in Wilhelm Wundt's laboratory in Germany. Using the technique of introspection, scientists attempted to understand conscious experience.
- *Introspection and Other Methods Led to Structuralism:* Structuralists used introspection to identify the basic underlying components of conscious experience. Structuralists attempted to understand conscious experience by reducing it to its structural elements.
- *Functionalism Addressed the Purpose of Behavior:* According to functionalists, the mind is best understood by examining its functions and purpose, not its structure.
- *Gestalt Psychology Emphasized Patterns and Context in Learning:* Gestalt psychologists asserted that the whole experience (the gestalt) is greater than the sum of its parts. As a result, they emphasized the subjective experience of perception.
- *Women Have Helped Shape the Field:* Women's early contributions to psychological science have been underacknowledged. Through the first half of the twentieth century, women in psychology struggled against sexism and other barriers to career success. Since then, women's participation in psychology has continued to increase and has affected the content of psychology.
- *Freud Emphasized the Power of the Unconscious:* Freud advanced the idea that unconscious processes are not readily available to our awareness but nevertheless

influence our behavior. This understanding had an enormous impact on psychology.

- *Behaviorism Studied Environmental Forces:* Discoveries that behavior is changed by its consequences caused behaviorism to dominate psychology until the 1960s.
- *Cognitive Approaches Emphasized Mental Activity:* The cognitive revolution and the computer analogy of the brain led to information processing theories. Cognitive neuroscience, which emerged in the 1980s, is concerned with the neural mechanisms that underlie thought, learning, and memory.
- *Social Psychology Studies How Situations Shape Behavior:* Work in social psychology has highlighted how situations and other people are powerful forces in shaping behavior.
- *Science Informs Psychological Therapy:* Psychological disorders are influenced by both nature (biological factors) and nurture (environmental factors). Scientific research has taught psychologists that no universal treatment exists for psychological disorders. Instead, different treatments are effective for different disorders.

1.3 What Are the Latest Developments in Psychology?

- *Biology Is Increasingly Important:* Tremendous advances in neuroscience have revealed the working brain. Mapping of the human genome has furthered the role of genetics in analyzing both behavior and disease. These advances are changing how we think about psychology.
- *Evolution Is Increasingly Important:* Evolution of the brain has helped solve survival and reproductive problems and helped us adapt to our environments. Many modern behaviors reflect adaptations to environmental pressures faced by our ancestors.
- *Culture Provides Adaptive Solutions:* Cultural norms specify how people should behave in different contexts. They reflect solutions to adaptive problems that have been worked out by a group of individuals, and they are transmitted through learning.
- *Psychological Science Now Crosses Levels of Analysis:* Psychologists examine behavior from various analytical levels: biological (brain systems, neurochemistry, genetics), individual (personality, perception, cognition), social (interpersonal behavior), and cultural (within a single culture, across several cultures). Psychology is characterized by numerous subfields. Within each subfield, psychologists may focus on one or more levels of analysis.

PUTTING IT ALL TOGETHER

Answer these questions to check your knowledge of the material in this chapter.

1. How might you use psychological science in your life?

2. Jon is very afraid of spiders. How might each of the following explain why he is afraid: evolutionary theory, Freudian theory, behaviorism?

3. Psychologists study behavior across different levels of analysis. Think of your favorite foods. Using each level of analysis presented in the textbook, describe why you eat that food.

ANSWER KEY FOR REINFORCE QUESTIONS

Section 1.1

1. a   p. 2
2. a   p. 4
3. b   p. 4
4. d   p. 3
5. d   p. 5
6. c   p. 2
7. b   p. 2

Section 1.2

1. d   p. 7
2. b   p. 8
3. a   p. 7
4. b   p. 7
5. a   p. 9
6. c   p. 10
7. a   p. 7
8. d   p. 9
9. d   p. 9
10. a   p. 8
11. d   p. 10
12. a   p. 11
13. a   p. 14
14. c   p. 14
15. a   p. 14
16. a   p. 16
17. b   p. 9
18. b   p. 15

Section 1.3

1. b   p. 20
2. c   pp. 18–19
3. a   p. 19
4. d   p. 20

5. b   p. 20
6. a   p. 20
7. b   p. 23
8. a   p. 22
9. d   pp. 21–22
10. b   p. 24
11. c   p. 20

HINTS FOR PUTTING IT ALL TOGETHER QUESTIONS

1. There are many ways to approach this question. You might consider what career you wish to pursue. In what ways will this career involve working with other people? In what ways will it involve critical thinking? Another way to approach this question is in terms of personal relationships. How may psychological science give you insight into dealing with friends or loved ones? You may also wish to look at the Table of Contents. Which chapters might be most relevant for your life now or for your future?

2. When discussing evolutionary theory, consider why a fear of spiders might be adaptive. How might the fear help one survive?

   When considering Freudian theory, address the unconscious. What hidden fears might the spider symbolically represent?

   When addressing behaviorism, discuss learning. What might have happened to Jon to cause him to learn to be afraid of spiders?

3. For the biological perspective, you might discuss why eating that food is adaptive.

   For the individual level, you might discuss why you like that food and other people do not.

   For the social level, discuss how others influence what you eat and enjoy.

   For the cultural level, consider how the culture or subculture you live in influences the foods you are exposed to and what you find acceptable to eat.

KEY TERMS EXERCISES

First, fill in your own definition and example for each term. Then check each term against the textbook's definition. These exercises can also be cut out and used as flash cards.

adaptations

Your Definition:
Your Example:
Textbook Definition:

critical thinking

Your Definition:
Your Example:
Textbook Definition:

behaviorism

Your Definition:
Your Example:
Textbook Definition:

culture

Your Definition:
Your Example:
Textbook Definition:

cognitive neuroscience

Your Definition:
Your Example:
Textbook Definition:

evolutionary theory

Your Definition:
Your Example:
Textbook Definition:

cognitive psychology

Your Definition:
Your Example:
Textbook Definition:

functionalism

Your Definition:
Your Example:
Textbook Definition:

Gestalt theory

Your Definition:
Your Example:
Textbook Definition:

introspection

Your Definition:
Your Example:
Textbook Definition:

mind/body problem

Your Definition:
Your Example:
Textbook Definition:

natural selection

Your Definition:
Your Example:
Textbook Definition:

nature/nurture debate

Your Definition:
Your Example:
Textbook Definition:

psychoanalysis

Your Definition:
Your Example:
Textbook Definition:

psychological science

Your Definition:
Your Example:
Textbook Definition:

social psychology

Your Definition:
Your Example:
Textbook Definition:

stream of consciousness

Your Definition:
Your Example:
Textbook Definition:

unconscious

Your Definition:
Your Example:
Textbook Definition:

structuralism

Your Definition:
Your Example:
Textbook Definition:

CHAPTER 2 | Research Methodology

CHAPTER OVERVIEW

Maybe you've read a headline that started with "Research shows . . ." or heard a news story introduced with "Scientists report . . . ," but maybe you didn't really understand what was behind those phrases. In this chapter you're going to get a crash course in the process that all scientists, including psychologists, use in making statements about phenomena in nature. In addition to helping you to be a better consumer of information, these methods may guide you toward making better decisions.

2.1 What Is Scientific Inquiry?

In reaching conclusions about natural phenomena, scientists use a process called the scientific method. This process encompasses a series of procedures and methods that help scientists make accurate statements about the area they are studying. The scientific method also helps scientists to develop theories and then to prove or disprove those theories.

At the beginning of each section in the Study Guide, there will be guiding questions. Before you read the chapter in your textbook, read through these questions and maybe even attempt to answer them based on either what you've already read or what you think the answer should be. Then as you study the chapter, you can use them to help guide your reading.

2.1 Guiding Questions

To guide your reading of the text, review the following questions. Then, as you read the chapter, look for the answers to these questions. You may want to note in your textbook where you find these answers.

1. Describe the scientific method.

2. Differentiate between theories, hypotheses, and research.

NOW READ Section 2.1 "What Is Scientific Inquiry?" keeping these questions in mind.

REVIEW: Now that you've read this section, go back to the 2.1 Guiding Questions and see if you can answer them based on what you've read. This is a check on your reading. If you can't answer a question, you need to go back to the text to reread that section.

VISUAL SUMMARY: Below is a summary of the major concepts in this section. To check your comprehension of the chapter, read the summary and ask yourself if you understand the concepts. If the concepts seem unfamiliar to you, you may want to go back to the book and reread those sections. This text is taken from the Visual Summaries on StudySpace at wwnorton.com/studyspace.

I. Scientific Inquiry
   A. Scientific inquiry is:
      i. a systematic method of collecting, analyzing, and interpreting data.
      ii. used to describe, predict, control, and explain why particular behaviors happen.

II. The Scientific Method Depends on Theories, Hypotheses, and Research
   A. A theory:
      i. asks questions about how an observable thing works.
      ii. consists of interconnected ideas.
   B. A hypothesis:
      i. is an attempt to answer a theory's questions.

ii. consists of a testable prediction that should be observed if the theory is correct.

C. Research is the systematic collection of data to prove or disprove hypothesis.

D. Replication is repeating an experiment to confirm results.

III. Unexpected Findings Can Be Valuable
A. Scientific research can proceed as experimenters expect, but serendipitous results can be useful.

REINFORCE: Are you ready to check your knowledge of this section? Answer the following multiple-choice questions with your textbook closed.

1. When researchers collect enough data to develop an explanation of why people behave as they do, the researchers are creating a(n):
   a. theory
   b. experiment
   c. hypothesis
   d. generalization

2. Jean Piaget observed children to see how they solved problems. Over the course of many studies, he was able to spot general patterns of behavior. This process led him to connect different concepts and behaviors within a single:
   a. theory
   b. hypothesis
   c. experiment
   d. sample

3. A specific prediction of behavior that is tested in an experiment is called a:
   a. theory
   b. hypothesis
   c. sample
   d. naturalistic observation

4. A researcher believes that presenting possible suspects in a lineup one at a time instead of in a group would lead to more accurate identification of the true suspect. This belief represents:
   a. a hypothesis
   b. an independent variable
   c. response performance
   d. a theory

5. Research that is done to test a theory:
   a. typically involves naturalistic observation
   b. has to rely on self-report methods
   c. involves systematic collection of data
   d. relies on positive correlations rather than negative correlations

6. When researchers document that a phenomenon is real by repeating a study done by another scientist, they are engaging in:
   a. meta-analysis
   b. experience sampling
   c. replication
   d. correlational research

7. Psychologists have greater confidence in research results when:
   a. the data involve stimulus judgments
   b. the research has used participant observation
   c. the results are replicated
   d. there is an experimenter expectancy effect

8. George is looking for a research project. In doing so, he could formulate and draw on a theory because:
   a. theories are shown to be true, so subsequent research is successful
   b. one of the benefits of theories is that they lead to testable hypotheses
   c. a theory can be successfully replicated by researchers
   d. theories are likely to result in serendipity, which leads to successful research

9. According to some psychologists, Sigmund Freud's theory of the meaning of dreams was not successful because:
   a. it was too socially controversial
   b. he developed the theory from previous ideas
   c. it did not lead to many testable hypotheses
   d. it was based on research later shown to be invalid

WHAT DID YOU MISS? Check your answers against the Answer Key at the end of this chapter of the Study Guide. The Answer Key also lists the page(s) in your text where each question is explained. If you missed any questions, go to the pages indicated in the Answer Key, reread those sections, go back to the questions, and see if you can answer them correctly this time.

ANOTHER OPPORTUNITY TO REVIEW: Answer these questions without your textbook. As a rule of thumb, if you can write only a few words about these questions, you probably need to go back and review.

1. Describe the scientific method. _____

_____

_____

2. Differentiate between theories, hypotheses, and research.

_____

_____

_____

WHAT DO I NEED TO KNOW? Based on what you've discovered above, what are the areas where you need to focus your studying? Which objectives do you need to spend more time mastering? Write this information down in your own words.

1. _____

2. _____

3. _____

4. _____

5. _____

6. _____

2.2 What Types of Studies Are Used in Psychological Research?

Scientific research in general, and psychological research in particular, has developed a set of research tools to help answer research questions and prove or disprove hypotheses. Different situations require different types of research methods. There are advantages and disadvantages to each of these techniques, and researchers choose the research method that can most accurately answer the question they are researching.

2.2 Guiding Questions

To guide your reading of the text, review the following questions. Then, as you read the chapter, look for the answers to these questions. You may want to note in your textbook where you find these answers.

1. Distinguish between descriptive studies, correlational studies, and experiments.

2. List the advantages and disadvantages of different research methods.

3. Explain why random sampling and random assignment are important when one is conducting research studies.

NOW READ Section 2.2 "What Types of Studies Are Used in Psychological Research?" keeping these questions in mind.

REVIEW: Now that you've read this section, go back to the 2.2 Guiding Questions and see if you can answer them based on what you've read. This is a check on your reading. If you can't answer a question, you need to go back to the text to reread that section.

TRY IT

Getting By with a Little Help from My Friends

Are you continuing with the Three Blessing exercise introduced in the last chapter? If you aren't, you may want to consider making the exercise part of your personal research project, which is mentioned later in this chapter.

Another way to improve your sense of well-being is to cultivate good friendships. There is a strong correlation (you'll learn more about that word in this chapter) between how you respond to a friend's good news and the quality of the relationship. Try these techniques to improve the quality of your close relationships: When a friend shares good news, listen attentively, share positive thoughts about the news, and respond constructively. As with all of the suggestions in this book, pay attention to how these techniques work for you. If they work, use them again.

VISUAL SUMMARY: Below is a summary of the major concepts in this section. To check your comprehension of the chapter, read the summary and ask yourself if you understand the concepts. If the concepts seem unfamiliar to you, you may want to go back to the book and reread those sections. This text is taken from the Visual Summaries on StudySpace at wwnorton.com/studyspace.

IV. Research Involves Variables: Things That Can Vary and That Researchers Can Measure

V. Descriptive Studies Involve Observing and Classifying Behavior
   A. Descriptive studies:
      i. involve observing and recording the behavior of people or other animals.
      ii. include:
         a. naturalistic studies (researcher remains separate and does not attempt to alter situation).
         b. participant observation (researcher is involved in situation rather than just observing).
         c. longitudinal studies (researcher studies same participants multiple times over years).
         d. cross-sectional studies (researcher compares participants of different ages at same time).
   B. Observer bias consists of research errors due to researcher's expectations (e.g., experimenter expectancy effect).

VI. Correlational Studies Examine How Variables Are Related

A. A correlational study examines natural relationships between variables with no attempt to alter them or assign causation.

B. A directionality problem makes uncertain which variable caused the other.

C. The third-variable problem makes uncertain if cause should be attributed to a third variable.

VII. An Experiment Involves Manipulating Conditions

A. Experiment: tests whether a change in the independent variable causes a change in the dependent variable.

B. The experimental (treatment) group receives some intervention or special treatment.

C. The control group does not receive an intervention or special treatment.

D. A confound: anything (other than the independent variable) that may change the dependent variable; a source of error.

VIII. Random Sampling and Random Assignment Are Important for Research

A. Random sampling: each member of the population has an equal chance of inclusion in the sample.

B. External validity: whether findings can be generalized to the real world.

C. Selection bias: unintended difference between participants in different groups.

D. Random assignment: gives each participant an equal chance of being assigned to either the control group or the experimental group of the independent variable.

REINFORCE: Are you ready to check your knowledge of this section? Answer the following multiple-choice questions with your textbook closed.

1. Something that can be measured or manipulated by an experimenter is considered:
   a. a descriptive statistic
   b. data
   c. a confound
   d. a variable

2. Something is considered a variable if it:
   a. has no operational definition
   b. can be manipulated by an experimenter
   c. involves random assignment
   d. is theoretical rather than concrete

3. If a researcher wanted to study the behavior of protesters who were in a closed group and did not easily admit new people, the researcher would probably use what approach to study them?
   a. naturalistic observation
   b. participant observation

   c. meta-analysis
   d. closed-ended questions

4. When a researcher joins a social group and talks to the members in order to study that group, the approach is referred to as:
   a. a self-report method
   b. participant observation
   c. experience sampling
   d. response performance

5. Paloma randomly assigns participants to two groups and compares the group that receives a treatment with the group that receives no treatment. The group that gets no treatment is the:
   a. variable group
   b. confounded group
   c. experimental group
   d. control group

6. Researchers investigated whether mood affects participants' ratings of jokes. Participants in the first mood group read sad statements. In the second group, participants read neutral statements. In this study, the participants who read the sad statements constituted the:
   a. control group
   b. population
   c. experimental condition
   d. observational group

7. When two variables are correlated, it is not clear which one is a causal variable and which is an effect. This ambiguity reflects:
   a. the third-variable problem
   b. random error
   c. selection bias
   d. the directionality problem

8. Data collection is particularly problematic when a researcher uses participant observation because:
   a. the researcher is able to make use of only closed-ended questions
   b. the researcher fails to recognize the third-variable problem
   c. random error occurs in the initial stages of observation
   d. the researcher loses objectivity in participating with a group

9. The variable that a researcher manipulates in an experiment is called the:
   a. independent variable
   b. dependent variable
   c. confounding variable
   d. stimulus

10. The variable that a researcher measures in an experiment to see if it has changed after a treatment is called the:
    a. independent variable
    b. dependent variable
    c. confounding variable
    d. stimulus

11. When confounds are present in an experiment, they result in:
    a. an increase in the possibility of selection bias
    b. a decrease in the reactivity of the experimental participants
    c. possible alternative explanations for the results of the experiment
    d. the same treatment for experimental and control groups in the experiment

12. A psychologist wants to create two groups that are as similar as possible at the beginning of an experiment. To do this, she should use:
    a. random sampling
    b. random assignment
    c. self-report methods
    d. participant observation

13. If a researcher wants to be able to generalize about a population using data pulled from a sample, it is best to use:
    a. a convenience sample
    b. experience sampling
    c. a descriptive study
    d. a random sample

14. In order to maximize the likelihood that experimental and control groups are similar before any treatment is applied, researchers typically use:
    a. naturalistic observation
    b. random assignment
    c. sampling
    d. participant observation

15. Which of the following would be best researched using a longitudinal study?
    a. the change in children's concepts of sharing from infancy through adolescence
    b. the difference between children and adults in their responses to a natural disaster
    c. the frequency with which people think about sources of stress in their lives over the course of a single day
    d. the rates of hospitalization of psychiatric patients over the course of the last century

WHAT DID YOU MISS? Check your answers against the Answer Key at the end of this chapter of the Study Guide. The Answer Key also lists the page(s) in your text where each question is explained. If you missed any questions, go to the

pages indicated in the Answer Key, reread those sections, go back to the questions, and see if you can answer them correctly this time.

ANOTHER OPPORTUNITY TO REVIEW: Answer these questions without your textbook. As a rule of thumb, if you can write only a few words about these questions, you probably need to go back and review.

1. Distinguish between descriptive studies, correlational studies, and experiments. _____
   _____
   _____

2. List the advantages and disadvantages of different research methods. _____
   _____
   _____
   _____

3. Explain why random sampling and random assignment are important when one is conducting research studies.
   _____
   _____
   _____

WHAT DO I NEED TO KNOW? Based on what you've discovered above, what are the areas where you need to focus your studying? Which objectives do you need to spend more time mastering? Write this information down in your own words.

1. _____

2. _____

3. _____

4. _____

5. _____

6. _____

2.3 What Are the Data Collection Methods of Psychological Science?

Just as there are various ways in which experimental procedures can be conducted, there are various ways in which data can be gathered. Each data collection method has advantages and disadvantages. Sometimes researchers use animals to conduct research that would not be possible with humans, and such techniques raise concerns about the humane use of animals for research. Whether research is conducted with humans or with animals, ethical guidelines exist to ensure that no harm comes to any participant in a research study.

2.3 Guiding Questions

To guide your reading of the text, review the following questions. Then, as you read the chapter, look for the answers to these questions. You may want to note in your textbook where you find these answers.

1. Distinguish between five methods of data collection.

2. List the advantages and disadvantages of different methods of data collection.

3. Discuss the use of animal models in psychological research.

4. Identify ethical issues associated with psychological research.

NOW READ Section 2.3 "What Are the Data Collection Methods of Psychological Science?" keeping these questions in mind.

REVIEW: Now that you've read this section, go back to the 2.3 Guiding Questions and see if you can answer them based on what you've read. This is a check on your reading. If you can't answer a question, you need to go back to the text to reread that section.

VISUAL SUMMARY: Below is a summary of the major concepts in this section. To check your comprehension of the chapter, read the summary and ask yourself if you understand the concepts. If the concepts seem unfamiliar to you, you may want to go back to the book and reread those sections. This text is taken from the Visual Summaries on StudySpace at wwnorton.com/studyspace.

IX. Observing Is an Unobtrusive Strategy
 A. Observation: careful and systematic assessment and coding of overt behavior.
 B. Reactivity: participants alter their behavior because they know they are being observed.

X. Case Studies Examine Individual Lives and Organizations
 A. Case study: intensive examination of a specific person or organization.

XI. Asking Takes a More Active Approach
 A. Self-report methods: questionnaires or surveys.

 B. Self-report bias: tendency to answer in socially desirable way; a form of error.

XII. Response Performance Measures the Processing of Information
 A. Response performance uses perceptual or cognitive processes to gather information.

XIII. Body/Brain Activity Can Be Measured Directly
 A. Body/brain activity can be measured through polygraphs, electroencephalographs, brain imaging (PET, MRI, fMRI), and can be temporarily altered using TMS.

XIV. Research with Animals Provides Important Data
 A. Important research findings can come through knowledge of genetics and of animals' behavior.

XV. There Are Ethical Issues to Consider
 A. Research must be monitored, informed consent obtained, relative risks explained, and data confidentiality ensured.

REINFORCE: Are you ready to check your knowledge of this section? Answer the following multiple-choice questions with your textbook closed.

1. When people are aware of being observed, they might change their behaviors. This phenomenon illustrates:
 a. variability
 b. experimenter expectancy
 c. random assignment
 d. reactivity

2. A study of the experiences of a synesthete—for example, a person who experiences a visual sensation when hearing a sound—is likely to use:
 a. random selection
 b. a case study
 c. cross-sectional research
 d. participant observation

3. Investigators who want to gain a lot of information about group attitudes quickly are likely to use what kind of research approach?
 a. case study
 b. psychophysical assessment
 c. participant observation
 d. self-report

4. A researcher would be likely to use a reaction-time study in order to see how quickly mental processes proceed when a person solves a problem. Reaction time is an example of:
 a. response performance
 b. stimulus judgment

c. response accuracy
d. experimental treatment

5. The most powerful imaging technique that measures the amount of energy released from brain tissue is:
   a. fMRI
   b. MRI
   c. psychophysiological assessment
   d. EEG recording

6. What approach have researchers used to document changes in metabolic activity in the brain during problem solving?
   a. EEG recording
   b. MRI
   c. fMRI
   d. PET scan

7. One issue that an institutional review board is likely to consider is:
   a. systematic error
   b. directionality problems
   c. relative risk
   d. experimenter expectancy

8. Before psychologists can begin a research project, they must receive approval from:
   a. the American Psychological Association
   b. the Association of Psychological Science
   c. the National Science Foundation
   d. the Institutional Review Board

9. Jamal wants to find out whether the customers of his coffee shop would prefer more booths or more tables and chairs. To be scientific, what kind of study should he use?
   a. participant observation
   b. self-report
   c. correlational
   d. experimental

10. Transcranial magnetic stimulation can be used to investigate the activity of a given region of the brain through the:
    a. monitoring of overall brain functioning and recording of increases in magnetic activity in the region of interest
    b. interrupting of brain functioning by sending a magnetic pulse to a specific area of the brain to explore the involvement of that region in a particular cognitive task
    c. recording of changing levels of oxygen flow in the area of interest in the brain
    d. monitoring of glucose use in the area of interest in the brain

WHAT DID YOU MISS? Check your answers against the Answer Key at the end of this chapter of the Study Guide. The Answer Key also lists the page(s) in your text where each question is explained. If you missed any questions, go to the pages indicated in the Answer Key, reread those sections, go back to the questions, and see if you can answer them correctly this time.

ANOTHER OPPORTUNITY TO REVIEW: Answer these questions without your textbook. As a rule of thumb, if you can write only a few words about these questions, you probably need to go back and review.

1. Distinguish between five methods of data collection.
   _____
   _____
   _____

2. List the advantages and disadvantages of different methods of data collection. _____
   _____
   _____
   _____

3. Discuss the use of animal models in psychological research. _____
   _____
   _____

4. Identify ethical issues associated with psychological research. _____
   _____
   _____

WHAT DO I NEED TO KNOW? Based on what you've discovered above, what are the areas where you need to focus your studying? Which objectives do you need to spend more time mastering? Write this information down in your own words.

1. _____

2. _____

3. _____

4. _____

5. _____

6. _____

TRY IT

My Own Research Project

You know that psychologists and other scientists use the scientific method to reach conclusions, but did you know that you can use this method yourself? In fact, you can use it on yourself. This process is called "single-subject design," and you are the subject. Below is an example of how one student used this method to reach some conclusions.

Although Tom had always heard that getting 8 hours of sleep was a good idea, he wondered if doing so would make a difference in his mood and academic productivity. He tried an experiment. For 2 weeks he slept his usual 4 to 6 hours a night. He also kept track on a daily basis of his mood and his academic productivity. He rated these factors on two scales, each ranging from 1 (worst) to 10 (best).

After 2 weeks of sleeping his usual amount, he switched and made the effort to sleep 8 hours or more a night while he continued to rate his mood and academic productivity. What do you think he found? As with every research tool, there are limitations to using a single-subject design, but you can nonetheless use this type of experiment to make changes in your life.

2.4 How Are Data Analyzed and Evaluated?

A crucial aspect of the scientific inquiry process is the evaluation of data. By using statistical methods, scientists can reach more-impartial conclusions about phenomena that exist in the world. Statistics is a large, comprehensive field with many techniques for analyzing data, so only a few of the most important concepts will be discussed in this section.

2.4 Guiding Questions

To guide your reading of the text, review the following questions. Then, as you read the chapter, look for the answers to these questions. You may want to note in your textbook where you find these answers.

1. Identify three characteristics that reflect the quality of data.

2. Describe measures of central tendency and variability.

3. Describe the correlation coefficient.

4. Discuss the rationale for inferential statistics.

NOW READ Section 2.4 "How Are Data Analyzed and Evaluated?" keeping these questions in mind.

REVIEW: Now that you've read this section, go back to the 2.4 Guiding Questions and see if you can answer them based on what you've read. This is a check on your reading. If you can't answer a question, you need to go back to the text to reread that section.

VISUAL SUMMARY: Below is a summary of the major concepts in this section. To check your comprehension of the chapter, read the summary and ask yourself if you understand the concepts. If the concepts seem unfamiliar to you, you may want to go back to the book and reread those sections. This text is taken from the Visual Summaries on StudySpace at wwnorton.com/studyspace.

XVI. Good Research Requires Valid, Reliable, and Accurate Data
   A. Internal validity: extent to which data collected address hypothesis.
   B. Reliability: extent to which measurement is stable over time in similar conditions.
   C. Accuracy: extent to which experimental measure is error free.

XVII. Descriptive Statistics Provide a Summary of the Data
   A. Central tendency: represents typical response or behavior of group as a whole.
   B. Measures of central tendency:
      i. mean: the average of a set of numbers.
      ii. median: the exact middle of a set of values.
      iii. mode: the most frequently occurring value.
   C. Variability: how widely dispersed the values are around the mean.
   D. Standard deviation: measure of how far each value is on average from the mean.

XVIII. Correlations Describe the Relationships between Variables
   A. Positive correlation: both variables either increase or decrease together.
   B. Negative correlation: one variable increases while the other variable decreases.

XIX. Inferential Statistics Permit Generalizations
   A. Statistical procedures: used to determine if differences actually exist between sets of numbers.
   B. Meta-analysis: analysis of the results from a variety of studies that examined the same/similar phenomenon to determine if a pattern of similar results exists to determine if hypothesis is true.

REINFORCE: Are you ready to check your knowledge of this section? Answer the following multiple-choice questions with your textbook closed.

1. Suppose a researcher intended to study people's level of happiness by monitoring how often they smile or laugh when watching a movie. If this measurement does not really indicate level of happiness, psychologists would say that the data are not:
   a. systematic
   b. reliable
   c. internally valid
   d. event-related

2. When researchers report a measure of central tendency, they might present:
   a. the standard deviation
   b. the median
   c. inferential statistics
   d. the correlation coefficient

3. If you list a set of scores from the lowest value to the highest, then take the middle value to indicate what is a typical score, you are using the:
   a. mean
   b. mode
   c. median
   d. range

4. If a researcher believes that participants in a single group will score very differently from one another on a task, that researcher can find out if that is true by looking at the:
   a. mean
   b. median
   c. correlation coefficient
   d. standard deviation

5. The mean, median, and mode are all examples of:
   a. inferential statistics
   b. measures of central tendency
   c. types of variability
   d. correlational measures

6. The range and standard deviation are examples of:
   a. inferential statistics
   b. measures of central tendency
   c. types of variability
   d. correlational measures

7. When you observe two variables, and as one increases so does the other, your data will show:
   a. a standardized range
   b. a positive correlation
   c. inferential statistics
   d. validity

8. When you observe two variables, and as one increases the other decreases, your data will show:
   a. a standardized range
   b. a negative correlation
   c. inferential statistics
   d. validity

9. If a researcher wants to test hypotheses about differences between populations by using a smaller sample, she would use:
   a. correlation coefficients
   b. measures of central tendency
   c. inferential statistics
   d. meta-analysis

10. When a researcher cannot manipulate variables in a project on the relationship between level of education and income, she will be forced to collect naturally occurring data. The data analysis would probably involve:
    a. a correlational analysis
    b. inferential statistics
    c. naturalistic observation
    d. selection bias

WHAT DID YOU MISS? Check your answers against the Answer Key at the end of this chapter of the Study Guide. The Answer Key also lists the page(s) in your text where each question is explained. If you missed any questions, go to the pages indicated in the Answer Key, reread those sections, go back to the questions, and see if you can answer them correctly this time.

ANOTHER OPPORTUNITY TO REVIEW: Answer these questions without your textbook. As a rule of thumb, if you can write only a few words about these questions, you probably need to go back and review.

1. Identify three characteristics that reflect the quality of data. _____

   _____

   _____

2. Describe measures of central tendency and variability.

   _____

   _____

   _____

3. Describe the correlation coefficient. _____

   _____

   _____

4. Discuss the rationale for inferential statistics.

   _____

   _____

   _____

WHAT DO I NEED TO KNOW? Based on what you've discovered above, what are the areas where you need to focus your studying? Which objectives do you need to spend more time mastering? Write this information down in your own words.

1. _____

2. _____

3. _____

4. _____

5. _____

6. _____

WHAT MATTERS TO ME: What facts in this chapter are personally relevant to you?

_____

_____

_____

_____

CHAPTER SUMMARY

2.1 What Is Scientific Inquiry?

- *The Scientific Method Depends on Theories, Hypotheses, and Research:* Scientific inquiry relies on objective methods and empirical evidence to answer testable questions. Interconnected ideas or models of behavior (theories) yield testable predictions (hypotheses), which are tested in a systematic way (research) by collecting and evaluating evidence (data).
- *Unexpected Findings Can Be Valuable:* Unexpected (serendipitous) discoveries sometimes occur, but only researchers who are prepared to recognize their importance will benefit from them.

2.2 What Types of Studies Are Used in Psychological Research?

- *Descriptive Studies Involve Observing and Classifying Behavior:* Researchers observe and describe naturally occurring behaviors to provide a systematic and objective analysis.
- *Correlational Studies Examine How Variables Are Related:* Correlational studies are used to examine how variables are naturally related in the real world, but cannot be used to establish causality or the direction of a relationship (which variable caused changes in another variable). Correlational reasoning occurs in many con-

texts, so readers need to be able to recognize correlational designs in everyday contexts, not just when reading research reports.
- *An Experiment Involves Manipulating Conditions:* In an experiment, researchers control the variations in the conditions that the participants experience (independent variables) and measure the outcomes (dependent variables) to gain an understanding of causality. Researchers need a control group to know if the experiment has had an effect.
- *Random Sampling and Random Assignment Are Important for Research:* Researchers sample participants from the population they want to study (e.g., drivers). They use random sampling when everyone in the population is equally likely to participate in the study, a condition that rarely occurs. To establish causality between an intervention and an outcome, random assignment must be used. When random assignment is used, all participants have an equal chance of being assigned to any level of the independent variable, and preexisting differences between the groups are controlled.

2.3 What Are the Data Collection Methods of Psychological Science?

- *Observing Is an Unobtrusive Strategy:* Data collected by observation must be defined clearly and collected systematically. Bias may occur in the data because the participants are aware they are being observed or because of the observer's expectations.
- *Case Studies Examine Individual Lives and Organizations:* A case study, one kind of descriptive study, examines an individual or an organization. An intensive study of an individual or organization can be useful for examining an unusual participant or unusual research question. Interpretation of a case study, however, can be subjective.
- *Asking Takes a More Active Approach:* Surveys, questionnaires, and interviews can be used to directly ask people about their thoughts and behaviors. Self-report data may be biased by the respondents' desire to present themselves in a particular way (e.g., smart, honest). Culturally sensitive research recognizes the differences among people from different cultural groups and from different language backgrounds.
- *Response Performance Measures the Processing of Information:* Measuring reaction times and response accuracy and asking people to make stimulus judgments are methods used to examine how people respond to psychological tasks.
- *Body/Brain Activity Can Be Measured Directly:* Electrophysiology (often using an electroencephalograph, or EEG) measures the brain's electrical activity. Brain imaging is done using positron emission tomography

(PET), magnetic resonance imaging (MRI), and functional magnetic resonance imaging (fMRI). Transcranial magnetic stimulation (TMS) disrupts normal brain activity, allowing researchers to infer the brain processing involved in particular thoughts, feelings, and behaviors.

- *Research with Animals Provides Important Data:* Research involving nonhuman animals provides useful, although simpler, models of behavior and of genetics. The purpose of such research may be to learn about animals' behavior or to make inferences about human behavior.
- *There Are Ethical Issues to Consider:* Ethical research is governed by a variety of principles that ensure fair and informed treatment of participants.

2.4 How Are Data Analyzed and Evaluated?

- *Good Research Requires Valid, Reliable, and Accurate Data:* Data must be meaningful (valid) and their measurement reliable (i.e., consistent and stable) and accurate.
- *Descriptive Statistics Provide a Summary of the Data:* Measures of central tendency and variability are used to describe data.
- *Correlations Describe the Relationships between Variables:* A correlation is a descriptive statistic that describes the strength and direction of the relationship between two variables. Correlations close to zero signify weak relationships; correlations near +1.0 or −1.0 signify strong relationships.
- *Inferential Statistics Permit Generalizations:* Inferential statistics allow us to decide whether differences between two or more groups are probably just chance variations (suggesting that the populations the groups were drawn from are the same) or whether they reflect true differences in the populations being compared. Meta-analysis combines the results of several studies to arrive at a conclusion.

PUTTING IT ALL TOGETHER

Answer these questions to check your knowledge of the material in this chapter.

1. Your roommate tells you that she or he can study only with music on in the background, but you find studying with music very distracting. Use your understanding of the five steps of the scientific method to develop a research plan to study this discrepancy.

2. Develop a correlational study using the hypothesis you developed in the previous question. Try to identify the directionality problem and/or the third variable problem

in your study. Then develop an experimental study using the same hypothesis, determining your independent and dependent variables. What potential confounds should you control in your experiment, and why?

3. Which data collection method (observational, survey, interview, response performance, brain imaging) would best test your research hypothesis developed above? Describe how you would create your study using that data collection method, and describe the role of ethics in your study. Then choose another data collection method and do the same.

4. Say you conduct a correlational study on the relationship between introversion and studying with music. You find a correlation coefficient of −.75. What does that result tell you about the relationship between introversion and whether someone studies with music? Can you make a causal claim? Why or why not?

ANSWER KEY FOR REINFORCE QUESTIONS

Section 2.1

1. a   p. 31
2. a   p. 31
3. b   p. 31
4. a   p. 31
5. c   p. 31
6. c   p. 32
7. c   p. 32
8. b   p. 32
9. c   p. 33

Section 2.2

1. d   p. 34
2. b   p. 34
3. a   p. 35
4. b   p. 35
5. d   p. 40
6. c   p. 40
7. d   p. 38
8. d   p. 35
9. a   p. 40
10. b   p. 40
11. c   p. 41
12. b   p. 45
13. d   p. 43
14. b   p. 45
15. a   p. 36

Section 2.3

1. d   p. 51
2. b   p. 52

HINTS FOR PUTTING IT ALL TOGETHER QUESTIONS

1. You might develop a theory that individual differences (e.g., personality, music preference, type of class studying for) influence whether people listen to music while studying. You can develop testable hypotheses from the theory (e.g., if someone is introverted, then she or he is more likely to be distracted by music). Test the hypothesis by conducting a research study (you will think of ways to test your hypothesis in the next questions), analyzing the collected data (typically using statistics), and think of ways you could share your results with the scientific community (e.g., research conferences, research papers).

2. A correlational study should examine the relationship between two variables, neither of which has been manipulated by the experimenter (e.g., in a sample of participants, record their level of introversion and record how distracted they are by listening to music while studying). Could a change in one variable be causing the other vari-able to change (i.e., directionality problem)? For example, does introversion cause higher distraction, or does distraction cause higher introversion? Could a change in both variables be caused by a variable you did not measure (i.e., third variable problem)? For example, an over-reactive nervous system could cause someone to be more introverted and more easily distracted. In an experimental study, you should manipulate your independent variable (e.g., randomly assign participants to a no-music control group or to a music experimental group). Then measure your dependent variable (e.g., level of distraction while studying a list of words). For potential confounds, think of some variables, other than your independent variable, that might influence the dependent variable (e.g., type of music the participant likes and the type of music you use in your experimental group).

3. If your hypothesis involves testing a correlational hypothesis, you are likely to use an observational, survey, or interview collection method (e.g., recording level of introversion and how distracted a person is by listening to music while studying could be collected using a written survey or an in-person interview). Alternatively, you are likely to text an experimental hypothesis using response performance and brain imaging (e.g., by using fMRI, brain activity in participants memorizing a list of words in silence can be compared with brain activity in participants memorizing a list of words with background music). Ethical issues vary depending on the type of data collection method. Informed consent is required whenever possible. Confidentiality is always required (i.e., researchers must not reveal individual participant responses to anyone), and anonymity is often possible when collecting survey data.

4. A correlation of −.75 indicates an inverse relationship between your two variables (i.e., as level of introversion increases, the chance of studying with music decreases, and vice versa). One cannot make a causal conclusion about the relationship between the two variables because causal conclusions can be based only on data from experimental studies that manipulate an independent variable and control other possible confounding variables. Directionality and third variable problems plague correlational studies.

KEY TERMS EXERCISES

First, fill in your own definition and example for each term. Then check each term against the textbook's definition. These exercises can also be cut out and used as flash cards.

accuracy

Your Definition:
Your Example:
Textbook Definition:

control group

Your Definition:
Your Example:
Textbook Definition:

case studies

Your Definition:
Your Example:
Textbook Definition:

correlational studies

Your Definition:
Your Example:
Textbook Definition:

central tendency

Your Definition:
Your Example:
Textbook Definition:

cross-sectional studies

Your Definition:
Your Example:
Textbook Definition:

confound

Your Definition:
Your Example:
Textbook Definition:

culturally sensitive research

Your Definition:
Your Example:
Textbook Definition:

data

Your Definition:
Your Example:
Textbook Definition:

dependent variable

Your Definition:
Your Example:
Textbook Definition:

descriptive statistics

Your Definition:
Your Example:
Textbook Definition:

descriptive studies

Your Definition:
Your Example:
Textbook Definition:

directionality problem

Your Definition:
Your Example:
Textbook Definition:

electroencephalograph (EEG)

Your Definition:
Your Example:
Textbook Definition:

experiment

Your Definition:
Your Example:
Textbook Definition:

experimental groups

Your Definition:
Your Example:
Textbook Definition:

experimenter expectancy effect

Your Definition:
Your Example:
Textbook Definition:

independent variable

Your Definition:
Your Example:
Textbook Definition:

external validity

Your Definition:
Your Example:
Textbook Definition:

inferential statistics

Your Definition:
Your Example:
Textbook Definition:

functional magnetic resonance imaging (fMRI)

Your Definition:
Your Example:
Textbook Definition:

institutional review boards (IRBs)

Your Definition:
Your Example:
Textbook Definition:

hypothesis

Your Definition:
Your Example:
Textbook Definition:

internal validity

Your Definition:
Your Example:
Textbook Definition:

longitudinal studies

Your Definition:
Your Example:
Textbook Definition:

meta-analysis

Your Definition:
Your Example:
Textbook Definition:

magnetic resonance imaging (MRI)

Your Definition:
Your Example:
Textbook Definition:

mode

Your Definition:
Your Example:
Textbook Definition:

mean

Your Definition:
Your Example:
Textbook Definition:

naturalistic observation

Your Definition:
Your Example:
Textbook Definition:

median

Your Definition:
Your Example:
Textbook Definition:

observational techniques

Your Definition:
Your Example:
Textbook Definition:

observer bias

Your Definition:
Your Example:
Textbook Definition:

random assignment

Your Definition:
Your Example:
Textbook Definition:

participant observation

Your Definition:
Your Example:
Textbook Definition:

reactivity

Your Definition:
Your Example:
Textbook Definition:

population

Your Definition:
Your Example:
Textbook Definition:

reliability

Your Definition:
Your Example:
Textbook Definition:

positron emission tomography (PET)

Your Definition:
Your Example:
Textbook Definition:

replication

Your Definition:
Your Example:
Textbook Definition:

research

Your Definition:
Your Example:
Textbook Definition:

scientific method

Your Definition:
Your Example:
Textbook Definition:

response performance

Your Definition:
Your Example:
Textbook Definition:

selection bias

Your Definition:
Your Example:
Textbook Definition:

sample

Your Definition:
Your Example:
Textbook Definition:

self-report methods

Your Definition:
Your Example:
Textbook Definition:

scatterplot

Your Definition:
Your Example:
Textbook Definition:

standard deviation

Your Definition:
Your Example:
Textbook Definition:

theory

Your Definition:
Your Example:
Textbook Definition:

variability

Your Definition:
Your Example:
Textbook Definition:

third-variable problem

Your Definition:
Your Example:
Textbook Definition:

variable

Your Definition:
Your Example:
Textbook Definition:

transcranial magnetic stimulation (TMS)

Your Definition:
Your Example:
Textbook Definition:

CHAPTER 3 | Biology and Behavior

CHAPTER OVERVIEW

Every thought, emotion, behavior, and intuition that you have is the result of the interaction among billions of neurons. As the result of thousands of years of human evolution, your brain is able to keep your heart beating, prepare your limbs to respond rapidly to threatening situations, conceive works of art, and even read this Study Guide. In this chapter, you will learn about the brain and the nervous system, from their most basic elements to the cooperation of various parts to create your experience of consciousness.

3.1 How Does the Nervous System Operate?

The basic unit of the nervous system is the neuron. The nervous system contains billions of these specialized cells, whose purpose is to communicate with other neurons to create the range of activity that makes up being human. This communication begins with an electrical change and then becomes chemical as a number of chemical messengers called neurotransmitters influence our thoughts, emotions, and behaviors.

At the beginning of each section in the Study Guide, there will be guiding questions. Before you read the chapter in your textbook, read through these questions and maybe even attempt to answer them based on either what you've already read or what you think the answer should be. Then as you study the chapter, you can use them to help guide your reading.

3.1 Guiding Questions

To guide your reading of the text, review the following questions. Then, as you read the chapter, look for the answers to these questions. You may want to note in your textbook where you find these answers.

1. Distinguish between the functions of distinct types of neurons.

2. Describe the structure of the neuron.

3. Describe the electrical and chemical changes that occur when neurons communicate.

4. Identify the major neurotransmitters and their primary functions.

NOW READ Section 3.1 "How Does the Nervous System Operate?" keeping these questions in mind.

REVIEW: Now that you've read this section, go back to the 3.1 Guiding Questions and see if you can answer them based on what you've read. This is a check on your reading. If you can't answer a question, you need to go back to the text to reread that section.

VISUAL SUMMARY: Below is a summary of the major concepts in this section. To check your comprehension of the chapter, read the summary and ask yourself if you understand the concepts. If the concepts seem unfamiliar to you, you may want to go back to the book and reread those sections. This text is taken from the Visual Summaries on StudySpace at wwnorton.com/studyspace.

I. Neurons
   A. Neurons are the basic unit of the nervous system.

B. Neurons receive, integrate, and transmit information.

II. Central Nervous System (CNS) Consists of the Brain and Spinal Cord

III. Peripheral Nervous System (PNS) Includes All Nerves That Are Not Part of CNS

IV. Neurons Are Specialized for Communication
   A. Types of neurons:
      i. sensory (afferent)
      ii. motor (efferent)
      iii. interneurons
   B. Neuron structure:
      i. dendrite
      ii. cell body
      iii. axon
      iv. terminal buttons
      v. synapse (synaptic cleft)
      vi. myelin sheath
      vii. nodes of Ranvier
   C. Resting membrane potential: when not active, neurons have negative electrical charge.
   D. Shift in the balance of sodium and potassium ions leads to polarization in neuron.

V. Action Potentials Cause Neural Communication
   A. Electrical signal passes along axon, causing release of chemicals in synapse.
   B. Excitatory signals reduce polarization, increasing likelihood of action potential.
   C. Inhibitory signals increase polarization, decreasing likelihood of action potential.
   D. Action potentials move down axon like a wave (propagation).
   E. All-or-none principle: neuron either fires (initiates action potential) with same potency or does not.

VI. Neurotransmitters Bind to Receptors across the Synapse
   A. Presynaptic neurons release neurotransmitters to postsynaptic neurons.
   B. Neurotransmitters: chemical substances that carry messages from one neuron to the next.
   C. Through reuptake, neurotransmitters are recycled back into the presynaptic neuron.
   D. Through enzyme deactivation, unused neurotransmitters in the synapse are destroyed.

VII. Neurotransmitters Influence Mental Activity and Behavior
   A. Agonist: drug or substance that mimics action of neurotransmitter.
   B. Antagonist: drug or substance that blocks action of neurotransmitter.

C. Neurotransmitters:
   i. acetylcholine
   ii. epinephrine
   iii. norepinephrine
   iv. serotonin
   v. dopamine
   vi. GABA
   vii. glutamate
   viii. endophins
   ix. substance P

REINFORCE: Are you ready to check your knowledge of this section? Answer the following multiple-choice questions with your textbook closed.

1. When Jon burned his finger on the stove, _____ neurons carried the message to the spinal cord and _____ neurons instructed the muscles in his arm to retract from the flame.
   a. motor; sensory
   b. inter; motor
   c. afferent; efferent
   d. efferent; afferent

2. Interneurons communicate:
   a. within local or short-distance circuits
   b. directly on muscles
   c. directly on sensory organs
   d. with glial cells

3. In general, a signal travels through a neuron in which of the following orders?
   a. dendrite, soma, axon, terminal buttons
   b. terminal buttons, axon, cell body, dendrite
   c. cell body, dendrite, axon, terminal buttons
   d. dendrite, axon, cell body, terminal buttons

4. What are the branchlike appendages that detect chemical signals from neighboring neurons?
   a. axons
   b. synapses
   c. cell bodies
   d. dendrites

5. The _____ capture(s) the incoming chemical signal; the _____ release(s) the chemical signal.
   a. terminal buttons; dendrites
   b. dendrites; terminal buttons
   c. cell body; axon
   d. axon; cell body

6. Thara's roommate has been complaining about having pain from a "pinched nerve" after moving some furniture. What she refers to as a "pinched nerve," neuroscientists are likely to describe as:

a. a single axon from a portion of her back to her spinal cord
b. a neuron that is part of her spinal cord
c. a bundle of axons from some nerves in her back
d. a neuron that connects to the pain center in her spine

7. Axons:
   a. transmit nerve impulses to terminal buttons and vary in length
   b. are always bundled with other axons to form nerves and are individually very short in length
   c. vary in length, depending on whether they send or receive information
   d. are uniform in size throughout the body, though capable of serving different functions

8. A myelin sheath is like:
   a. the tuning dial of a radio
   b. the insulation of a wire
   c. the layers of a cake
   d. the thermostat of a heater

9. What happens when the action potential reaches the terminal button?
   a. The signal terminates, or ends.
   b. The signal causes the vesicles to release the neurotransmitter.
   c. The terminal button sends it down the axon.
   d. The signal causes reuptake of neurotransmitters in the synapse.

10. Another term for neural firing is:
    a. action potential
    b. somatic potential
    c. resting membrane potential
    d. efferent arc

11. What is the state of the electrical charge when a neuron is said to be at resting potential?
    a. Inside the neuron is more positive than outside the neuron.
    b. Inside the neuron is more negative than outside the neuron.
    c. Both the inside and the outside of the neuron are of equal electrical charge.
    d. The electrical charges inside and outside the neuron are equal.

12. There are three ways that a neurotransmitter is removed from the synapse. Which of the following is NOT one of these ways?
    a. The neurotransmitter is taken back into the presynaptic neuron.
    b. Enzymes in the synapse destroy the neurotransmitter.
    c. The neurotransmitter "plugs" into a receptor in the presynaptic neuron.

d. The neurotransmitter alters its structure after release from the synaptic vesicle.

13. Using a key to open the front door of your house is analogous to the:
    a. randomness of neural activation
    b. unique chemical structure of a neurotransmitter that fits certain receptor sites
    c. neurotransmitters that carry a secret code to neurons
    d. activity log that the nervous system maintains

14. How do neurons communicate?
    a. Terminal buttons plug into receptor sites on adjacent dendrites.
    b. Neurotransmitters cross the synapse and bind with receptors on the postsynaptic dendrite.
    c. Electric signals jump across the synapse to the adjacent neuron.
    d. Chemicals released into the synapse are converted to neurotransmitters that bind with receptors.

15. Another way to think of agonists and antagonists, with respect to their involvement in the actions of neurotransmitters, is that agonists _____, whereas antagonists _____ the action of neurotransmitters.
    a. block; mimic
    b. mimic; block
    c. alter; maintain
    d. maintain; alter

16. Which of the following neurotransmitters would be most involved in enabling nerves that connect with muscles as you raise your arms above your head?
    a. acetylcholine
    b. epinephrine
    c. serotonin
    d. norepinephrine

17. Drugs that treat _____ make serotonin more available by blocking reuptake.
    a. motor disturbances
    b. memory disturbances and hallucinations
    c. eating disorders and depression
    d. pain management and hypersensitivity

18. Drugs that enhance the effects of GABA:
    a. are used to treat depression
    b. affect the location of reception
    c. are used to treat anxiety and insomnia
    d. may cause seizures and hallucinations

19. Narcotics, such as heroin and morphine, are probably rapidly addictive because they:
    a. block neural transmission
    b. cause a placebo effect

c. activate the release of substance P

d. bind to endorphin receptors

20. Capsaicin rubs, Tiger balm, and other salves used by athletes to soothe muscle injuries create a burning sensation. This effect is likely due to the release of which neurotransmitter, which transmits signals about pain to the brain?

    a. substance P
    b. dopamine
    c. GABA
    d. cholecystokinin

WHAT DID YOU MISS? Check your answers against the Answer Key at the end of this chapter of the Study Guide. The Answer Key also lists the page(s) in your text where each question is explained. If you missed any questions, go to the pages indicated in the Answer Key, reread those sections, go back to the questions, and see if you can answer them correctly this time.

ANOTHER OPPORTUNITY TO REVIEW: Answer these questions without your textbook. As a rule of thumb, if you can write only a few words about these questions, you probably need to go back and review.

1. Distinguish between the functions of distinct types of neurons. _____

    _____

    _____

2. Describe the structure of the neuron. _____

    _____

    _____

3. Describe the electrical and chemical changes that occur when neurons communicate. _____

    _____

    _____

4. Identify the major neurotransmitters and their primary functions. _____

    _____

    _____

    _____

WHAT DO I NEED TO KNOW? Based on what you've discovered above, what are the areas where you need to focus your studying? Which objectives do you need to spend more time mastering? Write this information down in your own words.

1. _____

2. _____

3. _____

4. _____

5. _____

6. _____

3.2 What Are the Basic Brain Structures and Their Functions?

The process of evolution has presented us with a remarkable structure called the brain. The older, more primitive sections of the brain help to control movement, emotion, and life functions. The newer portions of the brain allow us to do the wide range of behaviors and thinking that characterize what it is to be human.

3.2 Guiding Question

To guide your reading of the text, review the following question. Then, as you read the chapter, look for the answers to this question. You may want to note in your textbook where you find these answers.

1. Identify the basic structures of the brain and their primary functions.

NOW READ Section 3.2 "What Are the Basic Brain Structures and Their Functions?" keeping this question in mind.

REVIEW: Now that you've read this section, go back to the 3.2 Guiding Question and see if you can answer it based on what you've read. This is a check on your reading. If you can't answer the question, you need to go back to the text to reread that section.

VISUAL SUMMARY: Below is a summary of the major concepts in this section. To check your comprehension of the chapter, read the summary and ask yourself if you understand the concepts. If the concepts seem unfamiliar to you, you may want to go back to the book and reread those sections. This text is taken from the Visual Summaries on StudySpace at wwnorton.com/studyspace.

VIII. The Brain Stem Houses the Basic Programs of Survival

　A. The brain stem:

　　　i. consists of the medulla oblongata, pons, and midbrain.

ii. controls life functions.
iii. houses reticular formation (responsible for alertness).

IX. The Cerebellum Is Essential for Movement
   A. The cerebellum coordinates movement and maintains balance.

X. Subcortical Structures Control Emotions and Basic Drives
   A. Hypothalamus:
      i. regulates functions of internal organs and bodily functions.
      ii. governs basic drives.
   B. Thalamus: receives all incoming sensory information before information reaches cortex.
   C. Hippocampus: associated with the formation of memories.
   D. Amygdala: responsible for emotional responding and processing emotional information.
   E. Basal ganglia: important in production of planned movement.

XI. The Cerebral Cortex Underlies Complex Mental Activity
   A. Cerebral cortex includes:
      i. occipital lobes (important for vision).
      ii. parietal lobes (important for touch and understanding spatial information).
      iii. temporal lobes (important for hearing, face and object recognition).
      iv. frontal lobes (important for attention, inhibition, decision making, and movement).

REINFORCE: Are you ready to check your knowledge of this section? Answer the following multiple-choice questions with your textbook closed.

1. The amygdala plays an important role in _____, whereas the hippocampus plays an important role in _____.
   a. fear or emotional reactions; spatial memory
   b. emotions; automatic behaviors
   c. spatial memory; fear or emotional reactions
   d. automatic behaviors; emotions

2. The basal ganglia comprise a system of subcortical structures critical for:
   a. planning and producing movement
   b. regulating emotions
   c. sensory awareness
   d. thinking

3. Which of the following is NOT correct?
   a. The frontal lobe plays a significant role in thinking and movement.
   b. The occipital lobe plays a significant role in vision.
   c. The parietal lobe plays a significant role in touch.
   d. The temporal lobe plays a significant role in voluntary movement.

4. Which of the following is NOT a characteristic of the cerebral cortex?
   a. It has a wrinkled appearance.
   b. It is the largest part of the human brain.
   c. The corpus callosum provides connections between the two hemispheres.
   d. Damage to this area typically results in death.

5. A young child is referred to Marco's psychology practice following a severe accident. The child had vision prior to the accident, but because of a blow to the head, she has damaged a lobe of her brain and is completely blind. Her eyes are still fully functional. Based on this information, Marco determines that the brain area most likely damaged in the accident is the:
   a. frontal lobe
   b. parietal lobe
   c. temporal lobe
   d. occipital lobe

6. Brad has experienced a relatively severe left hemisphere stroke. As a result, he is unable to move his right arm and has a great deal of difficulty planning and maintaining attention. The location of his stroke is most likely the:
   a. frontal lobe
   b. parietal lobe
   c. temporal lobe
   d. occipital lobe

7. Anne is working in a laboratory and comes across a rat that is grossly overweight and seems unable to stop eating. The researcher tells Anne this rat has a brain lesion. Which part of the brain most likely has the lesion?
   a. amygdala
   b. hypothalamus
   c. frontal lobe
   d. brain stem

8. A study in which taxi drivers had to memorize the routes on which they traveled demonstrated that a particular part of the brain became larger the more they memorized. Which part of the brain was it, and why?
   a. frontal lobe; quick motor reactions
   b. hippocampus; greater and more accurate representations of the spatial world
   c. cerebellum; quick motor reactions
   d. thalamus; greater and more accurate representations of the spatial world

9. Jonas has experienced a relatively severe right hemisphere stroke. As a result, he is unable to notice anything on the left side of his body. The stroke is most likely within the:
   a. frontal lobe
   b. parietal lobe
   c. temporal lobe
   d. occipital lobe

10. Which part of the brain is involved in the maintenance of life functions?
    a. cortex
    b. limbic system
    c. brain stem
    d. peripheral nervous system

WHAT DID YOU MISS? Check your answers against the Answer Key at the end of this chapter of the Study Guide. The Answer Key also lists the page(s) in your text where each question is explained. If you missed any questions, go to the pages indicated in the Answer Key, reread those sections, go back to the questions, and see if you can answer them correctly this time.

ANOTHER OPPORTUNITY TO REVIEW: Answer these questions without your textbook. As a rule of thumb, if you can write only a few words about these questions, you probably need to go back and review.

1. Identify the basic structures of the brain and their primary functions.

   A. The brain stem _____

   _____

   _____

   B. The cerebellum _____

   _____

   _____

   C. Subcortical structures:

   1. hypothalamus _____

   2. thalamus _____

   3. amygdala _____

   4. basal ganglia _____

   D. Cerebral cortex:

   1. occipital lobes _____

   2. parietal lobes _____

   3. temporal lobes _____

   4. frontal lobes _____

WHAT DO I NEED TO KNOW? Based on what you've discovered above, what are the areas where you need to focus your studying? Which objectives do you need to spend more time mastering? Write this information down in your own words.

1. _____

2. _____

3. _____

4. _____

5. _____

6. _____

3.3 How Does the Brain Communicate with the Body?

What is the difference between a neuron and a nerve? How does the body communicate with the brain to allow you, for instance, to know that you've stepped on a tack? What about the hormones that have an impact on behavior and bodily changes? What is the link between these hormones and the brain? This section addresses these questions.

3.3 Guiding Questions

To guide your reading of the text, review the following questions. Then, as you read the chapter, look for the answers to these questions. You may want to note in your textbook where you find these answers.

1. Differentiate between the divisions of the nervous system.

2. Identify the primary structures of the endocrine system.

3. Explain how the nervous system and the endocrine system communicate to control thought, feeling, and behavior.

NOW READ Section 3.3 "How Does the Brain Communicate with the Body?" keeping these questions in mind.

REVIEW: Now that you've read this section, go back to the 3.3 Guiding Questions and see if you can answer them based on what you've read. This is a check on your reading. If you can't answer a question, you need to go back to the text to reread that section.

VISUAL SUMMARY: Below is a summary of the major concepts in this section. To check your comprehension of the chapter, read the summary and ask yourself if you understand the concepts. If the concepts seem unfamiliar to you, you may want to go back to the book and reread those sections. This text is taken from the Visual Summaries on StudySpace at wwnorton.com/studyspace.

XII. The PNS Includes the Somatic and Autonomic Systems
   A. Somatic nervous system transmits sensory and motor information to and from CNS.
   B. Autonomic nervous system regulates internal states.
   C. Sympathetic division prepares the body for action.
   D. Parasympathetic division returns body to its resting state.

XIII. The Endocrine System Communicates through Hormones
   A. The pituitary gland is the "master gland" in the body.
   B. Gonads produce androgen and estrogen that affect sexual behavior.

XIV. Actions of the Nervous System and Endocrine System Are Coordinated
   A. Pituitary gland triggers endocrine glands to release hormones.
   B. The hypothalamus of the nervous system signals the pituitary gland to send signals to other endocrine glands.

REINFORCE: Are you ready to check your knowledge of this section? Answer the following multiple-choice questions with your textbook closed.

1. The spinal cord is part of the _____ system.
   a. sensory
   b. peripheral nervous
   c. somatic nervous
   d. central nervous

2. As Beatriz rakes leaves in her yard, she works up a pretty good sweat. This effect is due in part to her:
   a. somatic nervous system
   b. autonomic nervous system
   c. central nervous system
   d. endocrine system

3. As Andre entered the room in which his introductory psychology exam would take place, his heart rate increased due to his _____. As he settled into the test, he calmed down due to his _____.
   a. endorphins; peripheral nervous system
   b. sympathetic system; parasympathetic system
   c. central nervous system; peripheral nervous system
   d. endocrine system; autonomic nervous system

4. Nasim is driving on a snow-covered road, and her car begins to slide. Her quick behavioral response and the increased heart rate and respiration she experiences are most likely due to the _____ nervous system; the feeling of relief and decrease in heart rate and respiration once she has the car under control again are most likely due to the _____ nervous system.
   a. parasympathetic; sympathetic
   b. sympathetic; parasympathetic
   c. autonomic; somatic
   d. somatic; autonomic

5. The _____ is a communication system that influences thoughts, behaviors, and actions via hormones.
   a. somatic nervous system
   b. sympathetic system
   c. parasympathetic system
   d. endocrine system

6. Hormones are to _____ as neurotransmitters are to _____.
   a. the endocrine system; the nervous system
   b. disease; dysfunction
   c. outside the skull; inside the skull
   d. sex; feelings

7. With respect to their relative functions, the endocrine and nervous systems:
   a. act separately and are specialized
   b. are interrelated; each system affects the other
   c. are identical, but the nervous system's effects are more diffuse
   d. have little to no overlap

8. The endocrine glands involved with sexual behavior are the:
   a. thymus
   b. penis and vagina
   c. gonads
   d. pituitary glands

9. You might think of the pituitary gland as the master gland because it:
   a. is in the brain and controls movement
   b. allows for the mastery of skills
   c. facilitates cognitive mastery of problems
   d. controls the release of hormones throughout the endocrine system

10. How does the hypothalamus influence physical growth?
   a. by affecting the release of growth hormone
   b. by activating calcium receptors in the bones and tissues

c. by directing the reception of growth hormone at the receptor sites

d. by overriding the action of the pituitary gland

WHAT DID YOU MISS? Check your answers against the Answer Key at the end of this chapter of the Study Guide. The Answer Key also lists the page(s) in your text where each question is explained. If you missed any questions, go to the pages indicated in the Answer Key, reread those sections, go back to the questions, and see if you can answer them correctly this time.

ANOTHER OPPORTUNITY TO REVIEW: Answer these questions without your textbook. As a rule of thumb, if you can write only a few words about these questions, you probably need to go back and review.

1. Differentiate between the divisions of the nervous system. _____

2. Identify the primary structures of the endocrine system. _____

3. Explain how the nervous system and the endocrine system communicate to control thought, feeling, and behavior. _____

WHAT DO I NEED TO KNOW? Based on what you've discovered above, what are the areas where you need to focus your studying? Which objectives do you need to spend more time mastering? Write this information down in your own words.

1. _____
2. _____
3. _____
4. _____
5. _____
6. _____

3.4 What Is the Genetic Basis of Psychological Science?

Just as you have inherited your natural hair color from your parents, you have also inherited aspects of your behavior. The genetic basis of your behavior, in combination with your environment, has produced the person you are today. By looking at people who are genetically close, such as identical twins, scientists reach conclusions about how behaviors are inherited and how social environments influence the development of those behaviors.

3.4 Guiding Questions

To guide your reading of the text, review the following questions. Then, as you read the chapter, look for the answers to these questions. You may want to note in your textbook where you find these answers.

1. Explain how genes are transmitted from parent to offspring.

2. Discuss the goals and methods of behavioral genetics.

3. Explain how both environmental factors and experience influence genetic expression.

NOW READ Section 3.4 "What Is the Genetic Basis of Psychological Science?" keeping these questions in mind.

REVIEW: Now that you've read this section, go back to the 3.4 Guiding Questions and see if you can answer them based on what you've read. This is a check on your reading. If you can't answer a question, you need to go back to the text to reread that section.

VISUAL SUMMARY: Below is a summary of the major concepts in this section. To check your comprehension of the chapter, read the summary and ask yourself if you understand the concepts. If the concepts seem unfamiliar to you, you may want to go back to the book and reread those sections. This text is taken from the Visual Summaries on StudySpace at wwnorton.com/studyspace.

XV. All of Human Development Has a Genetic Basis
   A. Human behavior is influenced by genes.
   B. Through genes, people inherit the disposition for both physical attributes and personality traits from their parents.

XVI. Heredity Involves Passing Along Genes through Reproduction
   A. Genes can be dominant or recessive.
   B. Genotype: genetic code.

C. Phenotype: observable result of genetic code.
D. Polygenic effects: results of multiple genes.

XVII. Genotypic Variation Is Created by Sexual Reproduction
A. Variations in traits result from combinations of genetic material at conception.

XVIII. Genes Affect Behavior
A. Behavioral genetics: interaction of genes and environment.
B. Behavioral genetics methods include twin studies and adoption studies.
C. Heritability: extent to which variations in a trait within a population is due to genetic factors.

XIX. Social and Environmental Contexts Influence Genetic Expression
A. Genetics and environment interact to produce unique behavioral manifestations.

XX. Genetic Expression Can Be Modified
A. Altering or changing even one gene can dramatically change behavior.

REINFORCE: Are you ready to check your knowledge of this section? Answer the following multiple-choice questions with your textbook closed.

1. Heredity is:
   a. the transmission of characteristics from parents to children through genetics
   b. the transmission of characteristics from parents to children through genetics and environment
   c. a statistical estimate of observed variation in a population caused by genetic variation
   d. the extent to which organisms differ from each other

2. Heritability refers to:
   a. the degree to which genes control a characteristic
   b. the degree to which shared environments account for a shared characteristic among siblings
   c. the degree to which a mother's characteristics are passed on versus a father's characteristics
   d. an estimate of how much of the variation in a characteristic is due to known genetic variation

3. What is the relationship between shared environments and siblings?
   a. Monozygotic twins have the same environment.
   b. Dizygotic twins have the same environment.
   c. Different-age siblings share the same environment, as do all twins.
   d. No siblings share the same exact environment.

4. The term genetics is used to describe how:
   a. only physical characteristics are passed on through inheritance
   b. only behavioral and personality characteristics are passed on through inheritance
   c. physical, behavioral, and personality characteristics are passed on through inheritance
   d. only physical and behavioral characteristics are passed on through inheritance

5. According to the Human Genome Project, humans have approximately how many genes?
   a. 1,000–5,000
   b. 20,000–30,000
   c. over 100,000
   d. three times as many as most animals

6. In considering a human characteristic, we could say that the _____ provides the options and the _____ determines which option is taken.
   a. gene; genome
   b. environment; genome
   c. genome; environment
   d. chromosome; genome

7. Darrius was visiting his cousin's dairy farm. His cousin pointed out that they were using selective breeding to increase milk production. What did he mean?
   a. They selected only certain cows to give milk.
   b. They bred cows for milking and cows for meat together.
   c. They used cows only for milking, not for meat.
   d. They controlled which cows bred, based on the cows' prior milk production.

8. A genotype is _____, whereas a phenotype is _____.
   a. underlying; observed
   b. expressed; inherited
   c. genetic; environmental
   d. dominant; recessive

9. People, even from the same family, can vary in skin color. This fact suggests that skin color is:
   a. controlled by a single gene
   b. a function of personality
   c. genetically determined
   d. polygenic

10. Why are gametes unique?
    a. They contain half of every chromosome pair.
    b. They allow a doubling of the paired chromosomes.
    c. They contain only X or Y chromosomes.
    d. They are fertilized zygotes.

11. Most behavioral geneticists are primarily interested in:
    a. mapping the human genome
    b. discovering how genes control psychological but not biological behaviors
    c. proving that genes have a stronger influence on behavior than does environment
    d. discovering the degree of genetic and environmental influence on psychological phenomena

12. The advantage of studying monozygotic twins is that:
    a. all of their behaviors are identical
    b. they are treated the same in their environment
    c. they are easy to locate and track for research
    d. they are genetically identical

13. Adoption studies are an important tool of behavioral genetics because they:
    a. allow us to examine the effects of non–genetically related mothering
    b. allow us to look at the contributions of environment and genetics on behavior
    c. are so rare
    d. show that environment overwhelms the effect of genes

14. According to the study conducted by Avshalom Caspi, boys who had been mistreated and showed the low-MAO gene were:
    a. least likely to commit a crime
    b. responsible for nearly half the crimes committed by the group
    c. no more likely to commit a crime than the boys without the low-MAO gene but who had been mistreated
    d. no more likely to commit a crime than boys with low-MAO genes who were not mistreated

15. Which of the following is NOT a purpose of a knock-out mouse?

    a. to determine the effects of a removed or disrupted gene on the genome
    b. to determine the effect of a removed or disrupted gene on other genes
    c. to determine how a removed gene might interact with the environment
    d. to reduce the need for MRIs and other invasive techniques to study brain development

WHAT DID YOU MISS? Check your answers against the Answer Key at the end of this chapter of the Study Guide. The Answer Key also lists the page(s) in your text where each question is explained. If you missed any questions, go to the pages indicated in the Answer Key, reread those sections, go back to the questions, and see if you can answer them correctly this time.

ANOTHER OPPORTUNITY TO REVIEW: Answer these questions without your textbook. As a rule of thumb, if you can write only a few words about these questions, you probably need to go back and review.

1. Explain how genes are transmitted from parent to offspring. _____

   _____

   _____

2. Discuss the goals and methods of behavioral genetics. _____

   _____

   _____

3. Explain how both environmental factors and experience influence genetic expression. _____

   _____

   _____

WHAT DO I NEED TO KNOW? Based on what you've discovered above, what are the areas where you need to focus your studying? Which objectives do you need to spend more time mastering? Write this information down in your own words.

1. _____

2. _____

3. _____

4. _____

5. _____

6. _____

3.5 How Does the Brain Change?

Genetics, environment, and experience all work together to create an individual's brain. Rather than being permanent, your brain has the ability to change and adapt to the environment and will continue to do so for your entire life. Culture contributes to this development. Whether you are male or female will also affect how your brain functions.

3.5 Guiding Questions

To guide your reading of the text, review the following questions. Then, as you read the chapter, look for the answers to these questions. You may want to note in your textbook where you find these answers.

1. Explain how environmental factors and experience influence brain organization.

2. Describe sex differences in brain structure and function.

NOW READ Section 3.5 "How Does the Brain Change?" keeping these questions in mind.

REVIEW: Now that you've read this section, go back to the 3.5 Guiding Questions and see if you can answer them based on what you've read. This is a check on your reading. If you can't answer a question, you need to go back to the text to reread that section.

VISUAL SUMMARY: Below is a summary of the major concepts in this section. To check your comprehension of the chapter, read the summary and ask yourself if you understand the concepts. If the concepts seem unfamiliar to you, you may want to go back to the book and reread those sections. This text is taken from the Visual Summaries on StudySpace at wwnorton.com/studyspace.

XXI. Plasticity Is the Tendency of the Brain to Change as a Result of Experience, Injury, or Substances

XXII. The Interplay of Genes and Environment Wires the Brain
   A. Plasticity reflects interactive nature of biological and environmental influences.
   B. Cell identity becomes fixed, but fetal cells can be transplanted to take over roles of dysfunctioning parts of brain.
   C. Experience fine-tunes neural connections: specific stimulation helps brain develop.

XXIII. Culture Affects the Brain
   A. Culture determines specific responses of the brain.

TRY IT

Do You Need Another Reason to Enjoy Yourself?

In this chapter, you learned about the sympathetic nervous system and how it prepares us to cope with potentially threatening and negative situations. Is there a role for positive emotions in helping us to cope more effectively in life? In what she calls the "broaden and build model," psychologist Barbara Fredrickson states that playing and enjoying ourselves can actually build our personal resources and make us into enhanced versions of ourselves. Think about your cat or dog as it plays with a ball or some other toy. Your pet is practicing a skill (hunting) that might help it were you not there to feed it. Although you probably won't need to hunt for your food, play can build new skills for humans also. So try some new activities, learn a new skill, and, in the process, laugh at yourself and try not to take yourself so seriously. You might find that you are building new sets of skills that will be helpful.

XXIV. The Brain Rewires Itself throughout Life
   A. Plasticity decreases with age, but neural connections are made throughout life span.
   B. Learning results in:
      i. neurogenesis.
      ii. formation of neural networks that fire together.
   C. Neural networks are affected by the amount of use.
   D. Synesthesia is:
      i. cross-sensory experience.
      ii. useful in research on brain organization and heredity.

XXV. Females' and Males' Brains Are Similar and Different
   A. Female and male brains have differences that are reflected in psychological functioning.

XXVI. The Brain Can Recover from Injury
   A. Recovery and reorganization can occur most easily in the brains of children.

REINFORCE: Are you ready to check your knowledge of this section? Answer the following multiple-choice questions with your textbook closed.

1. Your friend Cal explains to you that when he looks at the names of the days of the week on his calendar, each day looks as if it is written in a different color. For example, Cal always sees Monday as written in a

light maroon color, whereas Tuesday is always in royal blue. Based on Cal's description, it is likely that he is a(n):
a. integrative perceptionist
b. synesthete
c. holistic reader
d. selective reader

2. Which of the following is a myth about brain plasticity across the life span?
a. Stressful experiences may interfere with neurogenesis.
b. Adult brains form no new cells.
c. Neurogenesis occurs across the life span.
d. Environmental conditions play a role in neurogenesis.

3. In the studies that deprived animals of early visual input, why did the visual cortex fail to develop?
a. Sufficient stimulation was not received within the critical developmental period.
b. The eyes stopped functioning, so no information was received in the visual cortex.
c. The animals were too young for visual cortex development.
d. Plasticity is not found in the visual cortex.

4. Jimmy's crossed eyes were not diagnosed and treated until he was an adolescent. Based on your knowledge of critical periods, what do you think would be the result of the crossed eyes on his adult vision?
a. The crossed eyes will have no effect on his adult vision.
b. The crossed eyes are likely to result in poorer adult vision because they were not corrected until after the critical period.
c. The crossed eyes are unlikely to result in poorer adult vision because they were corrected within the critical period.
d. He will be blind because the correction occurred after the critical period.

5. Based on the study on enriched environments, what might you predict would be the effects of a superior preschool program versus an inferior preschool program on the mental development of human children?
a. There should be no effect, as intelligence is primarily genetic in humans.
b. The inferior program should result in greater mental development because the children would have to work harder to learn, providing an enriched experience.
c. The superior program should result in greater mental development, because the children would have experienced an enriched environment during their critical period.

d. There should be no effect because both preschool programs would occur outside the critical period for mental development in children.

6. Cultural neuroscience is least likely to involve:
a. the study of how dominant genes affect bone growth and development
b. analyses of social and emotional processes in the perception of faces
c. measurements of eye movements toward particular objects in individuals residing in Japan versus England
d. examining brain scans of individuals from Western and Eastern cultures as they listen to voices

7. According to research on people's responses to facial expressions of emotion, which of the following is NOT true?
a. People are best at identifying emotions in the faces of people from their same culture.
b. People across cultures recognize a general set of basic human facial emotions.
c. People from Eastern cultures are unable to recognize neutral versus fearful facial expressions.
d. People from different cultures show some variation in their recognition of human facial emotions.

8. Which of the following would be the best example of phantom limb syndrome?
a. not remembering that you have lost your arm
b. experiencing intense sensations in your leg, even though the leg has been amputated
c. dreaming about your missing limb as if it were still there
d. using a prosthetic limb

9. Which of the following phenomena is the best explanation for synesthesia?
a. Because of the proximity of the two brain areas involved in seeing colors and understanding numbers, some of these areas have cross connections.
b. Individuals with synesthesia have an extra cortical lobe in the brain.
c. Because of the proximity of the two brain areas involved in seeing color and understanding numbers, there is a short circuit between the two causing the confusion.
d. Individuals with synesthesia are missing a portion of the cortex used to process color, so the auditory area of the brain must process the information.

10. Which is an example of sexual dimorphism?
    a. differences in cognitive functioning between men and women
    b. existence of homosexuality
    c. changes in the size of the corpus callosum in left-handers versus right-handers
    d. hermaphrodite syndromes

11. Men and women have been shown to differ on all but which of the following?
    a. how they solve complex problems
    b. the degree to which they use language-related brain regions
    c. the size of the brain
    d. intelligence

12. Which statement best summarizes the research examining differences between men's and women's brains?
    a. Men have larger and thus superior brains.
    b. Women have denser and thus superior brains.
    c. The brains of men and women may differ such that they accomplish the same task equally but in different ways.
    d. There are no differences between the brains of men and the brains of women.

13. What is the typical outcome for young children who, due to disease or injury, have an entire brain hemisphere removed during a hemispherectomy?
    a. The remaining hemisphere eventually takes on most of the lost hemisphere's function.
    b. The children are most likely profoundly cognitively disabled.
    c. The children will be able to sit but not walk.
    d. There is no change in any function immediately after the surgery, due to immediate neural plasticity.

WHAT DID YOU MISS? Check your answers against the Answer Key at the end of this chapter of the Study Guide. The Answer Key also lists the page(s) in your text where each question is explained. If you missed any questions, go to the pages indicated in the Answer Key, reread those sections, go back to the questions, and see if you can answer them correctly this time.

ANOTHER OPPORTUNITY TO REVIEW: Answer these questions without your textbook. As a rule of thumb, if you can write only a few words about these questions, you probably need to go back and review.

1. Explain how environmental factors and experience influence brain organization. _____

_____

_____

2. Describe sex differences in brain structure and function. _____

_____

_____

WHAT DO I NEED TO KNOW? Based on what you've discovered above, what are the areas where you need to focus your studying? Which objectives do you need to spend more time mastering? Write this information down in your own words.

1. _____

2. _____

3. _____

4. _____

5. _____

6. _____

WHAT MATTERS TO ME: What facts in this chapter are personally relevant to you?

_____

_____

_____

_____

CHAPTER SUMMARY

3.1 How Does the Nervous System Operate?

- *Neurons Are Specialized for Communication:* Neurons are the basic building blocks of the nervous system. They receive and send chemical messages. All neurons have the same basic structure, but neurons vary by function and by location in the nervous system.
- *Action Potentials Cause Neural Communication:* Changes in a neuron's electrical charge are the basis of an action potential, or neural firing. Firing is the means of communication within networks of neurons.
- *Neurotransmitters Bind to Receptors across the Synapse:* Neurons do not touch; they release chemicals

(neurotransmitters) into the synaptic cleft, a small gap between the neurons. Neurotransmitters bind with the receptors of postsynaptic neurons, thus changing the charge in those neurons. Neurotransmitters' effects are halted by reuptake of the neurotransmitters into the presynaptic neurons, by enzyme deactivation, or by autoreception.

- *Neurotransmitters Influence Mental Activity and Behavior:* Neurotransmitters have been identified that influence aspects of the mind and behavior in humans. For example, neurotransmitters influence emotions, motor skills, sleep, dreaming, learning and memory, arousal, pain control, and pain perception. Drugs and toxins can enhance or inhibit the activity of neurotransmitters by affecting their synthesis, their release, and the termination of their action in the synaptic cleft.

3.2 What Are the Basic Brain Structures and Their Functions?

- *The Brain Stem Houses the Basic Programs of Survival:* The top of the spinal cord forms the brain stem, which is involved in basic functions such as breathing and swallowing. The brain stem contains the reticular formation, a network of neurons that influences general alertness and sleep.
- *The Cerebellum Is Essential for Movement:* The cerebellum ("little brain"), the bulging structure connected to the back of the brain stem, is essential for movement and controls balance.
- *Subcortical Structures Control Emotions and Appetitive Behaviors:* The subcortical structures play a key part in psychological functions because they control vital functions (the hypothalamus), sensory relay (the thalamus), memories (the hippocampus), emotions (the amygdala), and the planning and producing of movement (the basal ganglia).
- *The Cerebral Cortex Underlies Complex Mental Activity:* The lobes of the cortex play specific roles in vision (occipital), touch (parietal), hearing and speech comprehension (temporal), and movement, rational activity, social behavior, and personality (frontal).

3.3 How Does the Brain Communicate with the Body?

- *The Peripheral Nervous System Includes the Somatic and Autonomic Systems:* The somatic system transmits sensory signals and motor signals between the central nervous system and the skin, muscles, and joints. The autonomic system regulates the body's internal environment through the sympathetic division, which responds to alarm, and the parasympathetic division, which returns the body to its resting state.
- *The Endocrine System Communicates through Hormones:* Endocrine glands produce and release chemical substances. These substances travel to body tissues through the bloodstream and influence a variety of processes, including sexual behavior.
- *Actions of the Nervous System and Endocrine System Are Coordinated:* The endocrine system is largely controlled through the actions of the hypothalamus and the pituitary gland. The hypothalamus controls the release of hormones from the pituitary gland. The pituitary gland controls the release of hormones from other endocrine glands in the body.

3.4 What Is the Genetic Basis of Psychological Science?

- *All of Human Development Has a Genetic Basis:* Human behavior is influenced by genes. Through genes, people inherit both physical attributes and personality traits from their parents. Chromosomes are made of genes, and the Human Genome Project has mapped the genes that make up humans' 23 chromosomal pairs.
- *Heredity Involves Passing Along Genes through Reproduction:* Genes may be dominant or recessive. An organism's genetic constitution is referred to as its genotype. The organism's observable characteristics are referred to as its phenotype. Many characteristics are polygenic.
- *Genotypic Variation Is Created by Sexual Reproduction:* An offspring receives half of its chromosomes from its mother and half of its chromosomes from its father. Because so many combinations of the 23 pairs of chromosomes are possible, there is tremendous genetic variation in the human species. Mutations resulting from errors in cell division also give rise to genetic variation.
- *Genes Affect Behavior:* Behavioral geneticists examine how genes and environment interact to influence psychological activity and behavior. Twin studies and research on adoptees provide insight into heritability.
- *Social and Environmental Contexts Influence Genetic Expression:* Genes and social contexts interact in ways that influence our observable characteristics.
- *Genetic Expression Can Be Modified:* Genetic manipulation has been achieved in mammals such as mice. Animal studies using the technique of "knocking out" genes to determine their effects on behavior and on disease are a valuable tool for understanding genetic influences.

3.5 How Does the Brain Change?

- *The Interplay of Genes and Environment Wires the Brain:* Chemical signals influence cell growth and cell function. Environmental experiences, particularly during critical periods, influence cell development and neural connections.
- *Culture Affects the Brain:* The influence of experience on brain development is reflected in the different patterns of brain activity of people from different cultures.
- *The Brain Rewires Itself throughout Life:* Although plasticity decreases with age, the brain retains the ability to rewire itself throughout life. This ability is the biological basis of learning. Anomalies in sensation and in perception, such as synesthesia, are attributed to the cross-wiring of connections in the brain.
- *Females' and Males' Brains Are Similar and Different:* Females' and males' brains are more similar than different. They are different, however: Males' brains are larger than females' (on average), and females' verbal abilities are organized more bilaterally (more equally in both hemispheres).
- *The Brain Can Recover from Injury:* The brain can reorganize its functions in response to brain damage, although this capacity decreases with age.

PUTTING IT ALL TOGETHER

Answer these questions to check your knowledge of the material in this chapter.

1. Imagine you are flipping through the television channels looking for something interesting to watch. How would your sensory and motor neurons operate while performing this task? Say you flip to a channel showing brain surgery. Which neurotransmitters would be released in your brain in response to the surgery, and why?

2. Explain the role different parts of your brain might play in your reaction of repulsion to seeing brain surgery on television as you are flipping through the channels. Try to organize your responses under the categories of: brainstem areas, subcortical areas, and cerebral cortex areas.

3. Describe how the central and peripheral components of the nervous system interact with each other and how they interact with the endocrine system. Use repulsion to seeing brain surgery on television as an example, and describe how all three systems could be involved.

4. A main theme of this section (and the textbook overall) is that nature and nurture are inextricably entwined. Someone who has strong anxiety reactions to gory stimuli (such as seeing brain surgery on television) is likely to have developed that anxiety through nature and nurture. Use your knowledge of genotype and phenotype to explain the inextricable entwinement of nature and nurture in this case.

5. Suppose that surgeons are performing a radical hemispherectomy on a patient with severe epilepsy. Based on what you know about sensitive periods, plasticity, and neurogenesis, explain whether a child or an adult would be more likely to recover from such a procedure, and why.

ANSWER KEY FOR REINFORCE QUESTIONS

Section 3.1

1. c	p. 76
2. a	p. 76
3. a	p. 77
4. d	p. 77
5. b	p. 77
6. c	p. 76
7. a	p. 77
8. b	p. 77
9. b	p. 79
10. a	p. 79
11. b	p. 77
12. d	p. 82
13. b	p. 82
14. b	p. 80
15. b	p. 82
16. a	p. 83
17. c	p. 84
18. c	p. 85
19. d	p. 84
20. a	p. 86

Section 3.2

1. a	p. 92
2. a	p. 92
3. d	p. 93
4. d	p. 93
5. d	p. 93
6. a	p. 93
7. b	p. 93
8. b	p. 93
9. b	p. 93
10. c	p. 90

Section 3.3

1. d	p. 98
2. b	p. 98

3. b   p. 99
4. b   p. 99
5. d   p. 100
6. a   p. 101
7. b   p. 102
8. c   p. 101
9. d   p. 102
10. a   p. 103

Section 3.4

1. a   p. 113
2. d   p. 113
3. d   p. 111
4. c   p. 105
5. b   p. 106
6. c   p. 105
7. d   p. 107
8. a   p. 107
9. d   p. 108
10. a   p. 109
11. d   p. 110
12. d   p. 111
13. b   p. 112
14. b   p. 114
15. d   p. 115

Section 3.5

1. b   p. 121
2. b   p. 120
3. a   p. 118
4. b   p. 118
5. c   p. 118
6. a   p. 119
7. c   p. 119
8. b   p. 121
9. a   p. 121
10. a   p. 124
11. d   p. 125
12. c   p. 125
13. a   p. 125

HINTS FOR PUTTING IT ALL TOGETHER QUESTIONS

1. Sensory neurons pick up sensory information from the environment and transmit that information to the central nervous system (e.g., sensory neurons in the eye receive visual input from the television and send it to the brain for interpretation). Motor neurons allow signals from the brain to be sent to the spinal cord, then on to the muscles to allow for movement (e.g., allows you to press the button on the remote to change the channel). If you find watching surgery repulsive, you might release norepinephrine (i.e., increased vigilance because it grabs your attention) and substance P (i.e., increased anxiety). If you find watching surgery fascinating and want to learn more about it, you might release acetylcholine and glutamate (i.e., learning and memory) or dopamine (i.e., find the experience rewarding), as well as norepinephrine and serotonin (mood).

2. Overall, the brain stem would be involved in automatic responses of the body in reaction to the image of brain surgery. Increased alertness (reticular formation), increased heart rate and breathing (medulla oblongata) might both be involved. Subcortical areas involved might be the amygdala (fear response), hypothalamus (fight-or-flight response), hippocampus (if the image is burned into your memory), and basal ganglia (to plan a motor response—maybe covering your eyes or immediately pressing the channel changer). The cerebral cortex structures involved would be the occipital and lower temporal lobes to process the visual information. The frontal lobe might also be involved to send signals to initiate movement and to focus your attention away from the visual information.

3. The brain (central nervous system) would interpret the visual input from the television. If repulsed, the hypothalamus might send a signal to the pituitary gland (master gland), which releases hormones that signal other glands in the endocrine system (adrenal, pancreas) to release specific hormones. The brain (central nervous system) could also send signals through the peripheral nervous system to muscles (somatic) to enact motor movement (e.g., covering eyes). Furthermore, the brain could send signals through the peripheral nervous system (autonomic this time) to glands (endocrine system) to enact increased hormone release, which could, for example, increase heart rate (sympathetic) or decrease it (parasympathetic).

4. The genes we are born with make up our genotype, whereas the observable characteristics of our behavior and mind make up our phenotype (e.g., eye color, intelligence). A person's level of anxiety is his or her phenotype, and this anxiety level is due to a combination of nature (genes) and nurture (environment). One way of demonstrating the inextricable entwinement of nature and nurture in this person may be: A person born with susceptibility to anxiety will likely have inherited that genetic predisposition from his or her parents, who in turn may provide a high-anxiety home environment for their child. Another possible example is: The child with an anxious predisposition may also be more likely to create an anxious environment outside of the home (e.g., nervous at preschool, making other children nervous

and creating an anxious environment in preschool). Genotypes influence environment, often creating situations in which it is impossible to separate the influence of nature and nurture on phenotype.

5. A radical hemispherectomy is surgery to remove one entire hemisphere of the cerebral cortex. After surgery, the remaining hemisphere will need to take over many functions of the removed hemisphere, which requires formation of new neurons (neurogenesis) and reorganization of old neurons, two processes that are much more likely to be successful in children than in adults. Brain plasticity (i.e., malleability) is greatest during childhood, especially if the child has not yet passed the sensitive period of development (time period in which brain development is still occurring).

KEY TERMS EXERCISES

First, fill in your own definition and example for each term. Then check each term against the textbook's definition. These exercises can also be cut out and used as flash cards.

acetylcholine (ACh)

Your Definition:
Your Example:
Textbook Definition:

amygdala

Your Definition:
Your Example:
Textbook Definition:

action potential

Your Definition:
Your Example:
Textbook Definition:

antagonists

Your Definition:
Your Example:
Textbook Definition:

agonists

Your Definition:
Your Example:
Textbook Definition:

autonomic nervous system (ANS)

Your Definition:
Your Example:
Textbook Definition:

all-or-none principle

Your Definition:
Your Example:
Textbook Definition:

axon

Your Definition:
Your Example:
Textbook Definition:

basal ganglia

Your Definition:
Your Example:
Textbook Definition:

central nervous system (CNS)

Your Definition:
Your Example:
Textbook Definition:

brain stem

Your Definition:
Your Example:
Textbook Definition:

cerebellum

Your Definition:
Your Example:
Textbook Definition:

Broca's area

Your Definition:
Your Example:
Textbook Definition:

cerebral cortex

Your Definition:
Your Example:
Textbook Definition:

cell body

Your Definition:
Your Example:
Textbook Definition:

chromosomes

Your Definition:
Your Example:
Textbook Definition:

dendrites

Your Definition:
Your Example:
Textbook Definition:

endocrine system

Your Definition:
Your Example:
Textbook Definition:

dizygotic twins

Your Definition:
Your Example:
Textbook Definition:

endorphins

Your Definition:
Your Example:
Textbook Definition:

dominant gene

Your Definition:
Your Example:
Textbook Definition:

epinephrine

Your Definition:
Your Example:
Textbook Definition:

dopamine

Your Definition:
Your Example:
Textbook Definition:

frontal lobes

Your Definition:
Your Example:
Textbook Definition:

GABA

Your Definition:
Your Example:
Textbook Definition:

gonads

Your Definition:
Your Example:
Textbook Definition:

genes

Your Definition:
Your Example:
Textbook Definition:

heritability

Your Definition:
Your Example:
Textbook Definition:

genotype

Your Definition:
Your Example:
Textbook Definition:

hippocampus

Your Definition:
Your Example:
Textbook Definition:

glutamate

Your Definition:
Your Example:
Textbook Definition:

hormones

Your Definition:
Your Example:
Textbook Definition:

hypothalamus

Your Definition:
Your Example:
Textbook Definition:

myelin sheath

Your Definition:
Your Example:
Textbook Definition:

interneurons

Your Definition:
Your Example:
Textbook Definition:

neurons

Your Definition:
Your Example:
Textbook Definition:

monozygotic twins

Your Definition:
Your Example:
Textbook Definition:

neurotransmitters

Your Definition:
Your Example:
Textbook Definition:

motor neurons

Your Definition:
Your Example:
Textbook Definition:

nodes of Ranvier

Your Definition:
Your Example:
Textbook Definition:

norepinephrine

Your Definition:
Your Example:
Textbook Definition:

peripheral nervous system (PNS)

Your Definition:
Your Example:
Textbook Definition:

occipital lobes

Your Definition:
Your Example:
Textbook Definition:

phenotype

Your Definition:
Your Example:
Textbook Definition:

parasympathetic division

Your Definition:
Your Example:
Textbook Definition:

pituitary gland

Your Definition:
Your Example:
Textbook Definition:

parietal lobes

Your Definition:
Your Example:
Textbook Definition:

plasticity

Your Definition:
Your Example:
Textbook Definition:

prefrontal cortex

Your Definition:
Your Example:
Textbook Definition:

reuptake

Your Definition:
Your Example:
Textbook Definition:

receptors

Your Definition:
Your Example:
Textbook Definition:

sensory neurons

Your Definition:
Your Example:
Textbook Definition:

recessive gene

Your Definition:
Your Example:
Textbook Definition:

serotonin

Your Definition:
Your Example:
Textbook Definition:

resting membrane potential

Your Definition:
Your Example:
Textbook Definition:

somatic nervous system

Your Definition:
Your Example:
Textbook Definition:

substance P

Your Definition:

Your Example:

Textbook Definition:

synesthesia

Your Definition:

Your Example:

Textbook Definition:

sympathetic division

Your Definition:

Your Example:

Textbook Definition:

temporal lobes

Your Definition:

Your Example:

Textbook Definition:

synapse

Your Definition:

Your Example:

Textbook Definition:

terminal buttons

Your Definition:

Your Example:

Textbook Definition:

synaptic cleft

Your Definition:

Your Example:

Textbook Definition:

thalamus

Your Definition:

Your Example:

Textbook Definition:

CHAPTER 4 | Sensation and Perception

CHAPTER OVERVIEW

Sight, hearing, touch, taste, and smell are the windows to our world. Rather than being mechanical receptors, our senses are affected by perceptual processes, which cause us to experience the world in unique ways. You will learn in this chapter about the mechanisms that allow us to sense the world and how our perceptions can be affected by psychological processes.

4.1 How Do We Sense Our Worlds?

The process by which each of our senses receives information about the world and how perception starts has similarities across all sensory systems. When do we start paying attention to information from our senses, and when we do we stop paying attention? In this section, you'll learn about these basics and about the theory that can explain these processes.

At the beginning of each section in the Study Guide, there will be guiding questions. Before you read the chapter in your textbook, read through these questions and maybe even attempt to answer them based on either what you've already read or what you think the answer should be. Then as you study the chapter, you can use them to help guide your reading.

4.1 Guiding Questions

To guide your reading of the text, review the following questions. Then, as you read the chapter, look for the answers to these questions. You may want to note in your textbook where you find these answers.

1. Distinguish between sensation and perception.

2. Describe the process of transduction.

3. Distinguish between an absolute threshold and a difference threshold.

4. Discuss sensory detection theory.

5. Define sensory adaptation.

NOW READ Section 4.1 "How Do We Sense Our Worlds?" keeping these questions in mind.

REVIEW: Now that you've read this section, go back to the 4.1 Guiding Questions and see if you can answer them based on what you've read. This is a check on your reading. If you can't answer a question, you need to go back to the text to reread that section.

VISUAL SUMMARY: Below is a summary of the major concepts in this section. To check your comprehension of the chapter, read the summary and ask yourself if you understand the concepts. If the concepts seem unfamiliar to you, you may want to go back to the book and reread those sections. This text is taken from the Visual Summaries on StudySpace at wwnorton.com/studyspace.

I. Sensation Is the Body's Detection of External Sensory Stimuli

II. Perception
   A. Perception is further processing, organizing, and interpreting of stimuli.
   B. Perception leads to internal representations and conscious experience.

III. Stimuli Must Be Coded to Be Understood by the Brain
   A. Sensory coding consists of transduction (translation of information from sensory organs into pattern of neuronal impulses).
   B. Each sensory system responds to unique stimuli, has unique sensory receptors, and has unique pathways to the brain.

IV. Psychophysics Measures the Relationship between Stimuli and Perception
   A. Psychophysics examines psychological experiences of physical stimuli.
   B. Absolute threshold is minimum intensity of sensory stimulation required before sensation is experienced.
   C. Difference threshold is minimum difference needed to detect change between two stimuli.
   D. According to Weber's law, difference threshold is proportional to original stimulus, not to fixed amount of difference.
   E. According to signal detection theory, detection of threshold is subjective, requires judgment, and may be affected by response bias.
   F. Sensory adaptation is the tendency for any sensory system to stop responding as strongly when level of stimulation remains constant.

REINFORCE: Are you ready to check your knowledge of this section? Answer the following multiple-choice questions with your textbook closed.

1. Amadi is listening to John play the guitar. When John plays a note, the vibrations of the air are picked up by auditory receptors in Amadi's ear and sent to his brain. In his brain, the information from the receptors is analyzed to produce the experience of a musical note. The pickup of information by receptors in the ear is:
   a. sensation
   b. psychophysics
   c. perception
   d. top-down processing

2. Taj wants to create a robot that has sensation but not perception. The robot should:
   a. react to light but not to the stimuli for taste, smell, or touch
   b. detect external light sources, but be unable to use the sensory information to understand the environment
   c. understand what things are, but be unable to respond to them
   d. construct useful information, but be unable to remember it

3. Sensory stimuli are translated into chemical and electrical signals that the brain can interpret in a process called:
   a. psychophysics
   b. transduction
   c. response bias
   d. sensory adaptation

4. Jason is doing a psychology experiment in which he is seated in an absolutely dark room. An initially undetected point of light in front of him is gradually made more intense. With each increase, he is asked if he can see the light. In this experiment, Jason's _____ is being measured.
   a. difference threshold
   b. absolute threshold
   c. just noticeable difference
   d. psychophysical limit

5. The law that states that the just noticeable difference between two stimuli is based on a proportion of the original stimulus is:
   a. Fechner's Law
   b. Weber's Law
   c. Koehler's Law
   d. Wernicke's Law

6. Hannah is having dinner at a Mexican restaurant. When she tries the three kinds of sauces to see how hot they are, she is assessing _____ differences between the sauces.
   a. just perceptible
   b. coded
   c. qualitative
   d. quantitative

7. When Petra jumps into a cold lake, she feels as though she is freezing. After a few minutes, she no longer notices the cold and feels comfortable in the water. This effect is an example of:
   a. coarse coding
   b. just noticeable difference
   c. sensory adaptation
   d. sensory threshold

8. Kendra loves spicy curry, but her husband does not. Starting with a bland curry, Kendra gradually increases the spiciness every time she cooks. Each time, she asks her husband if the curry seems hotter, and one day her husband says yes. Kendra is assessing her husband's:
   a. difference threshold
   b. absolute threshold
   c. sensory adaptation
   d. psychophysical limit

9. People stop responding to unchanging stimuli because:
   a. people's attention is continually detecting new and possibly important stimuli
   b. people's sense organs become fatigued
   c. the stimuli exceed people's attentional capacity
   d. the sensory system has malfunctioned

10. On Monday, Manuel interviewed for a job that he really wants. The interviewer told Manuel that he would call on Friday to tell Manuel if he got the job. On late Friday afternoon, Manuel is trying to study, but whenever he hears a sound, he jumps up and thinks it is the phone. Manuel is showing which of the following?
    a. correct rejection
    b. sensory adaptation
    c. response bias
    d. sensory attenuation

WHAT DID YOU MISS? Check your answers against the Answer Key at the end of this chapter of the Study Guide. The Answer Key also lists the page(s) in your text where each question is explained. If you missed any questions, go to the pages indicated in the Answer Key, reread those sections, go back to the questions, and see if you can answer them correctly this time.

ANOTHER OPPORTUNITY TO REVIEW: Answer these questions without your textbook. As a rule of thumb, if you can write only a few words about these questions, you probably need to go back and review.

1. Distinguish between sensation and perception. _____
   _____
2. Describe the process of transduction. _____
   _____
   _____
3. Distinguish between an absolute threshold and a difference threshold. _____
   _____
   _____
4. Discuss sensory detection theory. _____
   _____
   _____
5. Define sensory adaptation. _____

WHAT DO I NEED TO KNOW? Based on what you've discovered above, what are the areas where you need to focus your studying? Which objectives do you need to spend more time mastering? Write this information down in your own words.

1. _____
2. _____
3. _____
4. _____
5. _____
6. _____

4.2 What Are the Basic Sensory Processes?

Each of the senses has a unique way of gathering information from the physical world and communicating that information to the brain. In this section, you will learn about the basic mechanisms of each sensory system. You will also learn about how we experience color and how acute and chronic pain differ in their patterns of neural activation.

4.2 Guiding Questions

To guide your reading of the text, review the following questions. Then, as you read the chapter, look for the answers to these questions. You may want to note in your textbook where you find these answers.

1. For each of the five major senses—taste, smell, touch, hearing, and vision—identify the type of receptor and trace the neural pathway to the brain.
2. Distinguish between the neural processes associated with the experience of immediate pain and the experience of chronic pain.
3. Discuss color perception.

NOW READ Section 4.2 "What Are the Basic Sensory Processes?" keeping these questions in mind.

REVIEW: Now that you've read this section, go back to the 4.2 Guiding Questions and see if you can answer them based on what you've read. This is a check on your reading. If you can't answer a question, you need to go back to the text to reread that section.

VISUAL SUMMARY: Below is a summary of the major concepts in this section. To check your comprehension of the

TRY IT

Looking Up and Looking Down

Although this chapter has been about the neurological and psychological processes of perception, perception also plays a role in how we experience life on a more complex level. Part of depression is a tendency to see more negative than positive events in one's life. Can we change this perception? Positive psychologists have come up with a number of techniques for changing our perceptions about the quality of our lives. One technique is called the "Gratitude Letter."

Choose someone in your life who has been important to you. Maybe you have told this person how important she or he was, or maybe you haven't. Write a letter telling the person why she or he has made a difference in your life. Send the letter or, even better, meet with the person and read the letter to her or him. Pay attention to how you felt in this process of writing the letter and then sharing the letter with the person. Did this process change your perception of your life? Did you feel better about yourself after this process? If you're like many people, you did, and you can continue this process of looking for events or relationships in your life for which to be thankful. Gratitude leads to feeling better about ourselves.

chapter, read the summary and ask yourself if you understand the concepts. If the concepts seem unfamiliar to you, you may want to go back to the book and reread those sections. This text is taken from the Visual Summaries on StudySpace at wwnorton.com/studyspace.

V. In Taste, Taste Buds Detect Chemicals
   A. The five tastes are sweet, sour, salty, bitter, and umami.
   B. Food preferences:
      i. are affected by culture.
      ii. can begin prenatally.

VI. In Smell, the Nasal Cavity Gathers Odorants
   A. Each odorant:
      i. makes contact with olfactory epithelium (which transmits information to the olfactory bulb, in the brain).
      ii. stimulates several receptors (resulting in pattern of neuronal activation).
   B. Perception of pheromones influences behaviors and physiological responses in animals and may also do so in humans.

VII. In Touch, Sensors in the Skin Detect Pressure, Temperature, and Pain

A. In touch, specific haptic receptors respond to:
   i. temperature.
   ii. pain.
   iii. pressure (vibration, light and fast pressure, light and slow pressure, stretching and steady pressure).
B. Two types of nerve fibers serve as pain receptors:
   i. fast fibers (myelinated) for sharp, immediate pain.
   ii. slow fibers (nonmyelinated) for chronic, dull, steady pain.

VIII. In Hearing, the Ear Detects Sound Waves
   A. Hearing (audition) results from:
      i. sound waves (pattern of changes in air pressure over time).
      ii. waves' amplitude (determines volume).
      iii. waves' frequency (determines pitch).
   B. Hearing pathway: sound waves → outer ear → ear drum (middle ear, where the hammer, anvil, and stirrup vibrate) → oval window (cochlea, in the inner ear) → basilar membrane → vibrates hair cells (primary receptors) → auditory nerve.
   C. Cochlear implants:
      i. restore hearing for people with loss of hair cells.
      ii. are controversial in the deaf community.

IX. In Vision, the Eye Detects Light Waves
   A. Retina has two types of receptors:
      i. rods (low light, no color, poor detail, 120 million, located at edge of retina).
      ii. cones (bright light, color, fine detail, 6 million, densely packed in fovea).
   B. Photopigments are light-sensitive chemicals that initiate transduction of light waves into electrical neural impulses.
   C. Visual pathway: transduction → bipolar, amacrine, horizontal cells, which converge on ganglion cells → optic nerve → optic chiasm → visual areas of thalamus → primary visual cortex (occipital lobe).
   D. There are two complementary models of color vision:
      i. According to trichromatic theory, color vision results from activity in S cones (responding to short wavelengths, blue-violet light), M cones (responding to medium wavelengths, yellow-green light), and L cones (responding to long wavelengths, red-orange light).
      ii. Opponent processes are exemplified when ganglion cells receive excitatory input from L cones but are inhibited by M cones

creating perception that some colors are opposites.

E. Color is determined by wavelength.

F. The three dimensions of color are hue (e.g., yellow), saturation (purity or mixture), and brightness (vividness).

G. Colors can be produced through additive color mixing or subtractive color mixing.

X. We Have Other Sensory Systems

A. Kinesthetic receptors in the muscles assist in both perception of the body's position in space and in voluntary movement.

B. Vestibular system uses information from the movement of fluid in the semicircular canals (ears) to determine balance.

XI. With the Exception of Olfaction, All Sensory Information Is Transduced into Electrical Impulses That Are Relayed from the Thalamus to a Specific Cortical Area (Primary Sensory Areas)

REINFORCE: Are you ready to check your knowledge of this section? Answer the following multiple-choice questions with your textbook closed.

1. Which of the following is NOT a basic quality of taste?
   a. sweet
   b. umami
   c. salty
   d. alkaline

2. Sadafa is careful about what he eats because it hurts his tongue when he eats very spicy food. Sadafa most likely:
   a. is a supertaster and has few taste buds in his mouth
   b. is a supertaster with a very large number of taste buds in his mouth
   c. is not a supertaster and has a large number of pain receptors in his mouth
   d. is not a supertaster and has few pain receptors in his mouth

3. Callie is pregnant. She has never liked vegetables and rarely eats them. However, she does not want her baby to have the same bad eating habits. If Callie wants her baby to grow up to enjoy the taste of vegetables, the most effective thing she can do is:
   a. eat vegetables while she is pregnant and nursing
   b. give the baby pureed meat as one of her first solid foods
   c. avoid eating large amounts of vegetables while she is pregnant and nursing
   d. limit the amount of meat the baby is fed when she starts to eat solid food

4. In a single person, gustation involves _____ taste buds.
   a. 500 to 1,000
   b. 1,000 to 5,000
   c. 5,000 to 10,000
   d. 500 to 1,500

5. Olfaction has the most direct route to the brain because it is the only sense that bypasses the:
   a. amygdala
   b. hypothalamus
   c. pineal gland
   d. thalamus

6. The most likely explanation for how an odor is encoded is that:
   a. each odor has a specialized receptor
   b. an activation pattern exists across several olfactory receptor types
   c. a single olfactory and a single gustatory receptor are necessary for perceiving an odor
   d. an activation pattern exists across several olfactory and gustatory receptor types

7. Our sense of touch comes from:
   a. a half-dozen receptors located in the skin
   b. millions of tiny nerves on the surface of the skin
   c. special glands for pressure, temperature, and pain
   d. stimulation of the tiny hairs that cover the body

8. Avi broke his ankle skiing. At first, he felt a sharp and intense pain. The next day, the sharp pain was gone, but his ankle throbbed almost all of the time. The sharp immediate pain was due to _____; the later throbbing pain was due to _____.
   a. unmyelinated axons; myelinated axons
   b. myelinated axons; unmyelinated axons
   c. occipital responses; temporal responses
   d. temporal responses; occipital responses

9. If a key is pressed on a piano, the frequency of the resulting sound will determine the _____, and the amplitude will determine the _____ of the perceived musical note.
   a. timbre; intensity
   b. intensity; timbre
   c. loudness; pitch
   d. pitch; loudness

10. Jeremy is deaf. Because the hair cells in his inner ear have been damaged, _____.
   a. sound waves cannot be transformed into nerve impulses
   b. sound waves cannot cause the oval window to vibrate

c. the tympanic membrane does not receive information from the basilar membrane

d. the cochlea has no fluid to generate sound vibrations

11. The attitude of a large segment of the deaf community to cochlear implants is that children:

a. should be given implants early enough to allow language development

b. should be given implants after they have learned to sign

c. should not be given implants in order to preserve deaf culture

d. should be given implants only if they have hearing parents

12. Encharta is sitting outside, looking at her beautiful garden. As the sun goes down, the colors become less bright and finally become shades of gray. This effect happens because:

a. the amount of photopigment decreases

b. the amount of photopigment increases

c. the cones take over for the rods

d. the rods take over for the cones

13. Where do molecules of photopigment reside?

a. in the iris

b. in the rods and cones

c. in the amacrine cells

d. in the ganglion cells

14. Susan is wearing a bright red skirt. She is trying to decide whether she wants to wear a pink top or a brown top with it. If she decides on the pink top, then the top and the skirt will vary in _____. If she decides on the brown top, then the top and the skirt will vary in _____.

a. hue; saturation

b. hue; wavelength

c. wavelength; hue

d. saturation; hue

15. Red and green appear to be opposite colors because of the activity of ganglion cells that are:

a. excited by L cones and inhibited by M cones

b. excited by S cones and inhibited by L cones

c. excited by L cones and inhibited by S and M cones

d. excited by S cones and inhibited by L and M cones

16. Yu-Ming becomes nauseated while driving down a curvy mountain road. His uncomfortable feeling is due to:

a. the feedback receptors of his kinesthetic system getting overloaded

b. conflicting signals from the visual and vestibular systems

c. conflicting signals from the visual and kinesthetic systems

d. the feedback receptors of his vestibular system getting overloaded

WHAT DID YOU MISS? Check your answers against the Answer Key at the end of this chapter of the Study Guide. The Answer Key also lists the page(s) in your text where each question is explained. If you missed any questions, go to the pages indicated in the Answer Key, reread those sections, go back to the questions, and see if you can answer them correctly this time.

ANOTHER OPPORTUNITY TO REVIEW: Answer these questions without your textbook. As a rule of thumb, if you can write only a few words about these questions, you probably need to go back and review.

1. For each of the five major senses, identify the type of receptor and trace the neural pathway to the brain.

   Taste _____

   Smell _____

   Touch _____

   Hearing _____

   Vision _____

2. Distinguish between the neural processes associated with the experience of immediate pain and the experience of chronic pain.

   Immediate pain _____
   _____

   Chronic pain _____
   _____

3. Discuss color perception. _____
   _____

WHAT DO I NEED TO KNOW? Based on what you've discovered above, what are the areas where you need to focus your studying? Which objectives do you need to spend more time mastering? Write this information down in your own words.

1. _____

2. _____

3. _____

4. _____

5. _____

6. _____

4.3 How Does Perception Emerge from Sensation?

The brain contains areas that are devoted to the processing of auditory, visual, and tactile information. These areas can be affected by previous experience so that our perceptions of pain, sound, and vision differ from person to person. In certain circumstances, the brain even has the capacity to ignore the sensory messages that it receives so that, for instance, we may not feel pain from an injury or we may not see objects that are right in front of us.

4.3 Guiding Questions

To guide your reading of the text, review the following questions. Then, as you read the chapter, look for the answers to these questions. You may want to note in your textbook where you find these answers.

1. Identify the primary sensory areas for touch, hearing, and vision.

2. Discuss the gate control theory of pain.

3. Explain how the brain localizes sound.

4. Distinguish between the "what" and "where" pathways of the visual system.

5. Describe blindsight.

NOW READ Section 4.3 "How Does Perception Emerge from Sensation?" keeping these questions in mind.

REVIEW: Now that you've read this section, go back to the 4.3 Guiding Questions and see if you can answer them based on what you've read. This is a check on your reading. If you can't answer a question, you need to go back to the text to reread that section.

VISUAL SUMMARY: Below is a summary of the major concepts in this section. To check your comprehension of the chapter, read the summary and ask yourself if you understand the concepts. If the concepts seem unfamiliar to you, you may want to go back to the book and reread those sections. This text is taken from the Visual Summaries on StudySpace at wwnorton.com/studyspace.

XII. In Touch, the Brain Integrates Sensory Information from Different Regions of the Body
  A. Touch is projected onto the somatosensory cortex, where:
    i. the body is mapped.
    ii. larger amounts of cortical tissue are devoted to more sensitive parts of the body.
  B. According to the gate control theory:
    i. pain involves biological, psychological, and cultural factors.
    ii. when pain receptors are activated, a neural "gate" opens in the spinal cord and allows pain signals to be carried by nerve fibers.
    iii. larger sensory nerve fibers can fire and close the gate, thus preventing pain perception.
    iv. cognitive factors such as distraction and positive moods can close the gate, whereas anxiety and stress can open the gate.

XIII. In Hearing, the Brain Integrates Sensory Information from the Ears
  A. Auditory neurons in thalamus extend their axons to primary auditory cortex, where neurons code frequency of auditory stimuli.
  B. Sound localization involves integration of information about magnitude of sound and which ear receives sound first.

XIV. In Vision, the Brain Processes Sensory Information from the Eyes
  A. What and where pathways:
    i. lower, ventral stream recognizes objects.
    ii. upper, dorsal stream locates objects in space.
  B. Blindsight: a person who is blind may have some visual ability but is unaware of this capability.

REINFORCE: Are you ready to check your knowledge of this section? Answer the following multiple-choice questions with your textbook closed.

1. When you touch a smooth surface, information on the surface first goes to the thalamus. After leaving the thalamus, axons project to the:
  a. frontal lobe
  b. temporal lobe
  c. primary somatosensory cortex
  d. primary motor cortex

2. Mick is getting a tattoo. The tattoo artist creates tiny points adjacent to each other on the skin to tattoo a line. The information from the needle pricks will be represented in the primary somatosensory cortex:
  a. by a single cell with a receptive field responsive to tactile lines
  b. as a pattern of neural responses that code indirectly for location
  c. in the same general area that processes tactile information from the arm
  d. in a line of adjacent points

3. Your friend suddenly looks shocked and asks, "What is that over there?" Your brain would need to use your _____ to locate the object.
   a. dorsal stream
   b. ventral stream
   c. temporal lobe
   d. parietal lobe

4. Kwamie has broken his wrist. His friend, Sam, has taken him to the ER. While they are waiting, Sam starts an argument with Kwamie about the presidential election. While they are arguing, Kwamie is feeling very little pain. This effect has most likely happened because:
   a. anger is incompatible with the experience of pain
   b. Kwamie ignored the pain to make his points
   c. Kwamie's intense focusing on the argument closed the pain gate
   d. Kwamie's nerve fibers thickened as a physical symptom of anger

5. The auditory neurons extending from the thalamus reach out with their axons to the primary auditory cortex in the _____ lobe.
   a. parietal
   b. temporal
   c. frontal
   d. occipital

6. During Little League practice, the third-base coach yells to the pitcher to try a fastball. The pitcher knows that it is the third-base coach, not the first-base coach, who is talking to him because the sound of the coach's voice reaches his left ear _____ than his right ear and is _____ in his left ear than his right ear.
   a. later; softer
   b. later; louder
   c. sooner; softer
   d. sooner; louder

7. Approximately what proportion of the cerebral cortex has been estimated to be involved in vision in some way?
   a. 10 percent
   b. 25 percent
   c. 50 percent
   d. 75 percent

8. Sanjay, who is fearful of injections, is going to get his flu shot. According to the gate control theory of pain, all of the following would be helpful in reducing his pain EXCEPT:
   a. rubbing the injection site prior to receiving the injection
   b. having a conversation with a friend about an upcoming vacation
   c. focusing on past unpleasant experiences with injections
   d. listening to a podcast of his favorite comedian

9. Pain medications such as Novocain work by:
   a. keeping pain stimuli from being received by sensory pain neurons
   b. blocking transmission from sensory pain neurons to the brain
   c. changing the brain's interpretation of information from sensory pain neurons
   d. diverting signals from the sensory pain neurons to the thalamus

10. If the ventral stream of your visual cortex was temporarily not working, you would be unable to understand _____ an object is, but if your dorsal stream was still functioning then you could understand _____ an object is.
    a. where; what
    b. what; where
    c. where; why
    d. what; why

WHAT DID YOU MISS? Check your answers against the Answer Key at the end of this chapter of the Study Guide. The Answer Key also lists the page(s) in your text where each question is explained. If you missed any questions, go to the pages indicated in the Answer Key, reread those sections, go back to the questions, and see if you can answer them correctly this time.

ANOTHER OPPORTUNITY TO REVIEW: Answer these questions without your textbook. As a rule of thumb, if you can write only a few words about these questions, you probably need to go back and review.

1. Identify the primary sensory areas for touch, hearing, and vision.

   Touch _____

   Hearing _____

   Vision _____

2. Discuss the gate control theory of pain. _____

   _____

   _____

3. Explain how the brain localizes sound. _____

   _____

   _____

4. Distinguish between the "what" and "where" pathways of the visual system. _____

_____

_____

5. Describe blindsight. _____

_____

WHAT DO I NEED TO KNOW? Based on what you've discovered above, what are the areas where you need to focus your studying? Which objectives do you need to spend more time mastering? Write this information down in your own words.

1. _____

2. _____

3. _____

4. _____

5. _____

6. _____

4.4 What Factors Influence Visual Perception?

Although perceptual processes can be unique, Gestalt psychologists have identified a number of principles that govern how most people put sensory experiences together in predictable ways. Our ability to experience depth, motion, and even to determine that there are no changes in the information from our senses also have predictable patterns. Optical illusions demonstrate how our perceptual systems can be "tricked."

4.4 Guiding Questions

To guide your reading of the text, review the following questions. Then, as you read the chapter, look for the answers to these questions. You may want to note in your textbook where you find these answers.

1. Describe the Gestalt principles of perceptual organization.

2. Identify the brain regions associated with facial perception.

3. Identify cues for depth perception.

4. Explain how the visual system perceives motion.

5. Discuss how perceptual constancy is achieved.

TRY IT

Sensation, Perception, and Your Favorite Flavor of Ice Cream

One characteristic of most sensory systems is habituation, the tendency for any sensory system to stop responding as strongly to sensory input over time. How can knowledge of habituation be helpful in daily life? Consider the common problem of trying to lose weight. As much as people want to curb their appetites, they also find it difficult to say no to favorite foods. Habituation might help people regulate their eating, as shown in this small experiment.

Choose your favorite forbidden food—say, ice cream, the really good full-fat version. Sit down with a dish and prepare to enjoy yourself. No TV, computer, or talking with friends, just you and a dish of your favorite ice cream. Now, take the first bite and focus on the flavor, maybe even describe it to yourself. Notice how intense the flavor is. After you've really savored that first bite, go on to take the second bite and follow the same process. And then the third. What do you notice? If you're like most people, the intensity of the flavor will lessen with each bite so that by the fourth bite or so you COULD choose to say, "I've had enough." Using this technique of enjoying food until the flavor diminishes can help you to eat less without depriving yourself. Try it!

NOW READ Section 4.4 "What Factors Influence Visual Perception?" keeping these questions in mind.

REVIEW: Now that you've read this section, go back to the 4.4 Guiding Questions and see if you can answer them based on what you've read. This is a check on your reading. If you can't answer a question, you need to go back to the text to reread that section.

VISUAL SUMMARY: Below is a summary of the major concepts in this section. To check your comprehension of the chapter, read the summary and ask yourself if you understand the concepts. If the concepts seem unfamiliar to you, you may want to go back to the book and reread those sections. This text is taken from the Visual Summaries on StudySpace at wwnorton.com/studyspace.

XV. Object Perception Requires Construction
    A. Optical illusions reveal how the visual system determines size and distance of objects and thus constructs three-dimensional image of the world.

B. Gestalt psychologists proposed laws to explain how the brain groups features of a scene into a comprehensible whole, including:
   i. figure-ground.
   ii. proximity.
   iii. similarity.
   iv. closure.
   v. good continuation.
   vi. illusory contours.
C. Bottom-up processing: information from sensory receptors is combined to make more complex and more recognizable patterns.
D. Top-down processing: what we expect to see (context) determines which sensory data we pay attention to.

XVI. Depth Perception Is Important for Locating Objects
A. Binocular vision cues:
   i. retinal disparity
   ii. convergence
B. Monocular vision cues:
   i. occlusion
   ii. relative size
   iii. familiar size
   iv. linear perspective
   v. texture gradient
   vi. position relative to horizon
C. Motion is a cue for depth perception.
D. Motion parallax is the relative movements of objects at various distances from observer.

XVII. Size Perception Depends on Distance Perception
A. Size of an object's retinal image depends on distance from observer.

XVIII. Motion Perception Has Internal and External Cues
A. Neurons fire when movement is detected.
B. Motion aftereffect, compensation for head and eye movement, and stroboscopic motion perception provide insights into motion perception.

XIX. Perceptual Constancies Are Based on Ratio Relationships
A. Perceptual constancy is the tendency to perceive sensory stimuli as constant despite conflicting sensory data.
B. Optical illusions demonstrate how the perception of size, shape, color, and lightness constancy:
   i. are based on underlying assumptions.
   ii. can be altered by misleading sensory data.

REINFORCE: Are you ready to check your knowledge of this section? Answer the following multiple-choice questions with your textbook closed.

1. Consider the pattern: XXY XXY XXY. People perceive this pattern as consisting of three groups of three letters each. Which Gestalt principle accounts for this outcome?
   a. similarity
   b. good continuation
   c. proximity
   d. common region

2. An artist is famous for leaving some objects in her paintings incompletely drawn. Yet when we look at her works, we perceive the complete objects. What organizational rule of perception is occurring?
   a. closure
   b. symmetry
   c. proximity
   d. similarity

3. On the table in front of you, there is a loaf of bread behind a container of milk. You see the bread as a single loaf rather than two half-loaves, one on either side of the milk container. Which Gestalt principle accounts for this outcome?
   a. similarity
   b. good continuation
   c. parallelism
   d. closure

4. Scotty makes dinner by looking at the ingredients in his refrigerator and then combining them into a meal. Scotty is cooking in a _____ manner.
   a. bottom-up
   b. top-down
   c. bottom-down
   d. top-up

5. Each eye sees more of the world on its own side of the visual field. A combination of the views from the two eyes provides humans with an adaptive advantage by creating a broader panorama of the scene. It also creates the depth cue of:
   a. linear perspective
   b. motion parallax
   c. occlusion
   d. disparity

6. As a result of an accident, David has only one eye. Which of the following depth cues would he NOT be able to use?
   a. relative size
   b. binocular disparity
   c. linear perspective
   d. occlusion

7. When driving on the freeway, you notice that the bushes at the side of the road appear to be passing very

quickly. In the distance, you can see a very tall tree, which it takes half an hour to drive past. What depth cue is causing this speed discrepancy?

   a. motion parallax
   b. compensatory movement
   c. stroboscopic movement
   d. changes in linear perspective

8. Gervase is staring at the blades of his ceiling fan, searching for inspiration for a paper that he is writing. When he turns off the fan, he is very surprised that the blades appear to be rotating in the opposite direction. You could reassure Gervase that he is not hallucinating from being overworked by telling him about:

   a. stroboscopic motion
   b. motion aftereffects
   c. compensatory motion
   d. motion parallax

9. Electronic signs create an illusion of movement by illuminating small adjacent lights in rapid succession. This effect is an example of:

   a. induced movement
   b. stroboscopic motion
   c. compensatory movement
   d. movement aftereffects

10. Illusions demonstrate what happens to our perceptual processes when:

   a. we use only one eye to view an object
   b. binocular disparity occurs
   c. our eyes fail to converge
   d. perceptual cues about size and distance are distorted

WHAT DID YOU MISS? Check your answers against the Answer Key at the end of this chapter of the Study Guide. The Answer Key also lists the page(s) in your text where each question is explained. If you missed any questions, go to the pages indicated in the Answer Key, reread those sections, go back to the questions, and see if you can answer them correctly this time.

ANOTHER OPPORTUNITY TO REVIEW: Answer these questions without your textbook. As a rule of thumb, if you can write only a few words about these questions, you probably need to go back and review.

1. Describe the Gestalt principles of perceptual organization. _____
   _____
   _____
   _____

2. Identify the brain regions associated with facial perception. _____

3. Identify cues for depth perception. _____
   _____
   _____
   _____

4. Explain how the visual system perceives motion. _____
   _____
   _____

5. Discuss how perceptual constancy is achieved. _____
   _____
   _____

WHAT DO I NEED TO KNOW? Based on what you've discovered above, what are the areas where you need to focus your studying? Which objectives do you need to spend more time mastering? Write this information down in your own words.

1. _____

2. _____

3. _____

4. _____

5. _____

6. _____

WHAT MATTERS TO ME: What facts in this chapter are personally relevant to you?

_____
_____
_____
_____

CHAPTER SUMMARY

4.1 How Do We Sense Our Worlds?

- *Stimuli Must Be Coded to Be Understood by the Brain:* Stimuli reaching the receptors are converted to neural impulses through the process of transduction.

- *Psychophysics Measures the Relationship between Stimuli and Perception:* By studying how people respond to different sensory levels, scientists can determine thresholds and perceived change (based on signal detection theory). Our sensory systems are tuned to both adapt to constant levels of stimulation and detect changes in our environment.

4.2 What Are the Basic Sensory Processes?

- *In Taste, Taste Buds Detect Chemicals:* The gustatory sense uses taste buds to respond to the chemical substances that produce at least five basic sensations: sweet, sour, salty, bitter, and umami (savory). The number and distribution of taste buds vary among individuals. Cultural taste preferences begin in the womb.
- *In Smell, the Nasal Cavity Gathers Odorants:* Receptors in the olfactory epithelium respond to chemicals and send signals to the olfactory bulb in the brain. Humans can discriminate among thousands of odors. Females are more accurate than males at detecting and identifying odors.
- *In Touch, Sensors in the Skin Detect Pressure, Temperature, and Pain:* The haptic sense relies on tactile stimulation to activate receptors for pressure, for temperature, and for distinct types of pain (immediate, sharp pain and chronic, dull pain).
- *In Hearing, the Ear Detects Sound Waves:* Sound waves activate hair cells in the inner ear. The receptors' responses depend on the sound waves' amplitude and frequency.
- *In Vision, the Eye Detects Light Waves:* Receptors (rods and cones) in the retina detect different forms of light waves. The lens helps the eye focus the stimulation on the retina for near versus far objects. Color is determined by wavelengths of light, which activate certain types of cones; by the absorption of wavelengths by objects; or by the mixing of wavelengths of light.
- *We Have Other Sensory Systems:* In addition to the five "basic" senses, humans and other animals have a kinesthetic sense (ability to judge where one's body and limbs are in space) and a vestibular sense (ability to judge the direction and intensity of head movements, associated with a sense of balance).

4.3 How Does Perception Emerge from Sensation?

- *In Touch, the Brain Integrates Sensory Information from Different Regions of the Body:* The primary sensory area for touch information is the primary somatosensory cortex in the parietal lobe. Neural "gates" in the spinal cord control pain. We can reduce pain perception by distracting ourselves, visualizing pain as more pleasant, being rested and relaxed, learning how to change the brain activity that underlies pain perception, and taking drugs that interfere with the neural transmission of pain.
- *In Hearing, the Brain Integrates Sensory Information from the Ears:* The primary sensory area for auditory information is the primary auditory cortex in the temporal lobe. The neurons at the front of the auditory cortex respond best to higher frequencies. The neurons at the rear of the auditory cortex respond best to lower frequencies. The brain localizes sound by comparing the times that a sound arrives at the individual ears and by comparing the magnitudes of the resulting sound waves at the ears.
- *In Vision, the Brain Processes Sensory Information from the Eyes:* The primary sensory area for visual information is the primary visual cortex in the occipital lobe. The visual system is characterized by a ventral stream that is specialized for object perception and recognition (what) and a dorsal stream that is specialized for spatial perception (where). Blindsight occurs when individuals who are blind retain some visual capacities of which they are unaware.

4.4 What Factors Influence Visual Perception?

- *Object Perception Requires Construction:* The Gestalt principles of organization account for some of the brain's perceptions of the world. The principles include distinguishing figure and ground, the grouping of objects on the basis of proximity and similarity, and the perception of "best" forms. Perception involves two processes: bottom-up processes (sensory information) and top-down processes (expectations about what we will perceive). Researchers have identified brain regions that are specialized for the perception of faces.
- *Depth Perception Is Important for Locating Objects:* The brain uses binocular cues, monocular cues, and motion cues to perceive depth. Binocular disparity and convergence are binocular depth cues. Pictorial depth cues such as occlusion, relative size, and linear perspective are monocular depth cues. Motion parallax is a motion depth cue.
- *Size Perception Depends on Distance Perception:* Illusions of size can be created when the retinal size conflicts with the known size of objects in the visual field, as in the Ames box illusion and the Ponzo illusion.
- *Motion Perception Has Internal and External Cues:* Motion detectors in the cortex respond to stimulation. The perceptual system establishes a stable frame of reference and relates object movement to it. Intervals of stimulation of repeated objects give the impression of

continuous movement. Motion aftereffects, which are opposite in motion from things that have been observed, tell us about the fatigue of neural receptors that fire in response to motion in certain directions.

• *Perceptual Constancies Are Based on Ratio Relationships:* We create expectations about the world that allow us to use information about the shape, size, color, and lightness of objects in their surroundings to achieve constancy.

PUTTING IT ALL TOGETHER

Answer these questions to check your knowledge of the material in this chapter.

1. Late one dark night, Christine, Becky, and Nawal were telling each other ghost stories. Suddenly Becky exclaimed, "Did you hear that groan?" Christine wasn't sure, but she figured Becky would not make things up, so she said, "YES! I heard it, too!" Nawal just shrugged and said she hadn't heard anything. Assuming there really was a groan, use signal detection theory to explain Christine's, Becky's, and Nawal's responses. Assuming there was NO groan, use signal detection theory to describe their responses.

2. When most people look at the stripes in the American flag, they see seven of them as red. When they look at the field behind the stars on the flag, most people see it as blue. If people stare at a flag made of green and white stripes with stars on a yellow background, then switch their focus to a white wall, they will see an afterimage of the American flag in red, white, and blue. Explain the theory of color vision that accounts for why we see a red, white, and blue afterimage after staring at a yellow, white, and green flag.

3. When children suffer bad falls and scrape their knees, they probably also experience pain. According to the gate control theory, why do the scrapes hurt? Based on gate control theory, what can people do to decrease their perception of pain?

4. People wear special glasses when watching 3-D movies. These glasses give each eye a slightly different view of the screen. Because of this, the picture seems to pop out. However, if people watch the movie without the glasses, they can still see that some objects on the screen appear closer than other objects because of occlusion and relative size. The glasses cause objects on the screen to pop out because of which depth cue? Define occlusion and relative size, including the types of depth cues they are.

ANSWER KEY FOR REINFORCE QUESTIONS

Section 4.1

1. a	p. 132
2. b	p. 133
3. b	p. 133
4. b	p. 135
5. b	p. 136
6. d	p. 134
7. c	p. 137
8. a	p. 135
9. a	p. 137
10. c	p. 136

Section 4.2

1. d	p. 140
2. b	p. 141
3. a	p. 141
4. c	p. 140
5. d	p. 143
6. b	p. 143
7. a	p. 145
8. b	pp. 146–147
9. d	p. 148
10. a	p. 148
11. c	p. 150
12. d	p. 151
13. b	p. 151
14. d	p. 154
15. a	pp. 153–154
16. b	p. 156

Section 4.3

1. c	p. 160
2. d	p. 160
3. a	pp. 162–163
4. c	pp. 160–161
5. b	p. 161
6. a	p. 162
7. c	p. 162
8. c	p. 161
9. b	p. 161
10. b	p. 162

Section 4.4

1. c	p. 166
2. a	p. 166
3. b	pp. 166–167
4. a	p. 167
5. d	p. 170

6. b p. 170
7. a p. 171
8. b p. 173
9. b p. 174
10. d p. 172

HINTS FOR PUTTING IT ALL TOGETHER QUESTIONS

1. Your answers for both parts of the question must describe whether the signal was present or absent. You must also include what response was given. Based on these, explain each type of response: hit, miss, false alarm, correct rejection. Be sure to address context when explaining why Christine agreed with Becky.

2. To explain why staring at a yellow, green, and white flag results in a red, white, and blue afterimage, you must describe the opponent process theory.

3. Include discussion of receptors, small fibers, the spinal cord, and the brain to explain the gate control theory of pain. When discussing what can be done to decrease pain, include closing the gate, large fibers, and some specific variables that will help the gate close.

4. To explain why the glasses make objects on the screen seem to pop out, include discussion of binocular depth perception, binocular disparity, and stereoscopic vision. To define occlusion and relative size, first explain monocular depth cues and pictorial depth cues. Then define occlusion and relative size specifically.

KEY TERMS EXERCISES

First, fill in your own definition and example for each term. Then check each term against the textbook's definition. These exercises can also be cut out and used as flash cards.

additive color mixing

Your Definition:
Your Example:
Textbook Definition:

blindsight

Your Definition:
Your Example:
Textbook Definition:

audition

Your Definition:
Your Example:
Textbook Definition:

bottom-up processing

Your Definition:
Your Example:
Textbook Definition:

binocular depth cues

Your Definition:
Your Example:
Textbook Definition:

cones

Your Definition:
Your Example:
Textbook Definition:

binocular disparity

Your Definition:
Your Example:
Textbook Definition:

convergence

Your Definition:
Your Example:
Textbook Definition:

cornea

Your Definition:
Your Example:
Textbook Definition:

haptic sense

Your Definition:
Your Example:
Textbook Definition:

eardrum

Your Definition:
Your Example:
Textbook Definition:

iris

Your Definition:
Your Example:
Textbook Definition:

fovea

Your Definition:
Your Example:
Textbook Definition:

kinesthetic sense

Your Definition:
Your Example:
Textbook Definition:

gustation

Your Definition:
Your Example:
Textbook Definition:

monocular depth cues

Your Definition:
Your Example:
Textbook Definition:

olfaction

Your Definition:
Your Example:
Textbook Definition:

perceptual constancy

Your Definition:
Your Example:
Textbook Definition:

olfactory bulb

Your Definition:
Your Example:
Textbook Definition:

pupil

Your Definition:
Your Example:
Textbook Definition:

olfactory epithelium

Your Definition:
Your Example:
Textbook Definition:

retina

Your Definition:
Your Example:
Textbook Definition:

perception

Your Definition:
Your Example:
Textbook Definition:

rods

Your Definition:
Your Example:
Textbook Definition:

sensation

Your Definition:
Your Example:
Textbook Definition:

taste buds

Your Definition:
Your Example:
Textbook Definition:

sensory adaptation

Your Definition:
Your Example:
Textbook Definition:

top-down processing

Your Definition:
Your Example:
Textbook Definition:

signal detection theory (SDT)

Your Definition:
Your Example:
Textbook Definition:

transduction

Your Definition:
Your Example:
Textbook Definition:

sound wave

Your Definition:
Your Example:
Textbook Definition:

vestibular sense

Your Definition:
Your Example:
Textbook Definition:

subtractive color mixing

Your Definition:
Your Example:
Textbook Definition:

CHAPTER 5 | Consciousness

CHAPTER OVERVIEW

Asleep, awake, concentrating, intoxicated, relaxed. What do these states have in common? They are forms of consciousness. In this chapter, you will learn how the brain creates consciousness and how psychologists have conducted experiments to further understand consciousness. Can we willingly alter consciousness? Yes, we can—for the better, as in sleep or with meditation, or for the worse, as by using substances such as alcohol or illicit drugs.

5.1 What Is Consciousness?

In this section, you will learn about consciousness and the various levels of consciousness. The brain creates the sense of consciousness, and research can be done with individuals who have had their corpora callosa severed to help understand the role that different parts of the brain play in consciousness. People don't necessarily have to be conscious of information for it to affect their emotions or behavior.

At the beginning of each section in the Study Guide, there will be guiding questions. Before you read the chapter in your textbook, read through these questions and maybe even attempt to answer them based on either what you've already read or what you think the answer should be. Then as you study the chapter, you can use them to help guide your reading.

5.1 Guiding Questions

To guide your reading of the text, review the following questions. Then, as you read the chapter, look for the answers to these questions. You may want to note in your textbook where you find these answers.

1. What is consciousness?

2. What are the various states of consciousness?

3. How does brain activity create consciousness?

4. How does research on split brains help us to understand the role of different hemispheres of the brain?

5. How do unconscious processes influence thought and behavior?

NOW READ Section 5.1 "What Is Consciousness?" keeping these questions in mind.

REVIEW: Now that you've read this section, go back to the 5.1 Guiding Questions and see if you can answer them based on what you've read. This is a check on your reading. If you can't answer a question, you need to go back to the text to reread that section.

VISUAL SUMMARY: Below is a summary of the major concepts in this section. To check your comprehension of the chapter, read the summary and ask yourself if you understand the concepts. If the concepts seem unfamiliar to you, you may want to go back to the book and reread those sections. This text is taken from the Visual Summaries on StudySpace at wwnorton.com/studyspace.

  I. Consciousness Is a Subjective Experience
   A. Consciousness:
       i. is moment-by-moment subjective experience.
       ii. results from activation of groups of neurons.

  II. There Are Variations in Conscious Experience
   A. Variations in consciousness range from:
       i. automatic to controlled processing of information.

ii. persistent vegetative states to minimal
consciousness to full consciousness.
B. Consciousness:
   i. allows performance of complex actions
with input from multiple parts of brain.
   ii. helps people connect by sharing thoughts
and feelings.
   iii. is required for complicated thinking.

III. Brain Activity Gives Rise to Consciousness
A. Global workspace model: level of consciousness depends on which brain region is
active.
B. Severing of corpus callosum leads to split
brain: two independently functioning half
brains.
C. Left hemisphere interpreter:
   i. makes sense of actions.
   ii. speculates about other actions.
D. Right brain experiences the world:
   i. with images.
   ii. spatially.
   iii. without narrative.

IV. Unconscious Processing Influences Behavior
A. Much behavior occurs automatically.
B. Information can be processed subliminally.
C. Unconscious information processing may
produce better decisions than conscious
processing.

REINFORCE: Are you ready to check your knowledge of
this section? Answer the following multiple-choice questions with your textbook closed.

1. Consciousness is best defined as:
a. moment-to-moment subjective experiences
b. focused attention
c. a state of wakefulness
d. the sum of your voluntary experiences

2. For an experienced driver, driving is generally a(n)
_____ process; for the same driver who
is getting used to a new car, driving may be a(n)
_____ process.
a. conscious; unconscious
b. automatic; controlled
c. unconscious; conscious
d. controlled; automatic

3. Psychologists call activities that require full awareness,
alertness, and concentration:
a. automatic processes
b. altered states
c. comas
d. controlled processes

4. After a car accident, John fell into a 10-year
coma. While in the coma, John was able to track
movement with his eyes and, on occasion, seemed to
try to communicate. After waking from the coma,
John was able to recall events that occurred during
his illness. For example, he remembered that his
niece had gotten married. John had most probably
been in a:
a. persistent vegetative state
b. minimally conscious state
c. semiconscious state
d. functionally conscious state

5. Angie has undergone some significant brain surgery
to reduce her out-of-control seizures. As a result of
this surgery, she is able to walk, talk, and think at
near normal levels. She is, however, unable to report
the name of an object shown to the left side of her
visual field. She does not show the inability to name
the object if it is shown to her right visual field. Based
on this information, it is likely that Angie's surgery
involved:
a. severing of the corpus callosum
b. severing of the frontal lobe
c. severing of the temporal lobe
d. a hemispherectomy

6. According to research on patient outcomes following
split-brain surgery, which of the following are likely to
improve with time?
a. right hemisphere language capabilities
b. left hemisphere language capabilities
c. left hemisphere spatial capabilities
d. right hemisphere spatial capabilities

7. According to your book, the interpreter effect is:
a. the propensity of the right hemisphere to construct a
world that makes sense
b. the propensity of the left hemisphere to construct a
world that makes sense
c. the ability of the right hemisphere to begin to
interpret language
d. the ability of the left hemisphere to interpret
language for the right hemisphere

8. After split-brain surgery, a picture of a chair is
shown to the right hemisphere of a patient. When
asked what she saw, the patient states she saw
_____; but when holding a pencil in her
left hand and asked to draw what she saw, she
draws _____.
a. a chair; nothing
b. nothing; a chair
c. a chair; a chair
d. nothing; nothing

9. Frank Tong and colleagues superimposed a house onto a face and asked participants to make judgments about what they saw. What were the participants' brain responses?
   a. The brain activity changed, depending on whether participants reported seeing a house or a face.
   b. The brain noticed both equally, meaning that eventually everything becomes conscious.
   c. The unconscious brain became confused, and thus the participants were able to see neither the house nor the face.
   d. The brain emitted large, slow-wave activity equally for both images.

10. Which of the following statements is true regarding unconscious decision making?
    a. Research has shown that unconscious thought conditions result in the best decisions regarding complex choices.
    b. Research has shown that conscious thought conditions result in the best decisions regarding complex choices.
    c. Research suggests that thinking about something for a long time results in better decision making than making a quick decision.
    d. Research suggests that people are unable to make wise unconscious decisions.

11. According to the _____ model, consciousness should be a function of _____.
    a. sensory neglect; the degree of damage to particular areas
    b. blindsight; visual processing
    c. global workspace; which brain circuits are active
    d. consciousness; the level of arousal

12. Which of the following would be consistent with the global workspace model?
    a. A person is blinded and seems acutely aware of her blindness.
    b. A person with hemineglect searches for the affected body part.
    c. If a person can't see something, she doesn't believe it exists.
    d. If a person can't see something, she doesn't feel compelled to search for it.

WHAT DID YOU MISS? Check your answers against the Answer Key at the end of this chapter of the Study Guide. The Answer Key also lists the page(s) in your text where each question is explained. If you missed any questions, go to the pages indicated in the Answer Key, reread those sections, go back to the questions, and see if you can answer them correctly this time.

ANOTHER OPPORTUNITY TO REVIEW: Answer these questions without your textbook. As a rule of thumb, if you can write only a few words about these questions, you probably need to go back and review.

1. What is consciousness? _____
   _____
   _____

2. What are the various states of consciousness? _____
   _____
   _____

3. How does brain activity create consciousness? _____
   _____
   _____

4. How does research on split brains help us to understand the role of different hemispheres of the brain? _____
   _____
   _____

5. How do unconscious processes influence thought and behavior? _____
   _____
   _____

WHAT DO I NEED TO KNOW? Based on what you've discovered above, what are the areas where you need to focus your studying? Which objectives do you need to spend more time mastering? Write this information down in your own words.

1. _____
2. _____
3. _____
4. _____
5. _____
6. _____

5.2 What Is Sleep?

During various stages of sleep, the electrical activity of the brain gradually slows. Periodically throughout those stages

of sleep, there are episodes of dreaming. Researchers have
proposed numerous theories as to why people dream. Despite
the importance of sleep, sleep disorders may interfere with
restful sleep.

5.2 Guiding Questions

To guide your reading of the text, review the following questions. Then, as you read the chapter, look for the answers to
these questions. You may want to note in your textbook where
you find these answers.

1. What are the different stages of sleep?

2. What are the common sleep disorders?

3. What is the function of sleeping?

4. What is the function of dreaming?

5. What are some theories about the purpose of dreaming?

NOW READ Section 5.2 "What Is Sleep?" keeping these
questions in mind.

REVIEW: Now that you've read this section, go back to the
5.2 Guiding Questions and see if you can answer them based
on what you've read. This is a check on your reading. If you
can't answer a question, you need to go back to the text to
reread that section.

VISUAL SUMMARY: Below is a summary of the major
concepts in this section. To check your comprehension of the
chapter, read the summary and ask yourself if you understand

the concepts. If the concepts seem unfamiliar to you, you
may want to go back to the book and reread those sections.
This text is taken from the Visual Summaries on StudySpace
at wwnorton.com/studyspace.

V. Sleep Is an Altered State of Consciousness
   A. Characterized by four stages of increasingly
      slower brain activity.
   B. REM sleep is:
      i. characterized by rapid eye movements.
      ii. typified by increased brain activity, body
          paralysis, and dreaming.
   C. Common sleep disorders include insomnia,
      apnea, narcolepsy, and REM behavior disorder.

VI. Sleep Is an Adaptive Behavior
   A. Three models explain adaptive nature of sleep:
      i. restorative theory: sleep allows brain to
         restore itself.
      ii. circadian rhythm theory: sleep limits
          activity of animals at times of day when
          threats of harm are greatest.
      iii. facilitation of learning: sleep promotes
           strengthening of neural connections.
   B. Sleep deprivation leads to:
      i. problems in mood and cognitive
         performance.
      ii. problems with immune system.
      iii. eventually, death.

VII. People Dream while Sleeping
   A. Non-REM sleep → brain deactivation +
      mundane dreams.
   B. REM sleep → brain activation + vivid, intense
      dreams.
   C. Three theories of dreaming:
      i. Freudian: dreaming reveals unconscious
         conflicts with manifest content and latent
         content; there is no evidence to support
         this theory.
      ii. activation-synthesis theory: dreams result
          from mind's attempts to make sense of
          random neural activity.
      iii. evolved threat-rehearsal theory: dreams
           are rehearsals of strategies for coping with
           threatening events.

REINFORCE: Are you ready to check your knowledge of
this section? Answer the following multiple-choice questions with your textbook closed.

1. If you are attentive but relaxed with your eyes while listening to a psychology lecture, what type of brain
   waves will appear on your EEG?
   a. beta waves
   b. alpha waves

c. theta waves

d. sleep spindles

2. Fast, short, irregular brain signals (beta waves) are an indication of:
   a. alertness
   b. epilepsy
   c. seizure
   d. hypertension

3. At what sleep stage does your breathing become more regular and your awareness of external stimulation decrease?
   a. REM
   b. stage 4
   c. stage 3
   d. stage 2

4. You have been asleep for approximately 90 minutes. What sleep stage are you likely to begin to enter?
   a. slow-wave sleep
   b. theta-wave sleep
   c. k-complex sleep
   d. paradoxical sleep

5. Your friend has been complaining about her inability to concentrate and her irritability. She mentions that she has not been able to fall asleep. What condition might your friend have?
   a. dementia
   b. insomnia
   c. melatonin
   d. paradoxical sleep

6. Which of the following phenomena is a major cause of insomnia?
   a. disrupted sleep cycles
   b. altered theta waves
   c. narcolepsy
   d. worrying about sleep

7. In the past, Evan has stopped breathing for temporary periods while asleep. Now, he wears a mask that blows air into his nose and mouth during sleep. It is likely that Evan has:
   a. sleep apnea
   b. sleep apraxia
   c. narcolepsy
   d. insomnia

8. Linnea had dreams about what she was going to wear to class and what pencil to bring. What type of sleep must she have been in during those dreams?
   a. non-REM
   b. REM
   c. luna
   d. SCN

9. Which of the following phenomena is NOT likely a purpose of sleep?
   a. strengthening of neuronal connections that serve as the basis for learning
   b. consolidation of information
   c. maintenance and strengthening of the immune system
   d. reducing the likelihood of schizophrenia

10. Although it usually has a negative effect, sleep deprivation may serve a useful purpose in treating which of the following problems?
    a. narcolepsy
    b. depression
    c. hypertension
    d. ADHD

11. Why do humans sleep at night instead of during the day?
    a. There is most danger at night, when we cannot see well.
    b. There is least danger at night, so we are safe to sleep.
    c. Our bodies, particularly our eyes, are not capable of functioning properly at night.
    d. There is no reason; it just became habitual in humans.

12. Which of the following is NOT involved in regulating sleep/wake cycles?
    a. pineal gland
    b. suprachiasmatic nucleus
    c. melatonin
    d. frontal cortex

13. Dreams occurring during REM sleep are often bizarre and emotional, whereas dreams occurring during non-REM sleep are:
    a. illogical
    b. dull and mundane
    c. likely to include auditory hallucinations
    d. likely to include visual hallucinations and illogical content

14. According to the activation-synthesis hypothesis, dreaming is the result of:
    a. the brain's attempt to make sense of random brain activity during sleep
    b. neural inhibition, which inhibits mechanisms that normally interpret visual input
    c. inhibition of the hypothalamus
    d. stimulation of the hypothalamus to process visual information

15. According to the evolutionary hypothesis of dreaming, which of the following phenomena would NOT be a function of dreams?
    a. Dreams serve as a means to simulate threatening events to allow people to rehearse coping strategies.

b. Dreams help people develop adaptive strategies to increase survival.

c. Dreams may be the result of unconscious processing of Freudian slips.

d. Dreams may involve practicing resolution of negative emotions.

WHAT DID YOU MISS? Check your answers against the Answer Key at the end of this chapter of the Study Guide. The Answer Key also lists the page(s) in your text where each question is explained. If you missed any questions, go to the pages indicated in the Answer Key, reread those sections, go back to the questions, and see if you can answer them correctly this time.

ANOTHER OPPORTUNITY TO REVIEW: Answer these questions without your textbook. As a rule of thumb, if you can write only a few words about these questions, you probably need to go back and review.

1. What are the different stages of sleep? _____

2. What are the common sleep disorders? _____

3. What is the function of sleeping? _____

4. What is the function of dreaming? _____

5. What are some theories about the purpose of dreaming? _____

WHAT DO I NEED TO KNOW? Based on what you've discovered above, what are the areas where you need to focus your studying? Which objectives do you need to spend more time mastering? Write this information down in your own words.

1. _____

2. _____

3. _____

4. _____

5. _____

6. _____

5.3 What Is Altered Consciousness?

People can willingly alter their states of consciousness through hypnosis and meditation. Both meditation and hypnosis have psychological and physical benefits. Even if people do not engage in meditation or hypnosis, by becoming immersed in any activity they can achieve a state called "flow." This self-induced alteration in consciousness can be positive or negative.

5.3 Guiding Questions

To guide your reading of the text, review the following questions. Then, as you read the chapter, look for the answers to these questions. You may want to note in your textbook where you find these answers.

1. What are the effects of hypnosis and meditation on consciousness?

2. What is the concept of flow?

3. What are the consequences of escaping the self?

NOW READ Section 5.3 "What Is Altered Consciousness?" keeping these questions in mind.

REVIEW: Now that you've read this section, go back to the 5.3 Guiding Questions and see if you can answer them based on what you've read. This is a check on your reading. If you can't answer a question, you need to go back to the text to reread that section.

VISUAL SUMMARY: Below is a summary of the major concepts in this section. To check your comprehension of the chapter, read the summary and ask yourself if you understand the concepts. If the concepts seem unfamiliar to you, you may want to go back to the book and reread those sections. This text is taken from the Visual Summaries on StudySpace at wwnorton.com/studyspace.

VIII. Hypnosis Is Induced through Suggestion
   A. Consciousness can be altered through hypnosis, meditation, and immersion in activity.
   B. Hypnosis:
      i. is a social interaction in which a person responds to suggestion.
      ii. involves hypnotic induction and posthypnotic suggestion.

Consciousness | 107

iii. can be useful for pain management.
  C. Two theories of hypnosis:
      i. socio-cognitive theory: person "acts" hypnotized.
      ii. dissociation theory: hypnosis is a trancelike state where awareness is separated from other aspects of consciousness; there is significant evidence to support this theory.

IX. Meditation Produces Relaxation
  A. Meditation:
      i. focuses attention on external object (concentrative) or sense of awareness (mindfulness).
      ii. leads to relaxation as well as physical and psychological benefits.

X. People Can Lose Themselves in Activities
  A. During flow:
      i. person becomes absorbed in activity (e.g., religion, exercise).
      ii. consciousness is altered.
  B. Escapist pursuits can reduce self-awareness, but can have negative results.

REINFORCE: Are you ready to check your knowledge of this section? Answer the following multiple-choice questions with your textbook closed.

1. Tom said, "I had a social interaction during which I, in response to the suggestions of someone else, experienced changes in memory, perception, and voluntary action." Tom has likely experienced which of the following?
  a. a hallucination
  b. meditation
  c. unconsciousness
  d. hypnosis

2. According to your textbook, which of the following variables INCREASES susceptibility to hypnosis?
  a. willpower
  b. a rich imagination
  c. gullibility
  d. fear

3. According to research on hypnosis, what is the most important factor for hypnosis to work?
  a. the ability of the hypnotist
  b. the suggestibility of the individual who is to be hypnotized
  c. both the suggestibility of the individual to be hypnotized and the ability of the hypnotist
  d. neither, as little evidence supports hypnosis as a real phenomenon

4. You are watching a movie in which the main character, Tom, agrees to be hypnotized by an evil hypnotist. While hypnotized, Tom is told by the hypnotist to carry out a bank robbery, which he later does. What is your educated response to this depiction of hypnosis?
  a. People who are hypnotized keep to their standards of moral behavior.
  b. A hypnotist could force a person to become hypnotized.
  c. Hypnosis can make a person do things he or she considers wrong.
  d. This technique works only if the person is frightened of the hypnotist.

5. According to the sociocognitive theory of hypnosis, people who are hypnotized are:
  a. merely acting out what they believe is expected of them
  b. simply following directions of the hypnotist to gain attention
  c. in a different sociocognitive state of consciousness, in which they become more compliant
  d. in an altered state of consciousness, one that reduces their social and cognitive abilities

6. According to the dissociation theory of hypnosis, the explanation of hypnosis states:
  a. that people merely act out what they believe is expected of them
  b. that people take on the role of following the directions of the hypnotist simply to gain attention to themselves
  c. that people experience a trancelike state in which there is separation or dissociation from conscious awareness
  d. that people are experiencing REM sleep and therefore dreaming

7. Which of the following is NOT a potential clinical use for hypnosis?
  a. analgesia
  b. relief from chronic pain
  c. speeding surgical recovery
  d. altering personality over a long period

8. A mental procedure that focuses attention on an external object or sense of awareness is:
  a. hypnosis
  b. automated behavior
  c. meditation
  d. concentrative consciousness

9. Which of the following is NOT a general form of meditation?
  a. focusing attention on one particular thing, such as your breathing pattern
  b. consciously trying to stop your inner thoughts
  c. repeating a mantra
  d. listening to your inner voice without responding

10. Susan is sitting quietly, observing the flow of thoughts, sensations, and awarenesses going through her mind without attempting to control her mind. In which of the following techniques is she likely engaging?
   a. concentrative meditation
   b. self-hypnosis
   c. mindfulness meditation
   d. TM

11. Which of the following is NOT a form of meditation?
   a. Zen
   b. yoga
   c. transcendental meditation
   d. hypnosis

12. According to research on the cognitive effects of meditation, which of the following is NOT correct?
   a. Meditation may improve attention and reduce stress.
   b. Long-term practicing of meditation may result in structural brain changes.
   c. Meditation may delay age-related cognitive declines.
   d. Meditation is identical to hypnosis.

13. Hector loves working in his garden. In fact, he finds gardening engrossing even though his plants don't look that good. In gardening for its own sake, he is likely experiencing which of the following?
   a. self-reinforcing behavior
   b. escapism
   c. flow
   d. runner's high

14. According to Roy Baumeister, why do people engage in self-destructive escapist pursuits?
   a. They want to decrease self-awareness.
   b. They want to increase moment-by-moment pleasure.
   c. They are actively looking for solutions to their problems.
   d. They are trying to strengthen their interpersonal relationships.

WHAT DID YOU MISS? Check your answers against the Answer Key at the end of this chapter of the Study Guide. The Answer Key also lists the page(s) in your text where each question is explained. If you missed any questions, go to the pages indicated in the Answer Key, reread those sections, go back to the questions, and see if you can answer them correctly this time.

ANOTHER OPPORTUNITY TO REVIEW: Answer these questions without your textbook. As a rule of thumb, if you can write only a few words about these questions, you probably need to go back and review.

1. What are the effects of hypnosis and meditation on consciousness? _____

_____

_____

2. What is the concept of flow? _____

_____

_____

_____

_____

3. What are the consequences of escaping the self? _____

_____

_____

_____

_____

_____

WHAT DO I NEED TO KNOW? Based on what you've discovered above, what are the areas where you need to focus your studying? Which objectives do you need to spend more time mastering? Write this information down in your own words.

1. _____

2. _____

3. _____

4. _____

5. _____

6. _____

5.4 How Do Drugs Affect Consciousness?

The use of legal and illegal substances to alter consciousness has been present since prehistoric times. The most commonly used and abused substances have a unique impact on neurochemical, psychological, and behavioral functioning. Some of these substances lead to tolerance, addiction, and the possibility of withdrawal symptoms.

5.4 Guiding Questions

To guide your reading of the text, review the following questions. Then, as you read the chapter, look for the answers to these questions. You may want to note in your textbook where you find these answers.

1. What are the neurochemical, psychological, and behavioral effects of marijuana?

2. What are the neurochemical, psychological, and behavioral effects of stimulants?

3. What are the neurochemical, psychological, and behavioral effects of opiates?

4. What are the neurochemical, psychological, and behavioral effects of alcohol?

5. What are the physiological and psychological factors associated with addiction?

6. What are the gender, social, and cultural differences in the use of alcohol?

NOW READ Section 5.4 "How Do Drugs Affect Consciousness?" keeping these questions in mind.

REVIEW: Now that you've read this section, go back to the 5.4 Guiding Questions and see if you can answer them based on what you've read. This is a check on your reading. If you can't answer a question, you need to go back to the text to reread that section.

VISUAL SUMMARY: Below is a summary of the major concepts in this section. To check your comprehension of the chapter, read the summary and ask yourself if you understand the concepts. If the concepts seem unfamiliar to you, you may want to go back to the book and reread those sections. This text is taken from the Visual Summaries on StudySpace at wwnorton.com/studyspace.

XI. Psychoactive Drugs
   A. Are mind-altering substances.
   B. Change the brain's neurochemistry by activating neurotransmitter systems.

XII. Stimulants
   A. Interfere with reuptake of dopamine.
   B. Increased release of dopamine → increased behavioral and mental activity.

XIII. People Use—and Abuse—Many Psychoactive Drugs
   A. Marijuana activates cannabinoid receptors → enhanced mental activity, memory impairment, and altered pain perception.
   B. Cocaine prevents reuptake of dopamine → confidence, alertness, and sociability.
   C. Amphetamines (e.g., methamphetamine):
      i. block reuptake of dopamine.
      ii. eventually damage frontal lobes.
   D. MDMA (ecstasy):
      i. is associated with serotonin release.
      ii. may lead to memory impairment.

TRY IT

Take a Break

Worried about taking a test? Having a problem with a friend? Just need to calm down a little? Try this technique for reducing your level of stress. It will take about 3–5 minutes.

1. Sit quietly and close your eyes.

2. Pay attention to your body, your thoughts. Notice where your attention goes. Rather than trying to calm yourself down or fix things, just note to yourself in a nonjudgmental fashion, "Oh well. That's how things are with me right now." Spend about a minute or so doing this. You don't have to look at a watch—just estimate.

3. Now bring your attention to your breath, watching how your body breathes in and out. Notice if the breath is smooth, even, long, short. Notice and observe rather than judge. When your attention wanders away from focusing on your breathing, bring it back gently. Again spend about a minute or so focusing on your breath.

4. Allow your focus to expand to include your entire body, just noticing how your body is at this moment. Do this for about a minute or so.

5. Open your eyes when you're ready.

   E. Opiates increase pleasure by binding with opiate receptors and activating dopamine receptors.

XIV. Alcohol Is the Most Widely Abused Drug
   A. Alcohol:
      i. activates dopamine receptors.
      ii. interferes with memory.
   B. Cross-culturally, men consume more alcohol than women:
      i. women do not metabolize alcohol as quickly.
      ii. because of body size, women consume less alcohol to achieve same effect.
   C. Expectations about impact of alcohol affect behavior while under influence of alcohol.

XV. Addiction Has Physical and Psychological Aspects
   A. Addiction: compulsive drug use despite negative consequences.
   B. Tolerance: need for more of drug to get same effect.
   C. Withdrawal: when failing to ingest an addictive substance leads to physiological and psychological symptoms.

D. Dependence: need for continued use of drug to avoid withdrawal.
E. Addiction:
    i. is likely caused by dopamine activity in limbic system.
    ii. may be related to genetic components and/or personality traits (high sensation seeking).
F. Influences on drug abuse include:
    i. observing others modeling use of drugs.
    ii. social context in which drug use occurs.

REINFORCE: Are you ready to check your knowledge of this section? Answer the following multiple-choice questions with your textbook closed.

1. A mind-altering substance that changes the brain's neurochemistry by activating neurotransmitter receptors is called a:
   a. neuromodulator
   b. neurotoxin
   c. psychoactive drug
   d. psychoendorphin

2. Marijuana has been known to produce memory effects in long-time users. This result is most likely due to the altering of a large percentage of _____ receptors in the _____ of the brain.
   a. THC; frontal lobe
   b. THC; hippocampus
   c. ACTH; frontal lobe
   d. ACTH; hippocampus

3. Which of the following relationships is NOT correct?
   a. marijuana—THC receptors
   b. cocaine—dopamine receptors
   c. opiates—opiate receptors
   d. MDMA—acetylcholine receptors

4. A drug works by blocking normal reuptake of dopamine, allowing released dopamine to remain in the synapse for a longer period of time. This drug must be a(n):
   a. stimulant
   b. depressant
   c. opiate
   d. antispsychotic

5. Which of the following drugs is NOT a stimulant?
   a. cocaine
   b. crack
   c. methamphetamine
   d. THC

6. Ecstacy (MDMA) differs from amphetamines in that it _____ and _____.
   a. increases dopamine release; decreases serotonin release
   b. decreases dopamine release; increases serotonin release
   c. increases dopamine release; decreases MDMA release
   d. decreases dopamine release; decreases MDMA release

7. Which of the following states is NOT an effect of opiates?
   a. euphoria
   b. pain relief or analgesia
   c. increased energy
   d. relaxation

8. Which drug(s) is (are) involved in more than half of fatal car accidents and often involved in risky sexual behavior?
   a. marijuana
   b. cocaine and methamphetamine
   c. opiates
   d. alcohol

9. Two areas of the brain that have been critically linked to the development of addiction are:
   a. the dopamine system and the insula
   b. the dopamine system and the forebrain
   c. the opiate system and the insula
   d. the opiate system and the forebrain

10. Brad told his counselor, "When I first started drinking, all I needed to get a buzz were two or three beers. Now it takes me about six or seven." Brad has likely developed:
    a. an addiction
    b. tolerance
    c. dependency
    d. immunity

11. You are asked to speak to your Public Health class about substance abuse and public health problems. In your presentation, you will want to include all of the following statements EXCEPT:
    a. 5 percent to 10 percent of people who experiment with drugs will go on to become addicted
    b. children attracted to novelty and risk taking are more likely to use psychoactive substances
    c. there is strong evidence that an "addiction gene" exists that will result in substance dependence
    d. imitating the behavior of parents and others can lead to substance abuse

12. According to the World Health Organization, data suggest that _____ are most likely to engage in binge and heavy drinking.
    a. men
    b. women
    c. university students
    d. none of the above; it varies by culture

13. Which of the following is NOT a theory suggested to explain gender differences in alcohol consumption?

a. Because women do not metabolize alcohol as quickly, they get the same psychoactive effect by consuming less.
b. Women may be as likely to drink, but they hide it better.
c. Drinking by men is more socially acceptable.
d. Women are less likely genetically to have addictive personalities.

WHAT DID YOU MISS? Check your answers against the Answer Key at the end of this chapter of the Study Guide. The Answer Key also lists the page(s) in your text where each question is explained. If you missed any questions, go to the pages indicated in the Answer Key, reread those sections, go back to the questions, and see if you can answer them correctly this time.

ANOTHER OPPORTUNITY TO REVIEW: Answer these questions without your textbook. As a rule of thumb, if you can write only a few words about these questions, you probably need to go back and review.

1. What are the neurochemical, psychological, and behavioral effects of marijuana? _____

_____

_____

2. What are the neurochemical, psychological, and behavioral effects of stimulants? _____

_____

_____

3. What are the neurochemical, psychological, and behavioral effects of opiates? _____

_____

_____

4. What are the neurochemical, psychological, and behavioral effects of alcohol? _____

_____

_____

5. What are the physiological and psychological factors associated with addiction? _____

_____

_____

6. What are the gender, social, and cultural differences in the use of alcohol? _____

_____

_____

WHAT DO I NEED TO KNOW? Based on what you've discovered above, what are the areas where you need to focus your studying? Which objectives do you need to spend more time mastering? Write this information down in your own words.

1. _____

2. _____

3. _____

4. _____

5. _____

6. _____

WHAT MATTERS TO ME: What facts in this chapter are personally relevant to you?

_____

_____

_____

_____

CHAPTER SUMMARY

5.1 What Is Consciousness?

- *Consciousness Is a Subjective Experience:* Consciousness is difficult to study because of the subjective nature of our experience of the world. Brain imaging research has shown that particular brain regions are activated by particular types of sensory information.
- *There Are Variations in Conscious Experience:* Consciousness is each person's unified and coherent experience of the world around him or her. At any one time, each person can be conscious of a limited number of things. A person's level of consciousness varies throughout the day and depends on the task at hand. Whereas people in a persistent vegetative state show no brain activity, people in minimally conscious states show brain activity. That activity indicates some awareness of external stimuli.
- *Brain Activity Gives Rise to Consciousness:* The global workspace model maintains that consciousness arises from activity in different cortical areas. The corpus callosum connects the brain's two sides; cutting it in half results in two independently functioning hemispheres. The left hemisphere is responsible primarily for language, and the right hemisphere is responsible primarily for images and spatial relations. The left hemisphere

strives to make sense of experiences, and its interpretations influence the way a person views and remembers the world.

- *Unconscious Processing Influences Behavior:* Research findings indicate that much of a person's behavior occurs automatically, without that person's conscious awareness. Thought and behavior can be influenced by stimuli that are not experienced at a conscious level.

5.2 What Is Sleep?

- *Sleep Is an Altered State of Consciousness:* Sleep is characterized by stages that vary in brain activity. REM sleep is marked by rapid eye movements, dreaming, and body paralysis. Sleep disorders include insomnia, sleep apnea, and narcolepsy.
- *Sleep Is an Adaptive Behavior:* Sleep allows the body, including the brain, to rest and restore itself. Sleep also protects animals from harm at times of the day when they are most susceptible to danger, and it facilitates learning through the strengthening of neural connections.
- *People Dream while Sleeping:* REM dreams and non-REM dreams activate and deactivate distinct brain regions. Sigmund Freud believed that dreams reveal unconscious conflicts. Evidence does not support this view. Activation-synthesis theory posits that dreams are the product of the mind's efforts to make sense of random brain activity during sleep. Evolved threat-rehearsal theory maintains that dreaming evolved as a result of its adaptive value. That is, dreaming may have enabled early humans to rehearse strategies for coping with threatening events.

5.3 What Is Altered Consciousness?

- *Hypnosis Is Induced through Suggestion:* Scientists have debated whether hypnotized people merely play the role they are expected to play or whether they experience an altered state of consciousness. Consistent with the latter view, brain imaging research has demonstrated changes in brain activity among hypnotized subjects.
- *Meditation Produces Relaxation:* The goal of meditation, particularly as it is practiced in the West, is to bring about a state of deep relaxation. Studies suggest that meditation can have multiple benefits for people's physical and mental health.
- *People Can Lose Themselves in Activities:* Exercise, religious practices, and other engaging activities can produce a state of altered consciousness called flow. In this state, people become completely absorbed in what they are doing. Flow is experienced as a positive state. In contrast to activities that generate flow, activities used to escape the self or reduce self-awareness can have harmful consequences.

5.4 How Do Drugs Affect Consciousness?

- *People Use—and Abuse—Many Psychoactive Drugs:* Stimulants, including cocaine and amphetamines, increase behavioral and mental activity. THC (the active ingredient in marijuana) produces a relaxed state, an uplifted mood, and perceptual and cognitive distortions. MDMA, or ecstasy, produces energizing and hallucinogenic effects. Opiates produce a relaxed state, analgesia, and euphoria.
- *Alcohol Is the Most Widely Abused Drug:* Alcohol impairs motor processes, informational processing, mood, and memory. Research has demonstrated that, across the globe, males consume more alcohol than females. A drinker's expectations can significantly affect his or her behavior while under the influence of alcohol.
- *Addiction Has Physical and Psychological Aspects:* Physical dependence occurs when the body develops tolerance for a drug. Psychological dependence occurs when someone habitually and compulsively uses a drug or engages in a behavior, despite its negative consequences.

PUTTING IT ALL TOGETHER

Answer these questions to check your knowledge of the material in this chapter.

1. Suppose you need to devise laboratory tests for split-brain patients. Specifically, you want to study the differing functions of the right and left hemispheres. With basic lab equipment, how might you observe the hemisphere's oral, visual, and tactile abilities?

2. Suppose you need to devise a program to educate college students about sleep. You want them to understand the importance of good sleep and to teach them techniques for sleeping better. What elements would your program consist of?

3. Your friend is very stressed out and is considering hypnosis to help her relax. What would you tell her about the research findings on the effectiveness of this technique?

4. An acquaintance, desperate for money to pay off his loans, is considering constructing a methamphetamine lab. You are horrified. To dissuade this person, what scientific research might you cite about the harmful effects of methamphetamine?

ANSWER KEY FOR REINFORCE QUESTIONS

Section 5.1

1. a   p. 183
2. b   p. 184

3. d   p. 184
4. b   p. 185
5. a   p. 187
6. a   p. 188
7. b   p. 189
8. b   p. 190
9. a   p. 185
10. a   p. 193
11. c   p. 185
12. a   p. 186

Section 5.2

1. b   p. 196
2. a   p. 196
3. d   p. 196
4. d   p. 197
5. b   p. 197
6. d   p. 198
7. a   p. 198
8. a   p. 202
9. d   p. 199
10. b   p. 199
11. a   p. 200
12. d   p. 195
13. b   p. 202
14. a   p. 203
15. c   p. 204

Section 5.3

1. d   p. 205
2. b   p. 206
3. b   p. 206
4. a   p. 206
5. a   p. 206
6. c   p. 206
7. d   p. 207
8. c   p. 207
9. b   p. 207
10. c   p. 207
11. d   p. 207
12. d   p. 208
13. c   p. 209
14. a   p. 210

Section 5.4

1. c   p. 212
2. b   p. 212
3. d   p. 213
4. a   p. 212
5. d   p. 213
6. b   p. 213
7. c   p. 214

TRY IT

Sleep and Study

College students, pressed for time, are often tempted to postpone study until the last minute and "cram." This approach can easily deprive students of much-needed sleep. Not surprisingly, researchers have found that sleeping is essential for learning. When you sleep, your brain stores what you have learned in a way that makes the material easier to recall. So, to maximize the impact of study, try a period of sleep between studying and when you need to take a test. You will likely find that you remember more.

---

8. d   p. 214
9. a   p. 217
10. b   p. 217
11. c   p. 218
12. a   p. 215
13. d   p. 215

HINTS FOR PUTTING IT ALL TOGETHER QUESTIONS

1. A good answer should include the ideas that objects shown briefly to the right visual field will be able to be articulated (left hemisphere), whereas those shown briefly in the left visual field will not (right hemisphere). Similarly, the left hand is processed by the right hemisphere and will have access to that information, whereas the tactile abilities of the left hemisphere will be identified by the right hand.

2. A good answer will include basic information about extended sleep deprivation, such as that it compromises the immune system, interferes with the consolidation of learning, and makes one less capable of rehearsing for negative life events.

   The techniques for sleeping better can be found in the chart on pp. 201–202 and include: plan your time; do not take on too many commitments; set a sleep pattern, including getting up at the same time every day; and refrain from worrying excessively.

3. A good answer will include the sociocognitive and dissociation theories of hypnosis and the research finding that some individuals are more susceptible to hypnosis than others are. The textbook suggests that a wiser path to relaxation is that of meditation, including Zen, yoga, and transcendental meditation. These techniques have been demonstrated to result in a reduction in stress and

increased relaxation, improvement in attention, and age-resistant structural changes in the brain.

4. A good answer should note facts such as: Methamphetamine becomes quite volatile during the cooking process, often leading to explosions. Because it increases dopamine levels in the brain (more dopamine becomes available in the synapse), meth is both highly pleasurable and highly addictive. Side effects include insomnia, anxiety, and heart, skin, and dental problems. Over time, meth damages various brain structures, including the frontal lobes. Eventually, it depletes dopamine levels. Prolonged use can lead to significant physical changes—for a shocking example, see the photos on p. 214 of your textbook.

KEY TERMS EXERCISES

First, fill in your own definition and example for each term. Then check each term against the textbook's definition. These exercises can also be cut out and used as flash cards.

activation-synthesis theory

Your Definition:
Your Example:
Textbook Definition:

hypnosis

Your Definition:
Your Example:
Textbook Definition:

circadian rhythms

Your Definition:
Your Example:
Textbook Definition:

insomnia

Your Definition:
Your Example:
Textbook Definition:

consciousness

Your Definition:
Your Example:
Textbook Definition:

interpreter

Your Definition:
Your Example:
Textbook Definition:

dreams

Your Definition:
Your Example:
Textbook Definition:

latent content

Your Definition:
Your Example:
Textbook Definition:

manifest content

Your Definition:
Your Example:
Textbook Definition:

meditation

Your Definition:
Your Example:
Textbook Definition:

narcolepsy

Your Definition:
Your Example:
Textbook Definition:

obstructive sleep apnea

Your Definition:
Your Example:
Textbook Definition:

REM sleep

Your Definition:
Your Example:
Textbook Definition:

split brain

Your Definition:
Your Example:
Textbook Definition:

subliminal perception

Your Definition:
Your Example:
Textbook Definition:

| Learning

CHAPTER OVERVIEW

What do learning how to tie your shoes by watching your brother tie his, the effects of parental discipline, and becoming nauseated when you see that restaurant where you ate the spoiled food have in common? They are all examples of learning, an essential survival process for all organisms. In this chapter, you will learn about the three major types of learning, which you will recognize as playing a major part in your life. You may also discover some ways to change your behavior or that of your pet.

6.1 What Ideas Guide the Study of Learning?

Pavlov, Watson, and Skinner, three important researchers in psychology, pioneered work on the process of learning. Pavlov discovered that both simple and complex organisms are prepared to make connections between external stimuli and biological stimuli or responses. Skinner and Watson discovered that organisms play an active role in acquiring new knowledge and in avoiding unpleasant situations. In this section, you'll learn about these different types of learning and about theories that can explain these processes.

At the beginning of each section in the Study Guide, there will be guiding questions. Before you read the chapter in your textbook, read through these questions and maybe even attempt to answer them based on either what you've already read or what you think the answer should be. Then as you study the chapter, you can use them to help guide your reading.

6.1 Guiding Questions

To guide your reading of the text, review the following questions. Then, as you read the chapter, look for the answers to these questions. You may want to note in your textbook where you find these answers.

1. Define classical conditioning.

2. Differentiate between US, UR, CS, and CR.

3. Describe the role of learning in the development and treatment of phobias and drug addiction.

4. Discuss the evolutionary significance of classical conditioning.

5. Describe the Rescorla-Wagner model of classical conditioning.

NOW READ Section 6.1 "What Ideas Guide the Study of Learning?" keeping these questions in mind.

REVIEW: Now that you've read this section, go back to the 6.1 Guiding Questions and see if you can answer them based on what you've read. This is a check on your reading. If you can't answer a question, you need to go back to the text to reread that section.

VISUAL SUMMARY: Below is a summary of the major concepts in this section. To check your comprehension of the chapter, read the summary and ask yourself if you understand the concepts. If the concepts seem unfamiliar to you, you may want to go back to the book and reread those sections. This text is taken from the Visual Summaries on StudySpace at wwnorton.com/studyspace.

   I. Learning Results from Experience
      A. Learning (also called conditioning):

i. is a relatively enduring change in behavior that results from experience.

ii. enables animals to better adapt to an environment, thus facilitates survival.

iii. involves forming associations between events.

II. Behavioral Responses Are Conditioned
   A. In classical conditioning:
      i. unconditioned stimulus (US) is a biological stimulus that reliably produces a biological response or reflex.
      ii. unconditioned response (UR) is a biological response that the organism does not have to learn.
      iii. neutral stimulus (NS) is a stimulus that does not evoke any response from the organism.
      iv. through conditioning trials, NS is presented along with the US.
      v. following the conditioning trials, critical trials occur; if NS has become conditioned stimulus (CS), it produces conditioned response (CR).
   B. Processes associated with classical conditioning:
      i. acquisition: formation of association between NS and US.
      ii. extinction: repeated presentation of the CS without the US leads to gradual loss of CR.
      iii. spontaneous recovery: after extinction, brief reappearance of extinguished response upon presentation of the CS.
      iv. generalization: stimulus similar to CS produces CR.
      v. discrimination: distinguishing between stimuli so only one CS produces CR.

III. Phobias and Addictions Have Learned Components
   A. Phobias: learned fear associations (classically conditioned).
   B. Counterconditioning: breaking connection between CS and US.
   C. Systematic desensitization: therapy based on counterconditioning.
   D. Addiction: can be explained by classical conditioning.

IV. Classical Conditioning Involves More Than Events Occurring at the Same Time
   A. Biological preparedness to fear specific objects helps animals avoid potential dangers and survive.

V. Learning Involves Cognition
   A. According to Rescorla-Wagner model of classical conditioning, strength of CS-US association is determined by unexpected or surprising nature of US.

REINFORCE: Are you ready to check your knowledge of this section? Answer the following multiple-choice questions with your textbook closed.

1. The best definition of learning is that learning:
   a. results entirely from maturation rather than experience
   b. must result in adaptation of behavior, but does not have to be enduring
   c. always results in adaptations in behavior
   d. is relatively enduring and results from experience

2. What psychological principle did Pavlov's experiments teach us?
   a. They demonstrated how a non–biologically salient stimulus can trigger the same natural response as a biologically salient stimulus.
   b. They demonstrated that all biological responses must be elicited by biologically salient stimuli.
   c. They demonstrated how important punishment and reinforcement are for learning to take place.
   d. They demonstrated that complex behaviors, such as fear of a stimulus, can be learned observationally.

3. A startling noise will always cause the human eye to blink. If one has learned to associate a blue light with a startling noise, what is the eyeblink elicited by the blue light known as?
   a. an unconditioned stimulus
   b. a conditioned response
   c. an unconditioned response
   d. a conditioned stimulus

4. If you trained a rat to fear a flashing light by pairing the light with a painful electric shock, what would be your conditioned stimulus?
   a. flashing light
   b. electric shock
   c. fear
   d. extinction

5. What is an unconditioned response?
   a. a learned pairing between two stimuli
   b. a learned nervous system reflex
   c. an unlearned, automatic behavior to a stimulus
   d. something that elicits an automatic behavior

6. What is an unconditioned stimulus?
   a. a learned response
   b. a reflexive action to a biologically relevant situation
   c. something that elicits a learned response
   d. something that elicits an unlearned response

7. What is a conditioned stimulus?
   a. something that naturally elicits a response
   b. something that elicits a response only after learning
   c. a previously extinct stimulus
   d. a second-order pairing of learned relations

8. What is the term used by behaviorists to describe the gradual forming of an association between an unconditioned stimulus and a conditioned stimulus?
   a. generalization
   b. discrimination
   c. deviation
   d. acquisition

9. What causes extinction?
   a. The conditioned response is no longer rewarding to the organism.
   b. The unconditioned stimulus no longer evokes a response from the organism.
   c. The organism learns that the conditioned stimulus no longer predicts the unconditioned stimulus.
   d. Spontaneous recovery fails to occur.

10. When slight differences in the form of conditioned stimuli still produce the same conditioned response, the learning phenomenon of _____ is occurring.
    a. generalization
    b. discrimination
    c. second-order conditioning
    d. operant conditioning

11. The ability to respond with an appropriate conditioned response to a conditioned stimulus and with no response to a very similar yet substantially different stimulus is known as:
    a. valence differentiation
    b. salience response
    c. stimulus generalization
    d. stimulus discrimination

12. How might behavioral techniques help treat phobias?
    a. by removing the central nucleus of the amygdala
    b. by conditioning a new unconditioned stimulus to the conditioned response, thus removing the initial conditioning
    c. by systematically desensitizing the threat by introducing new conditioned responses
    d. by punishing unwanted conditioned responses to the phobic unconditioned stimulus

13. Behaviorism has helped psychologists gain an understanding of drug tolerance by showing that:
    a. cues in the environment predictive of the drug can produce physiological reactions similar to actions of the drug
    b. increased levels of reward produced by the drug itself become needed for responding to any reinforcement over time
    c. punishment is an effective but controversial treatment for overcoming drug withdrawal
    d. drug therapies such as methadone need to be conditioned to be effective

14. The theory that animals are genetically programmed to fear particular things that threaten their survival is known as:
    a. tolerance conditioning
    b. biological preparedness
    c. evolutionary significance
    d. second-order conditioning

15. To which food would you be more likely to show conditioned taste aversion?
    a. a highly familiar food; because it was unusual that it made you ill
    b. a highly familiar food; because you have learned that this food is safe
    c. a novel food; because it was unusual and those new characteristics of the food became paired with your becoming ill
    d. a novel food; because it was unusual and those new characteristics became paired with its being a safe food

16. Sunil wishes to classically condition his dog to fear skunks so he doesn't get sprayed again. This task should be much easier than teaching the dog to fear a houseplant because:
    a. the dog is biologically prepared to fear certain types of objects
    b. the dog is highly intelligent
    c. the dog is biologically conditioned to fear skunks
    d. the dog's mind cannot physically be trained to fear plants

17. The Rescorla-Wagner model of the cognitive components of conditioning states that the strength of the conditioned stimulus–unconditioned stimulus association depends on how _____ the unconditioned stimulus is.
    a. rewarding
    b. evolutionarily significant
    c. fearful
    d. unexpected

WHAT DID YOU MISS? Check your answers against the Answer Key at the end of this chapter of the Study Guide. The Answer Key also lists the page(s) in your text where each question is explained. If you missed any questions, go to the pages indicated in the Answer Key, reread those sections, go back to the questions, and see if you can answer them correctly this time.

ANOTHER OPPORTUNITY TO REVIEW: Answer these questions without your textbook. As a rule of thumb, if you can write only a few words about these questions, you probably need to go back and review.

1. Define classical conditioning. _____
_____

2. Differentiate between US, UR, CS, and CR. _____

_____

3. Describe the role of learning in the development and treatment of phobias and drug addiction. _____

_____

_____

_____

4. Discuss the evolutionary significance of classical conditioning. _____

_____

_____

5. Describe the Rescorla-Wagner model of classical conditioning. _____

_____

_____

WHAT DO I NEED TO KNOW? Based on what you've discovered above, what are the areas where you need to focus your studying? Which objectives do you need to spend more time mastering? Write this information down in your own words.

1. _____

2. _____

3. _____

4. _____

5. _____

6. _____

6.2 How Does Operant Conditioning Differ from Classical Conditioning?

What do driving over the speed limit, studying hard to do well on a test, and cleaning your room so that your mother stops yelling at you have in common? They are all ways in which behavior can be reinforced or punished. In this section, you'll learn about operant conditioning and how the concepts from this type of learning can be used to increase or decrease many types of behavior.

6.2 Guiding Questions

To guide your reading of the text, review the following questions. Then, as you read the chapter, look for the answers to these questions. You may want to note in your textbook where you find these answers.

1. Define operant conditioning.

2. Distinguish between positive reinforcement, negative reinforcement, positive punishment, and negative punishment.

3. Distinguish between schedules of reinforcement.

4. Identify biological and cognitive factors that influence operant conditioning.

NOW READ Section 6.2 "How Does Operant Conditioning Differ from Classical Conditioning?" keeping these questions in mind.

REVIEW: Now that you've read this section, go back to the 6.2 Guiding Questions and see if you can answer them based on what you've read. This is a check on your reading. If you can't answer a question, you need to go back to the text to reread that section.

VISUAL SUMMARY: Below is a summary of the major concepts in this section. To check your comprehension of the chapter, read the summary and ask yourself if you understand the concepts. If the concepts seem unfamiliar to you, you may want to go back to the book and reread those sections. This text is taken from the Visual Summaries on StudySpace at wwnorton.com/studyspace.

VI. Reinforcement Increases Behavior
  A. In classical conditioning, organism does not know it is making associations.
  B. In operant conditioning, organism acts to receive reward.
  C. Shaping: reinforcing behaviors that successively approximate desired behavior.
  D. Reinforcers may be primary (satisfy biological needs) or secondary (do not satisfy biological needs).

VII. Both Reinforcement and Punishment Can Be Positive or Negative
  A. Positive reinforcement: by addition of reward, increases probability of behavior reoccurring.
  B. Negative reinforcement: by removal of negative stimulus, increases probability of behavior reoccurring.
  C. Positive punishment: by addition of negative consequence, decreases probability of behavior reoccurring.

D. Negative punishment: by removal of positive consequence, decreases probability of behavior reoccurring.

VIII. Operant Conditioning Is Influenced by Schedules of Reinforcement
A. Continuous reinforcement → rewarding for each behavior → fastest behavior acquisition but fastest extinction if reinforcement stops.
B. Partial reinforcement → intermittent rewarding of behavior → enduring, stable behavior.
C. Four partial reinforcement schedules:
   i. fixed ratio schedule: reinforcement given after certain number of responses.
   ii. fixed interval schedule: reinforcement given after certain amount of time.
   iii. variable ratio schedule: reinforcement given after random number of responses.
   iv. variable interval schedule: reinforcement given after random amount of time.

IX. Biology and Cognition Influence Operant Conditioning
A. Biological constraints: animal's behavior can be shaped if desired behavior is within animal's behavior repertoire.
B. Learning can take place without reinforcement: even without reinforcement, rats develop cognitive maps (latent learning) and learn by observation.

REINFORCE: Are you ready to check your knowledge of this section? Answer the following multiple-choice questions with your textbook closed.

1. What is the main difference between classical conditioning and operant conditioning?
   a. Classical conditioning uses reward-based learning, whereas operant conditioning is caused by reflexive actions.
   b. Classical conditioning is caused by reflexive actions, whereas operant conditioning requires cognitive evaluation.
   c. Classical conditioning requires learning that two events are related, whereas operant conditioning demonstrates that behavior leads to a consequence.
   d. Classical conditioning demonstrates that behavior leads to a consequence, whereas operant conditioning is caused by reflexive actions.

2. In which of the following examples from your textbook has an animal NOT been trained based on Skinner's principles?
   a. Seeing Eye dogs
   b. navy dolphins trained to seek explosives

   c. dogs salivating to a bell
   d. dogs trained to sniff for drugs

3. The idea that the consequences of our actions determine the likelihood that we will perform those actions in the future underlies:
   a. the operant conditioning model
   b. the classical conditioning model
   c. the Rescorla-Wagner model
   d. the social learning model

4. In what technique are successive approximations used?
   a. shaping
   b. taste aversion
   c. biological preparedness
   d. punishment

5. Which behavioral term is used to describe something that will increase the likelihood of a behavior?
   a. positive
   b. negative
   c. reinforcement
   d. punishment

6. Which of the following events could be classified as a reinforcer?
   a. receiving a cookie after washing the dishes
   b. cowering when your teacher places her fingernails on the blackboard
   c. not walking under ladders
   d. having a sunny day on your wedding

7. Which of the following items would most likely be defined as a primary reinforcer?
   a. a new set of china dishes
   b. a bottle of water
   c. a vacation
   d. money

8. Getting $1 for every correct answer on this test would be a form of:
   a. positive reinforcement
   b. negative reinforcement
   c. positive punishment
   d. negative punishment

9. The $75 fine for driving too fast is an example of:
   a. positive reinforcement
   b. negative reinforcement
   c. positive punishment
   d. negative punishment

10. Taking away a child's video games for bad behavior is a form of:
    a. positive reinforcement
    b. negative reinforcement

TRY IT

Mindfulness

> "Life is what happens to you while you're busy making other plans."
> —John Lennon

How often do you start off your day with a series of "things to do"? Although being organized is important, we often miss the moments of our lives because we're so focused on the next item on our "to do" list. Mindfulness and savoring are two ways to develop a greater appreciation of the moments of our lives by focusing on what is really important. How can we be mindful? You probably do it more than you realize. When you look at your baby's face or really pay attention to your friends as they are talking, rather than thinking about past events or the future, you are probably practicing mindfulness, being completely absorbed in that moment. Whether you're walking to work, waiting at the stoplight, eating your dinner with your family, maybe attending a psychology lecture, *choose* to be fully there throughout the moments of your day. Sometimes using your breath as a way to help you focus can make this process easier. Imagining yourself breathing into each moment as a way to anchor yourself to the moment can be helpful. Psychologists have found that by practicing mindfulness people experience lower levels of anxiety and depression. Try it and see for yourself.

---

   c. positive punishment
   d. negative punishment

11. Receiving a reduced jail sentence for good behavior is a form of:
   a. positive reinforcement
   b. negative reinforcement
   c. positive punishment
   d. negative punishment

12. The term _____ is used to describe intermittent or occasional reinforcements.
   a. partial reinforcement
   b. continuous reinforcement
   c. positive rewards
   d. negative punishments

13. Sue works in a toy factory and is paid for each toy she completes. Which of the following reinforcement schedules are the factory owners using?
   a. fixed interval
   b. variable interval
   c. fixed ratio
   d. variable ratio

14. Golf course owners put their sprinklers on a _____ schedule so that people can know when they can play on the course without getting wet.
   a. fixed interval
   b. variable ratio
   c. fixed ratio
   d. variable interval

15. Gambling on a slot machine involves rewards on a _____ schedule.
   a. fixed interval
   b. fixed ratio
   c. variable interval
   d. variable ratio

16. Getting paid monthly is what type of reinforcement schedule?
   a. fixed interval
   b. fixed ratio
   c. variable interval
   d. variable ratio

17. Three of the following phenomena are instinctive behaviors. Which one is a learned behavior?
   a. an ant following a food trail through a maze
   b. a dog sitting in order to receive a biscuit
   c. a raccoon picking up and "washing" a coin
   d. a pigeon flying up and over a wall

18. Why is Skinner's dream of solving all social problems through operant conditioning impossible?
   a. Biology places constraints on our learning.
   b. Operant conditioning isn't effective for learning.
   c. Operant conditioning doesn't apply to observational learning.
   d. Operant conditioning doesn't take into account learning from classical conditioning.

WHAT DID YOU MISS? Check your answers against the Answer Key at the end of this chapter of the Study Guide. The Answer Key also lists the page(s) in your text where each question is explained. If you missed any questions, go to the pages indicated in the Answer Key, reread those sections, go back to the questions, and see if you can answer them correctly this time.

ANOTHER OPPORTUNITY TO REVIEW: Answer these questions without your textbook. As a rule of thumb, if you can write only a few words about these questions, you probably need to go back and review.

1. Define operant conditioning. _____
_____
_____

2. Distinguish between positive reinforcement, negative reinforcement, positive punishment, and negative punishment. _____

_____

_____

3. Distinguish between schedules of reinforcement. _____

_____

_____

4. Identify biological and cognitive factors that influence operant conditioning. _____

_____

_____

WHAT DO I NEED TO KNOW? Based on what you've discovered above, what are the areas where you need to focus your studying? Which objectives do you need to spend more time mastering? Write this information down in your own words.

1. _____

2. _____

3. _____

4. _____

5. _____

6. _____

6.3 How Does Watching Others Affect Learning?

What do learning how to drive, cooking your favorite food, and tying your shoes have in common? You probably did not learn to perform any of these actions by reading about them or through reinforcement. You probably saw someone perform the actions, and you learned to perform them initially through observation. We can learn by observing others and also by cultural transmission.

6.3 Guiding Questions

To guide your reading of the text, review the following questions. Then, as you read the chapter, look for the answers to these questions. You may want to note in your textbook where you find these answers.

TRY IT

Savoring

Although we often think of savoring in terms of food, this term can also be used to describe the experience of more deeply appreciating our lives. Here are some methods to enhance your savoring or enjoyment of life:

The first is to be as fully absorbed in the experience as possible, whether you are spending time with a friend, enjoying a piece of cake, or even reading your Study Guide.

The second is to focus on one sensation, maybe by describing what you're experiencing.

The third way is to build memories, remembering these moments of savoring or joy.

The fourth way is to share these positive experiences with other people.

The fifth way is to congratulate yourself—in moderation—for taking the time to savor the moments of your life.

Try these methods this week. What effects do you notice?

---

1. Describe the concept of the meme.

2. Define observational learning.

3. Generate examples of observational learning, modeling, and vicarious learning.

4. Discuss contemporary evidence regarding the role of mirror neurons in learning.

NOW READ Section 6.3 "How Does Watching Others Affect Learning?" keeping these questions in mind.

REVIEW: Now that you've read this section, go back to the 6.3 Guiding Questions and see if you can answer them based on what you've read. This is a check on your reading. If you can't answer a question, you need to go back to the text to reread that section.

VISUAL SUMMARY: Below is a summary of the major concepts in this section. To check your comprehension of the chapter, read the summary and ask yourself if you understand the concepts. If the concepts seem unfamiliar to you, you may want to go back to the book and reread those sections. This text is taken from the Visual Summaries on StudySpace at wwnorton.com/studyspace.

X. Learning Can Be Passed On through Cultural Transmission

A. Memes (units of cultural knowledge) are selectively passed on from generation to generation.

XI. Learning Can Occur through Observation and Imitation
 A. Children learn behavior by observing adults.
 B. Demonstration and imitation: humans (and some other animals) teach young through imitation and demonstration.
 C. Modeling: imitating observed behavior; most likely if model is attractive, of high status, and similar to observer.
 D. Mirror neurons: activated in the brain when one person watches another perform action; can also be active when observer performs the action.

REINFORCE: Are you ready to check your knowledge of this section? Answer the following multiple-choice questions with your textbook closed.

1. What is the term for the cultural transmission of knowledge from one generation to another?
 a. epic
 b. era
 c. meme
 d. gene

2. How does the transmission of cultural memes relate to learning?
 a. They can be learned by reinforcement or by observation.
 b. They are useful economic models for explaining behavior.
 c. They are innate and reflexive.
 d. They operate only after consequences.

3. Ian, age 2, was watching his father hammer a nail. His father hit his own thumb and then used several expletives. As his father went into the house for a Band-Aid, Ian went over to the nail, picked up the hammer, pretended to hit his finger and repeated the expletives. This scenario exemplifies what kind of learning?
 a. meme learning
 b. observational learning
 c. operant learning
 d. classic learning

4. Bandura's study of children's play habits with the "Bobo" doll provided evidence that:
 a. learning depends on consequences
 b. meme-based learning can be transmitted observationally
 c. aggressive behavior can be learned through observation

d. intracranial self-stimulation can activate reward circuits

5. Billy has watched many movies in which the hero smokes cigarettes. When Billy identifies with these heroes and begins to smoke, what psychological term might be used to describe his behavior?
 a. vicarious reinforcement
 b. modeling
 c. positive reinforcement
 d. meme-based transmission

6. Evidence for observational learning in nonhumans is present in all of the following examples EXCEPT:
 a. lab-raised monkeys becoming fearful of a snake after watching a wild monkey's reactions
 b. a puppy learning to get into the cupboard with the dog food after watching the older dog open the door
 c. animals who injure rather than kill their prey in order to teach their young how to hunt
 d. a cat learning to come at the sound of a can opener because the sound predicts food

7. Learning that occurs when one learns the consequences of an action by observing another's consequences is called:
 a. vicarious learning
 b. indifferent learning
 c. occupational learning
 d. amplitude learning

8. Which factor may account for the relation between children observing violence in the media and their later likelihood of showing aggression?
 a. The children learn how to be aggressive. Without media they would not know how to be aggressive.
 b. Media reinforce the children's own biological tendency toward aggression.
 c. Individuals who engage in violence in the media are typically rewarded, and thus the observing children are also vicariously reinforced.
 d. There is no relation between observing violence in the media and the later likelihood of showing aggression.

9. Which of the following characteristics applies to a "model" that does NOT facilitate a person's imitating him or her?
 a. attractiveness
 b. high status
 c. similarity to oneself
 d. extroversion

10. Imitation learning is facilitated by special brain structures known as:
 a. motor cortices
 b. sensory cortices

c. mirror neurons

d. NMDA receptors

WHAT DID YOU MISS? Check your answers against the Answer Key at the end of this chapter of the Study Guide. The Answer Key also lists the page(s) in your text where each question is explained. If you missed any questions, go to the pages indicated in the Answer Key, reread those sections, go back to the questions, and see if you can answer them correctly this time.

ANOTHER OPPORTUNITY TO REVIEW: Answer these questions without your textbook. As a rule of thumb, if you can write only a few words about these questions, you probably need to go back and review.

1. Describe the concept of the meme. _____
   _____
   _____

2. Define observational learning. _____
   _____
   _____

3. Generate examples of observational learning, modeling, and vicarious learning. _____
   _____
   _____

4. Discuss contemporary evidence regarding the role of mirror neurons in learning. _____
   _____
   _____

WHAT DO I NEED TO KNOW? Based on what you've discovered above, what are the areas where you need to focus your studying? Which objectives do you need to spend more time mastering? Write this information down in your own words.

1. _____

2. _____

3. _____

4. _____

5. _____

6. _____

6.4 What Is the Biological Basis of Learning?

How does the process of learning take place? Cognitive scientists now know that the neurotransmitter dopamine plays a major role in the process of learning. Also, the strength of the connections between neurons explains the process of learning at a neurological level. Interestingly, this process takes place whether you are learning through classical conditioning, operant conditioning, or observational learning.

6.4 Guiding Questions

To guide your reading of the text, review the following questions. Then, as you read the chapter, look for the answers to these questions. You may want to note in your textbook where you find these answers.

1. Discuss the role of dopamine and the nucleus accumbens in the experience of reinforcement.

2. Define habituation, sensitization, and long-term potentiation.

3. Describe the neural basis of habituation, sensitization, long-term potentiation, and fear conditioning.

NOW READ Section 6.4 "What Is the Biological Basis of Learning?" keeping these questions in mind.

REVIEW: Now that you've read this section, go back to the 6.4 Guiding Questions and see if you can answer them based on what you've read. This is a check on your reading. If you can't answer a question, you need to go back to the text to reread that section.

VISUAL SUMMARY: Below is a summary of the major concepts in this section. To check your comprehension of the chapter, read the summary and ask yourself if you understand the concepts. If the concepts seem unfamiliar to you, you may want to go back to the book and reread those sections. This text is taken from the Visual Summaries on StudySpace at wwnorton.com/studyspace.

XII. Dopamine Activity Underlies Reinforcement
   A. Nucleus accumbens has dopamine receptors activated by pleasurable behaviors.
   B. Secondary reinforcers can produce dopamine activation through classical conditioning.

XIII. Habituation and Sensitization Are Simple Models of Learning

A. Learning results from alterations in synaptic connections: firing of one neuron increasingly likely to cause firing of another neuron.

B. Habituation: reduction in neurotransmitters → decrease in behavioral response after exposure to nonthreatening stimulus.

C. Sensitization: increase in neurotransmitters → increase in behavioral response after exposure to threatening stimulus.

XIV. Long-Term Potentiation Is a Candidate for the Neural Basis of Learning

A. Long-term potentiation:
   i. is the strengthening of synaptic connections so stimulation of one neuron leads to increased likelihood that another (postsynaptic) neuron will fire.
   ii. occurs in many parts of the brain including the hippocampus (learning and memory) and amygdala (fear conditioning).

REINFORCE: Are you ready to check your knowledge of this section? Answer the following multiple-choice questions with your textbook closed.

1. The neurotransmitter that is most important for reinforcement learning is:
   a. serotonin
   b. glutamate
   c. dopamine
   d. Norepinepherine

2. The neural structure responsible for releasing dopamine in response to reward or reinforcement is:
   a. the nucleus accumbens
   b. the insula
   c. the raphe system
   d. the orbitofrontal cortex

3. Donald Hebb's finding that alterations in synaptic connections can occur as a result of learning has been summed up in the saying "Cells that fire together, _____."
   a. learn forever
   b. learn together
   c. wire together
   d. form a tether

4. The first time you pick up your pet hamster, it recoils in fear. After a week of handling, your hamster is not bothered anymore. What change came over your hamster through the simple act of repetitive handling?
   a. long-term potentiation
   b. learned helplessness
   c. sensitization
   d. habituation

5. You are driving to school when suddenly an ambulance rushes past you with its siren blaring, shocking you so much that you fear that you might lose control of your car. A minute later, you hear a siren in the distance and increase your vigilance to be prepared for another emergency vehicle on the road. What change has come over your normal reaction to sirens?
   a. Hebbian learning
   b. sensitization
   c. habituation
   d. fight or flight

6. Long-term potentiation is:
   a. the action of glutamate opening NMDA receptors
   b. the summation of potentials on an axon hillock
   c. the strengthening of a synaptic connection between neurons
   d. the sustained release of neurotransmitters in a synapse

7. The NDMA receptor is involved in which of the following processes?
   a. vesicle release
   b. long-term potentiation
   c. influx of calcium in terminals
   d. increase in the protein kinase

8. Eric Kandel's study of learning in invertebrate animals provided evidence for neuronal alteration during the behaviors of:
   a. habituation and sensitization
   b. fight or flight
   c. orienting and defensive reactions
   d. reward and punishment

9. Seeing a good friend, getting a paycheck, or receiving an "A" for a course will activate which of the following neurotransmitter systems?
   a. norepinephrine
   b. endorphin
   c. serotonin
   d. dopamine

10. Long-term potentiation (LTP) has also been demonstrated to function outside the hippocampus. What brain structure uses LTP for fear-specific learning?
   a. the amygdala
   b. the septum
   c. the thalamus
   d. the basal ganglia

WHAT DID YOU MISS? Check your answers against the Answer Key at the end of this chapter of the Study Guide. The Answer Key also lists the page(s) in your text where each question is explained. If you missed any questions, go to the pages indicated in the Answer Key, reread those sections, go back to the questions, and see if you can answer them correctly this time.

ANOTHER OPPORTUNITY TO REVIEW: Answer these questions without your textbook. As a rule of thumb, if you can write only a few words about these questions, you probably need to go back and review.

1. Discuss the role of dopamine and the nucleus accumbens in the experience of reinforcement. _____

_____

_____

_____

2. Define habituation, sensitization, and long-term potentiation. _____

_____

_____

3. Describe the neural basis of habituation, sensitization, long-term potentiation, and fear conditioning. _____

_____

_____

WHAT DO I NEED TO KNOW? Based on what you've discovered above, what are the areas where you need to focus your studying? Which objectives do you need to spend more time mastering? Write this information down in your own words.

1. _____

2. _____

3. _____

4. _____

5. _____

6. _____

WHAT MATTERS TO ME: What facts in this chapter are personally relevant to you?

_____

_____

_____

_____

CHAPTER SUMMARY

6.1 What Ideas Guide the Study of Learning?

- *Learning Results from Experience:* Learning is a relatively enduring change in behavior that results from experience. Learning enables animals to better adapt to the environment, and thus it facilitates survival. Learning involves understanding the associations between events. These associations are acquired through classical conditioning and operant conditioning.

- *Behavioral Responses Are Conditioned:* Pavlov established the principles of classical conditioning. Through classical conditioning, associations are made between two stimuli, such as the clicking of a metronome and a piece of meat. What is learned is that one stimulas predicts another. Acquisition, extinction, spontaneous recovery, generalization, discrimination, and second-order conditioning are processes associated with classical conditioning.

- *Phobias and Addictions Have Learned Components:* Phobias are learned fear associations. Similarly, addiction involves a conditioned response, which can result in withdrawal symptoms at the mere sight of drug paraphernalia. Addiction also involves tolerance: the need for more of a drug, particularly when that drug is administered in a familiar context, to get a high comparable to the one obtained earlier.

- *Classical Conditioning Involves More Than Events Occurring at the Same Time:* Not all stimuli are equally potent in producing conditioning. Animals are biologically prepared to make connections between stimuli that are potentially dangerous. This biological preparedness to fear specific objects helps animals avoid potential dangers, and thus it facilitates survival.

- *Learning Involves Cognition:* Animals are predisposed to form predictions that enhance survival, such as judging the likelihood that food will continue to be available at one location. The Rescorla-Wagner model maintains that the strength of a CS-US association is determined by the extent to which the US is unexpected or surprising.

6.2 How Does Operant Conditioning Differ from Classical Conditioning?

- *Reinforcement Increases Behavior:* A behavior's positive consequences will make it more likely to occur. Shaping is a procedure in which successive approximations of a behavior are reinforced, leading to the desired behavior. Reinforcers may be primary (those that satisfy biological needs) or secondary (those that do not directly satisfy biological needs)

- *Both Reinforcement and Punishment Can Be Positive or Negative:* For positive reinforcement and positive punishment, a stimulus is delivered after the animal responds. For negative reinforcement and negative punishment, a stimulus is removed after the animal responds. Positive and negative reinforcement increase the likelihood that a behavior will recur. Positive and negative punishment decrease the likelihood that a behavior will recur.
- *Operant Conditioning Is Influenced by Schedules of Reinforcement:* Learning occurs in response to continuous reinforcement and partial reinforcement. Partial reinforcement may be delivered on a ratio schedule or an interval schedule. Moreover, partial reinforcement may be fixed or variable. Partial reinforcement administered on a variable-ratio schedule is particularly resistant to extinction. Behavior modification involves the use of operant conditioning to eliminate unwanted behaviors and replace them with desirable behaviors.
- *Biology and Cognition Influence Operant Conditioning:* An organism's biological makeup restricts the types of behaviors the organism can learn. Latent learning takes place without reinforcement. Latent learning may not influence behavior until a reinforcer is introduced.

6.3 How Does Watching Others Affect Learning?

- *Learning Can Be Passed On through Cultural Transmission:* Memes (units of knowledge transmitted within a culture) are analogous to genes in that memes are selectively passed on from generation to generation.
- *Learning Can Occur through Observation and Imitation:* Observational learning is a powerful adaptive tool. Humans and other animals learn by watching the behavior of others. The imitation of observed behavior is referred to as modeling. Vicarious learning occurs when people learn about an action's consequences by observing others being reinforced or punished for their behavior. Mirror neurons are activated when a behavior is observed and performed and may be the neural basis of imitation learning.

6.4 What Is the Biological Basis of Learning?

- *Dopamine Activity Underlies Reinforcement:* The brain has specialized centers that produce pleasure when stimulated. Behaviors that activate these centers are reinforced. The nucleus accumbens (a part of the limbic system) has dopamine receptors, which are activated by pleasurable behaviors. Through conditioning, secondary reinforcers can also activate dopamine receptors.
- *Habituation and Sensitization Are Simple Models of Learning:* Habituation is a decrease in behavioral response after repeated exposure to a nonthreatening stimulus. In contrast, sensitization is an increase in behavioral response after exposure to a new and threatening stimulus.
- *Long-Term Potentiation Is a Candidate for the Neural Basis of Learning:* Long-term potentiation refers to the strengthening of synaptic connections. Long-term potentiation has been observed in the hippocampus (learning and memory) and amygdala (fear conditioning). The receptor NMDA is involved in long-term potentiation.

PUTTING IT ALL TOGETHER

Answer these questions to check your knowledge of the material in this chapter.

1. Imagine the following scenarios occurring back when our ancestors were mainly hunters and gatherers. Two young hunters go out into the wild and encounter a bear, an animal they have never seen before. The bear kills one of the hunters as the other looks on. The surviving hunter now associates the bear with feelings of anxiety and anguish. How do these events exemplify classical conditioning?

   To find food for his family, the hunter returns to the wild. He hears a rustling in the leaves behind him, turns around, and sees the bear again. He escapes, but from this point on, whenever he is in the wild and hears rustling leaves, he feels anxious and his heart races. How do these events exemplify second-order conditioning?

2. To collect fruit, the gatherers go to a particular area where the fruit has proved plentiful. How would positive and negative reinforcement have led the gatherers to return to the same location? Use examples. How would positive and negative punishment have led the gatherers to avoid picking fruit at other locations? Again, use examples.

3. The hunter/gatherer's children spend most of their time with the gatherers. What aspects of gathering fruit might the children learn through observational learning? What aspects of gathering fruit might they learn from other children through vicarious learning?

4. The gatherers have spent the day picking blueberries from the nearby bushes. Not only are the blueberries sweet and delicious, but they also grow on low bushes without thorns. If the hunter/gatherers really enjoy eating the blueberries, what reaction would you expect to occur in their brains? The next day, the gatherers go out and find only thorny raspberry bushes and sour raspberries. Based on what you know about sensitization, what would happen when the gatherers start to collect raspberries and get pricked by the thorns? Based on what you know about habituation, what response do you expect the hunter/gatherers to have over time when eating the sour raspberries?

ANSWER KEY FOR REINFORCE QUESTIONS

Section 6.1

1. d   p. 225
2. a   p. 227
3. b   p. 227
4. a   p. 227
5. c   p. 227
6. d   p. 227
7. b   p. 227
8. d   p. 228
9. c   p. 229
10. a   p. 230
11. d   p. 230
12. c   pp. 232–233
13. a   pp. 233–234
14. b   p. 235
15. c   p. 234
16. a   p. 236
17. d   p. 236

Section 6.2

1. c   p. 239
2. c   p. 241
3. a   p. 239
4. a   p. 241
5. c   p. 240
6. a   p. 242
7. b   p. 242
8. a   p. 242
9. c   p. 243
10. d   p. 243
11. b   p. 242
12. a   p. 245
13. c   p. 245
14. a   p. 245
15. d   p. 245
16. a   p. 245
17. b   p. 247
18. a   p. 247

Section 6.3

1. c   p. 251
2. a   p. 251
3. b   p. 251
4. c   p. 252
5. b   p. 254
6. d   p. 251
7. a   p. 255
8. c   p. 255
9. d   p. 254
10. c   p. 255

Section 6.4

1. c   p. 257
2. a   p. 259
3. c   p. 260
4. d   p. 260
5. b   p. 261
6. c   p. 261
7. b   p. 262
8. a   pp. 260–261
9. d   p. 260
10. a   p. 263

HINTS FOR PUTTING IT ALL TOGETHER QUESTIONS

1. In the first occurrence of seeing the bear, the bear was a neutral stimulus. The surviving hunter saw the bear (neutral) kill his friend (UCS), and this experience produced anxiety and anguish (UCR). Now, if he were to encounter the bear (CS), he would feel anxiety and anguish (CR). This scenario exemplifies classical conditioning because an initially neutral stimulus (bear) now evokes an involuntary, conditioned response (fear). If the hunter returned to the wild and heard rusting leaves, that rustling would initially be a neutral stimulus. But because the bear (CS) followed the presentation of the rustling, the bear led to a CR (fear). Now the rustling leaves become a second-order CS, which predicts the occurrence of the bear and by itself leads to the CR (fear).

2. Reinforcement always leads to an increase in behavior, regardless of whether it is positive or negative reinforcement. Going to the same area to pick fruit could be due to positive reinforcement if the gatherers obtained a reward when they did so (e.g., they found fruit was plentiful there or the fruit there tasted particularly delicious). They may continue to gather fruit in the same place due to negative reinforcement if they avoided an unfavorable outcome by going to that location (e.g., they avoided hunger). Punishment always leads to a decrease in behavior, regardless of whether it is positive or negative punishment. Avoiding certain areas to gather fruit could be due to positive punishment if the gatherers found noxious stimuli at those locations (e.g., rotten fruit, dangerous animals, poison ivy). They may also avoid gathering fruit in some locations due to negative punishment if a reward was taken away when they went to that location (e.g., valuable baskets were stolen by enemies or a gatherer fell into a mud pit and died).

3. By watching their elders, the children can learn which fruits are edible, at what point of ripeness the fruit should be picked, how to eat the fruit (peel, cut, scrape

with rock), and many other important aspects of behavior. Vicarious learning involves learning whether to perform a behavior based on another person's being rewarded or punished for that behavior. If another child finds a big, ripe fruit and is rewarded with praise by his or her mother, the onlooking child will likely search for a big, ripe fruit as well, to earn the same reward (praise).

4. If the villagers really enjoy the blueberries, this experience is likely to activate pleasure centers in the brain (e.g., nucleus accumbens) through the release of the neurotransmitter dopamine. When picking raspberries and pricking their fingers on the thorns, the gatherers will likely retract their hands quickly. Sensitization, increased response to a noxious stimulus, is likely to be demonstrated by quicker withdrawal of their hands as well as possibly a retraction that involves a greater proportion of the body (e.g., pulling away the entire arm or body from the bush). When the villagers eat the sour raspberries, they are likely to notice the sour taste a lot at first. But after eating the raspberries again and again, the response to the non-threatening stimulus should decrease (so that the villagers notice the sour taste less and less).

KEY TERMS EXERCISES

First, fill in your own definition and example for each term. Then check each term against the textbook's definition. These exercises can also be cut out and used as flash cards.

acquisition

Your Definition:

Your Example:

Textbook Definition:

conditioned response (CR)

Your Definition:

Your Example:

Textbook Definition:

behavior modification

Your Definition:

Your Example:

Textbook Definition:

conditioned stimulus (CS)

Your Definition:

Your Example:

Textbook Definition:

classical conditioning (Pavlovian conditioning)

Your Definition:

Your Example:

Textbook Definition:

continuous reinforcement

Your Definition:

Your Example:

Textbook Definition:

cognitive map

Your Definition:

Your Example:

Textbook Definition:

extinction

Your Definition:

Your Example:

Textbook Definition:

fixed schedule

Your Definition:

Your Example:

Textbook Definition:

law of effect

Your Definition:

Your Example:

Textbook Definition:

habituation

Your Definition:

Your Example:

Textbook Definition:

learning

Your Definition:

Your Example:

Textbook Definition:

interval schedule

Your Definition:

Your Example:

Textbook Definition:

long-term potentiation (LTP)

Your Definition:

Your Example:

Textbook Definition:

latent learning

Your Definition:

Your Example:

Textbook Definition:

meme

Your Definition:

Your Example:

Textbook Definition:

mirror neurons

Your Definition:
Your Example:
Textbook Definition:

observational learning

Your Definition:
Your Example:
Textbook Definition:

modeling

Your Definition:
Your Example:
Textbook Definition:

operant conditioning (instrumental conditioning)

Your Definition:
Your Example:
Textbook Definition:

negative punishment

Your Definition:
Your Example:
Textbook Definition:

partial reinforcement

Your Definition:
Your Example:
Textbook Definition:

negative reinforcement

Your Definition:
Your Example:
Textbook Definition:

partial-reinforcement extinction effect

Your Definition:
Your Example:
Textbook Definition:

phobia

| Your Definition: |
| Your Example: |
| Textbook Definition: |

reinforcer

| Your Definition: |
| Your Example: |
| Textbook Definition: |

positive punishment

| Your Definition: |
| Your Example: |
| Textbook Definition: |

Rescorla-Wagner model

| Your Definition: |
| Your Example: |
| Textbook Definition: |

positive reinforcement

| Your Definition: |
| Your Example: |
| Textbook Definition: |

sensitization

| Your Definition: |
| Your Example: |
| Textbook Definition: |

ratio schedule

| Your Definition: |
| Your Example: |
| Textbook Definition: |

shaping

| Your Definition: |
| Your Example: |
| Textbook Definition: |

spontaneous recovery

Your Definition:

Your Example:

Textbook Definition:

stimulus discrimination

Your Definition:

Your Example:

Textbook Definition:

stimulus generalization

Your Definition:

Your Example:

Textbook Definition:

unconditioned response (UR)

Your Definition:

Your Example:

Textbook Definition:

unconditioned stimulus (US)

Your Definition:

Your Example:

Textbook Definition:

variable schedule

Your Definition:

Your Example:

Textbook Definition:

vicarious learning

Your Definition:

Your Example:

Textbook Definition:

CHAPTER 7 | Attention and Memory

CHAPTER OVERVIEW

Whether you're solving an algebra problem, finding your way home, or tying your shoelaces, memory enables you to retain the information you need to accomplish any task. Thanks to memory, you can function in the world. In fact, much of what you are doing in college is acquiring information that you are then storing in your memory. How the process of acquiring and storing information works, how reliable it is, and some techniques that can make this process easier and thus improve your study skills are the focus of this chapter.

7.1 What Is Memory?

The process of memory begins with encoding a memory and then storing it in specific parts of the brain. It is then transferred into long-term memory through the process of consolidation. Finally, for a memory to be used, it must be retrieved from long-term memory. This section describes the process of memory and the parts of the brain that are involved in storing memories.

At the beginning of each section in the Study Guide, there will be guiding questions. Before you read the chapter in your textbook, read through these questions and maybe even attempt to answer them based on either what you've already read or what you think the answer should be. Then as you study the chapter, you can use them to help guide your reading.

7.1 Guiding Questions

To guide your reading of the text, review the following questions. Then, as you read the chapter, look for the answers to these questions. You may want to note in your textbook where you find these answers.

1. Describe the three phases of memory.

2. Identify brain regions involved in learning and memory.

3. Describe the processes of consolidation and reconsolidation.

NOW READ Section 7.1 "What Is Memory?" keeping these questions in mind.

REVIEW: Now that you've read this section, go back to the 7.1 Guiding Questions and see if you can answer them based on what you've read. This is a check on your reading. If you can't answer a question, you need to go back to the text to reread that section.

VISUAL SUMMARY: Below is a summary of the major concepts in this section. To check your comprehension of the chapter, read the summary and ask yourself if you understand the concepts. If the concepts seem unfamiliar to you, you may want to go back to the book and reread those sections. This text is taken from the Visual Summaries on StudySpace at wwnorton.com/studyspace.

I. Memory Is the Nervous System's Capacity to Acquire and Retain Usable Skills and Knowledge
   A. Memory enables organisms to store information from experiences for retrieval.

II. Memory Is the Processing of Information
   A. Information processing model:
      i. is based on computer functioning.
      ii. consists of encoding, storage, and retrieval.

III. Memory Is the Result of Brain Activity
   A. Memory is stored in the:

i. hippocampus.
ii. cerebellum.
iii. amygdala.
iv. temporal lobes.
B. Consolidation: transfer of memories into long-term storage:
   i. leads to formation and reinforcement of neural networks.
   ii. is aided by sleep.
C. Reconsolidation: alteration of memories during retrieval.

REINFORCE: Are you ready to check your knowledge of this section? Answer the following multiple-choice questions with your textbook closed.

1. Yesterday you taught your dog a new trick. If the dog is to perform this trick tomorrow, which of the following sequences will have to occur?
  a. encode, store, retrieve
  b. store, encode, retrieve
  c. rehearse, store, retrieve
  d. store, rehearse, retrieve

2. A car drives away from the scene of an accident. Even though you have just seen the license plate, you cannot remember the number. The number was probably not _____ in your memory.
  a. encoded
  b. ignored
  c. reconsolidated
  d. processed

3. The false assumption that memory is distributed equally throughout the brain is called:
  a. concurrent storage
  b. equity of distribution
  c. connectivity
  d. equipotentiality

4. The phase of information processing that is most similar to a Google search is:
  a. encoding
  b. storage
  c. retrieval
  d. rehearsal

5. The amygdala and hippocampus are located in which part of the brain?
  a. the posterior parietal lobe
  b. the medial temporal lobe
  c. the left frontal lobe
  d. the right temporal lobe

6. Changes in the strength of neural connections and construction of new synapses cause:
  a. retrieval
  b. encoding

  c. consolidation
  d. rehearsal

7. Digitally editing a photograph on a computer is analogous to which memory process?
  a. spreading activation
  b. elaborative rehearsal
  c. reconsolidation
  d. retrieval

WHAT DID YOU MISS? Check your answers against the Answer Key at the end of this chapter of the Study Guide. The Answer Key also lists the page(s) in your text where each question is explained. If you missed any questions, go to the pages indicated in the Answer Key, reread those sections, go back to the questions, and see if you can answer them correctly this time.

ANOTHER OPPORTUNITY TO REVIEW: Answer these questions without your textbook. As a rule of thumb, if you can write only a few words about these questions, you probably need to go back and review.

1. Describe the three phases of memory. _____

  _____

  _____

2. Identify brain regions involved in learning and memory.

  _____

  _____

3. Describe the processes of consolidation and reconsolidation. _____

  _____

  _____

WHAT DO I NEED TO KNOW? Based on what you've discovered above, what are the areas where you need to focus your studying? Which objectives do you need to spend more time mastering? Write this information down in your own words.

1. _____

2. _____

3. _____

4. _____

5. _____

6. _____

7.2 How Does Attention Determine What We Remember?

Paying attention to any sensory information is the first step in storing the information for eventual retrieval. But with all the sensory information bombarding us, how do we decide which information is important? In answering this question, this section will discuss why multitasking isn't such a good idea and how our attention can be "tricked."

7.2 Guiding Questions

To guide your reading of the text, review the following questions. Then, as you read the chapter, look for the answers to these questions. You may want to note in your textbook where you find these answers.

1. Distinguish between parallel processing and serial processing.
2. Describe filter theory.
3. Define change blindness.

NOW READ Section 7.2 "How Does Attention Determine What We Remember?" keeping these questions in mind.

REVIEW: Now that you've read this section, go back to the 7.2 Guiding Questions and see if you can answer them based on what you've read. This is a check on your reading. If you can't answer a question, you need to go back to the text to reread that section.

VISUAL SUMMARY: Below is a summary of the major concepts in this section. To check your comprehension of the chapter, read the summary and ask yourself if you understand the concepts. If the concepts seem unfamiliar to you, you may want to go back to the book and reread those sections. This text is taken from the Visual Summaries on StudySpace at wwnorton.com/studyspace.

IV. Our Visual Attention Works Selectively and Serially
   A. Parallel processing: attending to and processing multiple types of information simultaneously.
   B. Because attention is limited, conducting different tasks at once is difficult and inefficient.

V. Our Auditory Attention Allows Us to Listen Selectively
   A. Cocktail party phenomenon: capturing of attention by particularly pertinent stimulus.

VI. Through Selective Attention, We Filter Incoming Information
   A. We pay more attention to personally relevant information.
   B. Change blindness: failure to notice major changes in an environment.

REINFORCE: Are you ready to check your knowledge of this section? Answer the following multiple-choice questions with your textbook closed.

1. In Anne Treisman's model of visual attention, primitive features—such as color, shape, and movement—can be analyzed in parallel because:
   a. a single system can handle all these primitive features simultaneously
   b. separate systems can analyze these different primitive features simultaneously
   c. separate systems do rapid serial processing that mimics nonspecific processing
   d. a single system focuses on a small subset of these primitive features simultaneously

2. Broadbent's filter theory of attention assumed that selective attention was necessary because people have limited capacity in short-term memory and thus must focus on the most _____ information.
   a. important
   b. complex
   c. transient
   d. simple

3. Children with attention deficit disorder are distracted by everything in the environment rather than being able to choose what they want to focus on. These children are lacking in:
   a. divided attention
   b. automatic processing
   c. selective attention
   d. simultaneous processing

4. Yelizaveta is talking to one of the caterers setting up for her sister's wedding. While she is answering her cell phone, a different member of the catering staff takes over. When Yelizaveta turns back to the conversation, she fails to notice that she is now talking to a different person. Yelizaveta is experiencing:
   a. divided attention
   b. change blindness
   c. selective attention
   d. serial processing

5. Olivia, a busy college student, always has more to do than there are hours in the day. As a result, she tends to doing several things at once, such as checking e-mail, text-messaging, doing homework, and watching television. Research on multitasking suggests that:
   a. her performance on all tasks will be diminished
   b. her performance on her homework will be diminished, but her performances on the other activities will not

c. her performance on the social tasks (e-mail and texting) will be diminished, but her performances on the other activities will not

d. her performance will not be diminished for any of the tasks

6. At a party, Frank was listening to his friend Eddy. Suddenly, Frank told Eddy to be quiet because he heard a pretty girl across the room mention his name and he wanted to listen in on her conversation. Frank's hearing his name from across the room reflects:

a. screened processing
b. unconscious inference
c. visual search
d. the cocktail party phenomenon

7. Pete is taking part in an experiment where different information is presented in each of his ears. His task is to repeat back information from only one ear. Research on auditory attention suggests that:

a. he will hear sound and understand meaning from the unattended ear
b. he will hear sound from the unattended ear, but not discern meaning
c. he won't be able to detect sound from the unattended ear
d. he won't be able to detect sound from the unattended ear and will have a very hard time repeating information from the ear he is listening to

WHAT DID YOU MISS? Check your answers against the Answer Key at the end of this chapter of the Study Guide. The Answer Key also lists the page(s) in your text where each question is explained. If you missed any questions, go to the pages indicated in the Answer Key, reread those sections, go back to the questions, and see if you can answer them correctly this time.

ANOTHER OPPORTUNITY TO REVIEW: Answer these questions without your textbook. As a rule of thumb, if you can write only a few words about these questions, you probably need to go back and review.

1. Distinguish between parallel processing and serial processing. _____

_____

_____

2. Describe filter theory. _____

_____

_____

3. Define change blindness. _____

_____

_____

WHAT DO I NEED TO KNOW? Based on what you've discovered above, what are the areas where you need to focus your studying? Which objectives do you need to spend more time mastering? Write this information down in your own words.

1. _____

2. _____

3. _____

4. _____

5. _____

6. _____

7.3 How Are Memories Maintained over Time?

Any sensory information to which we pay attention is initially stored in sensory memory. If we choose to pay more attention, it's transferred to working memory, and under certain circumstances information is transferred to long-term memory. You'll also learn some helpful techniques to make you a more efficient learner in this section.

7.3 Guiding Questions

To guide your reading of the text, review the following questions. Then, as you read the chapter, look for the answers to these questions. You may want to note in your textbook where you find these answers.

1. Distinguish between sensory memory, short-term memory, and long-term memory.

2. Describe working memory and chunking.

3. Review evidence that supports the distinction between working memory and long-term memory.

4. Explain how information is transferred from working memory to long-term memory.

NOW READ Section 7.3 "How Are Memories Maintained over Time?" keeping these questions in mind.

REVIEW: Now that you've read this section, go back to the 7.3 Guiding Questions and see if you can answer them based on what you've read. This is a check on your reading. If you can't answer a question, you need to go back to the text to reread that section.

VISUAL SUMMARY: Below is a summary of the major concepts in this section. To check your comprehension of the chapter, read the summary and ask yourself if you understand the concepts. If the concepts seem unfamiliar to you, you may want to go back to the book and reread those sections. This text is taken from the Visual Summaries on StudySpace at wwnorton.com/studyspace.

VII. Atkinson and Schiffrin's Three-part Model
   A. Sensory memory is brief:
      i. tied to visual or auditory information in pure sensory form.
   B. Working (short-term) memory is active:
      i. has limited capacity and short duration.
      ii. can be improved by chunking.
   C. Long-term memory is relatively permanent:
      i. is unlimited in capacity.

REINFORCE: Are you ready to check your knowledge of this section? Answer the following multiple-choice questions with your textbook closed.

1. When you read, your eyes fixate for a fraction of a second, then jump to a new point in the text. You experience reading continuous text because during the jump, the information from the last eye fixation is held in:
   a. short-term memory
   b. working memory
   c. sensory memory
   d. long-term memory

2. Animation works by presenting still pictures rapidly enough that they merge in sensory memory. How much time can elapse between each successive picture if animation is to work?
   a. several minutes
   b. several seconds
   c. a few fractions of a second
   d. variable amounts of time

3. Colt is an excellent quarterback. One skill that contributes to his ability is that he sees the players not just as individuals but as units that can be called on to make different plays. This skill enables him to process the game more efficiently and to hold more information about the game in his short-term memory. Colt is using the memory strategy of:
   a. visualization
   b. imaging
   c. chunking
   d. linking

4. A friend gives you her new address over the phone, and you realize that you do not have a pen to write it down. Approximately how long can it take for you find a pen before her address will vanish from your short-term memory (working memory)?
   a. several seconds
   b. several minutes
   c. less than 0.5 second
   d. less than 1 second

5. Professor Smith is doing research on fish. He refuses to learn his students' names because he believes that the names take up space in his long-term memory that could be better used for fish information. He is incorrect because:
   a. names of people are stored in the frontal lobes and names of animals (fish) are stored in the occipital lobes
   b. the students' names would have been stored in short-term memory
   c. long-term memory can hold essentially unlimited amounts of information
   d. the students' names that are preserved in long-term memory could be replaced later with different information

6. Stuart and Laura are studying for an upcoming midterm exam. Whereas Stuart reads over and reviews his notes every day, Laura takes as many practice tests on the material as she can. According to your text, which person is likely to have a better mastery of the material?
   a. Stuart
   b. Laura
   c. Both will likely perform equally well.
   d. Neither technique is effective in the mastery of new information.

7. According to evolutionary theory, the brain is selective about the information that gets stored in long-term memory because:
   a. only a limited amount of space is available in long-term memory
   b. information that aids in reproduction and survival is emphasized
   c. increased selectivity is associated with greater intelligence
   d. selectivity improves the organization of information in long-term memory

WHAT DID YOU MISS? Check your answers against the Answer Key at the end of this chapter of the Study Guide. The Answer Key also lists the page(s) in your text where each question is explained. If you missed any questions, go to the pages indicated in the Answer Key, reread those sections, go back to the questions, and see if you can answer them correctly this time.

ANOTHER OPPORTUNITY TO REVIEW: Answer these questions without your textbook. As a rule of thumb, if you can write only a few words about these questions, you probably need to go back and review.

1. Distinguish between sensory memory, short-term memory, and long-term memory. _____

_____

_____

2. Describe working memory and chunking. _____

_____

_____

3. Review evidence that supports the distinction between working memory and long-term memory. _____

_____

_____

4. Explain how information is transferred from working memory to long-term memory. _____

_____

_____

WHAT DO I NEED TO KNOW? Based on what you've discovered above, what are the areas where you need to focus your studying? Which objectives do you need to spend more time mastering? Write this information down in your own words.

1. _____

2. _____

3. _____

4. _____

5. _____

6. _____

7.4 How Is Information Organized in Long-Term Memory?

There are many specific and efficient ways to store information in long-term memory. Understanding how information is stored will help you figure out the most efficient ways for you to study. And if you study more efficiently, you may not have to study for as much time!

7.4 Guiding Questions

To guide your reading of the text, review the following questions. Then, as you read the chapter, look for the answers to

these questions. You may want to note in your textbook where you find these answers.

1. Discuss the levels of processing model.

2. Explain how schemas influence memory.

3. Describe spreading activation models of memory.

4. Identify retrieval cues.

5. Identify common mnemonics.

NOW READ Section 7.4 "How Is Information Organized in Long-Term Memory?" keeping these questions in mind.

REVIEW: Now that you've read this section, go back to the 7.4 Guiding Questions and see if you can answer them based on what you've read. This is a check on your reading. If you can't answer a question, you need to go back to the text to reread that section.

VISUAL SUMMARY: Below is a summary of the major concepts in this section. To check your comprehension of the chapter, read the summary and ask yourself if you understand the concepts. If the concepts seem unfamiliar to you, you may want to go back to the book and reread those sections. This text is taken from the Visual Summaries on StudySpace at wwnorton.com/studyspace.

VIII. Long-Term Storage Is Based on Meaning
   A. Studies that examine serial position effect help distinguish between short-term memory and long-term memory.
   B. Information:
      i. the more meaningful, the more likely to be stored in long-term memory.
      ii. enters permanent storage through rehearsal.
      iii. is more likely to be stored if it promotes adaptation, promotes survival, or enhances reproductive capability.
   C. Elaborative rehearsal: deeper processing encodes information more meaningfully and effectively.
   D. Maintenance rehearsal: information is repeated over and over.

IX. Schemas Provide an Organizational Framework
   A. Schemas:
      i. are cognitive maps or structures that help organize information in memory.
      ii. are affected by culture, thus prone to distortion and biased encoding.

X. Information Is Stored in Association Networks
   A. Association network:
      i. basic unit is a node.
      ii. information is arranged in categories for easier retrieval.

B. Spreading of activation model: memory nodes may have multiple associations thus activating one node may lead to activation of other networks.

XI. Retrieval Cues Provide Access to Long-Term Storage
   A. Retrieval cue: anything that helps recall information from long-term memory.
   B. Encoding specificity principle: any part of a memory may serve as a retrieval cue.
   C. Mnemonics: learning strategies that improve recall through retrieval cues.

REINFORCE: Are you ready to check your knowledge of this section? Answer the following multiple-choice questions with your textbook closed.

1. The best argument that long-term memory and short-term memory (currently referred to as working memory) are separate entities is that:
   a. brain damage can leave one but not the other memory intact
   b. recent events are remembered better than most past events
   c. recalling past events, but not recent events, requires retrieval cues
   d. the recency effect, but not the primacy effect, can be disrupted

2. According to levels of processing theory, information that is more deeply encoded is remembered better than less deeply encoded information because:
   a. it has greater rehearsal
   b. it is stored longer in short-term memory storage
   c. it is more meaningful
   d. it is entered into long-term memory more logically

3. Geoff is trying to remember his shopping list by repeating the items over and over again to himself. He is using:
   a. maintenance rehearsal
   b. acoustic rehearsal
   c. elaborative rehearsal
   d. linkage rehearsal

4. According to the encoding specificity principle, _____.
   a. only similar kinds of information can be encoded together
   b. anything encoded with information can be a retrieval cue for that information
   c. similar kinds of information are encoded into common schemas
   d. associative networks are formed of similarly encoded pieces of information

---

TRY IT

Memory and Forgiveness

If you're like many people, you have some memories that you would just as soon forget. For example, you might have felt wounded by another person or let yourself down by your actions. Whatever the circumstances, forgiveness may be a helpful response to unwanted memories. Let's debunk some myths about forgiving.

1. Despite the topic of this chapter, forgiving is not forgetting. Even though you may not forget, you can choose to forgive yourself or other people.

2. To forgive a person, you don't need to have moved past all the painful emotions involved in the situation.

3. Forgiveness is not about excusing somebody (or yourself) for the hurtful behavior.

4. Forgiveness does not mean you need to continually allow someone to hurt you.

5. Just because you forgive someone does not mean that you pretend nothing ever happened.

In some cases, even with forgiveness, you may choose to never be involved with the person ever again, or you may acknowledge that the relationship will have to be rebuilt. Rather than being a one-time event, forgiveness is an ongoing process that psychologists have found can lead to improvements in psychological and physical well-being.

---

5. Sergio tells Monica that his roommate goes to a lot of parties. After this conversation, Monica tells Genevra that Sergio's roommate drinks a great deal. Monica believes this statement about Sergio's roommate because:
   a. she used her schema of a party person
   b. she did not remember what Sergio had told her
   c. she is biased against people who like to party
   d. her elaboration made the story more interesting

6. Karl's late grandmother used to cook wonderful food from her native Poland. One day, Karl walks by a Polish restaurant and is flooded with memories of his grandmother. The food served as a _____ for Karl's memories of his grandmother.
   a. mnemonic
   b. mental image
   c. frame
   d. retrieval cue

7. On his way to get an afternoon snack, Jed walks by a billboard advertising hamburgers. He had intended to

get an ice cream cone but instead orders French fries. According to the spreading activation model, the hamburger made Jed want French fries because:

a. hamburgers and French fries are part of the prospective memory

b. hamburgers activated the nodes for French fries

c. hamburgers were encoded with French fries

d. hamburgers and French fries are part of the same procedural memory

WHAT DID YOU MISS? Check your answers against the Answer Key at the end of this chapter of the Study Guide. The Answer Key also lists the page(s) in your text where each question is explained. If you missed any questions, go to the pages indicated in the Answer Key, reread those sections, go back to the questions, and see if you can answer them correctly this time.

ANOTHER OPPORTUNITY TO REVIEW: Answer these questions without your textbook. As a rule of thumb, if you can write only a few words about these questions, you probably need to go back and review.

1. Discuss the levels of processing model. _____

_____

_____

2. Explain how schemas influence memory. _____

_____

_____

3. Describe spreading activation models of memory. _____

_____

_____

4. Identify retrieval cues. _____

_____

_____

5. Identify common mnemonics. _____

_____

_____

WHAT DO I NEED TO KNOW? Based on what you've discovered above, what are the areas where you need to focus your studying? Which objectives do you need to spend more time mastering? Write this information down in your own words.

1. _____

2. _____

3. _____

4. _____

5. _____

6. _____

7.5 What Are the Different Long-Term Memory Systems?

What do knowing how to serve a tennis ball, what month Labor Day is in, and when your first kiss was have in common? They are all different types of memory. In this section, you will learn the characteristics of these ways of organizing memory.

7.5 Guiding Questions

To guide your reading of the text, review the following questions. Then, as you read the chapter, look for the answers to these questions. You may want to note in your textbook where you find these answers.

1. Distinguish between episodic, semantic, implicit, explicit, and prospective memories.

2. Generate examples of each of these types of memory.

NOW READ Section 7.5 "What Are the Different Long-Term Memory Systems?" keeping these questions in mind.

REVIEW: Now that you've read this section, go back to the 7.5 Guiding Questions and see if you can answer them based on what you've read. This is a check on your reading. If you can't answer a question, you need to go back to the text to reread that section.

VISUAL SUMMARY: Below is a summary of the major concepts in this section. To check your comprehension of the chapter, read the summary and ask yourself if you understand the concepts. If the concepts seem unfamiliar to you, you may want to go back to the book and reread those sections. This text is taken from the Visual Summaries on StudySpace at wwnorton.com/studyspace.

XII. Explicit Memory Involves Conscious Effort
  A. Explicit memory:
    i. the system underlying conscious memories.
    ii. divided into episodic memories (personally relevant events), declarative memories (memories that can be verbalized), and semantic memories (general information).

XIII. Implicit Memory Occurs without Deliberate Effort
  A. Implicit memory: system underlying unconscious memory.

B. Procedural memory: memory for motor skills and behavior.

C. Declarative memory: memories that can be verbalized (declared).

XIV. Prospective Memory Is Remembering to Do Something

A. Prospective memory: related to future action, involves unconscious and conscious processes.

REINFORCE: Are you ready to check your knowledge of this section? Answer the following multiple-choice questions with your textbook closed.

1. Akila's brother asks her if she knows the names of the capitals of Texas and Montana. She instantly knows that the capital of Texas is Austin, but she does not know the capital of Montana. Akila is using her _____ memory to try to retrieve _____ memories.
   a. explicit; declarative
   b. implicit; tacit
   c. episodic; autobiographical
   d. procedural; semantic

2. If you can remember exactly what you did yesterday but have trouble remembering the names of the 50 states, then you have excellent _____ memory but somewhat poor _____ memory.
   a. episodic; semantic
   b. semantic; episodic
   c. procedural; explicit
   d. explicit; procedural

3. If someone asks you who is running for president, you will answer from your _____ memory. If someone asks who you plan to vote for, you will answer from your _____ memory.
   a. episodic; semantic
   b. semantic; episodic
   c. procedural; explicit
   d. explicit; procedural

4. Many movies involve product placement; for example, the main actor may drink only Dr. Pepper. Companies pay for product placement because they assume that it increases the likelihood that audience members will later buy the product even if they did not notice the frequency of their exposure to Dr. Pepper during the movie. If this technique actually works, its success is likely due to existence of the item in:
   a. explicit memory
   b. semantic memory
   c. implicit memory
   d. procedural memory

5. Ivaylo goes skiing after many years away from the sport. What kind of memory makes it possible for him to get back on the slopes without taking new skiing lessons?
   a. declarative memory
   b. episodic memory
   c. explicit memory
   d. procedural memory

6. Understanding and being able to state the steps involved in the process of serving a tennis ball involve _____ memory, but actually serving the ball involves _____ memory.
   a. declarative; procedural
   b. episodic; procedural
   c. procedural; declarative
   d. procedural; episodic

7. Which of the following is an example of prospective memory?
   a. learning history dates for your test tomorrow
   b. daydreaming about your date next Friday night
   c. planning to stop for a library book on your way home
   d. deciding which of several things you will do this weekend

WHAT DID YOU MISS? Check your answers against the Answer Key at the end of this chapter of the Study Guide. The Answer Key also lists the page(s) in your text where each question is explained. If you missed any questions, go to the pages indicated in the Answer Key, reread those sections, go back to the questions, and see if you can answer them correctly this time.

ANOTHER OPPORTUNITY TO REVIEW: Answer these questions without your textbook. As a rule of thumb, if you can write only a few words about these questions, you probably need to go back and review.

1. Distinguish between episodic, semantic, implicit, explicit, and prospective memories. _____

_____

2. Generate examples of each of these types of memory. ___

_____

_____

WHAT DO I NEED TO KNOW? Based on what you've discovered above, what are the areas where you need to focus your studying? Which objectives do you need to spend more time mastering? Write this information down in your own words.

1. _____

2. _____

3. _____

4. _____

5. _____

6. _____

7.6 When Do People Forget?

Have you ever wondered why you couldn't remember a telephone number or a particular answer to a quiz question? In this section, you will learn about the common reasons people forget information and how to prevent this from happening. You'll also learn about amnesia, a more severe form of memory loss.

7.6 Guiding Questions

To guide your reading of the text, review the following questions. Then, as you read the chapter, look for the answers to these questions. You may want to note in your textbook where you find these answers.

1. List the seven sins of memory.

2. Explain transience, blocking, and absentmindedness.

3. Distinguish between retrograde and anterograde amnesia.

4. Discuss methods to reduce persistence.

NOW READ Section 7.6 "When Do People Forget?" keeping these questions in mind.

REVIEW: Now that you've read this section, go back to the 7.6 Guiding Questions and see if you can answer them based on what you've read. This is a check on your reading. If you can't answer a question, you need to go back to the text to reread that section.

VISUAL SUMMARY: Below is a summary of the major concepts in this section. To check your comprehension of the chapter, read the summary and ask yourself if you understand the concepts. If the concepts seem unfamiliar to you, you may want to go back to the book and reread those sections. This text is taken from the Visual Summaries on StudySpace at wwnorton.com/studyspace.

XV. Forgetting: Inability to Retrieve Information from Long-term Memory

XVI. Seven Sins of Memory: Transience, Absentmindedness, Blocking, Persistence, Misattribution, Suggestibility, and Bias

XVII. Transience Is Caused by Interference
  A. Transience: forgetting over time because of interference from other information.
  B. Proactive interference: old information interferes with ability to remember new information.
  C. Retroactive interference: new information interferes with ability to remember old information.

XVIII. Blocking Is Temporary
  A. Blocking: temporary inability to remember information.

XIX. Absentmindedness Results from Shallow Encoding
  A. Absentmindedness:
    i. is failure to encode information effectively.
    ii. can occur through either inattention or shallow encoding.

XX. Amnesia Is a Deficit in Long-Term Memory
  A. Amnesia results from disease, brain injury, or psychological trauma.
  B. Retrograde amnesia: loss of past memories.
  C. Anterograde amnesia: inability to form new memories.

XXI. Persistence Is Unwanted Remembering
  A. Persistence: unwanted remembering of usually traumatic memories.

REINFORCE: Are you ready to check your knowledge of this section? Answer the following multiple-choice questions with your textbook closed.

1. According to your text, which of the following individuals is likely to have problems related to the persistence of memories?
   a. Tom, who is depressed
   b. Steve, who has posttraumatic stress disorder
   c. Laura, who has schizophrenia
   d. Lynn, who has a social phobia

2. You are following the plot of a complicated Shakespeare play quite clearly while you are watching it. However, the next week, you cannot remember the details. Your loss of memory is most likely due to:
   a. persistence
   b. interference
   c. blocking
   d. absentmindedness

3. Aaron took calculus as a freshman in high school, but he is now taking it again as a college senior to fulfill requirements for his major. The material is likely to take _____ in his college class as it did in his high school class.
   a. as much effort and as much time to learn
   b. less effort but as much time to learn
   c. as much effort but less time to learn
   d. less effort and less time to learn

4. Jacob learned French in high school and is now learning Spanish in college. Sometimes when he intends to write a Spanish word, he instead writes a French word. Jacob's problem is due to:
   a. blocking
   b. persistence
   c. proactive interference
   d. retroactive interference

5. Nadia changed her computer password on Monday. On Friday, she realizes that she failed to change the password in one system. When she tries to get in with her old password, she cannot remember it; her new password keeps coming to mind. Nadia's problem is due to:
   a. blocking
   b. persistence
   c. proactive interference
   d. retroactive interference

6. A character on a TV show wanders into a hospital seeking help because he cannot remember who he is or where he is from. If the doctor on the show knows anything about memory, she will diagnose the man with:
   a. a concussion
   b. retrograde amnesia
   c. anterograde amnesia
   d. Absentmindedness

7. After a plane crash, Sherrod wakes up in the hospital and can remember everything about his life. The doctor comes in, introduces himself, and explains the course of treatment. The next day, Sherrod believes that he has never met the doctor and asks him to explain the proposed treatment. The doctor is likely to diagnose Sherrod with:
   a. a concussion
   b. retrograde amnesia
   c. anterograde amnesia
   d. absentmindedness

WHAT DID YOU MISS? Check your answers against the Answer Key at the end of this chapter of the Study Guide. The Answer Key also lists the page(s) in your text where each question is explained. If you missed any questions, go to the pages indicated in the Answer Key, reread those sections, go back to the questions, and see if you can answer them correctly this time.

ANOTHER OPPORTUNITY TO REVIEW: Answer these questions without your textbook. As a rule of thumb, if you can write only a few words about these questions, you probably need to go back and review.

1. List the seven sins of memory. _____

2. Explain transience, blocking, and absentmindedness. ___

3. Distinguish between retrograde and anterograde amnesia.

4. Discuss methods to reduce persistence. _____

WHAT DO I NEED TO KNOW? Based on what you've discovered above, what are the areas where you need to focus your studying? Which objectives do you need to spend more time mastering? Write this information down in your own words.

1. _____
2. _____
3. _____
4. _____
5. _____
6. _____

7.7 How Are Memories Distorted?

Do we always remember everything accurately? Can we always trust eyewitness testimonies? To both questions, the answer is no. What about this question: Is it possible to plant a false memory in someone's long-term memory?

7.7 Guiding Questions

To guide your reading of the text, review the following questions. Then, as you read the chapter, look for the answers to these questions. You may want to note in your textbook where you find these answers.

1. Define memory bias.
2. Generate examples of source misattribution.
3. Identify factors that contribute to errors in eyewitness testimony.
4. Discuss susceptibility to false memories.

TRY IT

An Exercise in Forgiveness

There are many ways to start the process of forgiveness, and here is a technique you may find helpful. Begin by writing about the event for which you wish to forgive someone. In describing your thoughts and feelings about the event, report as much detail as you can. How has the event affected your life, your self-esteem, your self-worth? If you feel lingering anger or resentment, how has this feeling affected how you feel and think and what you do? In this process, don't edit or correct your writing; just put your pen to paper and write. Choose to forgive this person in your heart and mind. If this person has hurt you, think of ways to avoid being hurt by this person or by other people in the future. Although you may feel some sense of relief, realize that forgiveness is a process, and you will likely need to make this choice to forgive more than one time. If you wish, you can share what you have written with a friend and discuss with him or her your decision to forgive the person who has hurt you. If your feelings are overwhelming, consider talking with a psychologist or counselor to get some assistance with this very common concern.

---

5. Describe contemporary views on repressed memories.

6. Discuss neuroscientific advancements in the identification of true and false memories.

NOW READ Section 7.7 "How Are Memories Distorted?" keeping these questions in mind.

REVIEW: Now that you've read this section, go back to the 7.7 Guiding Questions and see if you can answer them based on what you've read. This is a check on your reading. If you can't answer a question, you need to go back to the text to reread that section.

VISUAL SUMMARY: Below is a summary of the major concepts in this section. To check your comprehension of the chapter, read the summary and ask yourself if you understand the concepts. If the concepts seem unfamiliar to you, you may want to go back to the book and reread those sections. This text is taken from the Visual Summaries on StudySpace at wwnorton.com/studyspace.

XXII. People Reconstruct Events to Be Consistent
    A. Memory bias: tendency to make memories consistent with current beliefs or attitudes.

XXIII. Flashbulb Memories Can Be Wrong
    A. Flashbulb memories: vivid but sometimes inaccurate memories of significant events.

XXIV. People Make Source Misattributions
    A. Source misattribution: misremembering the time, place, person, or circumstances of a memory.
    B. Source amnesia: having a memory of an event without knowing from where the memory originated.
    C. Cryptomnesia: thinking an idea is new but really retrieving a stored idea without remembering its source.

XXV. People Are Bad Eyewitnesses
    A. Cross-ethnic identification: tendency to have more difficulty identifying people of other ethnicities than of one's own ethnicity.
    B. Suggestibility: development of biased memories based on misleading information.
    C. Confabulation: creation of false memories through unintended recollection of episodic memories.
    D. Repressed or recovered memories represent examples of memory distortion and bias.

REINFORCE: Are you ready to check your knowledge of this section? Answer the following multiple-choice questions with your textbook closed.

1. Yu-Ting vividly remembers the day that her husband took her completely by surprise when he proposed to her. She believes that she remembers every detail of the proposal. Although Yu-Ting believes her memory for the event is more accurate than ordinary memories, research suggests that this _____ memory is _____ ordinary memories.
    a. photographic; more accurate than
    b. photographic; as accurate as
    c. flashbulb; more accurate than
    d. flashbulb; as accurate as

2. As you are telling a funny story, your boyfriend keeps interrupting you to say things like, "No, it was Sarah who said that, not LaToya." Either you or your boyfriend is experiencing:
    a. absentmindedness
    b. cryptomnesia
    c. source misattribution
    d. the sleeper effect

3. Laken takes a class in which her professor talks about Virginia Woolf's novel *To the Lighthouse*. The next semester, for a different class, she writes a paper on Virginia Woolf. In her paper, Laken uses ideas that her earlier professor had presented while believing that she has developed these ideas herself. Laken's behavior exemplifies:
    a. absentmindedness
    b. cryptomnesia

c. persistence

d. the sleeper effect

4. The police have put an Asian American suspect in a lineup of Asian Americans. The identification is most likely to be accurate if the eyewitness is:

   a. Caucasian

   b. Asian American

   c. African American

   d. Latino

5. Many people convicted of crimes based on eyewitness testimony are later found, through DNA evidence, not to be guilty. Which of the following statements is a common reason that eyewitness testimony may lead to false convictions?

   a. Eyewitness testimony is not always accurate, even when the eyewitness reports confidence in her or his testimony.

   b. Eyewitnesses are usually not questioned seriously enough by the defense.

   c. Eyewitnesses frequently lie to make their stories more dramatic.

   d. Judges instruct juries to prioritize eyewitness testimony over other evidence.

6. Jaimie has a very vivid memory of her first birthday party. She remembers that she wore a frilly pink dress, had a cake shaped like a pony, and received a big white teddy bear as a gift. Based on what is known about childhood amnesia, Jaimie's detailed memory is probably due to:

   a. the uniqueness of the memory

   b. the strong emotional content

   c. stories her family told her

   d. an abundance of retrieval cues

7. If you are recalling an episode that never really happened, you are experiencing:

   a. confabulation

   b. false recognition

   c. absentmindedness

   d. memory bias

WHAT DID YOU MISS? Check your answers against the Answer Key at the end of this chapter of the Study Guide. The Answer Key also lists the page(s) in your text where each question is explained. If you missed any questions, go to the pages indicated in the Answer Key, reread those sections, go back to the questions, and see if you can answer them correctly this time.

ANOTHER OPPORTUNITY TO REVIEW: Answer these questions without your textbook. As a rule of thumb, if you can write only a few words about these questions, you probably need to go back and review.

1. Define memory bias. _____

_____

_____

2. Generate examples of source misattribution. _____

_____

_____

3. Identify factors that contribute to errors in eyewitness testimony. _____

_____

4. Discuss susceptibility to false memories. _____

_____

_____

5. Describe contemporary views on repressed memories.

_____

_____

6. Discuss neuroscientific advancements in the identification of true and false memories. _____

_____

_____

WHAT DO I NEED TO KNOW? Based on what you have discovered above, what are the areas where you need to focus your studying? Which objectives do you need to spend more time mastering? Write this information down in your own words.

1. _____

2. _____

3. _____

4. _____

5. _____

6. _____

WHAT MATTERS TO ME: What facts in this chapter are personally relevant to you?

_____

_____

_____

_____

CHAPTER SUMMARY

7.1 What Is Memory?

- *Memory Is the Nervous System's Capacity to Acquire and Retain Usable Skills and Knowledge:* Memory enables organisms to take information from experiences and store it for retrieval at a later time.
- *Memory Is the Processing of Information:* Memory involves three phases. The first phase, encoding, is the processing of information so that it can be stored. The second phase, storage, is the retention of encoded information. The third phase, retrieval, is the recall of previously encoded and stored information.
- *Memory Is the Result of Brain Activity:* Multiple brain regions have been implicated in memory, including the hippocampus, temporal lobes, cerebellum, amygdala, prefrontal cortex, and the brain structures involved in perception. Through consolidation, immediate memories become lasting memories. Through reconsolidation, memories may be altered.

7.2 How Does Attention Determine What We Remember?

- *Our Visual Attention Works Selectively and Serially:* Simple searches for stimuli that differ in only one primary factor (e.g., shape, motion, size, color, orientation) occur automatically and rapidly through parallel processing. In contrast, searches for objects that are the conjunction of two or more properties (e.g., red and X shaped) occur slowly and serially.
- *Our Auditory Attention Allows Us to Listen Selectively:* We can attend to more than one message at a time, but we cannot do this well. There is evidence that we weakly process some unattended information.
- *Through Selective Attention, We Filter Incoming Information:* We often do not notice large changes in an environment because we fail to pay attention. This phenomenon is known as change blindness.

7.3 How Are Memories Maintained over Time?

- *Sensory Memory Is Brief:* Visual, auditory, olfactory, gustatory, and tactile memories are maintained long enough to ensure continuous sensory experiences.
- *Working Memory Is Active:* Working memory is an active processing system that keeps information available for current use. Chunking reduces information into units that are easier to remember. Research suggests that working memory may be limited to as few as four chunks of information.
- *Long-Term Memory Is Relatively Permanent:* Long-term memory is a relatively permanent, virtually limitless store. Information that is repeatedly retrieved, that is deeply processed, or that helps us adapt to an environment is most likely to enter long-term memory.

7.4 How Is Information Organized in Long-Term Memory?

- *Long-Term Memory Is Based on Meaning:* Maintenance rehearsal involves repetition. Elaborative rehearsal involves encoding information more meaningfully—for example, on the basis of semantic meaning. Elaborative rehearsal is more effective for long-term remembering than maintenance rehearsal.
- *Schemas Provide an Organizational Framework:* Schemas are cognitive structures that help people perceive, organize, and process information. Thus schemas influence memory. Culture shapes schemas. As a result, people from distinct cultures process information in different ways.
- *Information Is Stored in Association Networks:* Networks of associations are formed by nodes of information. The nodes are linked together and activated through spreading activation.
- *Retrieval Cues Provide Access to Long-Term Storage:* According to the encoding specificity principle, any stimulus encoded along with an experience can later trigger the memory of the experience. Mnemonics are learning aids or strategies that use retrieval cues to improve recall. Examples include the method of loci and verbal mnemonics.

7.5 What Are the Different Long-Term Memory Systems?

- *Explicit Memory Involves Conscious Effort:* Explicit, declarative memories that we consciously remember include personal events (episodic memory) and general, factual knowledge (semantic memory).
- *Implicit Memory Occurs without Deliberate Effort:* Procedural (motor) memories of how to do things automatically are implicit.
- *Prospective Memory Is Remembering to Do Something:* Prospective memory has "costs" in terms of reducing working memory capacity and reducing attention.

7.6 When Do People Forget?

- *Transience Is Caused by Interference:* Forgetting over time occurs because of interference from old information and new information.
- *Blocking Is Temporary:* The tip-of-the-tongue phenomenon is a person's temporary trouble retrieving the right word. This phenomenon is usually due to interference from a similar word.
- *Absentmindedness Results from Shallow Encodng:* Inattentive or shallow processing causes memory failure.

- *Amnesia Is a Deficit in Long-Term Memory:* Disease, injury, or psychological trauma can result in amnesia. Retrograde amnesia is the inability to recall past memories. Anterograde amnesia is the inability to form new memories.
- *Persistence Is Unwanted Remembering:* Persistence is the recurrence of unwanted memories. This problem is common among individuals with posttraumatic stress disorder. Researchers are investigating methods to erase unwanted memories.

7.7 How Are Memories Distorted?

- *People Reconstruct Events to Be Consistent:* People exhibit memory bias. That is, over time they make their memories consistent with their current beliefs or attitudes.
- *Flashbulb Memories Can Be Wrong:* The strong emotional response that attends a flashbulb memory may affect the memory's strength and accuracy.
- *People Make Source Misattributions:* People can misremember the time, place, person, or circumstances involved with a memory (source misattribution). In source amnesia, a person cannot remember where she or he encountered the information associated with a memory. In cryptomnesia, a person believes that he or she came up with a new idea, but only retrieved the idea from memory.
- *People Are Bad Eyewitnesses:* Poor eyewitness recall occurs because people often fail to pay attention to events and are suggestible to misleading information. People are particularly poor at identifying those whose ethnicities are different from their own.
- *People Have False Memories:* False memories can be implanted. Children are particularly susceptible to false memories. Confabulation, or "honest lying," is associated with some forms of brain damage.
- *Repressed Memories Are Controversial:* Psychologists continue to debate the validity of repressed memories. Some therapeutic techniques are highly suggestive and may contribute to the occurrence of false repressed memories.
- *Neuroscience May Make It Possible to Distinguish between "True" and "False" Memories:* By examining brain activity during encoding and retrieval, researchers hope to distinguish between true and false memories. Further research is needed in this emerging area of neuroscience.

PUTTING IT ALL TOGETHER

Answer these questions to check your knowledge of the material in this chapter.

1. In this section you learned about the current understanding of memory's relation to the brain. Based on this information, give some reasons why Karl Lashey's search for the *engram* in the brain was in vain.

2. Use Anne Treisman's theory about visual attention to explain why it is so difficult to find Waldo in a "Where's Waldo?" scene. Also, say you are trying to find Waldo while sitting in a busy coffee shop. What types of information might distract you, and why?

3. You are still at the coffee shop, but you decide to switch from finding Waldo to studying for your upcoming psychology exam. What are some ways to study for your test (based on what you read in this section of the textbook) that will lead to the best long-term memory of the information? Also, if you study for 3 hours, will you best remember the information from the first, second, or third hour?

4. As you are studying for your psychology exam in the coffee shop, you learn about context-dependent and state-dependent memory. You want to use your knowledge of both effects to improve your psychology grade. How might you take advantage of context-dependent memory? What about state-dependent memory?

5. One of your friends enters the coffee shop and asks what you're studying. You tell your friend about the different types of long-term memory systems, and your friend asks for examples of semantic, episodic, procedural, and prospective memories. As you look around the coffee shop, what examples of each type of memory might you see in the shop?

6. As you and your friend consider the ways that people can forget long-term memories, you become worried that proactive interference and absentmindedness might cause you to forget what you are studying. What are these two influences on forgetting? How might you diminish their effects on your memory of the psychology material you are studying in the coffee shop?

7. As you and your friend discuss psychological concepts, you realize that some of his understandings are wrong. Based on your knowledge about the memory distortions of source misattribution and suggestibility, explain why you might accidently use one of friend's wrong understandings when you are taking your psychology exam.

ANSWER KEY FOR REINFORCE QUESTIONS

Section 7.1

1. a   p. 269
2. a   p. 269

3. d   p. 270
4. d   p. 270
5. b   p. 271
6. c   p. 271
7. c   p. 272

Section 7.2

1. b   p. 274
2. a   p. 275
3. c   p. 276
4. b   p. 276
5. a   p. 273
6. d   p. 275
7. b   p. 275

Section 7.3

1. c   pp. 279–281
2. c   pp. 280–281
3. c   p. 282
4. a   p. 281
5. c   p. 283
6. b   p. 285
7. b   p. 286

Section 7.4

1. a   p. 284
2. c   p. 288
3. a   p. 288
4. b   p. 290
5. a   p. 288
6. d   p. 290
7. b   p. 290

Section 7.5

1. a   p. 294
2. a   p. 294
3. b   p. 294
4. c   p. 296
5. d   p. 295
6. a   p. 295
7. c   p. 296

Section 7.6

1. b   p. 301
2. b   p. 298
3. d   p. 298
4. c   p. 299
5. d   p. 299
6. b   p. 301
7. c   p. 301

Section 7.7

1. d   pp. 303–304
2. c   p. 304
3. b   p. 305
4. b   p. 305
5. a   p. 307
6. c   p. 308
7. a   p. 308

HINTS FOR PUTTING IT ALL TOGETHER QUESTIONS

1. Karl Lashley was searching for a single location where memory was stored in the cerebral cortex; that is, he was searching for the *engram*. When he found that removal of no one brain region caused complete memory impairment, he suggested that memories are stored throughout the brain. We now know that different types of memories are stored in different parts of the brain, so removal of just one brain region would not impair all memory. Some examples include the hippocampus (allows encoding of new memories not involving fear or motor movements), the amygdala (fear memories), and the cerebellum (motor memories). Also, memories are often stored in the same locations that are involved in perception. For example, the brain region responsible for processing people's faces (fusiform face area) is the same region where we store memories of people's faces. The brain region responsible for processing music is the same region where we store memories of music.

2. Anne Treisman developed a theory of visual attention that suggested that sometimes visual information can "pop out" or be captured easily by attention. It is unlikely that Waldo will "pop out" because he is the same size, color, and shape as most of the other objects in the scene. Therefore, to find Waldo requires processing that is serial (you need to systematically scan the entire scene) and effortful (you need to direct all your attention). Many types of information are likely to distract you: for example, overhearing your name or a story about someone you know (social relevance), feeling hunger or pain (physical discomfort), being stared at by someone who wants your seat (threatening face), hearing someone crying or yelling (emotional relevance).

3. This section mentions a variety of study tips that can help you better remember the material you are studying. For example, taking practice tests can improve memory more than simply studying or organizing the material. However, the more you think about the meaning of information and its personal relevance to you, the more likely

you are to remember it. Trying to recall the information, rather than just repeating it over and over, will lead to better recall, as will studying for several short periods of time rather than studying for one long period of time. If a person is studying for 3 hours, it is likely that—due to the serial position effect—the information from the first and third hours of studying will be remembered better than the information from the second hour. Information from the first hour is most likely to be consolidated into long-term memory because it has been extensively rehearsed and thereby stored in long-term memory. Information from the latter part of the third hour, on the other hand, is most likely to still be in working memory (short-term memory) and thereby also more easily remembered.

4. Context-dependent memory relies on your encoding information in the same context (environment or situation) as you will retrieve the information. For example, if you are taking a traditional class on a campus, you will likely retrieve the information (i.e., take the exam) in a classroom setting. It would be best for you to then encode the information in a setting as similar as possible to a classroom. However, if you are taking an online course, you might be encoding information in a coffee shop. For context-dependent memory to work, you would do best to retrieve the information in a setting as much like a coffee shop as possible. State-dependent memory relies on your internal state being similar at encoding and retrieval. If you drink coffee while studying for your exam, you should re-create the internal effect of the coffee (i.e., increase your energy, heart rate, and blood pressure) when you intend to retrieve the information (i.e., during the exam).

5. Semantic memories are factual knowledge. Any examples that relate to general knowledge about objects in the coffee shop (e.g., you are sitting on *chairs*, you are drinking *coffee* out of *cups*) or general knowledge about how a coffee shop operates (e.g., you stand in line, order your coffee, pay for your drink, wait for your name to be called) or any other pieces of general knowledge about the coffee shop (e.g., it likely has two restrooms, one for men and one for women) are good examples. Episodic memories are of specific events that occurred in one's life. Any examples about events in your life (e.g., the next day, when you recall meeting your friend today at the coffee shop) or about events related to the people around you (e.g., people telling stories about their lives to their friends;

the cashier has worked at the coffee shop for two months, but can recall her first day of work) are good examples of episodic memories. Procedural memories are automatic, unconscious memories for how to perform motor skills and actions. Good examples include the experienced barista making a cappuccino, likely relying on procedural memories to grind the coffee beans, brew the coffee, steam the milk, and combine these components without consciously thinking of every step in the process; anyone using a laptop, relying on procedural memory type on the keyboard; people walking; and people using forks, knives, and spoons. The final type of memory, prospective, applies to tasks one has to do in the future. Any examples related to yourself (e.g., you need to remember to stop at the library on your way home) or the workers (e.g., the cashier needs to remember to ask the manager for quarters; the barista needs to get more milk from the storage room) should be good.

6. Proactive interference occurs as newly formed memories cause forgetting of previously formed memories. To avoid this influence on your memory for psychology, you can study just psychology until your exam occurs. Studying another subject (i.e., forming new memories) before your psychology test could lead to worse memory for psychology (i.e., forgetting previously formed memories). Absent-mindedness is the forgetting of memories because, due to inattention, they were never fully formed. The best way to avoid absentmindedness is to pay full attention to the information you are studying—perhaps by studying in a quiet section of the coffee shop, taking extensive notes in your own words, and rereading passages that you know you weren't attending to.

7. When someone commits a source misattribution error, he or she can remember information but remember neither when the memory was formed nor from where or whom the memory originated. In this case, you might remember the example from your friend (which was incorrect), but might misattribute it to being from the textbook or from your professor (both typically reliable sources). Therefore, you might think that the bad example is actually a viable answer. On the other hand, someone who commits a suggestibility error changes his or her memory based on misinformation from another source. In this case, you might already have a good example of a psychological concept in your mind, but your friend gives you a bad example, and you add some of your friend's misinformation to your example.

KEY TERMS EXERCISES

First, fill in your own definition and example for each term. Then check each term against the textbook's definition. These exercises can also be cut out and used as flash cards.

absentmindedness

Your Definition:
Your Example:
Textbook Definition:

change blindness

Your Definition:
Your Example:
Textbook Definition:

amnesia

Your Definition:
Your Example:
Textbook Definition:

chunking

Your Definition:
Your Example:
Textbook Definition:

anterograde amnesia

Your Definition:
Your Example:
Textbook Definition:

confabulation

Your Definition:
Your Example:
Textbook Definition:

blocking

Your Definition:
Your Example:
Textbook Definition:

consolidation

Your Definition:
Your Example:
Textbook Definition:

cryptomnesia

Your Definition:
Your Example:
Textbook Definition:

episodic memory

Your Definition:
Your Example:
Textbook Definition:

declarative memory

Your Definition:
Your Example:
Textbook Definition:

explicit memory

Your Definition:
Your Example:
Textbook Definition:

encoding

Your Definition:
Your Example:
Textbook Definition:

flashbulb memories

Your Definition:
Your Example:
Textbook Definition:

encoding specificity principle

Your Definition:
Your Example:
Textbook Definition:

forgetting

Your Definition:
Your Example:
Textbook Definition:

implicit memory

Your Definition:
Your Example:
Textbook Definition:

mnemonics

Your Definition:
Your Example:
Textbook Definition:

long-term memory

Your Definition:
Your Example:
Textbook Definition:

parallel processing

Your Definition:
Your Example:
Textbook Definition:

memory

Your Definition:
Your Example:
Textbook Definition:

persistence

Your Definition:
Your Example:
Textbook Definition:

memory bias

Your Definition:
Your Example:
Textbook Definition:

proactive interference

Your Definition:
Your Example:
Textbook Definition:

procedural memory

Your Definition:

Your Example:

Textbook Definition:

prospective memory

Your Definition:

Your Example:

Textbook Definition:

reconsolidation

Your Definition:

Your Example:

Textbook Definition:

retrieval

Your Definition:

Your Example:

Textbook Definition:

retrieval cue

Your Definition:

Your Example:

Textbook Definition:

retroactive interference

Your Definition:

Your Example:

Textbook Definition:

retrograde amnesia

Your Definition:

Your Example:

Textbook Definition:

schemas

Your Definition:

Your Example:

Textbook Definition:

semantic memory

Your Definition:
Your Example:
Textbook Definition:

source amnesia

Your Definition:
Your Example:
Textbook Definition:

sensory memory

Your Definition:
Your Example:
Textbook Definition:

source misattribution

Your Definition:
Your Example:
Textbook Definition:

serial position effect

Your Definition:
Your Example:
Textbook Definition:

storage

Your Definition:
Your Example:
Textbook Definition:

short-term memory

Your Definition:
Your Example:
Textbook Definition:

suggestibility

Your Definition:
Your Example:
Textbook Definition:

transience

Your Definition:	
Your Example:	
Textbook Definition:	

working memory

Your Definition:	
Your Example:	
Textbook Definition:	

CHAPTER 8 | Thinking and Intelligence

CHAPTER OVERVIEW

How do you make decisions about which school to attend, which brand of toothpaste to buy, or how to best solve a conflict with a friend? How we think, solve problems, and make decisions is the focus of this chapter. We will consider questions such as these: What does it mean to be intelligent? Are there different ways of being intelligent? Are there differences between genders in terms of intelligence? What differences in intellectual functioning exist among racial and ethnic groups? Finally, is intelligence something you inherit or something you acquire from your environment, or is it a combination of both?

8.1 What Is Thought?

The world is full of information. Humans must find ways to simplify and use this information. Concepts, analogies, and symbols are ways in which we do this so that we can apply information to new experiences. We also develop schemas and scripts to help us apply information to new situations so that our past experiences will help us in responding to new events in our lives.

At the beginning of each section in the Study Guide, there will be guiding questions. Before you read the chapter in your textbook, read through these questions and maybe even attempt to answer them based on either what you've already read or what you think the answer should be. Then as you study the chapter, you can use them to help guide your reading.

8.1 Guiding Questions

To guide your reading of the text, review the following questions. Then, as you read the chapter, look for the answers to these questions. You may want to note in your textbook where you find these answers.

1. Distinguish between analogical and symbolic representations.

2. Describe the defining attribute, prototype, and exemplar models of concepts.

3. Discuss the positive and negative consequences of using schemas and scripts.

NOW READ Section 8.1 "What Is Thought?" keeping these questions in mind.

REVIEW: Now that you've read this section, go back to the 8.1 Guiding Questions and see if you can answer them based on what you've read. This is a check on your reading. If you can't answer a question, you need to go back to the text to reread that section.

VISUAL SUMMARY: Below is a summary of the major concepts in this section. To check your comprehension of the chapter, read the summary and ask yourself if you understand the concepts. If the concepts seem unfamiliar to you, you may want to go back to the book and reread those sections. This text is taken from the Visual Summaries on StudySpace at wwnorton.com/studyspace.

I. Thinking Is the Manipulation of Mental Representations
   A. Cognition: mental activity that includes thinking and language.

II. Thinking Involves Two Types of Mental Representations
   A. Analogical representations:
      i. correspond to images.
      ii. have some characteristics of actual objects.

B. Symbolic representations:
  i. correspond to words.
  ii. do not have physical features of an object or idea.
C. Mental maps combine analogical and symbolic representations.

III. Concepts Are Symbolic Representations
  A. Concept: a mental representation that categorizes objects, events, or relations around a common theme.
  B. Defining attribute model: concepts are characterized by features necessary to determine if they belong to a category.
  C. Prototype model of concepts: based on the best example (prototype) for a category of concepts.
  D. Exemplar model: all members of a category are examples of the concept.

IV. Schemas Organize Useful Information about Environments
  A. Schemas are cognitive structures that influence how we perceive, process, and organize information.
  B. Stereotypes are influenced by our schemas about the attributes of members of specific groups.
  C. Scripts are a type of schema. They address the appropriate order of events in a sequence.

V. Three Approaches: Reasoning, Decision Making, and Problem Solving

REINFORCE: Are you ready to check your knowledge of this section? Answer the following multiple-choice questions with your textbook closed.

1. A picture of a carrot is an example of a(n) _____ representation; the word *carrot* is a(n) _____ representation.
   a. symbolic; analogical
   b. analogical; symbolic
   c. analogical; analogical
   d. symbolic; symbolic

2. Analogical representations _____ correspond to characteristics of the object that they represent. Symbolic representations _____ correspond to characteristics of the object that they represent.
   a. do; do
   b. do not; do not
   c. do; do not
   d. do not; do

3. Her 5-year-old nephew asks Hallel what an aardvark looks like. Hallel finds a picture in a children's book about animals and shows it to him. Hallel's approach is similar to using a(n):
   a. analogical representation
   b. symbolic representation
   c. defining attribute
   d. categorization

4. Mandy e-mails her roommate to tell her that she has adopted a kitten. Even though the e-mail says nothing more, Mandy's roommate knows that the kitten will be small, furry, have a tail, purr, meow, drink milk, and need a litter box. Mandy knows all of this because of which memory process?
   a. symbolic representation
   b. analogical representation
   c. mental imaging
   d. categorization

5. Yang believes that a whale is a fish because a whale swims. Yang's misconception suggests that he is using a(n) _____ model for the fish category.
   a. prototype
   b. categorization
   c. defining attribute
   d. exemplar

6. According to the defining attribute model, which is the most important feature of the category *horse*?
   a. It can gallop.
   b. It can bear live young.
   c. It can breathe.
   d. They are all equally important.

7. Which of the following statements about categorization is a problem for the defining attribute model?
   a. Attributes have different degrees of importance.
   b. It is difficult to specify defining attributes.
   c. Category membership is not all-or-none.
   d. Categories cannot be well specified by attributes alone.

8. The main difference between the exemplar model and the prototype model is that the prototype model is defined by _____ of the category and the exemplar model is defined by _____ of the category.
   a. the best example; all the examples
   b. all the examples; the best example
   c. the most unusual example; the best set of examples
   d. the best set of examples; the most common example

9. In New York City, it might be a dress shoe. In Texas, it could be a cowboy boot. In Florida, it might be a sandal. In Montana, it could be a hiking boot. Each of these is a(n) _____ of the shoe category for the culture of that state.

a. exemplar
b. prototype
c. schema
d. representation

10. Political commentators often stress the importance of a candidate's appearing presidential, a quality that characterizes past presidents but is not equated with any one of them. Which theory of categorization could best explain this concept of being presidential?
    a. defining attributes
    b. exemplar
    c. prototype
    d. schema

11. You borrowed your neighbor's car without asking him. Your neighbor is upset because borrowing a car without asking is not part of our social:
    a. schema
    b. structure
    c. prototype
    d. concept

12. A grocery store manager decides to combat shoplifting by requiring customers to pay somewhat more than the estimated cost of their groceries when they enter the store and receive their change—or pay more, if necessary—when they leave. Customers are confused and unhappy about this change in the process of shopping because it violates our social:
    a. reasoning
    b. script
    c. prototype
    d. concept

13. A(n) _____ is a(n) _____ of a sequence of events.
    a. procedure; outline
    b. schema; script
    c. script; schema
    d. outline; procedure

14. The expectation that a minister will give a sermon in church, whereas a professor will give a lecture in class, comes from the property of schemas that:
    a. categories contain exemplars
    b. concepts contain prototypes
    c. situations have unpredictable attributes
    d. people have specific roles in situations

15. A problem with schemas such as gender roles is that they can easily:
    a. promote stereotypes
    b. incorrectly categorize examples
    c. confuse prototypes and exemplars
    d. miss defining attributes

WHAT DID YOU MISS? Check your answers against the Answer Key at the end of this chapter of the Study Guide. The Answer Key also lists the page(s) in your text where each question is explained. If you missed any questions, go to the pages indicated in the Answer Key, reread those sections, go back to the questions, and see if you can answer them correctly this time.

ANOTHER OPPORTUNITY TO REVIEW: Answer these questions without your textbook. As a rule of thumb, if you can write only a few words about these questions, you probably need to go back and review.

1. Distinguish between analogical and symbolic representations. _____

   _____

   _____

2. Describe the defining attribute, prototype, and exemplar models of concepts. _____

   _____

   _____

3. Discuss the positive and negative consequences of using schemas and scripts. _____

   _____

   _____

WHAT DO I NEED TO KNOW? Based on what you've discovered above, what are the areas where you need to focus your studying? Which objectives do you need to spend more time mastering? Write this information down in your own words.

1. _____

2. _____

3. _____

4. _____

5. _____

6. _____

8.2 How Do We Make Decisions and Solve Problems?

What do these two situations have in common: the ways detectives solve problems on television shows and how you figure out how to change your tire when you can't find the right tools? They require specific and sometimes creative ways of solving problems. We can change the way we view a problem, and such a change may lead to a more rapid decision. When it comes to making decisions, however, having too many choices may paradoxically make choosing one more difficult.

8.2 Guiding Questions

To guide your reading of the text, review the following questions. Then, as you read the chapter, look for the answers to these questions. You may want to note in your textbook where you find these answers.

1. Distinguish between deductive and inductive reasoning.

2. Distinguish between normative and descriptive models of decision making.

3. Explain how heuristics, framing, and affective forecasting influence decision making.

4. Review strategies that facilitate insight and problem solving.

NOW READ Section 8.2 "How Do We Make Decisions and Solve Problems?" keeping these questions in mind.

REVIEW: Now that you've read this section, go back to the 8.2 Guiding Questions and see if you can answer them based on what you've read. This is a check on your reading. If you can't answer a question, you need to go back to the text to reread that section.

VISUAL SUMMARY: Below is a summary of the major concepts in this section. To check your comprehension of the chapter, read the summary and ask yourself if you understand the concepts. If the concepts seem unfamiliar to you, you may want to go back to the book and reread those sections. This text is taken from the Visual Summaries on StudySpace at wwnorton.com/studyspace.

VI. People Use Deductive and Inductive Reasoning
   A. Deductive reasoning: using general rules to draw conclusions about specific situations.
   B. Inductive reasoning: using specific situations to draw conclusions about general rules.
   C. Inductive and deductive reasoning are often combined.
   D. Reasoning and the scientific method suggest caution in the use of inductive reasoning.

VII. Decision Making Often Involves Heuristics
   A. Decision making models:
      i. normative: views humans as optimal, rational decision makers.
         a. includes the Expected Utility model where people rank order alternatives and select the one with the most *utility* or value.
      ii. descriptive: views humans as frequently irrational and illogical in decision making.
   B. Approaches to problem solving:
      i. heuristic: short cuts (rules of thumb) to reduce thinking involved in decision making.
         a. availability: making decision based on answer that comes to mind.
         b. representativeness: categorizing based on similarity to a prototype.
      ii. algorithm: a procedure that will always lead to a correct answer.
   C. Framing effects: the presentation of information can affect perception/ interpretation.
   D. Affective forecasting: people are not good at predicting how they will feel in the future about choices.
   E. Paradox of choice: unlimited options makes people miserable.

VIII. Problem Solving Achieves Goals
   A. Organization of subgoals refers to the solving of problems in steps.
   B. Sudden insight: the sudden realization of a solution to a problem.
   C. Restructuring the problem is thinking about a problem in a new way.
   D. Mental sets: problem solving strategies that have worked in the past.
   E. Conscious strategies:
      i. working backward.
      ii. finding an appropriate analogy.

REINFORCE: Are you ready to check your knowledge of this section? Answer the following multiple-choice questions with your textbook closed.

1. Jamail is trying to decide whether to major in biology or psychology. Kevin is trying to figure out what type of part time job he can get that will let him continue with college. Jamail is engaged in _____; Kevin is engaged in _____.
   a. problem solving; decision making
   b. inductive reasoning; deductive reasoning
   c. decision making; problem solving
   d. deductive reasoning; inductive reasoning

2. In problem solving, a person:
   a. moves from a present state to a goal state
   b. selects among a set of alternatives
   c. evaluates a conclusion for validity
   d. reasons from general to specific information

3. Because you loved all the previous Batman movies, you decide to see the new one. You have made this decision using:
   a. heuristic decision making
   b. problem solving
   c. deductive reasoning
   d. inductive reasoning

4. A syllogism determines whether the conclusion:
   a. is equivalent to the premise
   b. incorporates the premise
   c. is true given the premise
   d. describes the premise

5. Almost all empirical psychology studies that employ sampling, hypothesis testing, and statistical analysis rely on the concept of _____ to generalize findings to a population.
   a. inductive reasoning
   b. deductive reasoning
   c. heuristic decision making
   d. algorithmic decision making

6. Kalil has read that small breeds of dogs were usually bred either as alert dogs or to attack rodents. When he sees a chihuahua, he expects the dog to be aggressive. What type of reasoning is he using?
   a. inductive reasoning
   b. deductive reasoning
   c. heuristic decision making
   d. algorithmic decision making

7. An economics professor and a psychology professor are discussing how people make decisions. The economics professor argues that people are optimal decision makers. The psychology professor counters that people are often irrational decision makers. The economics professor believes in a _____ model of human decision making; the psychology professor believes in a _____ model.
   a. normative; descriptive
   b. normative; normative
   c. descriptive; descriptive
   d. descriptive; normative

8. When a friend asks you to recommend a restaurant, you send her to the place you ate last Saturday because it comes most quickly to mind. This exchange exemplifies:
   a. confirmation bias
   b. the framing effect
   c. the representativeness heuristic
   d. the availability heuristic

9. Nkeis decides to buy a small car because it is good for the environment. When she looks at small cars, she expects to be very basic and uncomfortable, so she is surprised that they come in luxury versions. Nkeis has been using:
   a. confirmation bias
   b. the framing effect
   c. the representativeness heuristic
   d. the availability heuristic

10. A grocery store owner places a new item at the front of each aisle every few days. He wants people to think that these items are in front because they are special or on sale. The grocery store owner is trying to use _____ to sell the items at the front.
    a. loss aversion
    b. framing effect
    c. confirmation bias
    d. prospect theory

11. Research has shown that people do not necessarily believe that "time heals all wounds" when something bad is about to happen to them. Instead, people tend to use _____ and anticipate the worst.
    a. affective forecasting
    b. projected regret
    c. confirmation biases
    d. subjective likelihoods

12. Marco never had to study in high school, and he starts college the same way. After his first exams, he realizes he needs to study. He decides to go to the library every night and study for six straight hours. When he can't study for that long, he does not know what to do and gives up. Marco's approach to solving his problems with studying failed because:
    a. he was using inductive reasoning inappropriately
    b. his solution was conscious and lacked insight
    c. he did not establish reasonable subgoals
    d. he did not have a clearly defined goal

13. After struggling to solve a math problem, you suddenly see the solution. For no apparent reason, the method for solving the problem just came to your mind. You have experienced:
    a. insight
    b. clarity
    c. restructuring
    d. fixedness

14. Restructuring a problem often reveals a new and more successful approach to solving it. That fact suggests that a critical and ESSENTIAL step in problem solving is:
    a. insight
    b. brainstorming strategies
    c. replicating potential solutions
    d. formulating the problem

15. People tend to become closed minded when asked to find a different use for an object that has a clear purpose. This mind-set is a result of:
    a. mental sets
    b. restructuring
    c. working backward
    d. functional fixedness

16. If you are shopping for a bathrobe and you buy the very first soft robe that you see, then you are likely a(n) _____. If you go on to look for robes in every store in town before purchasing one, then you are likely a(n) _____.
    a. minimizer; optimizer
    b. optimizer; minimizer
    c. maximizer; satisficer
    d. satisficer; maximizer

WHAT DID YOU MISS? Check your answers against the Answer Key at the end of this chapter of the Study Guide. The Answer Key also lists the page(s) in your text where each question is explained. If you missed any questions, go to the pages indicated in the Answer Key, reread those sections, go back to the questions, and see if you can answer them correctly this time.

ANOTHER OPPORTUNITY TO REVIEW: Answer these questions without your textbook. As a rule of thumb, if you can write only a few words about these questions, you probably need to go back and review.

1. Distinguish between deductive and inductive reasoning.
   _____
   _____

2. Distinguish between normative and descriptive models of decision making. _____
   _____
   _____

3. Explain how heuristics, framing, and affective forecasting influence decision making. _____
   _____
   _____

4. Review strategies that facilitate insight and problem solving. _____
   _____
   _____

WHAT DO I NEED TO KNOW? Based on what you've discovered above, what are the areas where you need to

focus your studying? Which objectives do you need to spend more time mastering? Write this information down in your own words.

1. _____

2. _____

3. _____

4. _____

5. _____

6. _____

8.3 How Do We Understand Intelligence?

How do you define intelligence? Do you know smart people who did poorly in school? Who are smarter, women or men? This section will broaden your understanding of intelligence, describe how intelligence is measured, and give you more information on how environment and genetics interact to form intelligence.

8.3 Guiding Questions

To guide your reading of the text, review the following questions. Then, as you read the chapter, look for the answers to these questions. You may want to note in your textbook where you find these answers.

1. Identify common measures of intelligence.

2. Discuss the validity of measures of intelligence.

3. Review theory and research related to general intelligence, fluid intelligence, crystallized intelligence, multiple intelligences, and emotional intelligence.

4. Discuss the relationship between intelligence and cognitive performance.

5. Summarize research examining genetic and environmental influences on intelligence.

6. Discuss sex and race differences in intelligence.

7. Define stereotype threat.

NOW READ Section 8.3 "How Do We Understand Intelligence?" keeping these questions in mind.

REVIEW: Now that you've read this section, go back to the 8.3 Guiding Questions and see if you can answer them based on what you've read. This is a check on your reading. If you can't answer a question, you need to go back to the text to reread that section.

VISUAL SUMMARY: Below is a summary of the major concepts in this section. To check your comprehension of the chapter, read the summary and ask yourself if you understand the concepts. If the concepts seem unfamiliar to you, you may want to go back to the book and reread those sections. This text is taken from the Visual Summaries on StudySpace at wwnorton.com/studyspace.

IX. Intelligence Is the Ability to Use Knowledge and Cognitive Processes to Effectively Adapt to Life's Challenges

X. Intelligence Is Assessed with Psychometric Tests
  A. Psychometric approach: looks at how people perform on standardized tests.
  B. Stanford-Binet test: measures intelligence as unitary.
  C. Wechsler scale: measures intelligence as combination of verbal and nonverbal skills.
  D. Intelligence quotient (IQ):
    i. mental age (MA): assessment of intellect based on comparison with age-mates.
    ii. IQ: MA/chronological age × 100.
    iii. average IQ = 100.
    iv. IQ testing predicts about 25 percent of performance at school/work.
    v. nonintellectual factors (education, SES, motivation) predict performance in school/work.
  E. Cultural bias: intelligence tests penalize people who belong to particular cultures or groups.

XI. General Intelligence Involves Multiple Components
  A. Fluid intelligence: the ability to problem solve in novel or complex circumstances.
  B. Crystallized intelligence: reflects acquisition of knowledge and the ability to use it.
  C. Multiple intelligences: according to Gardner, there are multiple types of intelligence that are independent of one another.
  D. According to Sternberg, there are three types of intelligence: analytical, creative, and practical.
  E. Emotional intelligence: social intelligence that uses emotions to guide thought and action.

XII. Intelligence Is Associated with Cognitive Performance
  A. Speed of mental processing, working memory, and brain size are associated with intelligence.
  B. Savant: developmentally delayed individual with a specific and exceptional ability.

XIII. Genes and Environment Influence Intelligence

  A. Intelligence:
    i. produced by interaction of genes with environment.
    ii. influenced by prenatal and postnatal factors.

XIV. Group Differences in Intelligence Have Multiple Determinants
  A. There is no indication that race or sex predicts differences in IQ.
  B. Differences in environment prevent adequate comparisons of intelligence between groups.
  C. Stereotype threat: the fear that one might confirm negative stereotypes about one's group.

REINFORCE: Are you ready to check your knowledge of this section? Answer the following multiple-choice questions with your textbook closed.

1. Our ability to learn, understand ideas, use knowledge to solve problems, and adapt to our environment is called:
  a. thought
  b. intelligence
  c. cognition
  d. insight

2. Dr. Bellasouva gives 500 students a battery of standardized tests. He analyzes the results to see which kinds of skills allow good performance on different parts of the exam. What approach is Dr. Bellasouva using toward the study of intelligence?
  a. biological
  b. analytical
  c. psychometric
  d. cognitive

3. The LSAT (Law School Admissions Test) is designed to measure someone's ability to think logically, which is predictive of success in law school and as a practicing attorney. The LSAT is a(n) _____ test.
  a. aptitude
  b. achievement
  c. general ability
  d. intelligence

4. Which intelligence test involves measuring verbal and performance skills?
  a. Miller Analogy
  b. Binet
  c. Stanford-Binet
  d. Wechsler

5. The Binet IQ test compares the difference between which of the following factors?

a. analytical and emotional intelligence
b. verbal and mathematical skills
c. mental and chronological age
d. analytical and pragmatic intelligence

6. Jose, who is 7 years old, takes the Binet test and scores at the level of a 9-year-old. Jose's intelligence quotient would be _____, and Jose would be considered _____ in intelligence.
   a. 128; above average
   b. 77; below average
   c. 128; below average
   d. 77; above average

7. What is the main concept behind Spearman's theory of general intelligence (g)?
   a. There are multiple intelligences.
   b. One intelligence factor operates in all intellectual tasks.
   c. The main intelligence factor is composed of many small unrelated intelligence factors.
   d. Both a and c are correct.

8. _____ intelligence is involved in reasoning, processing novel events, and thinking flexibly.
   a. Pragmatic
   b. Crystallized
   c. Fluid
   d. Analytic

9. Joel is fantastic at solving logic problems and analogies, but he does not have a very good vocabulary and could not find most countries on a map. Joel would probably score _____ on a test of crystallized intelligence and _____ on a test of fluid intelligence.
   a. low; low
   b. low; high
   c. high; high
   d. high; low

10. Dr. Cisneros found in her research that people who score high in mathematical ability are usually gifted musicians. For which theory of intelligence is this a problematic finding?
    a. Sternberg
    b. Spearman
    c. Gardner
    d. both a and c

11. In terms of Sternberg's theory of intelligence, an architect who draws blueprints of a STANDARD house is showing _____ intelligence; the contractor who builds the house is showing _____ intelligence.
    a. analytical; creative
    b. creative; practical

c. practical; analytical
d. analytical; practical

12. Alina is a straight A student in an honors business program and has had very prestigious internships. During her job interviews, however, Alina comes across as arrogant about her abilities. She fails to see that her interviewers are looking for team players, not independent superstars. It is likely that Alina scores low on:
    a. intrapersonal intelligence
    b. general intelligence
    c. fluid intelligence
    d. emotional intelligence

13. Which memory system is most closely related to intelligence test scores?
    a. sensory
    b. working
    c. semantic
    d. episodic

14. A larger volume of neuronal cell bodies in areas that support attentional control is related to _____ intelligence but not to _____ intelligence.
    a. general; emotional
    b. emotional; general
    c. crystallized; fluid
    d. fluid; crystallized

15. Which of the following questions best summarizes the modern version of the nature/nurture question about intelligence?
    a. Is intelligence primarily determined by genetics?
    b. Is intelligence primarily determined by environment?
    c. To what extent do genes and environment duplicate each other in their effects?
    d. What roles do genes and environment play in intelligence?

16. Which of the following statements represents the best evidence that genetics plays an important role in determining intelligence?
    a. The IQs of identical twins raised apart tend to be more similar than the IQs of fraternal twins raised together.
    b. The IQs of fraternal twins raised together tend to be more similar than the IQs of nontwin siblings raised together.
    c. Children's IQs tend to be more similar to the IQs of their siblings than to the IQs of their parents.
    d. Children adopted from different biological parents but raised by the same adoptive parents have fairly similar IQs as young children.

17. A recent study has found that women do as well as men in math courses at all levels. If Heather read

this story before taking her calculus final, she would be _____ likely to do well because of
_____.

    a. less; positive role models
    b. more; positive role models
    c. more; reduced stereotype threat
    d. less; reduced stereotype threat

WHAT DID YOU MISS? Check your answers against the Answer Key at the end of this chapter of the Study Guide. The Answer Key also lists the page(s) in your text where each question is explained. If you missed any questions, go to the pages indicated in the Answer Key, reread those sections, go back to the questions, and see if you can answer them correctly this time.

ANOTHER OPPORTUNITY TO REVIEW: Answer these questions without your textbook. As a rule of thumb, if you can write only a few words about these questions, you probably need to go back and review.

1. Identify common measures of intelligence. _____

2. Discuss the validity of measures of intelligence. _____

3. Review theory and research related to general intelligence, fluid intelligence, crystallized intelligence, multiple intelligences, and emotional intelligence. _____

4. Discuss the relationship between intelligence and cognitive performance. _____

5. Summarize research examining genetic and environmental influences on intelligence. _____

6. Discuss sex and race differences in intelligence. _____

7. Define stereotype threat. _____

WHAT DO I NEED TO KNOW? Based on what you've discovered above, what are the areas where you need to focus your studying? Which objectives do you need to spend more time mastering? Write this information down in your own words.

1. _____

2. _____

3. _____

4. _____

5. _____

6. _____

WHAT MATTERS TO ME: What facts in this chapter are personally relevant to you?

_____

_____

_____

_____

CHAPTER SUMMARY

8.1 What Is Thought?

- *Thinking Is the Manipulation of Mental Representations:* Cognitive psychology is the study of thought. Thinking involves the manipulation of mental representations of the objects that we encounter in our environments. Cognition includes thinking and the understandings that result from thinking.

- *Thinking Involves Two Types of Representations:* Mental representations of objects may be analogical or symbolic. Analogical representations have some of the physical characteristics of objects; they usually correspond to images. Symbolic representations are abstract and do not have the physical features of objects; they usually correspond to words.

- *Concepts Are Symbolic Representations:* Concepts are categories of items organized around common themes. Concepts may be characterized by defining attributes, prototypes, or exemplars.

- *Schemas Organize Useful Information about Environments:* Schemas are cognitive structures that help us perceive, organize, and process information. Scripts are schemas that allow us to form expectations about the sequence of events in a given context. Schemas and

---

TRY IT

Improving Your Emotional Intelligence

One of the wealthiest women in the world today, Oprah Winfrey, has arguably made her fortune by using her emotional intelligence. Oprah skyrocketed from local news broadcaster to major media figure in part by understanding other people. Would you like to improve your emotional intelligence? If so, try the three techniques below to improve your knowledge of others and yourself and help you regulate your emotions, one of the hallmarks of emotional intelligence.

1. Take a daily vacation. Taking care of yourself is an important step in being able to regulate or manage your own emotions. If you are fatigued and stressed out, it's hard to be the best you can be. Take anywhere from a 15-minute to 60-minute break every day. Do something enjoyable. It doesn't have to be big; it just has to be something that you are doing for YOU.

2. We don't function in a vacuum. We need friends and family both in the difficult times and because they generally make us feel better about ourselves. Who are the important people in your life, and when was the last time you checked in with them? Make time to communicate with these people. Not only will you receive emotional benefits from being in touch, but your presence will likely be nurturing to your friends and family.

3. We live and breathe in a sea of positive things. There are more good things happening in most of our lives than we are aware. In Alice Walker's book *The Color Purple*, one character recommends not walking by a field of purple flowers without taking a moment to be grateful. As you walk through your life, what good things are happening? Can you take a moment to acknowledge them?

---

scripts minimize the attention needed to navigate familiar environments, but they can lead to stereotypical ways of thinking and behaving.

8.2 How Do We Make Decisions and Solve Problems?

- *People Use Deductive and Inductive Reasoning:* Reasoning involves the evaluation of information, arguments, and beliefs to draw a conclusion. Deductive reasoning proceeds from a general statement to specific conclusions. For example: If all psychology textbooks are fun to read and this is a psychology textbook, then this textbook will be fun to read. Inductive reasoning proceeds from specific statements to a general conclusion. For example: If you find this book interesting, you can infer that psychology books generally are interesting.

- *Decision Making Often Involves Heuristics:* Decision making involves choosing between alternatives. Normative models assume people behave according to logical processes, such as always selecting the outcome that will yield the greatest reward. Descriptive models highlight reasoning shortcomings, specifically the use of heuristics (mental shortcuts) that sometimes lead to faulty decisions. The framing of information and our predictions (forecasts) of our future emotions can influence the decisions that we make.

- *Problem Solving Achieves Goals:* Problem solving involves overcoming obstacles to reach a goal. Insight often comes suddenly, when we see elements of a problem in new ways. Breaking a problem down into subgoals, restructuring, working backward, and finding appropriate analogies aid solutions; mental sets and functional fixedness inhibit solutions.

8.3 How Do We Understand Intelligence?

- *Intelligence Is Assessed with Psychometric Tests:* The Binet-Simon Intelligence Test was the first modern test of mental ability and led to the concept of IQ as a ratio of mental age and chronological age. This test was later normed to a distribution with a mean of 100 and standard deviation of 15. Therefore, most people's IQ scores fall between 85 and 115. The validity of intelligence tests continues to be questioned. The validity of such tests among members of nonmainstream cultural groups is of particular concern, as intelligence tests may be culturally biased.

- *General Intelligence Involves Multiple Components:* Charles Spearman concluded that a general intelligence component exists, known as g. Fluid intelligence refers to our ability to quickly process information. Crystallized intelligence refers to the knowledge that we have acquired through experience and our ability to apply this knowledge. Howard Gardner has proposed a theory of multiple intelligences that includes linguistic, mathematical/logical, spatial, bodily-kinesthetic, intrapersonal, and interpersonal abilities. Robert Sternberg has proposed a theory of three intelligences: analytical, creative, and practical. Emotional intelligence refers to the ability to manage, recognize, and understand emotions and use emotions to guide appropriate thought and action.

- *Intelligence Is Associated with Cognitive Performance:* Intelligence is related to speed of mental processing (e.g., reaction time, inspection time) and working memory.

The association between intelligence and working memory appears to involve attention. Intelligence may also be related to the size of the brain and specific brain regions, including the frontal lobes. Importantly, research examining the relation between intelligence and brain size is correlational. As a result, we cannot infer that brain size necessarily causes differences in intelligence.

- *Genes and Environment Influence Intelligence:* Behavioral genetics has demonstrated that genes influence intelligence. However, environmental factors—including nutrition, parenting, schooling, and intellectual opportunities—influence the expression of genes associated with intelligence.
- *Group Differences in Intelligence Have Multiple Determinants:* One of the most contentious areas in psychology is group differences in intelligence. Females and males score similarly on measures of general intelligence, but some sex differences emerge on specific factors related to intelligence, such as writing ability and visuospatial processing. Race differences in intelligence are confounded with a multitude of environmental differences, including income, health care, and discrimination. Additionally, many scientists question the validity of race as a means by which to distinguish between groups of people.

PUTTING IT ALL TOGETHER

Answer these questions to check your knowledge of the material in this chapter.

1. Most adults have no trouble identifying a papillon and a Great Dane as dogs, even though the papillon is very small and long haired whereas the Great Dane is very large and short haired. Explain how the defining attribute model, the prototype model, and the exemplar model account for people's ability to identify these animals as dogs.

2. Young children's first jokes often take the form of "Why did the _____ cross the road?" For example, many 8-year-olds find the following joke funny:

   Question: Why did the skeleton NOT cross the road?
   Answer: No guts.

   What do jokes of this kind suggest about young children's schemas about jokes? What elements might the schemas include? How might the schemas enable the children to recognize and understand jokes?
   Of course, some children will not get the skeleton joke right away. They will need prompts such as: Do skeletons have insides? What else can "guts" mean? How do such prompts enable the children to understand the joke?

3. Dr. X is a very successful economics professor. After rereading the textbook's presentation on the validity of IQ tests, describe general factors that may account for Dr. X's success.

ANSWER KEY FOR REINFORCE QUESTIONS

Section 8.1

1. b   p. 319
2. c   p. 319
3. a   p. 319
4. d   p. 321
5. c   p. 321
6. d   p. 321
7. a   p. 321
8. a   p. 321
9. b   p. 321
10. b   p. 323
11. a   p. 324
12. b   p. 325
13. c   p. 325
14. d   p. 324
15. a   p. 324

Section 8.2

1. c   p. 329
2. a   p. 329
3. c   p. 329
4. c   p. 330
5. a   p. 331
6. b   p. 329
7. a   p. 332
8. d   p. 334
9. c   p. 334
10. b   p. 333
11. a   p. 336
12. c   p. 339
13. a   p. 339
14. d   p. 340
15. d   p. 341
16. d   p. 338

Section 8.3

1. b   p. 344
2. c   p. 344
3. a   p. 344
4. d   p. 345
5. c   p. 345
6. a   p. 345
7. b   p. 348
8. c   p. 349

9. b   p. 349
10. c   p. 349
11. d   p. 350
12. d   p. 351
13. b   p. 352
14. d   p. 353
15. d   p. 354
16. a   p. 355
17. c   p. 359

HINTS FOR PUTTING IT ALL TOGETHER QUESTIONS

1. In discussing the defining attribute model, you must describe specific features of dogs. When addressing the prototype model, consider what might be best examples of dogs and how these relate to papillons and Great Danes. For the exemplar model, address the types of dogs most people may be exposed to and how these instances make possible the identification of other dogs.

2. When addressing schemas, explain how schemas help people organize and process information. Include how recognizing the form of the joke enables children to use particular schemas. To explain why prompting enables some children to get the joke, discuss changing representation, restructuring, and sudden insight. You might also consider whether jokes without sudden insight are funny.

3. Your answer should include discussion of the relationships between both IQ and careers and IQ and success. You should also include how factors other than IQ—such as motivation, social background, work ethic, and self-control—influence success.

KEY TERMS EXERCISES

First, fill in your own definition and example for each term. Then check each term against the textbook's definition. These exercises can also be cut out and used as flash cards.

analogical representations

Your Definition:
Your Example:
Textbook Definition:

crystallized intelligence

Your Definition:
Your Example:
Textbook Definition:

availability heuristic

Your Definition:
Your Example:
Textbook Definition:

decision making

Your Definition:
Your Example:
Textbook Definition:

cognition

Your Definition:
Your Example:
Textbook Definition:

deductive reasoning

Your Definition:
Your Example:
Textbook Definition:

concept

Your Definition:
Your Example:
Textbook Definition:

defining attribute model

Your Definition:
Your Example:
Textbook Definition:

emotional intelligence (EI)

Your Definition:
Your Example:
Textbook Definition:

general intelligence (g)

Your Definition:
Your Example:
Textbook Definition:

exemplar model

Your Definition:
Your Example:
Textbook Definition:

heuristics

Your Definition:
Your Example:
Textbook Definition:

fluid intelligence

Your Definition:
Your Example:
Textbook Definition:

inductive reasoning

Your Definition:
Your Example:
Textbook Definition:

framing

Your Definition:
Your Example:
Textbook Definition:

insight

Your Definition:
Your Example:
Textbook Definition:

intelligence

Your Definition:
Your Example:
Textbook Definition:

multiple intelligences

Your Definition:
Your Example:
Textbook Definition:

intelligence quotient (IQ)

Your Definition:
Your Example:
Textbook Definition:

problem solving

Your Definition:
Your Example:
Textbook Definition:

mental age

Your Definition:
Your Example:
Textbook Definition:

prototype model

Your Definition:
Your Example:
Textbook Definition:

mental sets

Your Definition:
Your Example:
Textbook Definition:

reasoning

Your Definition:
Your Example:
Textbook Definition:

representativeness heuristic

Your Definition:
Your Example:
Textbook Definition:

stereotype threat

Your Definition:
Your Example:
Textbook Definition:

restructuring

Your Definition:
Your Example:
Textbook Definition:

symbolic representations

Your Definition:
Your Example:
Textbook Definition:

stereotypes

Your Definition:
Your Example:
Textbook Definition:

thinking

Your Definition:
Your Example:
Textbook Definition:

CHAPTER 9 | Human Development

CHAPTER OVERVIEW

Where are you in the grand scheme of your life—just out of adolescence, middle-aged, older? How has life seemed to you so far? When you look back at your early emotional experiences, do you see how they have affected who you are today?

The pathway from birth to old age is one of continuing change. Just as our bodies develop, so our brains and, consequently, our cognitive capacities change. This chapter discusses our physical states and our emotional states across the life span. It ends by showing the advantages, some of them perhaps unexpected, of adulthood and old age.

9.1 What Shapes Us during Childhood?

Beginning prenatally, biology and environment work together to create an individual with specific cognitive and physical abilities. The capacity of the brain changes through the life span. Normally, as the brain changes, the ability to learn is enhanced. In addition, our relationships with our parents and other caregivers affect our emotional and social development.

At the beginning of each section in the Study Guide, there will be guiding questions. Before you read the chapter in your textbook, read through these questions and maybe even attempt to answer them based on either what you've already read or what you think the answer should be. Then as you study the chapter, you can use them to help guide your reading.

9.1 Guiding Questions

To guide your reading of the text, review the following questions. Then, as you read the chapter, look for the answers to these questions. You may want to note in your textbook where you find these answers.

1. Describe how the prenatal environment can affect development.

2. Explain how dynamic systems theory illuminates the ways biology and environment work together to shape development.

3. Describe key processes in infant brain development and how these processes affect learning.

4. Describe the types of attachment infants have to their caregivers.

5. Explain how attachment and emotion regulation are related.

NOW READ Section 9.1 "What Shapes Us during Childhood?" keeping these questions in mind.

REVIEW: Now that you've read this section, go back to the 9.1 Guiding Questions and see if you can answer them based on what you've read. This is a check on your reading. If you can't answer a question, you need to go back to the text to reread that section.

VISUAL SUMMARY: Below is a summary of the major concepts in this section. To check your comprehension of the chapter, read the summary and ask yourself if you understand the concepts. If the concepts seem unfamiliar to you, you may want to go back to the book and reread those sections. This text is taken from the Visual Summaries on StudySpace at wwnorton.com/studyspace.

I. Developmental Psychology Is the Study of Changes Over the Life Span, in Physiology, Cognition, Emotion, and Social Behavior

II. Development Starts in the Womb
   A. Conception → zygote → embryo → fetus.
   B. The embryo or fetus can be affected by:
      i. hormones.
      ii. teratogens (harmful environmental agents).

III. Biology and Environment Influence Developmental Milestones
   A. Dynamic systems theory: behavior emerges through interactions between a child and cultural and environmental contexts.

IV. Brain Development Promotes Learning
   A. Early brain growth is characterized by increases in:
      i. myelination.
      ii. synaptic connections.
      iii. synaptic pruning.
   B. During sensitive periods, brain development and environment facilitate acquisition of skills.

V. Children Develop Attachment and Emotion Regulation
   A. Attachment:
      i. is strong emotional connection, usually to caregivers, that persists over time.
      ii. is adaptive.
      iii. is present in other species (imprinting).
      iv. can be secure (65 percent of U.S. children).
      v. can be insecure (35 percent of U.S. children).
   B. Oxytocin plays a role:
      i. in infant/caregiver attachment.
      ii. later in romantic relationships.

REINFORCE: Are you ready to check your knowledge of this section? Answer the following multiple-choice questions with your textbook closed.

1. Maternal hormones:
   a. have little effect on a fetus's development because the fetus is isolated from the mother's blood supply
   b. can affect physical development, such as the time at which a child begins to walk, but not mental variables, such as IQ
   c. can have important effects on variables such as intellectual development and birth weight
   d. affect a fetus's development only in the first trimester

2. Which of the following statements is NOT true of teratogens?
   a. Teratogens may include any chemical in the environment that negatively affects a developing embryo or fetus.

   b. Teratogens are recessive genes that affect the child in the womb.
   c. Teratogens include alcohol, prescription drugs, and environmental chemicals.
   d. Teratogens are often avoidable.

3. Which of the following is a preventable birth defect?
   a. Down syndrome
   b. fetal alcohol syndrome
   c. hemophilia, a genetic bleeding disorder
   d. schizophrenia

4. Myelination:
   a. occurs in all brain regions at roughly the same time
   b. increases the speed at which a neuron can transmit hormones
   c. is not complete in the brain areas involved in abstract thought until early childhood
   d. increases the speed at which a neuron can transmit signals and is not complete in the brain areas involved in abstract thought until young adulthood

5. Synaptic pruning is:
   a. the brain's way of doing away with synaptic connections that are not being used
   b. a process induced by teratogens that negatively affects development
   c. a process that occurs only in understimulated children
   d. a process that is detrimental to normal brain development

6. At day care, Tom's 4-year-old daughter, Maya, is being taught partly in Chinese. Tom wants to be able to speak Chinese with Maya, so he enrolls in a Chinese-language course. On the basis of the concept of "sensitive periods" in learning, you would predict:
   a. that Maya will learn the language more easily than Tom will
   b. that since Tom has had more experience with language, he will learn Chinese faster than Maya
   c. that Tom will master Chinese vocabulary faster than Maya, but will have problems with the grammar
   d. nothing, since acquisition of a second language is unrelated to age of exposure to the language

7. An infant's attachment to its caregivers is primarily a function of:
   a. genetic inheritance
   b. parental treatment
   c. which of Piaget's stages of development the child has achieved
   d. how complicated the birth process was

8. Which of the following statements is NOT true of attachment?

a. Attachment is important because it promotes survival.

b. Attachment occurs in humans and some other animal species.

c. Attachment can occur at any age and does not show the typical sensitive period.

d. Behaviors that indicate the strength of attachment include separation anxiety.

9. Which of the following statements is NOT true of imprinting?

a. There is a critical period in which imprinting occurs.

b. Imprinting occurs only in humans.

c. Imprinting is a biological behavior.

d. If the mother bird is not available, the baby bird can imprint on any available female of that species.

10. Harlow did an experiment with infant rhesus monkeys, requiring them to choose between an imitation mother that provided contact comfort or one that provided food. The results demonstrated that for this species:

a. food is the most important reinforcement

b. food is used to reduce tension in the young

c. tactile comfort is more important than food, particularly during stress

d. infants were distressed because the "mother" providing contact comfort did not also supply food

11. Approximately what percentage of children develop what Ainsworth called a secure attachment style?

a. 15 percent

b. 25 percent

c. 45 percent

d. 65 percent

12. If your mother was emotionally or behaviorally inconsistent with you, you are likely to have a(n) _____ attachment style.

a. secure

b. complex

c. insecure

d. imprinted

13. In the strange-situation test, a securely attached infant differs from one who is insecurely attached in terms of:

a. what each infant does when the attachment figure leaves

b. how each infant responds to strangers

c. what each infant does when the attachment figure returns after an absence

d. all of the above

14. The strange-situation test was designed to allow psychologists to assess:

a. the quality of a child's attachment to her or his mother

b. an infant's tendency to seek or avoid novelty

c. a mother's response to a fearful infant

d. the level of social skill an infant has acquired

15. A hormone that has recently been shown to play an important role in mother/infant attachment is:

a. testosterone

b. oxytocin

c. epinephrine

d. norepinephrine

WHAT DID YOU MISS? Check your answers against the Answer Key at the end of this chapter of the Study Guide. The Answer Key also lists the page(s) in your text where each question is explained. If you missed any questions, go to the pages indicated in the Answer Key, reread those sections, go back to the questions, and see if you can answer them correctly this time.

ANOTHER OPPORTUNITY TO REVIEW: Answer these questions without your textbook. As a rule of thumb, if you can write only a few words about these questions, you probably need to go back and review.

1. Describe how the prenatal environment can affect development. _____

_____

_____

2. Explain how dynamic systems theory illuminates the ways biology and environment work together to shape development. _____

_____

_____

3. Describe key processes in infant brain development and how these processes affect learning. _____

_____

_____

4. Describe the types of attachment infants have to their caregivers. _____

_____

5. Explain how attachment and emotion regulation are related. _____

_____

_____

WHAT DO I NEED TO KNOW? Based on what you've discovered above, what are the areas where you need to focus your studying? Which objectives do you need to spend more time mastering? Write this information down in your own words.

1. _____

2. _____

3. _____

4. _____

5. _____

6. _____

9.2 As Children, How Do We Learn about the World?

How do psychologists make discoveries about the inner world of the infant? How have psychologists revised their assumptions about that inner world over time? During childhood—a time of rapid physical growth—language, cognitive abilities, and sense of self develop to meet the demands of the particular child's environment.

9.2 Guiding Questions

To guide your reading of the text, review the following questions. Then, as you read the chapter, look for the answers to these questions. You may want to note in your textbook where you find these answers.

1. Provide examples of techniques psychologists use to find out what infants know and can do.

2. Explain how memory changes over time as children grow and learn.

3. List and describe the stages of development proposed by Piaget.

4. Explain how empathy and understanding others' viewpoints influence changes in moral reasoning over time.

5. Trace the development of language in infants and in older children.

NOW READ Section 9.2 "As Children, How Do We Learn about the World?" keeping these questions in mind.

REVIEW: Now that you've read this section, go back to the 9.2 Guiding Questions and see if you can answer them based on what you've read. This is a check on your reading. If you can't answer a question, you need to go back to the text to reread that section.

VISUAL SUMMARY: Below is a summary of the major concepts in this section. To check your comprehension of the chapter, read the summary and ask yourself if you understand the concepts. If the concepts seem unfamiliar to you, you may want to go back to the book and reread those sections. This text is taken from the Visual Summaries on StudySpace at wwnorton.com/studyspace.

VI. Perception Introduces the World
 A. Infant research is conducted using:
  i. preferential looking.
  ii. orienting reflex.
  iii. habituation.
 B. Infants:
  i. respond more to high contrast, complex visual patterns.
  ii. have memory for voices.
  iii. prefer their mothers' voices.

VII. Memory Improves during Childhood
 A. Inability to remember events from early childhood (infantile amnesia) may be related to:
  i. incomplete development of autobiographical memory.
  ii. incomplete language acquisition.
  iii. incomplete ability to perceive contexts well enough to store memories accurately.
 B. Inaccurate memory:
  i. may be due to underdeveloped source memory.
  ii. may be reflected by confabulation.

VIII. Piaget Emphasized Stages of Cognitive Development
 A. During the sensorimotor stage (birth–2 years):
  i. infants acquire information about the world through senses and motor skills.
  ii. children come to understand object permanence.
 B. During the preoperational stage (2–7 years), children:
  i. can think symbolically.
  ii. reason based on intuition and superficial appearance rather than logic.
  iii. do not understand law of conservation.
 C. During the concrete operational stage (7–12 years), children:
  i. can think logically.
  ii. understand law of conservation.
 D. During the formal operational stage (12 years–adulthood):
  i. people can think abstractly, critically, and hypothetically.
 E. People develop and refine schemas through:
  i. assimilation (placing new experiences into existing schemas).
  ii. accommodation (altering existing schema to include new information).

F. Children understand concepts of math and physics at much younger ages than Piaget's stages suggest.

IX. We Learn from Interacting with Others
   A. Theory of mind: ability to understand another's mental state and thus predict and explain the person's behavior.
   B. Kohlberg's levels of moral development:
       i. preconventional: moral behavior determined by self-interest or pleasurable outcomes.
       ii. conventional: moral behavior determined by laws or winning approval of others.
       iii. postconventional: moral behavior based on abstract principles about value of life.
   C. Moral emotions (empathy and sympathy):
       i. are facilitated by self-awareness and inductive reasoning by adults.
       ii. may be based in physiological mechanisms of decision making.

X. Language Develops in an Orderly Way
   A. Language: a system of using sounds and symbols according to grammatical rules (syntax).
       i. telegraphic speech: basic, bare-bones sentences that convey meaning (e.g. "Throw ball!").
       ii. overextending a grammatical rule when not appropriate reflects attempt to understand language rules.
   B. All languages are based on universal grammar.
   C. Learning and language acquisition are influenced by sociocultural context.
   D. Animals can use language but cannot express novel thoughts and ideas.

REINFORCE: Are you ready to check your knowledge of this section? Answer the following multiple-choice questions with your textbook closed.

1. The orienting reflex is the tendency for an infant to:
   a. pay more attention to novel stimuli than to stimuli he or she is familiar with
   b. move toward any breastlike stimulus
   c. prefer subtle patterns to bold patterns
   d. look away less quickly when the stimulus is familiar

2. A toymaker wants to determine which of three colors infants like best. Which of the following techniques would be best for assessing this preference?
   a. strange-situation test
   b. preferential looking technique
   c. visual acuity tests
   d. There is no good technique, as infants cannot distinguish colors.

3. Visual acuity reaches adult levels in a child:
   a. within weeks after birth
   b. at approximately 1 year
   c. by the first grade
   d. at about 10 years of age

4. Infants less than 10 days old:
   a. will alter their behavior if the alteration enables them to hear their mother's voice
   b. have the auditory acuity of an adult
   c. can see stimuli in depth
   d. begin to learn vocabulary audiovisually

5. Which of the following is true of young infants?
   a. They show no preferences for particular stimuli because they cannot discriminate among them.
   b. They prefer familiar to unfamiliar stimuli.
   c. They prefer novel rather than familiar stimuli.
   d. They prefer circular rather than rectangular stimuli.

6. What does Piaget call the process of changing or modifying a schema in response to environmental factors?
   a. assimilation
   b. accommodation
   c. maturation
   d. conservation

7. What is the correct ordering of Piaget's stages of cognitive development?
   a. formal operational, concrete operational, preoperational, sensorimotor
   b. concrete operational, preoperational, sensorimotor, formal operational
   c. preoperational, concrete operational, sensorimotor, formal operational
   d. sensorimotor, preoperational, concrete operational, formal operational

8. Object permanence refers to the child's awareness that:
   a. the mass of an object does not change when its shape changes
   b. objects exist even when you cannot see them
   c. broken objects can be repaired
   d. objects that cannot be seen may be similar to those that can

9. A child pours one bucket of sand into a short, fat container and a second bucket into a tall, thin container. When asked which container holds more sand, the child points to the tall, thin container. This response suggests that the child is at Piaget's _____ stage of cognitive development.
   a. formal operational
   b. preoperational
   c. sensorimotor
   d. concrete operational

10. Piaget's conclusion that young children have no inherent sense of mathematical principles:
    a. was contradicted by the results of his own marble test
    b. has been called into question by research showing that children under 3 understand concepts such as *more than* and *less than*
    c. has largely been supported, though such principles are acquired earlier than he postulated
    d. has been supported in a manner highly consistent with his initial proposal

11. Theory of mind is:
    a. our ability to recognize that others have mental states that might explain their behavior
    b. the tendency to explain our own behavior in terms of environmental factors and the behavior of others in terms of their mental states
    c. the belief that nonhumans have minds that are much like our own
    d. the fact that the mind cannot be observed directly but must be inferred

12. The development of a theory of mind is linked to development in which area of the brain?
    a. limbic system
    b. amygdala
    c. prefrontal region
    d. cerebellum

13. Given an ethical dilemma regarding a behavior, a child conforms to the societal rules of law and order and focuses on others' disapproval of the behavior. According to Kohlberg's stage theory, in which stage is this child most likely functioning?
    a. preconventional
    b. conventional
    c. concrete operations
    d. postconventional

14. Which of the following is an example of telegraphic speech?
    a. "Ball."
    b. "Ba Ba Ba Ba."
    c. "Daddy, Ball!"
    d. "Daddy, please throw the ball."

15. Chomsky has argued that children:
    a. must learn the grammatical rules of any language through a trial-and-error process
    b. quickly grasp the surface structure of a language, but have great difficulty with what he termed the deep structure of language
    c. have a built-in preparedness to acquire grammar
    d. have an innate tendency to name objects

WHAT DID YOU MISS? Check your answers against the Answer Key at the end of this chapter of the Study Guide. The Answer Key also lists the page(s) in your text where each question is explained. If you missed any questions, go to the pages indicated in the Answer Key, reread those sections, go back to the questions, and see if you can answer them correctly this time.

ANOTHER OPPORTUNITY TO REVIEW: Answer these questions without your textbook. As a rule of thumb, if you can write only a few words about these questions, you probably need to go back and review.

1. Provide examples of techniques psychologists use to find out what infants know and can do. _____

    _____

    _____

2. Explain how memory changes over time as children grow and learn. _____

    _____

    _____

3. List and describe the stages of development proposed by Piaget. _____

    _____

    _____

4. Explain how empathy and understanding others' viewpoints influence changes in moral reasoning over time.

    _____

    _____

5. Trace the development of language in infants and in older children. _____

    _____

    _____

WHAT DO I NEED TO KNOW? Based on what you've discovered above, what are the areas where you need to focus your studying? Which objectives do you need to spend more time mastering? Write this information down in your own words.

1. _____

2. _____

3. _____

4. _____

5. _____

6. _____

9.3 How Do We Progress from Childhood to Adolescence?

As we move from childhood through adolescence on our way to adulthood, we face physical and psychological challenges. How is our sense of self affected by puberty, our peers, our parents, and culture?

9.3 Guiding Questions

To guide your reading of the text, review the following questions. Then, as you read the chapter, look for the answers to these questions. You may want to note in your textbook where you find these answers.

1. Describe the key challenges faced in each of Erik Erikson's first five stages of psychosocial development.

2. Describe how biology and environment interact to influence puberty.

3. Explain key factors that influence gender identity development and gender-specific behaviors.

4. Describe how parents, peers, and cultural forces shape the sense of self.

NOW READ Section 9.3 "How Do We Progress from Childhood to Adolescence?" keeping these questions in mind.

REVIEW: Now that you've read this section, go back to the 9.3 Guiding Questions and see if you can answer them based on what you've read. This is a check on your reading. If you can't answer a question, you need to go back to the text to reread that section.

VISUAL SUMMARY: Below is a summary of the major concepts in this section. To check your comprehension of the chapter, read the summary and ask yourself if you understand the concepts. If the concepts seem unfamiliar to you, you may want to go back to the book and reread those sections. This text is taken from the Visual Summaries on StudySpace at wwnorton.com/studyspace.

XI. Erikson's "Crisis"-Oriented Stages
   A. Trust versus mistrust (0–20)
   B. Autonomy versus shame (2–3)
   C. Initiative versus guilt (4–6)
   D. Industry versus inferiority (7–12)
   E. Identity versus role confusion (13–19)
   F. Intimacy versus isolation (20s)
   G. Generativity versus stagnation (30s–50s)
   H. Integrity versus despair (60 and beyond)

XII. Physical Changes and Cultural Norms Influence the Development of Identity
   A. Identity is influenced by:
      i. biological changes (puberty).
      ii. culture (gender roles, identity, and schema).
   B. Biology has a strong effect on gender identity.
   C. Cultural norms can make the process of establishing ethnic identity challenging.

XIII. Peers and Parents Help Shape the Sense of Self
   A. Adolescent identity development is shaped by:
      i. adults' perceptions.
      ii. peers' influences.
      iii. teens' active exploration of the world.

REINFORCE: Are you ready to check your knowledge of this section? Answer the following multiple-choice questions with your textbook closed.

1. In terms of the influence of peers and parents on children's social development and personality, psychologists tend to agree that:
   a. parents play the primary role
   b. peers play the primary role
   c. peers and parents play complementary roles
   d. genes override the influences of both parents and peers

2. Which of the following factors has the greatest impact on parent/child interactions?
   a. family norms and values
   b. the fit between the biologically based temperament of the child and parental behaviors
   c. the temperament the child learns from his or her parents
   d. parental frustration with the child's temperament

3. Marissa is worried about the occasional conflicts she has with her adolescent-aged daughter Karin. What could you tell her about these interactions?
   a. She should avoid conflicts because adolescents usually do not listen to their parents.
   b. Conflicts are likely to lead to the escalation of antisocial behavior.
   c. She should not worry because conflicts have little or no impact on adolescents.
   d. Parent/child conflicts can lead to the development of negotiation skills and empathy in adolescents.

4. All of the following statements describe the adolescent brain EXCEPT:
   a. The frontal cortex is not fully myelinated.
   b. Gray matter is decreasing in quantity.
   c. The limbic system is more active than the frontal cortex.
   d. Synaptic connections are being refined.

5. Some psychologists use the term *gender* to refer to:
   a. biological differences between the sexes
   b. differences that are an outgrowth of socialization practices
   c. sexual functioning
   d. all of the above

6. Gender roles are _____ , whereas gender schemas are _____ .
   a. culturally defined norms that differentiate the behavior and attitudes of men and women; cognitive structures that influence how people interpret the behavior of men and women
   b. cognitive structures that influence how people interpret the behavior of men and women; culturally defined norms that differentiate the behavior and attitudes of men and women
   c. biologically defined norms that differentiate the behavior and attitudes of men and women; cognitive structures that influence how people interpret the behavior of men and women
   d. biological structures that influence how people interpret the behavior of men and women; culturally defined norms that differentiate the behavior and attitudes of men and women

7. All of the following changes in adolescents cause them to question who they are EXCEPT:
   a. shifts in physical appearance
   b. greater sophistication in cognitive processes
   c. greater emotional stability
   d. societal pressures to prepare for the future

8. The case of Bruce, who was surgically and hormonally reassigned to a female identity (Brenda), illustrates that:
   a. gender identity does not totally depend on how one is treated
   b. gender is highly changeable if biological changes are also made
   c. how a person thinks about his or her gender identity is less important than the person's biological sex
   d. surgical reassignment to the other sex is usually successful

9. By middle school, children are most likely to:
   a. be able to label their ethnic or racial groups, but not express the societal attributes attached to their ethnic or racial groups
   b. both label their ethnic or racial groups and express the societal attributes attached to their ethnic or racial groups
   c. reject the values of their ethnic or racial groups
   d. form strong attachments to the values of their ethnic or racial groups

10. Which of the following is/are associated with competent parenting?
    a. flexibility
    b. considering both the child's temperament and the parents' personalities
    c. considering the impact of the particular situation
    d. all of the above

11. According to Erikson's theory of development:
    a. most of the important challenges occur before puberty
    b. once adulthood is reached, the important issue is how to maintain the cognitive and social gains made to that point
    c. important cognitive and social changes occur across the life span
    d. development can best be thought of as a continuous process rather than something that proceeds in stages

12. Erikson argues that most adults are motivated by what he calls generativity. By this, he means that people:
    a. wish to be creative
    b. wish to produce as much as possible
    c. want to give something of themselves to future generations
    d. all of the above

13. Erikson's final stage of adult development is focused on the issues of:
    a. stagnation versus productivity
    b. isolation versus intimacy
    c. competence versus incompetence
    d. integrity versus despair

14. Which of the following theorists is noted for arguing that development continues across the life span?
    a. Jean Piaget
    b. Sigmund Freud
    c. John Bowlby
    d. Erik Erikson

15. From Erikson's point of view, what is the major goal of development during the adolescent period?
    a. learning to deal with sexual issues
    b. developing a sense of identity
    c. resolving the intimacy-versus-isolation crisis
    d. identifying sexual orientation

WHAT DID YOU MISS? Check your answers against the Answer Key at the end of this chapter of the Study Guide. The Answer Key also lists the page(s) in your text where each question is explained. If you missed any questions, go to the pages indicated in the Answer Key, reread those sections, go back to the questions, and see if you can answer them correctly this time.

ANOTHER OPPORTUNITY TO REVIEW: Answer these questions without your textbook. As a rule of thumb, if you can write only a few words about these questions, you probably need to go back and review.

1. Describe the key challenges faced in each of Erik Erikson's first five stages of psychosocial development.

_____

_____

_____

_____

_____

2. Describe how biology and environment interact to influence puberty. _____

_____

_____

3. Explain key factors that influence gender identity development and gender-specific behaviors. _____

_____

_____

4. Describe how parents, peers, and cultural forces shape the sense of self. _____

_____

_____

WHAT DO I NEED TO KNOW? Based on what you discovered above, what are the areas where you need to focus your studying? Which objectives do you need to spend more time mastering? Write this information down in your own words.

1. _____

2. _____

3. _____

4. _____

5. _____

6. _____

TRY IT

Taking a Moment to Say Thanks

Thinking about life stages—infancy, childhood, adolescence, and adulthood—may lead you to think about yourself at the various stages of your life. It may also lead you to think about the people who were important to you at various points in your life. Maybe you haven't seen or thought about these people for a while. As discussed in a previous chapter, one technique that positive psychologists use is the "Gratitude Letter" to a person who has been important to the letter writer.

Choose someone in your life who has been important to you. Maybe you have told this person how she or he changed your life or helped you, or maybe you haven't. Write the person a letter about her or his influence on your life. Send the letter to the person or read it aloud to him or her, in person or on the telephone. How does writing the letter and sharing it make you feel? According to the research conducted by positive psychologists, this technique can lead to a greater sense of well-being, greater appreciation of life, and lower levels of psychological distress.

9.4 What Brings Us Meaning in Adulthood?

This chapter considers the following questions: What are the hallmarks of adulthood physically, socially, and cognitively? What do you think about marriage and children? Do you think they contribute to well-being or can be a challenge to well-being? What changes and what stays the same as we age?

9.4 Guiding Questions

To guide your reading of the text, review the following questions. Then, as you read the chapter, look for the answers to these questions. You may want to note in your textbook where you find these answers.

1. Describe the key challenges of the last three of Erikson's stages of psychosocial development.

2. Contrast an egosystem perspective with an ecosystem perspective.

3. Describe the physical changes that occur as we age.

4. Explain key research findings on the benefits of a healthy marriage and how to keep a marriage healthy after the birth of a child.

5. Describe the cognitive changes that occur as we age.

NOW READ Section 9.4 "What Brings Us Meaning in Adulthood?" keeping these questions in mind.

REVIEW: Now that you've read this section, go back to the 9.4 Guiding Questions and see if you can answer them based on what you've read. This is a check on your reading. If you can't answer a question, you need to go back to the text to reread that section.

VISUAL SUMMARY: Below is a summary of the major concepts in this section. To check your comprehension of the chapter, read the summary and ask yourself if you understand the concepts. If the concepts seem unfamiliar to you, you may want to go back to the book and reread those sections. This text is taken from the Visual Summaries on StudySpace at wwnorton.com/studyspace.

XIV. Adulthood Presents Psychosocial Challenges
    A. According to Erikson, major life challenges in adulthood include:
        i. establishing intimate relationships.
        ii. finding sense of meaning in life.
        iii. facing life review that comes with old age.
    B. Egosystem: focus on building and maintaining other people's impressions of yourself.
    C. Ecosystem: perceiving yourself to be interconnected with others.

XV. Adults Are Affected by Life Transitions
    A. In midlife, a sense of generativity is associated with:
        i. having a successful marriage.
        ii. having children.

XVI. The Transition to Old Age Can Be Rewarding
    A. Attitudes toward aging are changing as people live long and fulfilling lives.
    B. Old age: characterized by deterioration in physical and cognitive abilities.
    C. Socioemotional selectivity theory: older people adjust their priorities to emphasize meaningful experiences.

XVII. Cognition Changes as We Age
    A. During aging:
        i. learning new things and retrieving memories become more difficult.
        ii. fluid intelligence declines and crystallized intelligence increases.
    B. People who are healthy and mentally active demonstrate less decline.

REINFORCE: Are you ready to check your knowledge of this section? Answer the following multiple-choice questions with your book closed.

1. In Alzheimer's-type dementia, which neurotransmitter has lower levels?
    a. dopamine
    b. serotonin
    c. acetylcholine
    d. norepinephrine

2. How are marriage and mental health related?
    a. Married individuals report greater happiness than do singles.
    b. Married females report greater happiness than do single women, but married males do not report greater happiness than do single males.
    c. Single males are mentally healthier than any other group.
    d. Marital status appears unrelated to mental health status.

3. Which type of woman is most likely to live the longest?
    a. single and never married
    b. divorced
    c. widowed
    d. currently married

4. What have psychologists discovered about the relationship between having children and marital happiness?
    a. Couples with children report being happier unless the number of offspring exceeds three.
    b. No consistent relationship between these variables has been found.
    c. Couples with children report less happiness than those without.
    d. It depends on the sex of the offspring; couples with female children are the happiest.

5. All of the following statements about the benefits of marriage or cohabiting are true EXCEPT:
    a. Married men derive greater health benefits from marriage than do married women.
    b. Married women report greater emotional satisfaction than do single women.
    c. Although married men report greater sexual satisfaction than do single or cohabiting men, women in these groups do not report any difference.
    d. Cohabitation and marriage confer equally strong health benefits.

6. Demographic statistics for Americans over the last several decades reveal that:
    a. people are living longer, are healthier, and are better educated
    b. the number of people in America over 65 has risen to 30 percent

c. because people are retiring younger, the relative contribution of older people to society is decreasing

d. all of the above

7. Your grandparents are increasingly focused on things that have emotional meaning for them and have begun spending more time with a smaller circle of friends. These developments are most consistent with:
   a. Erikson's stage theory
   b. Freud's psychodynamic theory
   c. Carstensen's socioemotional selectivity theory
   d. Piaget's stages of development

8. Imagine that a psychologist tests you every year in regard to your mental processing speed. For example, how long it takes you to push a lever when a light comes on is measured. If you age normally you should show:
   a. no reduction in speed of response until after about age 60
   b. an increase in speed until about age 35 and then a slow decline
   c. a slight decrease by the mid-20s that accelerates as you age further
   d. an ability to perform this task throughout your life at roughly the same speed as long as your visual acuity is high

9. Which of the following statements is true about the memory processes of the elderly versus those of young adults?
   a. The elderly are better able to remember things that happened to them yesterday, but have more difficulty recalling things from childhood.
   b. The elderly are better at keeping multiple things in mind simultaneously.
   c. Whether the information is positive or negative has a greater impact on recall in the elderly.
   d. Memory is equal in both groups, but the elderly require less time to recall negative information.

10. Crystallized intelligence is to fluid intelligence as:
    a. abstract is to concrete
    b. general is to specific
    c. fact is to analogy
    d. young is to old

11. Which of the following statements is true about crystallized intelligence and fluid intelligence?
    a. Crystallized intelligence remains stable across the life span, whereas fluid intelligence begins to decline around age 30.
    b. Both crystallized and fluid intelligence remain relatively stable across the life span.

c. Both types of intelligence begin to decline around age 30, with crystallized intelligence showing bigger losses.

d. Both types of intelligence remain stable until about age 60 and then decline dramatically.

12. Specific knowledge about important events during World War II exemplifies:
    a. crystallized intelligence
    b. fluid intelligence
    c. generative intelligence
    d. conceptual intelligence

13. The ability to quickly calculate a 10 percent discount on an item exemplifies:
    a. crystallized intelligence
    b. fluid intelligence
    c. generative intelligence
    d. conceptual intelligence

14. Dementia can be caused by:
    a. a genetic predisposition
    b. small strokes
    c. excessive alcohol intake
    d. all of the above

15. Attempts to use cognitive training strategies to reduce memory deficits in the elderly:
    a. have tended not to work, probably because the deficits are a result of brain deterioration
    b. show some ability to postpone the memory problems associated with aging
    c. work, but only if they also serve to increase activation of the right hemisphere
    d. have worked better with females than with males

WHAT DID YOU MISS? Check your answers against the Answer Key at the end of this chapter of the Study Guide. The Answer Key also lists the page(s) in your text where each question is explained. If you missed any questions, go to the pages indicated in the Answer Key, reread those sections, go back to the questions, and see if you can answer them correctly this time.

ANOTHER OPPORTUNITY TO REVIEW: Answer these questions without your textbook. As a rule of thumb, if you can write only a few words about these questions, you probably need to go back and review.

1. Describe the key challenges of the last three of Erikson's stages of psychosocial development. _____

2. Contrast an egosystem perspective with an ecosystem perspective. _____

_____

_____

3. Describe the physical changes that occur as we age.

_____

_____

4. Explain key research findings on the benefits of a healthy marriage and how to keep a marriage healthy after the birth of a child. _____

_____

_____

5. Describe the cognitive changes that occur as we age.

_____

_____

WHAT DO I NEED TO KNOW? Based on what you've discovered above, what are the areas where you need to focus your studying? Which objectives do you need to spend more time mastering? Write this information down in your own words.

1. _____

2. _____

3. _____

4. _____

5. _____

6. _____

WHAT MATTERS TO ME: What facts in this chapter are personally relevant to you?

_____

_____

_____

_____

CHAPTER SUMMARY

9.1 What Shapes Us during Childhood?

- *Development Starts in the Womb:* Many factors in the prenatal environment, such as nutrition and hormones, can affect development. Exposure to teratogens (e.g., drugs, alcohol, viruses) can result in death, deformity, or mental disorders.

- *Biology and Environment Influence Developmental Milestones:* Infants have many sensory abilities. For example, they can discriminate smells, tastes, and sounds. Infant physical development follows a consistent pattern across cultures, but cultural practices can affect the timing of milestones, such as walking. Dynamic systems theory helps us see how every new development occurs due to complex interactions between biology, environment, and personal agency.

- *Brain Development Promotes Learning:* Brain development involves both maturation and experience. The brain's plasticity allows changes in the development of connections and in the synaptic pruning of unused neural connections. The timing of experiences necessary for brain development is particularly important in the early years.

- *Children Develop Attachment and Emotion Regulation:* The emotional bond that develops between a child and a caregiver increases the child's chances of survival. Attachment styles are generally categorized as secure or insecure. Insecure attachment can be avoidant or ambivalent. Secure attachments are related to better adjustment later in life, including good emotion regulation skills and social relationships.

9.2 As Children, How Do We Learn about the World?

- *Perception Introduces the World:* Experiments using habituation and the preferential-looking technique have revealed infants' considerable perceptual ability. Vision and hearing develop rapidly as neural circuitry develops.

- *Memory Improves during Childhood:* Infantile memory is limited by a lack of both language ability and autobiographical reference. Source amnesia is common in children. Confabulation, common in young children, may result from underdevelopment of the frontal lobes.

- *Piaget Emphasized Stages of Development:* Jean Piaget proposed that through interaction with the environment, children develop mental schemas and proceed through stages of cognitive development. In the sensorimotor stage, children experience the world through their senses and develop object permanence. In the preoperational stage, children's thinking is dominated by the appearance of objects rather than by logic. In the concrete operational stage, children learn the logic of concrete objects. In the formal operational stage, children become capable of abstract, complex thinking.

- *We Learn from Interacting with Others:* Being able to infer another's mental state is known as theory of mind. Through socialization, children move from egocentric thinking to being able to take another's perspective.

- *Language Develops in an Orderly Way:* Infants can discriminate phonemes. Language proceeds from sounds to words to telegraphic speech to sentences. According to Noam Chomsky, all human languages are governed by universal grammar, an innate set of relations between linguistic elements. According to Lev Vygotsky, social interaction is the force that develops language. For language to develop, a child must be exposed to it during the sensitive period of the first few months and years of life.

9.3 How Do We Progress from Childhood to Adolescence?

- *Physical Changes and Cultural Norms Influence the Development of Identity:* The biological changes of puberty affect social and emotional development. Those changes can also be influenced by social events. The adolescent's brain is undergoing important reorganization, which may lead to impulsive or risky behaviors governed by an overactive limbic system and immature frontal cortex. Gender identity develops in children and shapes their behaviors (i.e. gender roles). Gender schemas develop as cognitive representations of appropriate gender characteristics in the culture each person belongs to. Ethnic identity also develops through social forces. A bicultural identity allows a teen of color to feel connected to his or her own culture as well as the dominant culture.

- *Peers and Parents Help Shape the Sense of Self:* Social comparisons help shape children's identity development. Based on feedback from peer groups and the larger community, teens develop a sense of belonging. Adults may view teens as belonging to homogeneous cliques, but teens emphasize their own individuality. Research shows that parents influence many areas of adolescents' lives, including religiosity, morality, identity, and how children experience emotions. Parents who use flexible parenting styles that respond to children's temperamental characteristics often have well-adjusted teens.

9.4 What Brings Us Meaning in Adulthood?

- *Adulthood Presents Psychosocial Challenges:* Erikson believed that people develop throughout the life span. He theorized that each stage of life presents important

social issues to be resolved. For adults, building intimacy with others, finding a sense of generativity, and facing the end of life with integrity are key challenges.

- *Adults are Affected by Life Transitions:* Adults experience many physical changes. Weight gain, poor diet, and lack of exercise become challenges to face if we do not adopt a healthy lifestyle in early adulthood. Marriage is a typical life transition for most adults and can provide a sense of security, health, and happiness. Married couples who understand each other's needs can adjust positively to the birth of a child, which can be a stressful transition for many.

- *The Transition to Old Age Can Be Rewarding:* As the population in many Western societies ages, more research is being done on aging, which inevitably brings physical and mental changes. Dementia has various causes, including Alzheimer's disease. Most older adults are healthy, remain productive, and become selective about their relationships and activities.

- *Cognition Changes as We Age:* Short-term memory, particularly when attention is divided or tasks are complex, is affected by aging. Crystallized intelligence increases; fluid intelligence declines in old age as processing speed declines. Being mentally active and socially engaged preserves cognitive functioning.

PUTTING IT ALL TOGETHER

Answer these questions to check your knowledge of the material in this chapter.

1. Explain how environment may influence prenatal development and the attainment of developmental milestones in infancy.

2. Describe the kinds of toys you think would be appropriate for children in each of Piaget's stages. Be sure to justify your answer based on Piaget's theory.

3. Define and give an example for each of the following: gender identity, gender roles, and gender schemas. How might environment influence these factors?

4. When is marriage good for people? Include the positive effects of marriage. When is marriage bad for people? Include the negative effects. How does having children influence marital happiness?

ANSWER KEY FOR REINFORCE QUESTIONS

Section 9.1

1. c   p. 367
2. b   p. 368
3. b   p. 368

4. d   p. 372
5. a   p. 372
6. a   p. 373
7. b   p. 374
8. c   p. 374
9. b   p. 375
10. c   p. 375
11. d   p. 377
12. c   p. 377
13. d   p. 377
14. a   p. 377
15. b   p. 379

Section 9.2

1. a   p. 381
2. b   p. 381
3. b   p. 382
4. a   p. 382
5. c   p. 381
6. b   p. 385
7. d   p. 385
8. b   p. 386
9. b   p. 387
10. b   p. 389
11. a   p. 390
12. c   p. 391
13. b   p. 391
14. c   p. 394
15. c   p. 395

Section 9.3

1. c   p. 405
2. b   p. 406
3. d   p. 406
4. b   p. 400
5. b   p. 401
6. a   p. 401
7. c   p. 404
8. a   p. 403
9. b   p. 404
10. d   p. 406
11. c   p. 398
12. c   p. 398
13. d   p. 398
14. d   p. 398
15. b   p. 398

Section 9.4

1. c   p. 413
2. a   p. 411
3. d   p. 411

4. c   p. 412
5. d   p. 411
6. a   p. 413
7. c   p. 414
8. c   p. 414
9. c   p. 415
10. c   p. 415
11. a   p. 416
12. a   p. 416
13. b   p. 416
14. d   p. 413
15. b   p. 415

HINTS FOR PUTTING IT ALL TOGETHER QUESTIONS

1. In your discussion of environmental effects on prenatal development, include discussion of teratogens and stress. When addressing developmental milestones, briefly discuss both dynamic systems theory and cultural differences in child rearing.

2. For children in the sensorimotor stage, knowledge is tied to action. When thinking of toys for children in this stage, focus on how they can physically manipulate the objects. Preoperational children can think about objects, and they can pretend. However, they are also egocentric. What kinds of toys are good for pretending? Will these egocentric children do well at games involving a lot of cooperation or competition? Concrete operational children can think logically but not abstractly. What kinds of board games, card games, or puzzles might be appropriate for these children? What games might be too abstract for this group? Individuals capable of formal operations think abstractly and generate and test hypotheses. Games involving strategies and trying to guess what other players' moves might be require formal thought.

3. In your answer, explain that people's beliefs about themselves make up gender identity, cultural norms define gender roles, and cognitive structures are related to gender schemas. When discussing environmental effects, describe our culture's expectations for males and females. Also discuss the kinds of models children are exposed to both in real life and through the media (e.g., television, movies, the Internet).

4. When discussing whether marriage is good or bad for someone, consider: What is the person's gender? Is the marriage happy or unhappy? When considering the effects of having a baby on marital happiness, include time, money, stress, and planning.

KEY TERMS EXERCISES

First, fill in your own definition and example for each term. Then check each term against the textbook's definition. These exercises can also be cut out and used as flash cards.

accommodation

Your Definition:
Your Example:
Textbook Definition:

assimilation

Your Definition:
Your Example:
Textbook Definition:

attachment

Your Definition:
Your Example:
Textbook Definition:

concrete operational stage

Your Definition:
Your Example:
Textbook Definition:

conventional level

Your Definition:
Your Example:
Textbook Definition:

developmental psychology

Your Definition:
Your Example:
Textbook Definition:

dynamic systems theory

Your Definition:
Your Example:
Textbook Definition:

formal operational stage

Your Definition:
Your Example:
Textbook Definition:

gender identity

Your Definition:
Your Example:
Textbook Definition:

insecure attachment

Your Definition:
Your Example:
Textbook Definition:

gender roles

Your Definition:
Your Example:
Textbook Definition:

object permanence

Your Definition:
Your Example:
Textbook Definition:

gender schemas

Your Definition:
Your Example:
Textbook Definition:

postconventional level

Your Definition:
Your Example:
Textbook Definition:

infantile amnesia

Your Definition:
Your Example:
Textbook Definition:

preconventional level

Your Definition:
Your Example:
Textbook Definition:

preoperational stage

Your Definition:
Your Example:
Textbook Definition:

synaptic pruning

Your Definition:
Your Example:
Textbook Definition:

secure attachment

Your Definition:
Your Example:
Textbook Definition:

telegraphic speech

Your Definition:
Your Example:
Textbook Definition:

sensitive periods

Your Definition:
Your Example:
Textbook Definition:

teratogens

Your Definition:
Your Example:
Textbook Definition:

sensorimotor stage

Your Definition:
Your Example:
Textbook Definition:

theory of mind

Your Definition:
Your Example:
Textbook Definition:

CHAPTER 10 | Emotion and Motivation

CHAPTER OVERVIEW

How do you feel right now? Excited? Anxious? Bored? If you are like most of us, your emotional life plays a fairly large role in your sense of well-being. Why do your emotions function as they do? In this chapter, you will find out which parts of the brain are responsible for your emotional life, and you will learn about some effective and ineffective techniques for managing your emotional life.

10.1 How Do We Experience Emotions?

Our experience of an emotion has a subjective interpretation, a physiological response, and associated thought processes. There are three major theories that explain the experience of an emotion. We have the capacity to regulate and manage our emotional experiences.

At the beginning of each section in the Study Guide, there will be guiding questions. Before you read the chapter in your textbook, read through these questions and maybe even attempt to answer them based on either what you've already read or what you think the answer should be. Then as you study the chapter, you can use them to help guide your reading.

10.1 Guiding Questions

To guide your reading of the text, review the following questions. Then, as you read the chapter, look for the answers to these questions. You may want to note in your textbook where you find these answers.

1. Distinguish between primary and secondary emotions.

2. Compare and contrast the James-Lange, Cannon-Bard, and Schacter-Singer two-factor theories of emotion.

3. Discuss the roles that the amygdala and prefrontal cortex play in emotional experience.

4. Define misattribution of arousal and excitation transfer.

5. Discuss common strategies that people use to regulate their emotional states.

NOW READ Section 10.1 "How Do We Experience Emotions?" keeping these questions in mind.

REVIEW: Now that you've read this section, go back to the 10.1 Guiding Questions and see if you can answer them based on what you've read. This is a check on your reading. If you can't answer a question, you need to go back to the text to reread that section.

VISUAL SUMMARY: Below is a summary of the major concepts in this section. To check your comprehension of the chapter, read the summary and ask yourself if you understand the concepts. If the concepts seem unfamiliar to you, you may want to go back to the book and reread those sections. This text is taken from the Visual Summaries on StudySpace at wwnorton.com/studyspace.

I. Emotions Are Feelings Comprised of Subjective Evaluation, Physiological Processes, and Cognitive Beliefs

II. Emotions Have a Subjective Component
   A. Primary emotions are:
      i. evolutionarily adaptive.
      ii. anger, fear, sadness, disgust, happiness, possibly surprise and contempt.

B. Secondary emotions are:
  i. blends of primary emotions.
  ii. remorse, guilt, submission, anticipation.
C. Negative affect and positive affect are independent but can co-occur.

III. Emotions Have a Physiological Component
A. James-Lange theory: perception of specific pattern of bodily responses leads to experience of emotion.
B. Facial feedback hypothesis: facial expressions trigger experience of emotion.
C. Cannon-Bard theory: environmental information leads to physical reaction and experience of emotion.
D. Amygdala: processes emotional significance and generates emotional/behavioral reactions.
E. Prefrontal cortex:
  i. right associated with negative affect.
  ii. left associated with positive affect.

IV. Emotions Have a Cognitive Component
A. Schachter-Singer two-factor theory: situation evokes physiological response (arousal) and cognitive interpretation (emotion label).
B. Excitation transfer: attribution of physical state to wrong emotion.

V. We Regulate Our Emotional States
A. Effective strategies: distraction (best) and humor.
B. Ineffective strategies: thought suppression and rumination.

REINFORCE: Are you ready to check your knowledge of this section? Answer the following multiple-choice questions with your textbook closed.

1. Which of the following is a secondary emotion?
   a. fear
   b. sadness
   c. shame
   d. happiness

2. Jason and Cora are riding on a roller coaster, which is producing high levels of arousal. They both attribute their aroused state to romantic feelings for each other. The arousal caused by the roller coaster is the _____ component of emotion.
   a. physiological
   b. subjective
   c. cognitive
   d. affective

3. Alexithymia occurs because damage to the _____ causes the physiological messages associated with emotions to fail to reach the brain centers that interpret emotions.
   a. amygdala
   b. limbic system
   c. temporal lobe
   d. prefrontal cortex

4. In the mythical country of Xacandra, people experience an emotion they call revzola. Revzola is associated with particular states of arousal, and the people who experience it strongly do better in Xacandran society. When Xacandran psychologists explored nearby countries, they discovered that every culture had an emotion like revzola, though they called it by different names. In terms of the circumplex model of emotions, revzola is a _____ emotion.
   a. nonadaptive
   b. primary
   c. secondary
   d. cross-culturally congruent

5. In a song from the musical *The King and I,* the lead character sings about whistling when she feels afraid to hide her fear and about finally losing her fear. The notion that acting as though you are not afraid keeps you from feeling afraid is compatible with which theory of emotion?
   a. Cannon-Bard
   b. James-Lange
   c. Schacter-Singer two-factor
   d. cerebral symmetry

6. As Jimmy meets his blind date for the first time, he becomes extremely happy as a result of his brain's interpreting the person as attractive and his heart's starting to pound at the same time. These responses can explained through which theory of emotion?
   a. Cannon-Bard
   b. James-Lange
   c. Schacter-Singer two-factor
   d. cerebral symmetry

7. Danny, who has a damaged amygdala, accidentally spilled kerosene on a campfire and got badly burned. Later, Danny:
   a. knows fire is dangerous and has a strong conditioned fear response to it
   b. does not think fire is dangerous and has no conditioned fear of it
   c. does not think fire is dangerous, but becomes terrified around it
   d. knows fire is dangerous but has no conditioned fear of it

8. Participants in a psychology experiment view photographs that elicit happiness, fear, or sadness. A week later, they view photographs and are asked to identify

the ones they have seen before. Their memories will be strongest for the:
a. sad pictures
b. happy pictures
c. frightening pictures
d. calm pictures

9. Contemporary thinking about the role of the amygdala in emotion holds that the fast path from the thalamus to the amygdala _____ , and the slow path from the thalamus to the sensory cortex to the amygdala _____.
   a. evaluates whether a threat exists; prepares someone to respond
   b. prepares someone to respond; evaluates whether a threat exists
   c. selects a response; determines if that is the appropriate response
   d. determines which response is appropriate; selects that response

10. Jason is fascinated by his physics course; he gets excited every time he walks into class. However, Jason has never cared about science, so he does not recognize his excitement as due to the class. Instead, he decides that he is attracted to his lab partner. Jason's misattribution of his arousal is compatible with which theory of emotion?
    a. Cannon-Bard
    b. James-Lange
    c. Schacter-Singer two-factor
    d. cerebral symmetry

11. Blake is waiting to hear whether he has been accepted to medical school. He is so anxious that he is having trouble working. To cope with the situation, he tries to keep himself from thinking about medical school or the admissions process. By doing this, Blake is attempting to:
    a. regulate his emotions
    b. distract himself from his anxiety
    c. use rumination
    d. use a highly effective technique for modifying mood

WHAT DID YOU MISS? Check your answers against the Answer Key at the end of this chapter of the Study Guide. The Answer Key also lists the page(s) in your text where each question is explained. If you missed any questions, go to the pages indicated in the Answer Key, reread those sections, go back to the questions, and see if you can answer them correctly this time.

ANOTHER OPPORTUNITY TO REVIEW: Answer these questions without your textbook. As a rule of thumb, if you can write only a few words about these questions, you probably need to go back and review.

1. Distinguish between primary and secondary emotions.

_____

_____

2. Compare and contrast the James-Lange, Cannon-Bard, and Schacter-Singer two-factor theories of emotion. ____

_____

_____

3. Discuss the roles that the amygdala and prefrontal cortex play in emotional experience. _____

_____

_____

4. Define misattribution of arousal and excitation transfer.

_____

_____

_____

5. Discuss common strategies that people use to regulate their emotional states. _____

_____

_____

WHAT DO I NEED TO KNOW? Based on what you've discovered above, what are the areas where you need to focus your studying? Which objectives do you need to spend more time mastering? Write this information down in your own words.

1. _____

2. _____

3. _____

4. _____

5. _____

6. _____

10.2 How Are Emotions Adaptive?

Cross-culturally, emotions are surprisingly similar and serve the same purpose. We use emotions coupled with our thoughts to help us in making decisions. We consider the emotional impact of our choices in the decision-making process. How do emotions such as guilt and embarrassment affect our

---

TRY IT

Be Here, Right Now

Think back to a time when you experienced strong negative emotions. How badly did you suffer? Would you have preferred to regulate your emotions? Controlling one's emotional life can be a great skill. As you've read in this chapter, however, trying to make emotions "go away" rarely works.

A technique that can be helpful in managing painful emotions is mindfulness. The core belief behind mindfulness is that if we are fully present to our emotions, they become easier to manage. What is so great about the "present moment"? You can't change the past. No matter how much you prepare for the future, it remains unknown and often doesn't turn out as expected. Consequently, the only point that you can know and change with certainty is the present moment, right now.

There are various ways in which you can practice this skill. All of these ways share the decision to inhabit the current moment rather than focus on the past or on the future. How can you practice this? Use your breath as an anchor. As you are working or thinking, imagine that you are breathing into each of your actions or thoughts. Even if your present moment is unpleasant, see what happens if you focus your breath on what you are experiencing. Be compassionate and gentle with yourself. See if you notice any differences in your mood as you do this. To start, try this technique for about 5 to 10 minutes at a stretch and then extend the time. The longer you practice this mindfulness skill, the more effective it will be.

---

interpersonal relationships? You might be surprised to learn that these emotions strengthen our relationships.

10.2 Guiding Questions

To guide your reading of the text, review the following questions. Then, as you read the chapter, look for the answers to these questions. You may want to note in your textbook where you find these answers.

1. Review research on the universality of emotional expressions.

2. Define display rules.

3. Discuss the impact of emotions on decision making and self-regulation.

4. Discuss the interpersonal functions of guilt and embarrassment.

NOW READ Section 10.2 "How Are Emotions Adaptive?" keeping these questions in mind.

REVIEW: Now that you've read this section, go back to the 10.2 Guiding Questions and see if you can answer them based on what you've read. This is a check on your reading. If you can't answer a question, you need to go back to the text to reread that section.

VISUAL SUMMARY: Below is a summary of the major concepts in this section. To check your comprehension of the chapter, read the summary and ask yourself if you understand the concepts. If the concepts seem unfamiliar to you, you may want to go back to the book and reread those sections. This text is taken from the Visual Summaries on StudySpace at wwnorton.com/studyspace.

VI. Facial Expressions Communicate Emotion
   A. Eyes, mouth, face, and context play roles in interpreting emotions.
   B. Facial expression of some emotions is similar across cultures.

VII. Display Rules Differ across Cultures and between the Sexes
   A. Cultural and sex-specific rules differ for appropriate expression of emotions.

VIII. Emotions Serve Cognitive Functions
   A. Speed of emotional responses makes separation of cognition and emotion impossible.
   B. Affect-as-information theory: we use current moods to make judgments.
   C. Somatic markers: bodily reactions arising from emotional evaluation of action's consequences.

IX. Emotions Strengthen Interpersonal Relations
   A. Guilt:
      i. discourages harmful behavior.
      ii. strengthens prosocial behavior.
      iii. can be used for manipulation.
   B. Embarrassment reaffirms close relationships after wrongdoing.

X. Emotions Are the Primary Source of Motivation

REINFORCE: Are you ready to check your knowledge of this section? Answer the following multiple-choice questions with your textbook closed.

1. The part of the face that best expresses emotion on its own is the:
   a. mouth
   b. eyes
   c. jaw
   d. brow

2. The strongest cross-cultural congruence in the identification of emotions seems to involve:
   a. fear
   b. happiness
   c. pain
   d. disgust

3. When Suellen learns that her roommate, Diana, is from Britain, she wonders if Diana is stiff and reserved. She is pleased, but very surprised, when Diana turns out to be bouncy and emotional. Suellen is surprised because Diana's behavior violates:
   a. cross-cultural dominance
   b. gender norms for emotionality
   c. display rules
   d. both a and c

4. Emotions influence decision making in all of the following ways EXCEPT:
   a. we can anticipate our future emotional states, and this anticipation helps guide decision making
   b. emotions provide feedback for quick decision making
   c. when emotions and cognitions are in conflict, cognitions have a stronger impact
   d. emotions influence our perception of risk

5. Tameri and Khai found a house to buy that they really like. The day that they found it, they had been having a wonderful time house hunting and planning their life together. A few days later, after having had a miserable day at work, Khai goes back to look at the house. Khai probably will like the house:
   a. more because it will remind him of Tameri
   b. more because of belief persistence
   c. less because of his bad day at work
   d. less because his second look will be more objective

6. Margarita is a brilliant student. The men that she has dated have had trouble dealing with her academic success. Margarita just won a full scholarship for her last two years of college. She is going to tell her boyfriend at dinner, and she feels nauseated every time she thinks about doing so. Margarita's nausea exemplifies:
   a. somatic marker theory
   b. thought suppression
   c. the dominance of emotions over cognition
   d. conflict between physiological responding and affect

7. Ahava has been working for a week in her company's London office. She finishes the project a day earlier than expected. Initially, she decides to take that free day and explore London. Then she thinks about how much it would please her husband if she came back early and starts to feel guilty. Which of the following factors helps to explain Ahava's feelings of guilt?
   a. She likely had parents who were cold and blaming.
   b. She has a diminished capacity for empathy.
   c. She likely has an overactive amygdala.
   d. She likely experienced warm and supportive parenting as a child.

8. Twin studies have shown that guilt is primarily influenced by:
   a. the social environment
   b. genetics
   c. hormonal fluctuations
   d. gender

9. Sadao makes the same mistakes over and over again. His friends are constantly telling him, "Don't do that. Remember how badly it turned out the last time!" But Sadao never listens. He insists, every time, that this situation is new. According to somatic marker theory, Sadao most likely has damage to his:
   a. amygdala
   b. hippocampus
   c. frontal lobes
   d. thalamus

10. Magdala regards her frequent blushing as a real social failing and wishes she could stop blushing. To help Magdala reconsider the value of her blushing, you might tell her that people who blush:
    a. have better social skills
    b. are more empathetic
    c. look more attractive to the people around them
    d. are more readily forgiven for their mistakes

WHAT DID YOU MISS? Check your answers against the Answer Key at the end of this chapter of the Study Guide. The Answer Key also lists the page(s) in your text where each question is explained. If you missed any questions, go to the pages indicated in the Answer Key, reread those sections, go back to the questions, and see if you can answer them correctly this time.

ANOTHER OPPORTUNITY TO REVIEW: Answer these questions without your textbook. As a rule of thumb, if you can write only a few words about these questions, you probably need to go back and review.

1. Review research on the universality of emotional expressions. _____

2. Define display rules. _____

3. Discuss the impact of emotions on decision making and self-regulation. _____

_____

_____

4. Discuss the interpersonal functions of guilt and embarrassment. _____

_____

_____

WHAT DO I NEED TO KNOW? Based on what you've discovered above, what are the areas where you need to focus your studying? Which objectives do you need to spend more time mastering? Write this information down in your own words.

1. _____

2. _____

3. _____

4. _____

5. _____

6. _____

10.3 How Does Motivation Energize, Direct, and Sustain Behavior?

Why do you want to go to college? Why do you want to be a good friend or partner? Motivations direct and drive us to meet our needs. Some needs are biological, and others are social. When we are deprived of any biological or psychological necessity, our need or drive for that necessity increases. One of our greatest needs is to feel connected to other humans.

10.3 Guiding Questions

To guide your reading of the text, review the following questions. Then, as you read the chapter, look for the answers to these questions. You may want to note in your textbook where you find these answers.

1. Distinguish between a motive, a need, and a drive.

2. Describe Maslow's hierarchy of needs.

3. Describe the Yerkes-Dodson law.

4. Distinguish between extrinsic motivation and intrinsic motivation.

5. Discuss the relationships between self-efficacy, the achievement motive, delayed gratification, and goal achievement.

6. Describe the need to belong theory.

NOW READ Section 10.3 "How Does Motivation Energize, Direct, and Sustain Behavior?" keeping these questions in mind.

REVIEW: Now that you've read this section, go back to the 10.3 Guiding Questions and see if you can answer them based on what you've read. This is a check on your reading. If you can't answer a question, you need to go back to the text to reread that section.

VISUAL SUMMARY: Below is a summary of the major concepts in this section. To check your comprehension of the chapter, read the summary and ask yourself if you understand the concepts. If the concepts seem unfamiliar to you, you may want to go back to the book and reread those sections. This text is taken from the Visual Summaries on StudySpace at wwnorton.com/studyspace.

XI. Multiple Factors Motivate Behavior
   A. Need: a biological or social deficiency.
   B. Need hierarchy: basic survival needs must be met before people want to satisfy higher needs.
   C. Self-actualization: the achievement of personal dreams or aspirations.
   D. Drives: psychological states that motivate organisms to satisfy needs.
   E. Homeostasis: the tendency for bodily functions to remain in equilibrium.
   F. Incentives: external objects/goals that motivate behaviors.
   G. Yerkes-Dodson law: performance increases with arousal up to an optimal point then decreases.
   H. Pleasure principle: according to Freud, people are driven to seek pleasure and avoid pain.
   I. We engage in pleasurable behaviors that do not necessarily satisfy biological needs.

XII. Some Behaviors Are Motivated for Their Own Sake
   A. Extrinsic motivation: performing an activity because of external goals.
   B. Intrinsic motivation: performing an activity because of associated value.
   C. Self-determination theory: people are motivated to satisfy needs for competence and relatedness.
   D. Self-perception theory: people draw conclusions based on their behavior, unaware of their motives.

XIII. We Set Goals to Achieve
  A. Self-regulation: changing one's behavior to attain personal goals.
  B. Focusing on short-term, concrete goals facilitates achieving long-term goals.
  C. Self-efficacy: expecting that goal-directed efforts will lead to success.
  D. Achievement motive: the desire to do well relative to standards of excellence.
  E. Delayed gratification: degree of self-control predicts physical health, substance dependence, higher grades, and financial solvency.

XIV. We Have a Need to Belong
  A. Need for interpersonal attachment:
    i. is fundamental and adaptive.
    ii. motivates development of strategies for making and maintaining attachments.
  B. In a stressful situation, people prefer to be with other people in same situation.

REINFORCE: Are you ready to check your knowledge of this section? Answer the following multiple-choice questions with your textbook closed.

1. Motivational states are directive, which means they:
  a. call attention to important goals
  b. activate us to do something
  c. guide us to behaviors that satisfy our goals
  d. determine a pattern of physiological activation

2. Bingwen does not like formal clothes, but he must buy a suit for his sister's wedding. He goes to seven stores before he finds a suit that he likes. Bingwen's going to buy a suit shows the _____ quality of motivation. His search through seven stores shows the _____ quality of motivation.
  a. energizing; directive
  b. energizing; persistent
  c. directive; energizing
  d. directive; persistent

3. Reiko has not slept for almost 2 days while she studies for finals. She finally realizes that she is exhausted and goes home from the library to sleep. Reiko's exhaustion reflects a(n) _____ for sleep.
  a. goal
  b. incentive
  c. need
  d. drive

4. Vincent is a brilliant but impoverished artist. He spends all day pushing the boundaries of his art and finds complete satisfaction in his achievements, but he has little to eat and lives in squalor. His wife has left him, and most of his friends keep their distance because they do not understand his art. Why would Vincent's life be problematic for Maslow's need hierarchy?
  a. Satisfaction is an emotion, not a need.
  b. Lower needs must be met before higher needs.
  c. Satisfying the need for achievement requires success.
  d. Lower and higher needs can't be organized in a single system.

5. Depti reads the paper every day only because she feels a need to keep current with world events. Jalila reads the paper every day only so that her friends and colleagues will be impressed by how well-informed she is. Depti reads the paper because of _____ motivation; Jalila reads the paper because of _____ motivation.
  a. extrinsic; intrinsic
  b. intrinsic; extrinsic
  c. achievement; affiliation
  d. affiliation; achievement

6. Maslow's need hierarchy has been criticized for:
  a. lacking empirical support
  b. being limited to Western cultures
  c. defining the nature of a need too broadly
  d. underestimating the role of physiological factors

7. The more that Jolene's mother criticizes Jolene's boyfriend, the more determined Jolene is to stay with her boyfriend. Jolene's behavior can be most clearly explained by:
  a. intrinsic motivation
  b. the pleasure principle
  c. self-perception theory
  d. psychological reactance

8. Ruth has weighed 130 pounds all of her adult life. During her recent pregnancy, she gained 10 pounds. Within a few months, Ruth's weight returned naturally to 130 pounds. For Ruth, 130 pounds was a(n) _____, and her body went back to it through a process of homeostasis.
  a. optimal weight
  b. equilibrium
  c. set-point
  d. incentive

9. Cesar has done so well in his economics class that he needs to earn only 43 of 100 points on the final exam to receive an A in the class. Cesar still studies a lot because he wants to get an A on the exam. Cesar's behavior is being motivated by a(n):
  a. drive
  b. need
  c. habit
  d. incentive

10. Pavati is a competitive gymnast who has made it to the final round of the Olympic trials. She is intensely motivated to perform at her absolute peak. Given your knowledge of the effects of arousal on performance, you might advise her to _____ because _____.
    a. calm down; very high arousal can hurt performance
    b. calm down; she will lose focus and hurt her performance
    c. stay intensely motivated; very high arousal will help performance
    d. stay intensely motivated; it will increase her focus and help performance

WHAT DID YOU MISS? Check your answers against the Answer Key at the end of this chapter of the Study Guide. The Answer Key also lists the page(s) in your text where each question is explained. If you missed any questions, go to the pages indicated in the Answer Key, reread those sections, go back to the questions, and see if you can answer them correctly this time.

ANOTHER OPPORTUNITY TO REVIEW: Answer these questions without your textbook. As a rule of thumb, if you can write only a few words about these questions, you probably need to go back and review.

1. Distinguish between a motive, a need, and a drive. _____

2. Describe Maslow's hierarchy of needs. _____

3. Describe the Yerkes-Dodson law. _____

4. Distinguish between extrinsic motivation and intrinsic motivation. _____

5. Discuss the relationships between self-efficacy, the achievement motive, delayed gratification, and goal achievement. _____

6. Describe the need to belong theory. _____

WHAT DO I NEED TO KNOW? Based on what you've discovered above, what are the areas where you need to focus your studying? Which objectives do you need to spend more time mastering? Write this information down in your own words.

1. _____
2. _____
3. _____
4. _____
5. _____
6. _____

10.4 What Motivates Eating?

Obesity is a major health problem in many countries. What motivates us to eat? What parts of the brain are associated with eating, and what hormones drive hunger or allow us to feel satiated? Does culture play a role in eating behavior?

10.4 Guiding Questions

To guide your reading of the text, review the following questions. Then, as you read the chapter, look for the answers to these questions. You may want to note in your textbook where you find these answers.

1. Discuss the impact of time, taste, and cultural learning on eating behavior.
2. Identify neural structures associated with eating.
3. Describe the glucostatic and lipostatic theories of eating.
4. Discuss the role that hormones play in regulating eating behavior.

NOW READ Section 10.4 "What Motivates Eating?" keeping these questions in mind.

REVIEW: Now that you've read this section, go back to the 10.4 Guiding Questions and see if you can answer them based on what you've read. This is a check on your reading. If you can't answer a question, you need to go back to the text to reread that section.

VISUAL SUMMARY: Below is a summary of the major concepts in this section. To check your comprehension of the chapter, read the summary and ask yourself if you understand the concepts. If the concepts seem unfamiliar to you, you may want to go back to the book and reread those sections. This text is taken from the Visual Summaries on StudySpace at wwnorton.com/studyspace.

XV. Time and Taste Set the Stage
   A. We have been classically conditioned to associate eating with mealtimes.
   B. Sensory-specific satiety: we grow tired of just one flavor.

XVI. Culture Plays a Role
   A. Food preferences:
       i. determined by familiarity.
       ii. reinforced by norms for what to eat (guidelines or cuisine).

XVII. Brain Structures, Homeostasis, and Hormones Direct the Action
   A. Hypothalamus and prefrontal cortex influence eating behavior.
   B. Glucostatic theory of eating: glucose level in bloodstream triggers hunger.
   C. Lipostatic theory of eating: loss of body fat leads to hunger.
   D. Hormonal activity:
       i. associated with maintenance of normal weight or weight loss.
       ii. associated with triggering of eating.

REINFORCE: Are you ready to check your knowledge of this section? Answer the following multiple-choice questions with your textbook closed.

1. A rat has been fed a single kind of rat chow and has maintained a steady weight. If the rat is offered high-fat junk food, such as cookies, candy, or potato chips, the rat will:
   a. refuse the junk food after the first day because it lacks nutrients
   b. supplement the rat chow with junk food and gradually gain weight
   c. initially eat huge amounts, then return to its set point weight
   d. eat huge amounts indefinitely and become obese

2. When Gavan arrives at his morning meeting, he is quite full. Everyone else is eating the delicious-looking pastries that are available. After a few minutes, Gavan feels quite hungry. The best explanation for Gavan's hunger comes from:
   a. a failure of satiety cues
   b. poor self-regulation
   c. classical conditioning
   d. observational learning

3. Which of the following actions will NOT increase the likelihood that a young child will learn to like an unfamiliar food?

TRY IT

Give Yourself a Boost

It can be very easy to focus on our problems, ignore our strengths, and feel anxious or depressed as a result. Therefore, it can be helpful to routinely remind ourselves about the good things that are happening to us and what our strengths are. Consider the following technique.

Whenever you feel down, remind yourself about three small or large blessings that you experienced recently. Then remind yourself about three of your accomplishments, keeping in mind that accomplishments can also be both large and small. Finally, remind yourself about three aspects of your personality that you like. To make this technique handy, remember the acronym BAT (blessings, accomplishments, and personality traits) (Frisch, 2006). See how you feel about yourself if you try this every day for a couple of weeks.

   a. The child is initially given small amounts of the food.
   b. The food is initially sweetened.
   c. The food is initially put inside a food that the child likes.
   d. The child watches a family member eat the food.

4. Damaging the ventromedial region of the hypothalamus of a rat will cause the rat to become:
   a. dangerously thin
   b. hyperactive
   c. comatose
   d. obese

5. Remy the rat has lost his appetite and is losing so much weight that he is in danger of dying. Remy most probably has damage to the _____ region of the hypothalamus.
   a. ventromedial
   b. lateral
   c. anterior
   d. superior

6. Morwenna had always been thin. After suffering a stroke, she became fascinated with food and consequently put on weight. A brain scan would likely show that Morwenna has:
   a. more activity in the limbic system
   b. less activity in the limbic system
   c. more activity in the ventromedial hypothalamus
   d. less activity in the ventromedial hypothalamus

7. Food preferences are affected most strongly by:
   a. protein content of the food
   b. carbohydrate content of the food

c. familiarity with the food

d. experiences with a wide variety of foods

8. Long-term regulation of body fat seems to involve which hormone?

   a. leptin

   b. glucose

   c. oxytocin

   d. estrogen

9. An animal that continues to eat despite an adequate diet may have a dysregulation in which hormone?

   a. glucose

   b. ghrelin

   c. oxytocin

   d. androgen

WHAT DID YOU MISS? Check your answers against the Answer Key at the end of this chapter of the Study Guide. The Answer Key also lists the page(s) in your text where each question is explained. If you missed any questions, go to the pages indicated in the Answer Key, reread those sections, go back to the questions, and see if you can answer them correctly this time.

ANOTHER OPPORTUNITY TO REVIEW: Answer these questions without your textbook. As a rule of thumb, if you can write only a few words about these questions, you probably need to go back and review.

1. Discuss the impact of time, taste, and cultural learning on eating behavior. _____

   _____

   _____

2. Identify neural structures associated with eating. _____

   _____

   _____

3. Describe the glucostatic and lipostatic theories of eating.

   _____

   _____

4. Discuss the role that hormones play in regulating eating behavior. _____

   _____

   _____

WHAT DO I NEED TO KNOW? Based on what you've discovered above, what are the areas where you need to focus your studying? Which objectives do you need to spend more time mastering? Write this information down in your own words.

1. _____

2. _____

3. _____

4. _____

5. _____

6. _____

10.5 What Motivates Sexual Behavior?

The sexual response of humans follows a predictable cycle. Hormones and neurotransmitters fuel the sexual response or, in some situations, dampen it. The sexual behavior of men and women is strongly affected by culture, and each culture includes scripts for appropriate behavior.

How is sexual identity determined, and how flexible is it?

10.5 Guiding Questions

To guide your reading of the text, review the following questions. Then, as you read the chapter, look for the answers to these questions. You may want to note in your textbook where you find these answers.

1. Review the four stages of the sexual response cycle.

2. Discuss the role that hormones play in sexual behavior.

3. Identify the primary neurotransmitters involved in sexual behavior.

4. Discuss sex differences in sexual behavior and in mate preferences.

5. Review contemporary theories of sexual orientation.

NOW READ Section 10.5 "What Motivates Sexual Behavior?" keeping these questions in mind.

REVIEW: Now that you've read this section, go back to the 10.5 Guiding Questions and see if you can answer them based on what you've read. This is a check on your reading. If you can't answer a question, you need to go back to the text to reread that section.

VISUAL SUMMARY: Below is a summary of the major concepts in this section. To check your comprehension of the chapter, read the summary and ask yourself if you understand the concepts. If the concepts seem unfamiliar to you, you may want to go back to the book and reread those sections. This text is taken from the Visual Summaries on StudySpace at wwnorton.com/studyspace.

XVIII. Biology Influences Sexual Behavior
   A. Sexual response cycle: excitement, plateau, orgasm, resolution.
   B. Sex hormones (androgens and estrogen):
      i. influence sexual behavior.
      ii. activate reproductive behavior.
   C. Neurotransmitters: dopamine, serotonin, and nitric oxide play roles in sexual behavior.
   D. Visual erotic stimulation:
      i. differs between men and women.
      ii. is related to neurotransmitters and menstrual cycle.

XIX. Cultural Scripts and Cultural Rules Shape Sexual Interactions
   A. Scripts: cognitive and cultural beliefs about enactment of sexual episodes.
   B. Regulation of sexual behavior:
      i. is cross-cultural.
      ii. may have various motivations.
   C. Men and women differ in level of sexual activity and sexual/mating strategies.
   D. Mate preference:
      i. differences exist between males and females.
      ii. social context plays a role.

XX. We Differ in Our Sexual Orientations
   A. Differences in sexual orientation do not appear related to environmental factors.
   B. Biology:
      i. prenatal exposure to hormones may play role in sexual orientation.
      ii. heritability of sexual orientation is greater for males than females.
   C. There is little evidence that sexual orientation can be changed.

REINFORCE: Are you ready to check your knowledge of this section? Answer the following multiple-choice questions with your textbook closed.

1. Which hormone influences sexual receptivity in many nonhuman female animals?
   a. oxytocin
   b. androgen
   c. nitric oxide
   d. estrogen

2. The most important hormone for sexual functioning in men is _____ and in women is _____.
   a. testosterone; estrogen

   b. estrogen; estrogen
   c. testosterone; testosterone
   d. androgen; progesterone

3. A group of rats has had an area of their brains damaged, resulting in a disruption of sexual behavior. The area that was damaged was most likely the:
   a. amygdala
   b. hypothalamus
   c. prefrontal cortex
   d. cerebellum

4. Women have more choice and control of their sexuality than females of many species. This difference is largely because of the lesser effect of _____ on women.
   a. oxytocin
   b. androgen
   c. nitric oxide
   d. estrogen

5. Massoud is an international student studying in America. In his culture, women are expected to be very modest. He really likes Hillary, an American girl whom he has gotten to know in his art history class. However, Massoud is distressed and is reevaluating his opinion of Hillary because she spontaneously kissed him on their second date. Though she probably did not realize it, Hillary has:
   a. offended Massoud's sense of his masculinity
   b. violated Massoud's cultural script
   c. implied a more serious relationship than Massoud assumed
   d. made Massoud fear being trapped

6. Cross-cultural comparisons of sexual motivation in men and women have found that:
   a. men and women have roughly equal sexual motivation
   b. women have equal sexual motivation, but are more culturally constrained
   c. men have a higher level of sexual motivation
   d. differences between men and women are culture specific

7. Susan is preparing her profile for an online dating service. According to the sexual strategies theory, she should emphasize which of the following characteristics to be more attractive to prospective males?
   a. intelligent
   b. high wage earner
   c. physically appealing
   d. well-educated

8. The finding that men would like to have more sexual partners than would women makes sense from the perspective of evolutionary psychology. This is because:

a. women lose value as potential mates with each additional partner

b. having multiple partners makes men appear more desirable

c. women are less likely to have healthy babies with multiple partners

d. men can increase their number of offspring with multiple partners

9. Who has the highest probability of having a same-sex sexual orientation?

a. Hui, who has an identical twin brother who is gay

b. Shanaz, who has an identical twin sister who is a lesbian

c. Carlos, who has a fraternal twin sister who is a lesbian

d. Hui and Shanaz have equal probabilities

10. One area of the hypothalamus typically differs in size between men and women. The size of this area in gay men is comparable to that of heterosexual women, and the size of this area in lesbians is comparable to that of heterosexual men. What is the most reasonable interpretation of these findings?

a. This area of the hypothalamus plays a role in the development of sexual orientation.

b. This area of the hypothalamus develops in response to sexual orientation.

c. This area of the hypothalamus is influenced by the same underlying genetic pattern as sexual orientation.

d. A causal connection cannot be deduced from this finding.

WHAT DID YOU MISS? Check your answers against the Answer Key at the end of this chapter of the Study Guide. The Answer Key also lists the page(s) in your text where each question is explained. If you missed any questions, go to the pages indicated in the Answer Key, reread those sections, go back to the questions, and see if you can answer them correctly this time.

ANOTHER OPPORTUNITY TO REVIEW: Answer these questions without your textbook. As a rule of thumb, if you can write only a few words about these questions, you probably need to go back and review.

1. Review the four stages of the sexual response cycle. ____

_____

_____

2. Discuss the role that hormones play in sexual behavior.

_____

_____

_____

3. Identify the primary neurotransmitters involved in sexual behavior. _____

_____

_____

4. Discuss sex differences in sexual behavior and in mate preferences. _____

_____

_____

5. Review contemporary theories of sexual orientation. ___

_____

_____

WHAT DO I NEED TO KNOW? Based on what you've discovered above, what are the areas where you need to focus your studying? Which objectives do you need to spend more time mastering? Write this information down in your own words.

1. _____

2. _____

3. _____

4. _____

5. _____

6. _____

WHAT MATTERS TO ME: What facts in this chapter are personally relevant to you?

_____

_____

_____

_____

CHAPTER SUMMARY

10.1 How Do We Experience Emotions?

- *Emotions Have a Subjective Component:* Primary emotions are evolutionarily adaptive and are universal across cultures. They include anger, fear, sadness, disgust, happiness, and possibly surprise and contempt. Secondary emotions are blends of the primary emotions. Emotions may be described using two dimensions: valence and activation. Negative affect and positive affect are independent.

- *Emotions Have a Physiological Component:* The James-Lange theory of emotion maintains that we perceive patterns of bodily responses and, as a result of our perceptions, experience emotion. The Cannon-Bard theory of emotion maintains that the mind and body experience emotion independently. Consistent with both theories, studies have demonstrated that emotions are associated with changes in bodily states. Research points to important roles of the amygdala and the prefrontal cortex in the production and experience of emotion.

- *Emotions Have a Cognitive Component:* According to the Schachter-Singer two-factor theory of emotion, emotions involve a physiological component and a cognitive component or interpretation. The interpretation determines the emotion that we feel. Misattribution of arousal occurs when people misidentify the source of their arousal. Excitation transfer occurs when residual arousal caused by one event is transferred to a new stimulus.

- *We Regulate Our Emotional States:* We use various strategies to regulate or manage our emotional states. Humor and distraction are effective strategies for regulating negative affect, whereas rumination and thought suppression are not effective strategies for regulating negative affect.

10.2 How Are Emotions Adaptive?

- *Facial Expressions Communicate Emotion:* Facial expressions of emotion are adaptive because they communicate how we feel. Across cultures, there are some expressions of emotion that are universally recognized. These include happiness, sadness, anger, and pride.

- *Display Rules Differ across Cultures and between the Sexes:* Display rules are learned through socialization and dictate how and when people express emotions. Females express emotions more readily, frequently, easily, and intensely than males, possibly as a consequence of display rules.

- *Emotions Serve Cognitive Functions:* We use our emotions as a guide when making decisions. Indeed, emotions often serve as heuristic guides, enabling quick decisions to be made. Somatic marker theory maintains that we use our bodily reactions to emotional events to regulate our behaviors. That is, we interpret our body's responses and use that information to help make decisions.

- *Emotions Strengthen Interpersonal Relations:* Emotions facilitate the maintenance and repair of social bonds. Guilt serves several functions. For example, it discourages people from engaging in actions that may harm their relationships and encourages people to engage in actions that will strengthen their relation-

ships. Embarrassment rectifies interpersonal awkwardness and restores social bonds after a social error or wrongdoing has been committed.

10.3 How Does Motivation Energize, Direct, and Sustain Behavior?

- *Multiple Factors Motivate Behavior:* Motives activate, direct, and sustain behaviors that will satisfy a need. Needs create arousal, and the response to being aroused is a drive to satisfy the need. Maslow's hierarchy proposes five needs: physiological, safety, belonging and love, esteem, and self-actualization needs. *Homeostasis* refers to the body's attempts to maintain a state of equilibrium. The Yerkes-Dodson law states that a person performs best when his or her level of arousal is neither too low nor too high.

- *Some Behaviors Are Motivated for Their Own Sake:* Behaviors that are extrinsically motivated are directed toward the achievement of an external goal. Behaviors that are intrinsically motivated fulfill no obvious purpose. They are performed simply because they are pleasurable. Extrinsic rewards decrease intrinsic motivation because they decrease our experience of autonomy and competence or because the reward replaces the goal of pleasure.

- *We Set Goals to Achieve:* Challenging and specific goals are most likely to lead to success. People who are high in self-efficacy and have a high need to achieve are more likely to set challenging but attainable goals. Moreover, those who are able to delay gratification as they work toward their goals are more likely to be successful. Several strategies facilitate delayed gratification, including distraction and the use of cold cognitions rather than hot cognitions.

- *We Have a Need to Belong:* Humans have a fundamental need to belong. Evolutionary theorists maintain that this need provided a survival advantage to our ancestors. Our need to belong facilitates the development of friendships, makes us sensitive to social exclusion, and produces feelings of emptiness and despair in the absence of other people. When we are anxious, we seek out similar others. Other people provide information that helps us determine if we are acting appropriately.

10.4 What Motivates Eating?

- *Time and Taste Set the Stage:* Eating is greatly affected by learning. Through classical conditioning, we associate eating with regular mealtimes. Having a variety of flavors results in more eating. Sensory-specific satiety refers to our tendency to eat less when there is little variety in our food choices.

- *Culture Plays a Role:* Culture determines what a person considers edible. Researchers have found that infants have an innate preference for sweet tastes, but children can learn to like most foods—particularly those foods offered by family members.

- *Brain Structures, Homeostasis, and Hormones Direct the Action:* The hypothalamus is the brain structure most closely identified with eating. Rats whose ventromedial hypothalami were damaged experienced hyperphagia. That is, they consumed huge quantities of food. By contrast, rats whose lateral hypothalami were damaged exhibited aphagia. That is, they stopped eating to the point of death. Other structures that influence our eating behavior include a region of the frontal lobes (sensory-specific satiety, processing of taste cues) and the limbic system (cravings). Blood glucose monitors, set-point sensors for body fat, and the hormones leptin and ghrelin also play important roles in determining how much we eat.

10.5 What Motivates Sexual Behavior?

- *Biology Influences Sexual Behavior:* The four stages of the human sexual response cycle are excitement, plateau, orgasm, and resolution. Testosterone and oxytocin influence the sexual behavior of both women and men. Among the neurotransmitters that affect sexual functioning among women and men are dopamine, serotonin, and nitric oxide. Although women's sexual behavior does not appear to vary across the menstrual cycle, some data show that heterosexual women's preferences for masculine-looking and self-assured men increases during ovulation.
- *Cultural Scripts and Cultural Rules Shape Sexual Interactions:* Sexual scripts are beliefs about how women and men should behave in sexual relationships. Sexual scripts are socially determined and differ across cultures. The double standard is one means by which sexual behavior is regulated in many cultures; it allows men greater sexual latitude than it allows women. Research has demonstrated that, around the world, men exhibit greater motivation for sexual activity and sexual variety than women. According to sexual strategies theory, women and men have evolved distinct mating strategies to maximize their reproductive potential. For example, women tend to be more selective in choosing partners because their investments in pregnancy and child care are intensive. In contrast, men are less selective in choosing partners because they are not required to invest as much in potential offspring. In addition, women tend to seek men who are good providers for their children because good providers will increase the likelihood that the women's offspring will survive. In contrast, men tend to seek attractive women because attractiveness suggests fertility.
- *We Differ in Our Sexual Orientations:* A number of biological theories of sexual orientation have been pro-

posed. In particular, theories have implicated prenatal hormone exposure, genes, and the hypothalamus in determining sexual orientation. Although research has emerged to support these theories, the data are largely correlational, precluding causal statements. Many contemporary researchers maintain that both biological and environmental factors influence sexual orientation.

PUTTING IT ALL TOGETHER

Answer these questions to check your knowledge of the material in this chapter.

1. Describe three ways in which the processing of emotional information can suffer due to damage to the amygdala. Give an example for each, demonstrating what an individual will be unable to do.

2. According to Ekman's research, an American traveling in China will be able to recognize which emotions? Of the five basic emotions described by Ekman, which would the American be most likely to recognize, and which would the American be least likely to recognize? Would you expect Chinese people to express emotions in the same way and the same situations as American people?

3. Tariq works very hard in school and earns excellent grades. How would extrinsic motivation explain his hard work? Give an example. How would intrinsic motivation explain Tariq's hard work? Give an example. Tariq's studying was found to decrease when he was given money for studying. Why would this happen?

4. Both culture and biology influence eating. Describe how the culture you live in influences the kinds of things you eat. Describe how different kinds of brain damage may influence how much someone eats.

5. William and Kate, both young adults, would like to have children. According to sexual strategies theory, what will be Kate's primary concerns about reproduction? What will be William's concerns? According to sexual strategies theory, how will Kate and William differ in what they look for in a mate? In what ways will they be similar? Do you think that sexual strategies theory is correct? Why or why not?

ANSWER KEY FOR REINFORCE QUESTIONS

Section 10.1

1. c   p. 423
2. a   p. 422
3. d   p. 423
4. b   p. 423
5. b   p. 424

6. a   p. 425
7. d   p. 425
8. c   p. 426
9. b   p. 426
10. c   pp. 428–429
11. a   pp. 430–431

Section 10.2

1. b   p. 433
2. b   p. 433
3. c   p. 434
4. c   p. 435
5. c   p. 437
6. a   p. 437
7. d   p. 439
8. a   pp. 438–439
9. c   p. 437
10. d   p. 439

Section 10.3

1. c   p. 440
2. d   p. 440
3. c   p. 441
4. b   p. 441
5. b   p. 444
6. a   p. 441
7. d   p. 446
8. c   p. 442
9. d   p. 442
10. a   p. 443

Section 10.4

1. d   p. 453
2. c   p. 452
3. c   p. 453
4. d   p. 454
5. b   p. 454
6. a   p. 454
7. c   p. 453
8. a   p. 455
9. b   p. 455

Section 10.5

1. d   pp. 457–458
2. c   p. 458
3. b   p. 458
4. d   p. 458
5. b   p. 459
6. c   p. 460
7. c   p. 461
8. d   p. 460
9. a   p. 463
10. d   p. 463

HINTS FOR PUTTING IT ALL TOGETHER QUESTIONS

1. Damage to the amygdala results in problems with conditioning (learning) of fear responses, memory of emotional events, and processing of facial expressions of emotion. Describe each of these problems, giving an example for each.

2. Present Ekman's findings on facial expressions across cultures, describing Ekman's five basic emotions. Also, draw on the research to explain which of these basic emotions are most likely to be recognized and which are least likely to be recognized. When discussing the differences in people's expression of emotion, refer to differences in display rules based on culture.

3. Refer to an external goal when describing extrinsic motivation. When describing intrinsic motivation, explain that the behavior satisfies Tariq in some way. When explaining why his studying decreased when rewarded, you need to include intrinsic motivation, self-determination theory, and self-perception theory. Make sure you address what motivates people according to each theory.

4. When addressing culture, include the roles of experience, parenting, exposure, and cultural taboos. When addressing brain damage, describe the effects of lesions in different parts of the hypothalamus.

5. Discuss how the bearing and raising of children makes the adaptive concerns of women different from those of men. Include how women's concerns with stability and men's concerns with fertility will influence mate selection. Also include the characteristics both men and women value and the characteristics both men and women avoid. When giving your opinion about whether you think sexual strategies theory is correct, try to think of examples (based either on your own observations or on things you see in the media) that support the theory. In addition, provide examples that do not support the theory.

REFERENCE

Frisch, M. (2006). *Quality of Life Therapy: Applying a Life Satisfaction Approach to Positive Psychology and Cognitive Therapy*. New York: John Wiley & Sons.

KEY TERMS EXERCISES

First, fill in your own definition and example for each term. Then check each term against the textbook's definition. These exercises can also be cut out and used as flash cards.

arousal

Your Definition:
Your Example:
Textbook Definition:

extrinsic motivation

Your Definition:
Your Example:
Textbook Definition:

display rules

Your Definition:
Your Example:
Textbook Definition:

homeostasis

Your Definition:
Your Example:
Textbook Definition:

drive

Your Definition:
Your Example:
Textbook Definition:

incentives

Your Definition:
Your Example:
Textbook Definition:

emotion

Your Definition:
Your Example:
Textbook Definition:

intrinsic motivation

Your Definition:
Your Example:
Textbook Definition:

motivation

Your Definition:
Your Example:
Textbook Definition:

primary emotions

Your Definition:
Your Example:
Textbook Definition:

need

Your Definition:
Your Example:
Textbook Definition:

secondary emotions

Your Definition:
Your Example:
Textbook Definition:

need hierarchy

Your Definition:
Your Example:
Textbook Definition:

self-actualization

Your Definition:
Your Example:
Textbook Definition:

need to belong theory

Your Definition:
Your Example:
Textbook Definition:

sexual response cycle

Your Definition:
Your Example:
Textbook Definition:

sexual strategies theory

Your Definition:
Your Example:
Textbook Definition:

somatic markers

Your Definition:
Your Example:
Textbook Definition:

Yerkes-Dodson law

Your Definition:
Your Example:
Textbook Definition:

CHAPTER 11 | Health and Well-Being

CHAPTER OVERVIEW

This chapter will consider questions such as: How can you maintain your sense of physical and psychological well-being throughout your life? Is there a connection between your thinking and your physical health? How might unmanaged stress affect your well-being? What is the latest thinking about threats to health such as obesity, smoking, and eating disorders? Do you have a plan for maintaining your health?

11.1 Can Psychosocial Factors Affect Health?

The most comprehensive way to understand the multiple factors involved in health is the biopsychosocial model. Illness or well-being can be approached from psychological, biological, and social perspectives. Most of the serious illnesses today result from poor behavioral choices. Even though contemporary medicine offers many treatments for these problems and others, the placebo effect has also been responsible for improvements in physical health.

At the beginning of each section in the Study Guide, there will be guiding questions. Before you read the chapter in your textbook, read through these questions and maybe even attempt to answer them based on either what you've already read or what you think the answer should be. Then as you study the chapter, you can use them to help guide your reading.

11.1 Guiding Questions

To guide your reading of the text, review the following questions. Then, as you read the chapter, look for the answers to these questions. You may want to note in your textbook where you find these answers.

1. Discuss the goals of health psychology.

2. Describe the biopsychosocial model of health.

3. Identify behaviors that contribute to the leading causes of death in industrialized societies.

4. Describe the placebo effect.

NOW READ Section 11.1 "Can Psychosocial Factors Affect Health?" keeping these questions in mind.

REVIEW: Now that you've read this section, go back to the 11.1 Guiding Questions and see if you can answer them based on what you've read. This is a check on your reading. If you can't answer a question, you need to go back to the text to reread that section.

VISUAL SUMMARY: Below is a summary of the major concepts in this section. To check your comprehension of the chapter, read the summary and ask yourself if you understand the concepts. If the concepts seem unfamiliar to you, you may want to go back to the book and reread those sections. This text is taken from the Visual Summaries on StudySpace at wwnorton.com/studyspace.

    I. Health Psychology
        A. Subdiscipline of psychology.
        B. Integrates research on health and on psychology.

   II. Well-being
        A. Well-being: a positive state in which we feel our best.

B. Includes striving for both optimal health and life satisfaction.

III. The Biopsychosocial Model of Health Incorporates Multiple Perspectives for Understanding and Improving Health
   A. This model integrates effects of biological, behavioral, and social factors on health.

IV. Behavior Contributes to the Leading Causes of Death
   A. People are most likely to die from causes that stem from their own behaviors.

V. Placebos Can Be Powerful Medicine
   A. The placebo effect consists of improvements in health following inert treatment.

REINFORCE: Are you ready to check your knowledge of this section? Answer the following multiple-choice questions with your textbook closed.

1. Dr. Haverford suggests to a patient that the patient's mood problems stem from serotonin dysregulation, but does not mention social or behavioral factors related to mood. Dr. Haverford is using which approach to understanding the patient's problems?
   a. the intradisciplinary model
   b. the behaviorist model
   c. the single stratum model
   d. the medical model

2. In contrast to the _____ model, the biopsychosocial model focuses on multiple aspects of health and well-being.
   a. single stratum
   b. medical
   c. componential
   d. interactive

3. A health care provider who uses the biopsychosocial model would endorse which of the following views of patient care?
   a. emphasis on disease states
   b. holistic
   c. physician managed
   d. patient as passive recipient of treatment

4. Health psychologists focus on all of the following factors EXCEPT:
   a. the conceptualization of health only as the absence of disease
   b. the role that lifestyle factors play in physical health
   c. using psychological principles to promote health
   d. psychological well-being

5. Sarah is trying to be the healthiest and most satisfied person she can possibly be. Sarah is concerned with her:
   a. positive emotionalism
   b. well-being

   c. health empowerment
   d. self-control

6. If Dr. Arzun is using the biopsychosocial model as a frame of reference for understanding psychological disorders, she will be MOST likely to prescribe which of the following treatments for a patient's anxiety?
   a. family therapy
   b. family therapy plus drug therapy
   c. drug therapy
   d. assertiveness training

7. Compared to the medical model of health, the biopsychosocial model:
   a. is more comprehensive
   b. ignores human biology
   c. is rarely used in practice
   d. is more simplistic

8. The interaction of thoughts, behaviors, biology, and environment describes elements of interest in the:
   a. medical model
   b. multistratum model
   c. circularity model
   d. biopsychosocial model

9. What do most of the common causes of death today have in common?
   a. Harmful behaviors are contributors.
   b. They result from emotional stress.
   c. They are related to psychological disorders.
   d. They are related to a particular personality style.

10. The fact that when you are sick you will almost always get better is an example of:
    a. problem-focused coping
    b. a facet of positive psychology
    c. the medical model of health
    d. the principle of regression to the mean

11. According to the principle of regression to the mean, if LeShaun received an award for academic excellence in grade 7 but never received awards before that point, how is he likely to perform in grades 8–12?
    a. He will continue to achieve academic excellence.
    b. He will return to an average level of performance.
    c. He will perform about the same as in grade 7.
    d. His performance will gradually get better and better throughout grades 8–12.

12. Joanie is in a research study in which she is told that a powerful new drug will dramatically increase her memory abilities. She is then administered the "drug," which is in fact a placebo. How will Joanie do on a memory test after taking the placebo?
    a. She will remember about the same amount as she would have without it.

b. She will remember more if she believes the "drug" is effective.

c. She will show memory interference because her expectation about the "drug" does not match the placebo effects.

d. She will remember more regardless of what she believes about the "drug."

13. Dr. Anh tests her newly developed drug, Sarzone, against a placebo in two randomly selected patient groups. In both groups, 20 percent of the patients report fewer symptoms. This finding illustrates that:

a. drugs are often ineffective in treating illness

b. Dr. Anh made mistakes in her research design

c. patient expectations have little to do with drug effects

d. patient expectations in the placebo group account for the drug effects

14. Jim suffers from chronic migraines. His doctor prescribes a pill, but doesn't tell Jim that it's really a placebo. Jim says, "Nothing has worked so far, but I'll try it." According to what you know about the placebo effect, the frequency and severity of Jim's headaches probably will _____ after taking the pills.

a. decrease moderately

b. increase moderately

c. not change

d. be worse than ever

15. Which of the following interventions would be most important to implement in terms of its potential for reducing the greatest number of adolescent deaths?

a. methamphetamine awareness

b. accident prevention

c. AIDS awareness

d. anorexia prevention

WHAT DID YOU MISS? Check your answers against the Answer Key at the end of this chapter of the Study Guide. The Answer Key also lists the page(s) in your text where each question is explained. If you missed any questions, go to the pages indicated in the Answer Key, reread those sections, go back to the questions, and see if you can answer them correctly this time.

ANOTHER OPPORTUNITY TO REVIEW: Answer these questions without your textbook. As a rule of thumb, if you can write only a few words about these questions, you probably need to go back and review.

1. Discuss the goals of health psychology. _____

_____

_____

2. Describe the biopsychosocial model of health. _____

_____

_____

3. Identify behaviors that contribute to the leading causes of death in industrialized societies. _____

_____

_____

4. Describe the placebo effect. _____

_____

_____

WHAT DO I NEED TO KNOW? Based on what you've discovered above, what are the areas where you need to focus your studying? Which objectives do you need to spend more time mastering? Write this information down in your own words.

1. _____

2. _____

3. _____

4. _____

5. _____

6. _____

11.2 How Do We Cope with Stress?

How do you manage stress? Stress can result from problems or from positive events such as a new job or a new baby. Responses to stress—which come about through communication between the brain and the body—follow a predictable sequence. Men and women respond to stress in different ways, and each person's personality style is related to how the person handles stress and to the person's general health.

11.2 Guiding Questions

To guide your reading of the text, review the following questions. Then, as you read the chapter, look for the answers to these questions. You may want to note in your textbook where you find these answers.

1. Define stress.

2. Describe the hypothalamic-pituitary-adrenal axis.

3. Discuss sex differences in responses to stressors.

4. Describe the general adaptation syndrome.

5. Discuss the association between personality traits and health.

6. Distinguish between emotion-focused coping and problem-focused coping.

7. Define hardiness.

NOW READ Section 11.2 "How Do We Cope with Stress?" keeping these questions in mind.

REVIEW: Now that you've read this section, go back to the 11.2 Guiding Questions and see if you can answer them based on what you've read. This is a check on your reading. If you can't answer a question, you need to go back to the text to reread that section.

VISUAL SUMMARY: Below is a summary of the major concepts in this section. To check your comprehension of the chapter, read the summary and ask yourself if you understand the concepts. If the concepts seem unfamiliar to you, you may want to go back to the book and reread those sections. This text is taken from the Visual Summaries on StudySpace at wwnorton.com/studyspace.

VI. Stress
  A. Stress: pattern of behavioral, psychological, and physiological responses to events that match or exceed an organism's ability to respond in a healthy way.
  B. Can be positive (eustress) or negative (distress).
  C. Can be caused by a major event or a minor hassle.
  D. Stressor: an environmental event or stimulus that threatens an organism.
  E. Coping response: any response an organism makes to avoid, escape from, or minimize an unpleasant stimulus.

VII. Stress Has Physiological Components
  A. Hypothalamic-pituitary-adrenal (HPA) axis is the biological system responsible for the stress response.
  B. Stress:
    i. damages organs and neurons.
    ii. affects working memory and capacity to retrieve memories.

VIII. There Are Sex Differences in How We Respond to Stressors
  A. Fight-or-flight response is physiological preparedness of animals to deal with danger.
    i. Men are more likely than women to respond to stress with the fight-or-flight response.

  B. Tend-and-befriend response:
    i. females' tendency to:
      a. protect and care for their offspring.
      b. form social alliances.
    ii. mediated by the release of oxytocin.

IX. The General Adaptation Syndrome Is a Bodily Response to Stress
  A. Stress:
    i. causes physical damage, such as to immune system.
    ii. reduces organism's ability to resist additional stressors.
  B. General adaptation syndrome has three stages:
    i. alarm.
    ii. resistance.
    iii. exhaustion.

X. Stress Affects Health
  A. Stress leads to:
    i. poor health behaviors.
    ii. overstimulation of sympathetic nervous system.
  B. Type A behavior pattern:
    i. competitive.
    ii. hostile.
    iii. restless.
  C. Type B behavior pattern:
    i. noncompetitive.
    ii. easygoing.
    iii. relaxed.
  D. Hostility predicts coronary disease.

XI. Coping Is a Process
  A. Through primary appraisals, we decide whether stimuli are stressful, benign, or irrelevant.
  B. Through secondary appraisals, we evaluate response options and choose coping behaviors.
  C. Emotion-based coping: trying not to respond emotionally to a stressor.
  D. Problem-focused coping: trying to confront or minimize a stressor.
  E. Two coping strategies use positive reappraisal:
    i. downward comparison: comparing oneself to people worse off.
    ii. creation of positive events: giving positive meaning to ordinary events.
  F. Some people are hardier and more resilient to effects of stress.
  G. Families can be helpful in increasing positive coping during illness.

REINFORCE: Are you ready to check your knowledge of this section? Answer the following multiple-choice questions with your textbook closed.

1. Psychologists use the term *stress* primarily to refer to situations in which:
   a. the demands placed on us exceed our abilities to respond to them
   b. we are emotionally aroused but don't know why
   c. the demands of a physical task exceed our capabilities
   d. we experience high levels of physiological arousal

2. A stressor is any event or stimulus that:
   a. threatens an organism and elicits a coping response
   b. cannot be coped with
   c. cannot be coped with in the short term
   d. always results in negative consequences

3. Harold is late for a doctor's appointment and can't find a parking place. He is experiencing:
   a. eustress
   b. a-stress
   c. a daily hassle
   d. a major life stressor

4. Research indicates that a stressor activates:
   a. the hypothalamic-pituitary-adrenal system
   b. the norepinephrine system but not the epinephrine system
   c. primarily the right brain hemisphere
   d. primarily the left brain hemisphere

5. Females under stress are likely to show a _____ response, whereas males under stress are more likely to show a _____ response.
   a. fight-or-flight; tend-and-befriend
   b. coping; noncoping
   c. tend-and-befriend; fight-or-flight
   d. flight; fight

6. All of the following stages make up the general adaptation syndrome EXCEPT:
   a. exhaustion
   b. resistance
   c. alarm
   d. compensation

7. According to Hans Selye, the general adaptation syndrome consists of three stages that occur in the following order:
   a. exhaustion, resistance, and alarm
   b. resistance, alarm, and exhaustion
   c. alarm, exhaustion, and resistance
   d. alarm, resistance, and exhaustion

8. Margot is an air force pilot stationed in a war zone. Compared to someone who has a less stressful job, Margot is likely to have _____ immune functioning.
   a. better
   b. worse

   c. about the same
   d. It's impossible to tell from this example.

9. If plotted on a graph, the correlation between stress and immune functioning would be:
   a. strong and positive
   b. strong and negative
   c. shaped like an inverted U
   d. random

10. Feeling hostile and impatient (i.e., part of Type A pattern behavior) is characteristic of people who may later develop:
    a. major depressive disorder
    b. heart disease
    c. an immune disorder
    d. an eating disorder

11. Recent research on predictors of heart disease suggests that people who are _____ are particularly vulnerable to cardiac problems.
    a. angry or depressed
    b. time-urgent and shy
    c. low in self-esteem
    d. low in cortisol production

12. Emotional coping strategies:
    a. work better over the short term than over the long term
    b. are usually better than problem-focused strategies
    c. work best in the face of a controllable stressor
    d. are productive and useful in most situations

13. The decision to use either emotion-focused or problem-focused coping often depends on:
    a. the intensity of the stressor
    b. the perceived ability to control the stressor
    c. the perceived ability to understand the stressor
    d. whether the stress is familiar or unfamiliar

14. If Amy is committed to her life tasks, feels challenged by barriers, and feels in control of her fate, she would be described as:
    a. Type A
    b. Type B
    c. hardy
    d. an externalizer

15. In looking at family-focused interventions for individuals with health problems, which of the following factors seems to predict whether intervention will be effective or ineffective?
    a. The patient has adequate social skills.
    b. Family members have enough information about the patient's illness.
    c. A medical practitioner or a family therapist conducts the intervention.
    d. Effectiveness depends on whether the patient or the family controls the situation.

WHAT DID YOU MISS? Check your answers against the Answer Key at the end of this chapter of the Study Guide. The Answer Key also lists the page(s) in your text where each question is explained. If you missed any questions, go to the pages indicated in the Answer Key, reread those sections, go back to the questions, and see if you can answer them correctly this time.

ANOTHER OPPORTUNITY TO REVIEW: Answer these questions without your textbook. As a rule of thumb, if you can write only a few words about these questions, you probably need to go back and review.

1. Define stress. _____

_____

_____

2. Describe the hypothalamic-pituitary-adrenal axis. _____

_____

_____

3. Discuss sex differences in responses to stressors. _____

_____

_____

4. Describe the general adaptation syndrome. _____

_____

_____

5. Discuss the association between personality traits and health. _____

_____

_____

6. Distinguish between emotion-focused coping and problem-focused coping. _____

_____

_____

7. Define hardiness. _____

_____

_____

WHAT DO I NEED TO KNOW? Based on what you've discovered above, what are the areas where you need to focus your studying? Which objectives do you need to spend more time mastering? Write this information down in your own words.

1. _____

2. _____

3. _____

4. _____

5. _____

6. _____

11.3 What Behaviors Affect Mental and Physical Health?

In most of the developed countries, obesity and smoking are two of the major threats to health. How can we reduce those threats? Does dieting work? How important is exercise? What are the consequences of smoking?

11.3 Guiding Questions

To guide your reading of the text, review the following questions. Then, as you read the chapter, look for the answers to these questions. You may want to note in your textbook where you find these answers.

1. Discuss the causes and consequences of obesity.

2. Review evidence to support the set-point regulation of body weight.

3. Contrast restrained and unrestrained eaters.

4. Compare and contrast anorexia nervosa and bulimia nervosa.

5. Discuss the causes and consequences of smoking.

6. Review the benefits of regular exercise.

7. Discuss ethnic differences in health behaviors.

NOW READ Section 11.3 "What Behaviors Affect Mental and Physical Health?" keeping these questions in mind.

REVIEW: Now that you've read this section, go back to the 11.3 Guiding Questions and see if you can answer them based on what you've read. This is a check on your reading. If you can't answer a question, you need to go back to the text to reread that section.

VISUAL SUMMARY: Below is a summary of the major concepts in this section. To check your comprehension of the chapter, read the summary and ask yourself if you understand the concepts. If the concepts seem unfamiliar to you, you may want to go back to the book and reread those sections. This text is taken from the Visual Summaries on StudySpace at wwnorton.com/studyspace.

XII. Most Causes of Premature Death Are Related to Lifestyle

XIII. Obesity Results from a Genetic Predisposition and Overeating
    A. Understanding obesity requires examining:
        i. behavior.
        ii. biology.
        iii. cognition.
        iv. societal context (e.g., cheap and tasty food).
    B. Over 300 genetic markers or genes play roles in obesity.
    C. Three maladaptive patterns of eating:
        i. restrictive eating: diets fail because the body naturally resists weight loss.
        ii. restrained eating: eating based on cognitive cues rather than internal states of hunger.
        iii. disordered eating: anorexia nervosa, bulimia nervosa.

XIV. Smoking Is a Leading Cause of Death
    A. Observation of attractive models of smoking leads many people to start smoking.
    B. Physiological dependence on nicotine may be related to genetics.

XV. Exercise Has Physical, Emotional, and Cognitive Benefits
    A. Exercise:
        i. helps control appetite.
        ii. aids metabolism.
        iii. burns calories.
        iv. affects neurotransmitter systems involved in reward, motivation, and emotion.

XVI. There Are Ethnic Differences in Health Behaviors
    A. Differences in health are related to genetics, access to health care, and cultural factors.

XVII. Health Can Be Maintained by Stopping Bad Habits
    A. Obesity and smoking can be managed with changes in behaviors.

REINFORCE: Are you ready to check your knowledge of this section? Answer the following multiple-choice questions with your textbook closed.

1. Claude Bouchard conducted research on the effects of overfeeding on weight gain and found that identical twins were similar in the amount of weight they gained. This study provides evidence for which of the following statements?
    a. Environment plays an important role in weight gain.
    b. Being an identical twin is stressful, and therefore weight gain is more likely.
    c. Weight gain is inevitable for most people if they overeat.
    d. Genes play an important role in weight gain.

2. One difference between anorexia nervosa and bulimia nervosa involves:
    a. the degree of psychological disturbance present
    b. the amount of food that is typically consumed
    c. whether periods of dieting occur
    d. the race and class of the people who engage in each

3. Obesity is:
    a. primarily linked to personality styles
    b. the body's way of regulating heartbeat
    c. primarily a result of overeating
    d. controlled more by genetic factors than by environment

4. Dieting:
    a. is successful in dealing with weight problems because it can be maintained easily for long periods of time
    b. is typically counterproductive for long-term weight loss
    c. is more effective if wide varieties of food are available
    d. is on the decline in developed countries

5. Evidence that humans have a set-point for weight is reflected in the fact that:
    a. when prisoners were fed large amounts of food they gained less weight than they should have and returned to their normal weight when they resumed a regular diet
    b. people who diet frequently wind up gaining more weight than those who do not
    c. semistarvation studies have shown that long-term reduction in food intake causes people to lose interest in food and eating
    d. as less food is consumed, the body's ability to use the energy contained in the food is reduced

6. Dieting as a method of controlling weight has proved ineffective in part because:
    a. the diet causes metabolism to increase such that the body becomes highly efficient in using the available calories
    b. weight gain occurs more rapidly after each episode of dieting
    c. the body lacks a set-point for regulating weight
    d. in most people, the set-point is set too high

7. As a long-term weight-loss strategy, controlling the amount you eat:
    a. is the best method yet discovered

b. works for only about 60 percent of people

c. can result in overeating when one perceives the diet has been "broken" by eating a forbidden food

d. works best for those who are very overweight rather than moderately overweight

8. People with anorexia nervosa and bulimia nervosa differ in that:

a. anorexia nervosa is associated with a higher mortality rate than bulimia

b. anorexia nervosa is more common among men than bulimia nervosa

c. persons suffering from anorexia nervosa tend to recover more quickly than those with bulimia nervosa

d. those with bulimia nervosa are very underweight and practice restrained eating

9. Research suggests that compared to nonsmokers, the average adult smoker:

a. can plan to live about a decade less than nonsmoking peers

b. underestimates the number of people who smoke

c. didn't try cigarettes until after college

d. overestimates the number of health problems he or she has

10. According to your textbook, enhancing one's self-image is a reason why people:

a. eat too much

b. engage in emotional coping

c. start smoking

d. develop a Type A personality

11. If people did not possess dopamine neurons, addiction to nicotine would be:

a. less likely

b. more likely

c. unaffected

d. strong at first and weak later

12. LaShawna, who is 13, has no siblings, and her parents do not smoke. Jayda, who is 15, has an older brother and mother who smoke. Who would be more likely to start smoking, and why?

a. LaShawna would be because her dopamine neurons are more sensitive to nicotine.

b. LaShawna would be because smoking would be a novel and exciting experience.

c. Jayda would be because her family members act as role models for smoking.

d. Both girls are equally likely to start smoking.

13. Approximately how many teenagers who start smoking will continue smoking into adulthood?

a. 10 percent

b. 30 percent

c. 50 percent

d. 80 percent

14. Based on what you know about the prevalence rates of smoking, where would you expect to find the most lung cancer deaths in the next 20 years?

a. urban cities in the United States

b. rural communities in the United States

c. China

d. France

15. Regular cardiovascular exercise has been shown to contribute to all of the following conditions EXCEPT:

a. improved mood and lowered depression

b. improved immune functioning

c. reduced storage of negative memories

d. speeded-up healing

WHAT DID YOU MISS? Check your answers against the Answer Key at the end of this chapter of the Study Guide. The Answer Key also lists the page(s) in your text where each question is explained. If you missed any questions, go to the pages indicated in the Answer Key, reread those sections, go back to the questions, and see if you can answer them correctly this time.

ANOTHER OPPORTUNITY TO REVIEW: Answer these questions without your textbook. As a rule of thumb, if you can write only a few words about these questions, you probably need to go back and review.

1. Discuss the causes and consequences of obesity. _____

_____

_____

2. Review evidence to support the set-point regulation of body weight. _____

_____

_____

3. Contrast restrained and unrestrained eaters. _____

_____

_____

4. Compare and contrast anorexia nervosa and bulimia nervosa. _____

_____

_____

5. Discuss the causes and consequences of smoking. _____

_____

_____

6. Review the benefits of regular exercise. _____

_____

_____

7. Discuss ethnic differences in health behaviors. _____

_____

_____

WHAT DO I NEED TO KNOW? Based on what you've discovered above, what are the areas where you need to focus your studying? Which objectives do you need to spend more time mastering? Write this information down in your own words.

1. _____
2. _____
3. _____
4. _____
5. _____
6. _____

11.4 Can a Positive Attitude Keep Us Healthy?

Can thinking and acting in a positive way improve our psychological and physical health? Yes, and the ways to bring this effect about are relatively easy. Other ways to improve your health—including friends, marriage, and spirituality—will also be covered in this section.

11.4 Guiding Questions

To guide your reading of the text, review the following questions. Then, as you read the chapter, look for the answers to these questions. You may want to note in your textbook where you find these answers.

1. Discuss the goals of positive psychology.

2. Describe the health benefits of positive affect, social support, marriage, trust, and spirituality.

NOW READ Section 11.4 "Can a Positive Attitude Keep Us Healthy?" keeping these questions in mind.

REVIEW: Now that you've read this section, go back to the 11.4 Guiding Questions and see if you can answer them

based on what you've read. This is a check on your reading. If you can't answer a question, you need to go back to the text to reread that section.

VISUAL SUMMARY: Below is a summary of the major concepts in this section. To check your comprehension of the chapter, read the summary and ask yourself if you understand the concepts. If the concepts seem unfamiliar to you, you may want to go back to the book and reread those sections. This text is taken from the Visual Summaries on StudySpace at wwnorton.com/studyspace.

XVIII. Positive Psychology Emphasizes Well-Being
    A. Positive psychology focuses on strengths and virtues that help maintain psychological well-being.

XIX. Being Positive Has Health Benefits
    A. Positive emotions can predict better mental and physical health.

XX. Social Support Is Associated with Good Health
    A. According to buffering hypothesis, direct emotional support from other people helps us cope with stressful events.
    B. Supportive marriages lead to better health.
    C. Supportive friendships lead to better health; may be related to oxytocin.

XXI. Spirituality Contributes to Well-Being
    A. Religious groups can help us maintain well-being through social and physical support.
    B. Religion or spirituality helps us derive meaning and purpose in life.

XXII. Taking Care of Mind and Body
    A. Eat natural foods.
    B. Watch portion size.
    C. Drink alcohol in moderation, if at all.
    D. Keep active.
    E. Do not smoke.
    F. Practice safe sex.
    G. Learn to relax.
    H. Learn to cope.
    I. Build a strong support network.
    J. Consider your spiritual life.
    K. Try some of the happiness exercises.

REINFORCE: Are you ready to check your knowledge of this section? Answer the following multiple-choice questions with your textbook closed.

1. Fewer colds and flus, a better-functioning immune system, and reduced risk of serious diseases such as heart disease can be expected from which of the following conditions?
    a. increasing the positive emotions one experiences

b. decreasing the number of people in one's social network

c. being single versus married

d. increasing one's social and work responsibilities

2. The most central goal of the positive psychology movement is to:
   a. promote positive change in society, as in advocating for peace
   b. convince people that they have much in life to be grateful for
   c. study and understand what makes people happy and have an overall sense of well-being
   d. train people to think positively and therefore be more-effective leaders

3. Dr. Zakaria, a young faculty member at XYZ University, is interested in how personal characteristics such as hopefulness, trustworthiness, and kindness affect self-perceived happiness. Dr. Zakaria is most likely a:
   a. cognitive psychologist
   b. positive psychologist
   c. psychoanalyst
   d. humanistic psychologist

4. Researchers who consider themselves to be part of the positive psychology movement would look to which well-known classical psychologist as a role model?
   a. Hans Selye
   b. Abraham Maslow
   c. B. F. Skinner
   d. Sigmund Freud

5. Which of the following states is NOT characterized as one of the three components of happiness by positive psychologists?
   a. being acknowledged by others as a successful person
   b. having meaning in life
   c. having positive emotions and pleasure
   d. being engaged in life

6. Serena would like to feel happier, so she goes to see a psychologist who specializes in helping people with mild depression. Which of the following activities might the psychologist recommend to elevate Serena's mood, at least for a few weeks?
   a. asking for a promotion at work
   b. making one new friend a day for a month or more
   c. writing a letter to someone expressing both positive and negative feelings about past events
   d. writing down three good things that happened every day and why they happened

7. Inspired by his reading about positive psychology, Adam writes a letter of thanks to his grandfather, whom he greatly admires. What should happen after Adam writes and delivers this letter?

a. He will experience greater happiness.

b. He will engage in downward comparisons.

c. His level of testosterone will increase.

d. The activity in his amygdala will increase.

8. If Aimee wants to live longer, which of the following activities should she engage in?
   a. Pampering herself.
   b. Increasing her social support network.
   c. Spending more time in nature.
   d. Spending more time on hobbies.

9. Mohamed is experiencing a large amount of work stress lately. His coworkers are helping him cope with the stress by encouraging him and telling him how much they appreciate his hard work. Because of his coworkers' actions, Mohamed is better able to deal with the stress. This scenario exemplifies:
   a. hardy friendships
   b. the social networking hypothesis
   c. positive stress
   d. the buffering hypothesis

10. Having a higher level of social support is:
    a. negatively correlated with health problems
    b. correlated with Type A personality
    c. important to health for children but less so for adults
    d. unrelated to gender

11. According to your textbook, the most effective mechanism for dealing with stressful events is:
    a. an emotion-focused approach to coping
    b. rumination
    c. seeking out information
    d. social support

12. Safia is a moderately healthy person. She has a small network of acquaintances and friends. If Safia wants to get all the health benefits associated with social support, she should increase:
    a. the size of her network and her level of social integration
    b. her buffering threshold and the number of new friends she makes
    c. the size of her network and her leadership capacity
    d. her social integration and dominance expressions

13. If human beings had more receptors for the hormone oxytocin, people would be:
    a. less trusting
    b. less curious
    c. more trusting
    d. more curious

14. Research has shown that the correlation between trust and physical health is:
    a. mostly positive
    b. mostly negative

c. mostly random

d. unable to be assessed scientifically

15. The relationship between spirituality and health can be described as:

a. basically negative

b. basically positive

c. basically random

d. difficult to infer

WHAT DID YOU MISS? Check your answers against the Answer Key at the end of this chapter of the Study Guide. The Answer Key also lists the page(s) in your text where each question is explained. If you missed any questions, go to the pages indicated in the Answer Key, reread those sections, go back to the questions, and see if you can answer them correctly this time.

ANOTHER OPPORTUNITY TO REVIEW: Answer these questions without your textbook. As a rule of thumb, if you can write only a few words about these questions, you probably need to go back and review.

1. Discuss the goals of positive psychology. _____

_____

_____

2. Describe the health benefits of positive affect, social support, marriage, trust, and spirituality._____

_____

_____

WHAT DO I NEED TO KNOW? Based on what you've discovered above, what are the areas where you need to focus your studying? Which objectives do you need to spend more time mastering? Write this information down in your own words.

1. _____

2. _____

3. _____

4. _____

5. _____

6. _____

WHAT MATTERS TO ME: What facts in this chapter are personally relevant to you?

_____

CHAPTER SUMMARY

11.1 Can Psychosocial Factors Affect Health?

- *The Biopsychosocial Model of Health Incorporates Multiple Perspectives for Understanding and Improving Health:* The biopsychosocial model describes the reciprocal and multiple influences of biological factors (e.g., genetic predispositions), behavioral factors (e.g., lifestyle), and social factors (e.g., social support) on health. In contrast to the traditional medical model, this model maintains that people are active participants in determining their health outcomes.

- *Behavior Contributes to the Leading Causes of Death:* The leading causes of death in industrialized societies are influenced by our behaviors. Lifestyle variables—such as overeating, poor diet, smoking, and lack of exercise—contribute to heart disease, the leading cause of death in the United States. Teenagers and young adults are most likely to die from accidents, homicide, and suicide. These causes of death are often preventable.

- *Placebos Can Be Powerful Medicine:* Placebos can have powerful effects on health and well-being. A placebo is effective, however, only if the person taking it believes in its ability to improve health. Research suggests that placebos activate the same neural processes as biologically active (nonplacebo) treatments.

11.2 How Do We Cope with Stress?

- *Stress Has Physiological Components:* Stressful events cause a cascade of physiological events—specifically, the release of hormones from the hypothalamus, the pituitary gland, and the adrenal glands. Stress-related hormones (e.g., cortisol, norepinephrine) circulate through the bloodstream, affecting organs throughout the body.

- *There Are Sex Differences in How We Respond to Stressors:* Women and men respond somewhat differently to stress. Women are more likely to tend and befriend, whereas men are more likely to fight or flee. Evolutionary psychology maintains that these distinct responses emerged as a consequence of the distinct challenges faced by women and men in our ancestral environment. Research suggests that the hormone oxytocin may play a role in the tend-and-befriend response.

- *The General Adaptation Syndrome Is a Bodily Response to Stress:* Selye outlined the general adaptation syndrome. This syndrome consists of the steps by which the body responds to stress. The initial response, alarm, is followed by resistance. If the stressor continues, the final response is exhaustion.

- *Stress Affects Health:* Excessive stress negatively affects health. Stress is associated with the occurrence of a wide variety of diseases, including heart disease. Heart disease is the leading cause of death of adults in the industrialized world. Individuals who are hostile or depressed are more likely to develop heart disease than those who are not.
- *Coping Is a Process:* We engage in cognitive appraisal of potential stressors. We may use emotion-focused and problem-focused coping strategies. Problem-focused coping strategies tend to be more effective for controllable stressors and under conditions of moderate stress. Emotion-focused coping strategies tend to be more effective for uncontrollable stressors and under conditions of high stress. Individuals who are hardy are more stress resilient. Having a sense of autonomy and control reduces the experience of stress and increases well-being.

11.3 What Behaviors Affect Mental and Physical Health?

- *Obesity Results from a Genetic Predisposition and Overeating:* In industrialized countries around the world, an increasing number of people are obese. Obesity results from a combination of a genetic predisposition and overeating. Restrictive diets rarely help obese people lose weight because weight is regulated around a set-point. Similarly, restrictive eating tends to fail because restrictive eaters are susceptible to overeating when they believe they have broken their diets. Extreme efforts to control weight and body shape may result in the onset of either anorexia nervosa or bulimia nervosa.
- *Smoking Is a Leading Cause of Death:* Smoking contributes to heart disease, cancer, and many other deadly diseases. People typically begin smoking as children or adolescents as a consequence of social influences or in an effort to display the positive characteristics that we associate with smokers (e.g., tough, independent).
- *Exercise Has Physical, Emotional, and Cognitive Benefits:* Exercise has positive effects on the heart and lungs. In addition, exercise has been shown to improve memory, enhance mood, and speed healing. Research has demonstrated that exercise can reduce cognitive decline in older adults.
- *There Are Ethnic Differences in Health Behaviors:* Racial and ethnic differences in health behaviors can explain some of the disparities in health outcomes. As groups become more acculturated to the mainstream culture, they tend to adopt the health behaviors of that culture, positive and negative.

- *Health Can Be Maintained by Stopping Bad Habits:* For changes in health behaviors to be successful, individuals need to incorporate those behaviors into permanent lifestyle changes.

11.4 Can a Positive Attitude Keep Us Healthy?

- *Positive Psychology Emphasizes Well-Being:* Positive psychology has its origins in the work of humanist psychologists. The early emphasis of this field was happiness. Today, positive psychologists emphasize the strengths and virtues associated with psychological well-being.
- *Being Positive Has Health Benefits:* According to a range of evidence, there are health benefits to having a positive, optimistic outlook.
- *Social Support Is Associated with Good Health:* Social support is critical to good health because when others care about us, they provide material and emotional support. Research has demonstrated enhanced well-being and reduced mortality among individuals who are in good marriages. Trust in others is critical to psychological and physical health. Oxytocin is secreted during trusting encounters and is involved in infant/parent attachments and love relationships.
- *Spirituality Contributes to Well-Being:* Spirituality contributes to a sense of well-being. Members of religious groups derive social and physical support from their faith communities. Many religions support healthy behaviors, and faith provides meaning to people's lives.

PUTTING IT ALL TOGETHER

Answer these questions to check your knowledge of the material in this chapter.

1. Given the known health risks of smoking cigarettes, it is surprising to walk around university campuses and see young adults smoking. However, as mentioned in this section of the textbook, people often make health decisions that go against known medical knowledge and common sense. Using the biopsychosocial model, explain why people smoke even though they understand the dangers of doing so.

2. Consider a hugely stressful event. For example, you might contemplate an impending flood that is sure to destroy a neighborhood. Based on what you learned in this section, explain how men and women—such as the inhabitants of the neighborhood—might react to that stressful event and explain how hormones might be related to their responses. What health effects might

occur in both sexes if the stressful event lasts for a long time (i.e., becomes chronic)?

3. Using the biopsychosocial model, discuss factors that influence weight.

4. What ways to improve your health did you learn about in this section? Will you employ any of these methods? Why or why not?

5. Think of two or three positive health habits you currently have. Discuss why you have them. Then find two or three negative health habits that have and would like to change. Develop a plan for adding those changes to your daily or weekly routine.

ANSWER KEY FOR REINFORCE QUESTIONS

Section 11.1

1. d	pp. 470–471
2. b	pp. 470–471
3. b	p. 470
4. a	p. 470
5. b	p. 470
6. b	p. 471
7. a	p. 471
8. d	p. 471
9. a	p. 471
10. d	p. 473
11. c	p. 473
12. b	p. 474
13. d	p. 474
14. c	p. 474
15. b	p. 472

Section 11.2

1. a	p. 476
2. a	p. 476
3. c	p. 477
4. a	p. 478
5. c	p. 479
6. d	p. 480
7. d	p. 480
8. b	p. 481
9. b	p. 481
10. b	p. 483
11. a	p. 483
12. a	p. 484
13. b	p. 484
14. c	p. 485
15. d	p. 486

TRY IT

Relaxing Your Body and Mind

Your textbook and this study guide discuss many techniques that psychologists and other scientists have developed for increasing people's well-being. Most of these techniques will work if used on a regular basis. Unfortunately, some people wait until they are in crises before they use the techniques. While the methods should work in difficult situations, they will work better over long periods of time.

To begin increasing your well-being, try to decrease your stress by relaxing your body and relaxing your mind. Your body and your mind are inseparable, of course, so if you relax one, you will relax the other. Still, techniques exist for relaxing each part separately.

Relaxing your body: Get yourself in a comfortable position, either lying down or sitting in a comfortable chair. Close your eyes and focus your attention on your feet and ankles. Imagine your feet and ankles becoming warm and heavy, warm and relaxed. You might even say to yourself, "I imagine my feet and ankles becoming warm and heavy, warm and relaxed." As you are saying this, imagine that you are focusing your breath on your feet and ankles, that you are breathing into your feet and ankles. Try five breaths or so. Now move up to your legs and imagine that they are becoming warm and heavy. Say and do the same things that you did with your feet and ankles. Next, focus on your hips and thighs, your abdomen and chest, your arms and shoulders, and your head and neck. Finally, imagine your entire body feeling warm and heavy. Imagine you are breathing into your entire body. Spend a few moments observing how you feel. What differences do you notice in your body or your mind?

Relaxing your mind: Get yourself in a comfortable position, either lying down or sitting in a comfortable chair. Either close your eyes or choose a spot on the wall on which to focus your sight. Breathe gently and shift your focus to what is going on in your mind. There may be pleasant thoughts or worrisome thoughts. Rather than judging or evaluating them, imagine as you are breathing that each of your thoughts is like a cloud floating in the sky. As a new thought comes into your mind, place it on a cloud and let it float by. Once you place a thought on a cloud, another thought will appear in your mind. Continue this process of breathing and watching your thoughts drift by on clouds for 5 to 10 minutes. Notice how you feel at the end of this exercise. What differences do you notice in your body or your mind?

Section 11.3

1. d   p. 491
2. b   pp. 494–495
3. d   p. 490
4. b   p. 493
5. a   p. 493
6. b   p. 493
7. c   p. 493
8. a   p. 495
9. a   p. 496
10. c   p. 497
11. a   p. 497
12. c   p. 497
13. c   p. 496
14. c   p. 496
15. c   p. 498

Section 11.4

1. a   p. 501
2. c   p. 501
3. b   p. 501
4. b   p. 501
5. a   p. 501
6. d   p. 502
7. a   p. 502
8. b   p. 503
9. d   p. 504
10. a   p. 503
11. d   p. 503
12. a   p. 503
13. c   p. 505
14. a   p. 505
15. b   p. 506

HINTS FOR PUTTING IT ALL TOGETHER QUESTIONS

1. First, consider biological factors that could influence why young adults smoke. Once people start smoking, they become addicted to the nicotine. They physically require the nicotine to feel normal, so they continue to smoke. But what biological factors might cause a person to start to smoke? Perhaps a physiological predisposition to high anxiety could lead someone to start smoking as a way to cope with his or her anxiety. Second, consider some psychological factors that could influence why young adults smoke. University students often have stressful lives, filled with too much work to do in their classes, stressful low-pay jobs, and tumultuous relationships. Young adults may continue smoking because it helps them *cope* with their stress. Also, another psycho-

logical factor is that some people *think* that smoking allows them to manage their weight. Furthermore, young adults may *think* they are young and have plenty of time to quit smoking when their lives are not as stressful. Finally, consider some social factors related to smoking. People raised in families with smokers are more likely to start smoking themselves. People with friends who smoke are also more likely to try smoking. Commercials, the media, and actors who portray smoking as attractive and desirable can also contribute to how people view smoking and can influence their smoking habits.

2. Men are more likely to demonstrate the fight-or-flight response in reaction to a stressful event, whereas women are more likely to demonstrate the tend-and-befriend response in reaction to a stressful event. Men's reactions would be due more to the release of the hormones epinephrine and cortisol, whereas women's reactions would be due more to the release of the hormone oxytocin. According to the theory, men might use their energy to "fight" the flood (e.g., use sand bags, pump pump, move their belongings to high ground) or "flight" from the flood (e.g., gather their things and seek higher ground). Women may be more likely to "tend" to their children (e.g., gather their children and their belongings, explain the dangers of the flood to their children) and "befriend" (e.g., ask for help from neighbors, friends, family). If stress becomes chronic, it can decrease immune system response (i.e., lead to increased illness and disease) and can lead to increased blood pressure, stomach ulcers, heart disease, and many other health-related issues (e.g., strokes, diabetes).

3. Biological factors related to weight gain include genetic predisposition. Indeed, genetics accounts for nearly half the variability in body weight and can affect metabolism, body shape, and the brain's reaction to food (e.g., increased activity in reward centers in the brain in overweight people compared to normal-weight people). Psychological factors correlated with weight gain include depression, anxiety, and low self-esteem (because these factors have been determined through correlational studies, we cannot say that they *cause* weight gain). Also, key factors in the development of anorexia nervosa include obsessive *thoughts* about weight gain and poor body image. Social factors include availability of low-cost and high-calorie food, large portion sizes at restaurants, and commercials for food. Also, the weight of our close friends influences the weight we consider acceptable for ourselves.

4. Positive attitude and positive affect can improve health. For example, high levels of hope and curiosity are

associated with low rates of diabetes and of high blood pressure. People who have a positive attitude, in general, develop fewer colds and live longer. Having social support—friends and family members who care about you—is also related to improved immune responses and longer lives. A good marriage has similar health benefits. Finally, trusting others and having a sense of spirituality also have been related to improvements in health.

5. The list of health habits includes these: eat natural foods, watch portion size, drink alcohol in moderation (if at all), keep active, do not smoke, practice safe sex, learn to relax, learn to cope, build a strong support network, consider your spiritual life, and try some of the happiness exercises. You can try to use positive reinforcement to add some of these healthy habits to your routine—reward yourself with something you really enjoy every time you perform a new healthy habit. Of course, make sure that your reward doesn't have negative consequences for your health.

KEY TERMS EXERCISES

First, fill in your own definition and example for each term. Then check each term against the textbook's definition. These exercises can also be cut out and used as flash cards.

anorexia nervosa

Your Definition:

Your Example:

Textbook Definition:

bulimia nervosa

Your Definition:

Your Example:

Textbook Definition:

biopsychosocial model

Your Definition:

Your Example:

Textbook Definition:

coping response

Your Definition:

Your Example:

Textbook Definition:

body mass index (BMI)

Your Definition:

Your Example:

Textbook Definition:

emotion-focused coping

Your Definition:

Your Example:

Textbook Definition:

buffering hypothesis

Your Definition:

Your Example:

Textbook Definition:

fight-or-flight response

Your Definition:

Your Example:

Textbook Definition:

general adaptation syndrome

Your Definition:
Your Example:
Textbook Definition:

health psychology

Your Definition:
Your Example:
Textbook Definition:

hypothalamic-pituitaryadrenal (HPA) axis

Your Definition:
Your Example:
Textbook Definition:

immune system

Your Definition:
Your Example:
Textbook Definition:

oxytocin

Your Definition:
Your Example:
Textbook Definition:

placebo effect

Your Definition:
Your Example:
Textbook Definition:

primary appraisals

Your Definition:
Your Example:
Textbook Definition:

problem-focused coping

Your Definition:
Your Example:
Textbook Definition:

secondary appraisals

Your Definition:

Your Example:

Textbook Definition:

stress

Your Definition:

Your Example:

Textbook Definition:

stressor

Your Definition:

Your Example:

Textbook Definition:

tend-and-befriend response

Your Definition:

Your Example:

Textbook Definition:

Type A behavior pattern

Your Definition:

Your Example:

Textbook Definition:

Type B behavior pattern

Your Definition:

Your Example:

Textbook Definition:

well-being

Your Definition:

Your Example:

Textbook Definition:

CHAPTER 12 | Social Psychology

CHAPTER OVERVIEW

Within just a few minutes of meeting someone new, you will "size this person up." How we anticipate people's actions, and to what degrees stereotypes and prejudices affect our perceptions, will all come into play in this situation.

In addition to considering the formation of attitudes, this chapter will discuss how other people influence us to be obedient or conform and how easily we can be persuaded to behave in ways that might be shocking to us. Finally, the chapter will look at how we form relationships and how we can keep our relationships together.

12.1 How Do We Form Our Impressions of Others?

Social psychology is the study of how we interact with other people. Our impressions of other people are usually formed quickly through verbal and nonverbal means. We make assumptions or attributions about people's behaviors, providing us with shortcuts to understanding people and their behaviors. However, our assumptions or attributions may be incorrect. Stereotypes and prejudices are shortcuts to understanding that are frequently incorrect.

At the beginning of each section in the Study Guide, there will be guiding questions. Before you read the chapter in your textbook, read through these questions and maybe even attempt to answer them based on either what you've already read or what you think the answer should be. Then as you study the chapter, you can use them to help guide your reading.

12.1 Guiding Questions

To guide your reading of the text, review the following questions. Then, as you read the chapter, look for the answers to these questions. You may want to note in your textbook where you find these answers.

1. Identify the goals of social psychology.

2. Discuss the role that nonverbal behavior plays in impression formation.

3. Define the fundamental attribution error and the actor/observer discrepancy.

4. Describe the functions and self-fulfilling effects of stereotypes.

5. Distinguish between prejudice and discrimination.

6. Distinguish between ingroups and outgroups.

7. Discuss strategies to inhibit stereotypes and reduce prejudice.

NOW READ Section 12.1 "How Do We Form Our Impressions of Others?" keeping these questions in mind.

REVIEW: Now that you've read this section, go back to the 12.1 Guiding Questions and see if you can answer them based on what you've read. This is a check on your reading. If you can't answer a question, you need to go back to the text to reread that section.

VISUAL SUMMARY: Below is a summary of the major concepts in this section. To check your comprehension of the chapter, read the summary and ask yourself if you understand the concepts. If the concepts seem unfamiliar to you, you may want to go back to the book and reread those sections. This text is taken from the Visual Summaries on StudySpace at wwnorton.com/studyspace.

I. Nonverbal Actions and Expressions Affect Our First Impressions
   A. Accurate judgments can be based on brief observations.
   B. Facial expressions and body movements influence impressions.

II. We Make Attributions about Others
   A. Attributions are explanations of motives, traits, and preferences.
   B. In explaining behavior, fundamental attribution error is the tendency to:
      i. overemphasize personality.
      ii. underestimate situation.
   C. Actor/observer discrepancy:
      i. in interpreting our own behavior, we focus on situation.
      ii. in interpreting others' behavior, we focus on personality.

III. Stereotypes Are Based on Automatic Categorization
   A. Stereotypes: mental shortcuts for rapid processing of social information.
   B. Self-fulfilling prophecy: the tendency to behave in ways that confirm stereotypes.

IV. Stereotypes Can Lead to Prejudice
   A. Prejudice: negative feelings, opinions, and beliefs associated with a stereotype.
   B. Discrimination: inappropriate, unjustified treatment of people based on prejudice.
   C. Ingroup/outgroup bias is the tendency to:
      i. positively evaluate groups we belong to.
      ii. negatively evaluate groups different from ours.

V. Cooperation Can Reduce Prejudice
   A. Shared goals that require cooperation reduce hostility and prejudice.

REINFORCE: Are you ready to check your knowledge of this section? Answer the following multiple-choice questions with your textbook closed.

1. Gamiel has taken Aliyah out to dinner for the first time. She is very surprised when he does not leave a tip for the waiter. If Aliyah decides that Gamiel did not leave a tip because he is stingy, she is making a _____ attribution; if Aliyah decides that Gamiel did not leave a tip because the service was terrible, she is making a _____ attribution.
   a. situational; personal
   b. personal; situational
   c. stable; variable
   d. variable; stable

2. Which of the following statements is the best example of the fundamental attribution error?
   a. "People live in ghettos because they lack the motivation to make anything of themselves."
   b. "She was born with a silver spoon in her mouth."
   c. "Prison guards are not mean people; they are just victims of a very difficult situation."
   d. "There, but for the grace of God, go I."

3. People make just world attributions mainly to:
   a. increase their senses of self-esteem
   b. make them feel safer
   c. let them avoid their own errors
   d. ease their consciences

4. In explaining her failure to be admitted to the graduate school of her choice and the failure of a classmate to get into graduate school, Cynthia uses the actor/observer discrepancy. Her reasoning involves which of the following sets of attributions?
   a. "I didn't get in because I'm not motivated to do well; my classmate isn't adequately motivated either."
   b. "I didn't get in because I was so swamped with coursework that I didn't have enough time to prepare my application packet; my classmate didn't get in because she's not motivated to do well."
   c. "I didn't get in because I'm not motivated to do well; my classmate didn't get in because she didn't have enough time to prepare her admissions packet."
   d. "I didn't get in because I didn't have enough time to prepare; my classmate didn't have enough time to prepare either."

5. The Stanford prison study demonstrates that people:
   a. are innately violent unless constrained by society
   b. are typically obedient to authority
   c. will never obey orders that violate their principles
   d. placed in all male groups will always create dominance hierarchies

6. In making attributions about the behavior of people around them, people from Western cultures tend to emphasize _____ factors, and people from Eastern cultures tend to emphasize _____ factors.
   a. personal; personal and situational
   b. personal and situational; personal
   c. situational; personal and situational
   d. personal and situational; situational

7. Employing a stereotype may mean judging a person in terms of his or her:

a. fundamental qualities
b. background
c. group membership
d. personal affiliations

8. Dr. Norton had heard from other teachers that five of his algebra students might require extra help. As a consequence, he tended to hover around these students, checked their answers more than he checked other students' answers, seemed to doubt their ability to understand the material, and often stopped them in the middle of their problem solving to tell them that they were working the problem incorrectly. All five students failed the class. Which of the following factors would, in part, explain their failure?
a. positive attributional bias
b. self-serving bias
c. self-fulfilling prophecy
d. group stereotype

9. If people are randomly assigned to groups A and B, the members of each group are likely to:
a. favor members of their own group because of ingroup bias
b. not favor members of their own group because of random assignment
c. not be hostile to members of the other group because of random assignment
d. favor neither members of their own group nor members of the other group

10. Mr. Ahkbar is the principal of a military school that has only had male students. For the first time this fall, girls are being admitted. The boys are very hostile to this decision, and Mr. Ahkbar is worried that there will be trouble. What would you advise Mr. Ahkbar to do in order to decrease hostility and better integrate the female students into the school?
a. make sure that all classes have a gender balance
b. have an open discussion of the situation
c. have mixed-gender groups work together on projects
d. start with single-gender classes and gradually mix the genders

WHAT DID YOU MISS? Check your answers against the Answer Key at the end of this chapter of the Study Guide. The Answer Key also lists the page(s) in your text where each question is explained. If you missed any questions, go to the pages indicated in the Answer Key, reread those sections, go back to the questions, and see if you can answer them correctly this time.

ANOTHER OPPORTUNITY TO REVIEW: Answer these questions without your textbook. As a rule of thumb, if you can write only a few words about these questions, you probably need to go back and review.

1. Identify the goals of social psychology. _____

2. Discuss the role that nonverbal behavior plays in impression formation. _____

3. Define the fundamental attribution error and the actor/observer discrepancy. _____

4. Describe the functions and self-fulfilling effects of stereotypes. _____

5. Distinguish between prejudice and discrimination. _____

6. Distinguish between ingroups and outgroups. _____

7. Discuss strategies to inhibit stereotypes and reduce prejudice. _____

WHAT DO I NEED TO KNOW? Based on what you've discovered above, what are the areas where you need to focus your studying? Which objectives do you need to spend more time mastering? Write this information down in your own words.

1. _____
2. _____
3. _____
4. _____
5. _____
6. _____

12.2 How Do Attitudes Guide Behavior?

Our attitudes influence our behavior, yet our attitudes often are not thought out or logical. How do we form our attitudes, and what factors influence them? How do we use knowledge of attitude formation in persuading other people to do things? How can we determine when people are trying to persuade us to do things?

12.2 Guiding Questions

To guide your reading of the text, review the following questions. Then, as you read the chapter, look for the answers to these questions. You may want to note in your textbook where you find these answers.

1. Explain how attitudes are formed.

2. Identify characteristics of attitudes that are predictive of behavior.

3. Distinguish between explicit and implicit attitudes.

4. Describe cognitive dissonance theory.

5. Identify factors that influence the persuasiveness of messages.

6. Describe the elaboration likelihood model.

NOW READ Section 12.2 "How Do Attitudes Guide Behavior?" keeping these questions in mind.

REVIEW: Now that you've read this section, go back to the 12.2 Guiding Questions and see if you can answer them based on what you've read. This is a check on your reading. If you can't answer a question, you need to go back to the text to reread that section.

VISUAL SUMMARY: Below is a summary of the major concepts in this section. To check your comprehension of the chapter, read the summary and ask yourself if you understand the concepts. If the concepts seem unfamiliar to you, you may want to go back to the book and reread those sections. This text is taken from the Visual Summaries on StudySpace at wwnorton.com/studyspace.

VI. Attitudes are evaluations of:
   A. objects.
   B. events.
   C. ideas.
VII. We Form Attitudes through Experience and Socialization
   A. Negative attitudes develop more rapidly than positive attitudes.

   B. Greater exposure leads to familiarity and therefore more positive attitudes.
VIII. Behaviors Are Consistent with Strong Attitudes
   A. Ease of attitude accessibility predicts behavior resistant to change.
IX. Attitudes Can Be Explicit or Implicit
   A. Explicit attitudes: because we know we hold them, we can report them to other people.
   B. Implicit attitudes: at an unconscious level, they influence feelings and behavior.

X. Discrepancies Lead to Dissonance
   A. Cognitive dissonance is:
      i. an uncomfortable mental state.
      ii. due to contradiction between two attitudes or between behavior and attitude.

XI. Attitudes Can Be Changed through Persuasion
   A. Persuasion is active and conscious effort to change attitude through transmission of message.
   B. According to the elaboration likelihood model, persuasive communication changes attitudes through a:
      i. central route: paying attention to the information presented.
      ii. peripheral route: minimal attention to information leads to impulsivity.

REINFORCE: Are you ready to check your knowledge of this section? Answer the following multiple-choice questions with your textbook closed.

1. Catalina has gotten an entirely new haircut that she can't wait to show her boyfriend. A social psychologist might advise her that her boyfriend may:
   a. not like the haircut because it is new
   b. not like the haircut because she did not ask his opinion first
   c. like the haircut just because she is so happy with it
   d. like the haircut because having her look different is exciting

2. Naomi was raised as a vegetarian. When she gets to college, she decides that she will eat meat so that she will be more like everyone else. Even though she really wants to stop being a vegetarian, Naomi finds that she can't bring herself to eat meat. Naomi's situation demonstrates the effect of _____ on attitudes.
   a. classical conditioning
   b. implicit attitudes
   c. actor/observer discrepancy
   d. unconscious influence

3. A presidential candidate's acceptance speech at the party convention greatly influences the way in which many voters see the candidate. Who will be most likely

to have a more favorable opinion of President Obama after his speech at the 2012 Democratic National Convention?

a. Zora, who has been an Obama supporter since he announced his first candidacy for president

b. Yancey, who is undecided, leans toward Democrat, but admits that he doesn't follow politics very much

c. Xenia, who became a strong Obama supporter after switching from the Republican Party

d. Will, who was a Rick Perry supporter but came to intensely dislike Perry's negative campaign

4. Which of the following does NOT increase the stability of an attitude?

a. the personal relevance of the attitude
b. the ease of accessibility of the attitude
c. the values expressed by the attitude
d. the specificity of the attitude

5. Even though Jacqueline attended a very expensive boarding school, she passionately believes that money and social class are irrelevant to how interesting or valuable a person is. At the first party in her college dorm, Jacqueline, without even realizing it, spends time with only the women who are very well dressed. Jacqueline's belief in social equality is a(n) _____, and her choice of people to spend time with reflects a(n) _____.

a. implicit attitude; explicit attitude
b. explicit attitude; implicit attitude
c. more accessible attitude; less accessible attitude
d. less accessible attitude; more accessible attitude

6. Kyle was raised in a vegan family. Before he goes to college, his mother tells him that it will probably be impossible for him to maintain a healthy vegan diet in a college dorm and that eating a healthy diet is more important in that situation than eating a vegan diet. Kyle's mom is trying to protect him from experiencing the unpleasant effects of:

a. conflicting behaviors
b. overcoming socialization
c. extinguishing a conditioned attitude
d. cognitive dissonance

7. In the central route to persuasion:

a. the appeal is to the central neurological paths
b. the most basic and direct arguments are used
c. rational cognitive arguments are used
d. the argument is directed only at the central point

8. In working on the campaign of the student body president, Tom wants to present his candidate in the best light to specific audiences. He has divided his audiences into two categories: those who are paying attention to the issues (the concerned or skeptical) and those who are not really concerned with the relevant issues (the unconcerned or gullible). If he were to structure speeches for each of these groups, which types of messages might be most appealing?

a. concerned: two-sided argument; unconcerned: two-sided argument

b. concerned: two-sided argument; unconcerned: one-sided argument

c. concerned: one-sided argument; unconcerned: two-sided argument

d. It is impossible to predict without knowing the cultural and religious backgrounds of the audience.

9. Sources of information who are _____ tend to be the most persuasive.

a. like the target audience
b. rational and emotional
c. attractive and credible
d. strongly partisan

10. When Saqui breaks up with her boyfriend, she cannot decide whether to date her best friend, Bradan, or a fascinating new man. Both men have different attractive qualities. After deciding on the new man, Saqui finds that she no longer likes Bradan. Even though he wants to continue their long friendship, she keeps finding more things to dislike about him. Saqui is experiencing:

a. cognitive dissonance
b. attributional bias
c. postdecisional dissonance
d. emergence of an implicit attitude

WHAT DID YOU MISS? Check your answers against the Answer Key at the end of this chapter of the Study Guide. The Answer Key also lists the page(s) in your text where each question is explained. If you missed any questions, go to the pages indicated in the Answer Key, reread those sections, go back to the questions, and see if you can answer them correctly this time.

ANOTHER OPPORTUNITY TO REVIEW: Answer these questions without your textbook. As a rule of thumb, if you can write only a few words about these questions, you probably need to go back and review.

1. Explain how attitudes are formed. _____

_____

_____

2. Identify characteristics of attitudes that are predictive of behavior. _____

_____

_____

3. Distinguish between explicit and implicit attitudes. _____

_____

_____

4. Describe cognitive dissonance theory. _____

_____

_____

5. Identify factors that influence the persuasiveness of messages. _____

_____

_____

6. Describe the elaboration likelihood model. _____

_____

_____

WHAT DO I NEED TO KNOW? Based on what you've discovered above, what are the areas where you need to focus your studying? Which objectives do you need to spend more time mastering? Write this information down in your own words.

1. _____

2. _____

3. _____

4. _____

5. _____

6. _____

12.3 How Do Others Influence Us?

What social pressures influence our behaviors? We tend to be affected by the groups we belong to or by people whose opinions matter to us. We may find ourselves behaving in ways that are very different from our normal behaviors or even in ways that are shocking.

12.3 Guiding Questions

To guide your reading of the text, review the following questions. Then, as you read the chapter, look for the answers to these questions. You may want to note in your textbook where you find these answers.

1. Define social facilitation, social loafing, deindividuation, group polarization, and groupthink.

2. Differentiate between conformity, compliance, and obedience.

3. Identify factors that increase or decrease conformity, compliance, and obedience.

NOW READ Section 12.3 "How Do Others Influence Us?" keeping these questions in mind.

REVIEW: Now that you've read this section, go back to the 12.3 Guiding Questions and see if you can answer them based on what you've read. This is a check on your reading. If you can't answer a question, you need to go back to the text to reread that section.

VISUAL SUMMARY: Below is a summary of the major concepts in this section. To check your comprehension of the chapter, read the summary and ask yourself if you understand the concepts. If the concepts seem unfamiliar to you, you may want to go back to the book and reread those sections. This text is taken from the Visual Summaries on StudySpace at wwnorton.com/studyspace.

XII. Groups Influence Individual Behavior
   A. Social facilitation: the presence of others enhances performance.
   B. Social loafing: the tendency to work less hard in a group than when alone.
   C. Deindividuation: reduced attention to personal standards when part of a group.

XIII. We Conform to Others
   A. Conformity:
      i. altering one's beliefs/behaviors to match those of other people.
      ii. happens because of:
         a. normative influence: going along with crowd to avoid looking foolish.
         b. informational influence: assuming crowd's behavior is correct.
   B. Social norms:
      i. expected standards of conduct
      ii. influence behavior

XIV. We Are Compliant
   A. Compliance:
      i. the tendency to do things requested by others
      ii. can be brought about by strategies:
         a. foot-in-the-door effect
         b. door in the face
         c. low-balling strategy

XV. We Are Obedient to Authority
   A. Milgram's famous study demonstrated the tendency to follow the directions of authority.

REINFORCE: Are you ready to check your knowledge of this section? Answer the following multiple-choice questions with your textbook closed.

1. Terriers were bred to chase small animals and in the process to dig holes. Susan adopted a terrier, but it played happily in her backyard without digging holes. To give that dog company, Susan adopted a second terrier. Within a week, both dogs were digging holes throughout the yard. The dogs' behavior exemplifies:
   a. social loafing
   b. deindividuation
   c. social facilitation
   d. the autokinetic effect

2. According to Zajonc, the presence of other people affects performance because it _____ , which leads the person to _____ .
   a. decreases arousal; respond less strongly
   b. increases arousal; select the adaptive response
   c. decreases arousal; seek further stimulation
   d. increases arousal; make a dominant response

3. Mr. Lahore has hired four college students to paint his house. Which set of conditions will be likely to produce the best work?
   a. Each student paints one room by himself or herself.
   b. All the students work together on each room.
   c. The students work in two-person teams.
   d. The students take turns painting and watching each other.

4. After Hurricane Katrina, people committed many acts of valor and bravery and many acts of looting and theft. According to the concept of deindividuation, all of the following factors probably contributed to the criminal acts EXCEPT:
   a. arousal
   b. anonymity
   c. confusion
   d. diffusion of responsibility

5. Microbiology students have been working on a semester-long project that will determine 50 percent of their course grade. A week before the project is due, they realize they have made a critical error and their results are useless. One member of the group argues strongly that they should falsify their results so they will be able to turn in a successful project. Though all the other members have doubts, none feels comfortable expressing doubt. The group ignores the possibility of being caught and falsifies the report. This scenario exemplifies:
   a. foot in the door technique
   b. social loafing

   c. the autokinetic effect
   d. groupthink

6. Jodie is a member of a jury that is trying to decide how much money to award the plaintiff in damages. Most of the jury favors an award of $5,000, but Jodie favors $10,000. When the foreman polls the jury, Jodie is the last person he polls. Which of the following factors is most likely to make Jodie maintain her view?
   a. There is little discussion before the jury is polled.
   b. One other juror votes for the larger award.
   c. All the other jurors are male.
   d. All the other jurors are female.

7. Cat wants to buy a new laptop, but she knows that her husband will think that it isn't a necessary expense. She initially proposes buying a $2,500 laptop. When her husband gets upset, she suggests that she could get by with a used laptop for $700. Cat is using the _____ approach, and it is likely that her husband _____ agree.
   a. foot-in-the-door; will
   b. foot-in-the-door; will not
   c. door-in-the-face; will not
   d. door-in-the-face; will

8. Cassie is joining a yoga studio because new memberships are quite inexpensive. When the director explains the plan to her, Cassie discovers that there are added costs for workshops, mats, and other items. Although Cassie would never have thought to sign up at the final price, she has become committed to the idea and does join the studio. The yoga studio has effectively used the _____ to sell Cassie a membership.
   a. foot-in-the-door technique
   b. low-balling strategy
   c. door-in-the-face technique
   d. gradual acquiescence strategy

9. In Milgram's obedience studies, about _____ of the participants administered maximum shock, and _____ of them tried to quit the study.
   a. 66 percent; almost all
   b. 50 percent; almost all
   c. 25 percent; 50 percent
   d. 15 percent; 50 percent

10. The main conclusion to be drawn from Milgram's studies is:
    a. ordinary people will do terrible things if ordered by an insistent authority
    b. ordinary people have an inherent violence that is easily released
    c. ordinary people will follow immoral orders only in artificial situations
    d. ordinary men but not ordinary women will obey immoral orders

WHAT DID YOU MISS? Check your answers against the Answer Key at the end of this chapter of the Study Guide. The Answer Key also lists the page(s) in your text where each question is explained. If you missed any questions, go to the pages indicated in the Answer Key, reread those sections, go back to the questions, and see if you can answer them correctly this time.

ANOTHER OPPORTUNITY TO REVIEW: Answer these questions without your textbook. As a rule of thumb, if you can write only a few words about these questions, you probably need to go back and review.

1. Define social facilitation, social loafing, deindividuation, group polarization, and groupthink. _____

_____

_____

2. Differentiate between conformity, compliance, and obedience. _____

_____

_____

3. Identify factors that increase or decrease conformity, compliance, and obedience. _____

_____

_____

WHAT DO I NEED TO KNOW? Based on what you've discovered above, what are the areas where you need to focus your studying? Which objectives do you need to spend more time mastering? Write this information down in your own words.

1. _____
2. _____
3. _____
4. _____
5. _____
6. _____

12.4 When Do We Harm or Help Others?

Why do people act aggressively, even violently? Often, their behavior is influenced by situation, culture, and biological determinants. What, then, brings about kindness and altru-

ism? Why do people sometimes choose to help others who are in trouble and sometimes choose not to? This section will address these and other questions.

12.4 Guiding Questions

To guide your reading of the text, review the following questions. Then, as you read the chapter, look for the answers to these questions. You may want to note in your textbook where you find these answers.

1. Identify biological, situational, and sociocultural determinants of aggression.

2. Discuss the association between steroid use and aggression.

3. Review evolutionary explanations for altruism.

4. Review explanations for the bystander intervention effect.

NOW READ Section 12.4 "When Do We Harm or Help Others?" keeping these questions in mind.

REVIEW: Now that you've read this section, go back to the 12.4 Guiding Questions and see if you can answer them based on what you've read. This is a check on your reading. If you can't answer a question, you need to go back to the text to reread that section.

VISUAL SUMMARY: Below is a summary of the major concepts in this section. To check your comprehension of the chapter, read the summary and ask yourself if you understand the concepts. If the concepts seem unfamiliar to you, you may want to go back to the book and reread those sections. This text is taken from the Visual Summaries on StudySpace at wwnorton.com/studyspace.

XVI. Many Factors Can Influence Aggression
   A. Aggression:
     i. any behavior intended to harm someone else
     ii. associated with amygdala and neurotransmitters (serotonin)
     iii. according to frustration-aggression hypothesis, predicted by aggression
     iv. affected by culture

XVII. Steroids May Play a Role in Some Violent Behavior
   A. Steroids (testosterone) may promote aggression.

XVIII. Many Factors Can Influence Helping Behavior
   A. Prosocial and altruistic behavior:
     i. likely genetic
     ii. adaptive in nature (help humans to survive)

XIX. Some Situations Lead to Bystander Apathy
   A. Bystander intervention effect: failure to offer help to someone in need.

REINFORCE: Are you ready to check your knowledge of this section? Answer the following multiple-choice questions with your textbook closed.

1. If the amygdala of a cat is stimulated with an electric probe, the cat will _____; if the amygdala of a cat is damaged, it will _____.
   a. explore feared objects; eat unusual things
   b. attack; become passive
   c. eat unusual things; explore feared objects
   d. become passive; attack

2. Human beings typically engage in prosocial, altruistic behavior. Why, according to your book, do we engage in these behaviors?
   a. to manage our public image
   b. to relieve our negative mood
   c. to help individuals in our gene pool
   d. all of the above

3. Which of the following is NOT associated with low levels of serotonin in people?
   a. disruptive behavior in children
   b. criminal behavior in adult males
   c. suicide through violent means
   d. violent behavior in adult males

4. As discussed in your textbook, a psychology study conducted in the 1970s compared men raised in the northern part of the United States to men raised in the South. When a confederate in the study was verbally aggressive, southern men responded by:
   a. exhibiting increases in cortisol and testosterone
   b. acting violently toward the confederate
   c. refusing to participate in the study
   d. challenging the confederate's bad behavior

5. Dillon arrives late at the airport because of a big accident on the highway, waits on the security line for almost an hour, and is in danger of missing his flight. The baggage inspector flags Dillon's bag to be hand searched. Although Dillon is usually very even-tempered, he starts to yell abusively at the inspector. Dillon's behavior can be readily explained by:
   a. low serotonin level
   b. the accumulated-stress hypothesis
   c. the frustration-aggression hypothesis
   d. a damaged amygdala

6. In the cognitive-neoassociationistic model, frustration leads to aggression by which of the following paths?
   a. frustration, related cognition, negative affect, aggression
   b. frustration, negative affect, related cognition, aggression
   c. frustration, fight-or-flight response, suppressed cognition, aggression
   d. frustration, suppressed cognition, fight-or-flight response, aggression

7. Cross-cultural comparisons of levels of violence support the conclusion that:
   a. humans have evolved to engage in certain kinds of violence
   b. aggressive acts such as murder derive from basically adaptive behavior
   c. cultural factors influence aggressive behavior
   d. genetic differences account for cross-cultural differences in aggression

8. According to the idea of kin selection, we tend to be:
   a. altruistic to people who give evidence of the best genes
   b. most altruistic toward people who share our genes
   c. most altruistic to relatives because we expect reciprocity
   d. altruistic to our kin group to avoid being ostracized

9. The value of reciprocal helping is that it increases the person's:
   a. potential value as a mate
   b. status within the group
   c. capability as an employee
   d. probability of survival

10. Shaina is walking to class when she sees a woman drop a large bag of groceries. Shaina is not inclined to help until she sees the woman look directly at her. Shaina then goes over to pick up groceries because she:
    a. has lost her anonymity
    b. feels guilty
    c. has little to lose
    d. has lost her anonymity and feels guilty

WHAT DID YOU MISS? Check your answers against the Answer Key at the end of this chapter of the Study Guide. The Answer Key also lists the page(s) in your text where each question is explained. If you missed any questions, go to the pages indicated in the Answer Key, reread those sections, go back to the questions, and see if you can answer them correctly this time.

ANOTHER OPPORTUNITY TO REVIEW: Answer these questions without your textbook. As a rule of thumb, if you can write only a few words about these questions, you probably need to go back and review.

1. Identify biological, situational, and sociocultural determinants of aggression. _____
_____
_____

TRY IT

Loving Kindness Meditation

Often we focus on our difficult relationships and tend to take our easy relationships for granted. All of these relationships—even those we don't think about, such as our relationship with the barrista who makes our coffee or the attendant at the gas station—are the threads that form the fabric of life. A traditional Buddhist approach to understanding and thus honoring relationships is a meditation technique called "Loving Kindness Meditation." This technique may help you see the commonalities in all relationships.

Begin by sitting in a relaxed position. With your eyes open or closed, bring to mind an image of yourself. Imagine looking yourself in the eye and saying, "May I be well. May I be safe and secure." With each breath, send this message to the image of yourself. Now bring to mind someone important to you or someone you love. Imagine looking this person in the eye and, with each breath, sending the message "May you be well. May you be safe and secure." Now bring to mind your family or another group of people who are important to you. Imagine sending them these wishes as you breathe. Now imagine members of your class, the people you work with, or other people with whom you are in contact; as you bring these images to mind, offer the wishes to this extended group. Finally, recognizing that people are more alike than they are different and that most of us want most of the same things, consider bringing to mind an even larger group, such as people in this country or another country, maybe even a country with which we are in conflict, and consider offering the wishes to the image you bring to mind. Conclude with a few moments of quiet breathing. What did you observe about this process? Did you notice any changes in your attitudes as a result of this exercise?

2. Discuss the association between steroid use and aggression.

_____

_____

3. Review evolutionary explanations for altruism. _____

_____

_____

4. Review explanations for the bystander intervention effect.

_____

_____

WHAT DO I NEED TO KNOW? Based on what you have discovered above, what are the areas where you need to focus your studying? Which objectives do you need to spend more time mastering? Write this information down in your own words.

1. _____

2. _____

3. _____

4. _____

5. _____

6. _____

12.5 What Determines the Quality of Relationships?

Why are we attracted to some people? What causes us to form close relationships? There are several types of love, and the love we have for someone may change over time. This section will present cognitive techniques that may help to keep your relationships alive and thriving.

12.5 Guiding Questions

To guide your reading of the text, review the following questions. Then, as you read the chapter, look for the answers to these questions. You may want to note in your textbook where you find these answers.

1. Identify factors that influence interpersonal attraction.

2. Distinguish between passionate and companionate love.

3. Discuss the function of idealization in romantic relationships.

4. Identify interpersonal styles and attributional styles that contribute to relationship dissatisfaction and dissolution.

NOW READ Section 12.5 "What Determines the Quality of Relationships?" keeping these questions in mind.

REVIEW: Now that you've read this section, go back to the 12.5 Guiding Questions and see if you can answer them based on what you've read. This is a check on your reading. If you can't answer a question, you need to go back to the text to reread that section.

VISUAL SUMMARY: Below is a summary of the major concepts in this section. To check your comprehension of the chapter, read the summary and ask yourself if you understand the concepts. If the concepts seem unfamiliar to you, you may want to go back to the book and reread those sections. This text is taken from the Visual Summaries on StudySpace at wwnorton.com/studyspace.

XX. Relationships Are Connections with Friends and with Romantic Partners

XXI. Situational and Personal Factors Influence Friendships
  A. Relationships are promoted by:
    i. proximity.
    ii. similarity.
    iii. admirable personality characteristics.
    iv. physical attractiveness.

XXII. Love Is an Important Component of Romantic Relationships
  A. Passionate love:
    i. is intense longing and sexual desire.
    ii. generally happens early in relationships.
  B. Companionate love:
    i. is strong commitment to caring for and supporting partner.
    ii. evolves in relationships.
  C. Love in relationships may be related to early attachment styles.

XXIII. Love Is Fostered by Idealization
  A. Viewing partner in unrealistically positive terms predicts early stability of relationship.

XXIV. Staying in Love Can Require Work
  A. Romantic discord is predicted by:
    i. criticism.
    ii. contempt.
    iii. defensiveness.
    iv. mental withdrawing.
  B. Romantic satisfaction is predicted by:
    i. care.
    ii. concern.
    iii. cooperative problem solving.
    iv. overlooking bad behavior or responding constructively.

REINFORCE: Are you ready to check your knowledge of this section? Answer the following multiple-choice questions with your textbook closed.

1. Sharrita has just started a new job. She is smart, attractive, funny, and reliable, yet her coworkers do not seem to like her. According to the literature on friendship formation, Sharrita might improve her relationships with her coworkers by:
   a. helping them with their projects
   b. dressing down to be less attractive
   c. stumbling and falling when she gets up to give a big presentation
   d. asking them for help she really does not need

2. People who are biracial tend to be _____ attractive because their faces _____.
   a. less; have incompatible features
   b. more; are more symmetrical
   c. less; look unfamiliar to most people
   d. more; seem more average

3. At age 5, Lokelani is stunningly beautiful. The research on physical attractiveness suggests that:
   a. people will tend to overestimate her intelligence and character
   b. she will be more successful and more interesting than most people
   c. she will never develop her other abilities and opportunities
   d. she will intimidate a lot of men

4. Alyssa and Orlando have been together for 3 years. The first year was overwhelming. They spent all of their time together, and every meeting was intense and arousing. Their relationship now is less intense, but involves deep caring and intimacy. According to Hatfield and Berscheid, Alyssa and Orlando have moved from _____ love to _____ love.
   a. romantic; consummate
   b. passionate; companionate
   c. infatuated; mature
   d. physical; friendly

5. Which of the following statements is true about conflict in a relationship?
   a. Happy couples keep their dissatisfactions to themselves.
   b. The less conflict there is in a relationship, the better the relationship is.
   c. The amount of conflict matters less than the way in which it is handled.
   d. Conflict is usually problematic, so denial of problems is most useful.

6. Renee and Yves have been together for just over a year. They are having sex much less frequently and feel much less passionately about each other. If their relationship is going to last, Renee and Yves need to:
   a. find a way to reignite the passion between them
   b. develop stronger bonds of support and intimacy
   c. restructure their relationship as a friendship
   d. get counseling to figure out why they are falling out of love

7. Romantic relationships are damaged by conflict in which the couple _____ and strengthened by conflict in which the couple _____.

a. insults or demeans each other; sees each other's point of view
b. withdraws emotionally; suppresses disagreements
c. suppresses disagreements; expresses mutual concern during the conflict
d. insults each other; is openly critical

8. Before she got married, Su-lin sought the advice of her grandmother, who had been happily married for over 50 years to a man who, Su-lin knew, could be difficult at times. Which of the following pieces of advice, according to your textbook, would Su-lin have received from her grandmother that might explain her years of happy marriage?
   a. "Live your own life, find your own interests, and ignore him as much as possible."
   b. "I always try to find the good things about him, and believe me, they're there."
   c. "You have to remember that he's a man and consequently has many weaknesses."
   d. "If you let him make the decisions in most things, then he'll be happy, and you'll be happy."

9. One morning, Leo and Jenny have a major argument. That night, he gives her a lovely necklace to apologize. Jenny thinks that he gave her the necklace not to make her happy but to make himself feel better. Jenny is making a(n) _____ attribution.
   a. partner-enhancing
   b. assimilation
   c. accommodation
   d. distress-maintaining

10. Lucia is recently divorced. She goes to lunch with her two closest friends and tells them that although she is sad, she is also optimistic that she will find another, better relationship. Lucia most likely had a(n) _____ attachment to her parents as a child.
    a. secure
    b. avoidant
    c. disorganized
    d. anxious-ambivalent

WHAT DID YOU MISS? Check your answers against the Answer Key at the end of this chapter of the Study Guide. The Answer Key also lists the page(s) in your text where each question is explained. If you missed any questions, go to the pages indicated in the Answer Key, reread those sections, go back to the questions, and see if you can answer them correctly this time.

ANOTHER OPPORTUNITY TO REVIEW: Answer these questions without your textbook. As a rule of thumb, if you can write only a few words about these questions, you probably need to go back and review.

1. Identify factors that influence interpersonal attraction.
   _____
   _____

2. Distinguish between passionate and companionate love.
   _____
   _____

3. Discuss the function of idealization in romantic relationships. _____
   _____
   _____

4. Identify interpersonal styles and attributional styles that contribute to relationship dissatisfaction and dissolution.
   _____
   _____

WHAT DO I NEED TO KNOW? Based on what you've discovered above, what are the areas where you need to focus your studying? Which objectives do you need to spend more time mastering? Write this information down in your own words.

1. _____
2. _____
3. _____
4. _____
5. _____
6. _____

WHAT MATTERS TO ME: What facts in this chapter are personally relevant to you?

_____
_____
_____
_____

CHAPTER SUMMARY

12.1 How Do We Form Our Impressions of Others?

- *Nonverbal Actions and Expressions Affect Our First Impressions:* Nonverbal behavior, sometimes referred to as body language, is interpreted quickly and provides valuable information. Important nonverbal cues include gait, facial expression, and eye contact.

- *We Make Attributions about Others:* We use personal dispositions and situational factors to explain other people's behavior. The fundamental attribution error occurs when personal attributions are favored over situational attributions in explaining other people's behavior. Our tendency to make personal attributions when explaining other people's behavior and situational attributions when explaining our own behavior is referred to as the actor/observer discrepancy.

- *Stereotypes Are Based on Automatic Categorization:* Stereotypes are cognitive schemas that allow for fast, easy processing of social information. Self-fulfilling prophecies occur when people behave in ways that confirm their own or other people's expectations. Stereotype threat is a self-fulfilling prophecy in which people behave in ways that confirm negative stereotypes of their group.

- *Stereotypes Can Lead to Prejudice:* Prejudice occurs when the feelings, opinions, and beliefs associated with a stereotype are negative. Prejudice can lead to discrimination, the inappropriate and unjustified treatment of others. We show a preference for members of ingroups versus members of outgroups. Stereotypes may be inhibited—for instance, by presenting people with positive examples of negatively stereotyped groups.

- *Cooperation Can Reduce Prejudice:* Sharing superordinate goals that require cooperation can lead to reduced prejudice and discrimination.

12.2 How Do Attitudes Guide Behavior?

- *We Form Attitudes through Experience and Socialization:* Attitudes are evaluations of objects, of events, or of ideas. Attitudes are influenced by familiarity (the mere exposure effect) and may be shaped by conditioning and socialization.

- *Behaviors Are Consistent with Strong Attitudes:* Attitudes that are strong, personally relevant, specific, formed through personal experience, and easily accessible are most likely to affect behavior.

- *Attitudes Can Be Explicit or Implicit:* Implicit attitudes operate at an unconscious level. Implicit attitudes may differ from explicit attitudes, or those attitudes that we are consciously aware of and can report. In situations that are socially sensitive, implicit attitudes tend to predict behavior better than explicit attitudes do.

- *Discrepancies Lead to Dissonance:* A contradiction between attitudes or between an attitude and a behavior produces cognitive dissonance. This state is characterized by anxiety, tension, and displeasure. People reduce dissonance by changing their attitudes or behaviors, or by rationalizing or trivializing the discrepancies.

- *Attitudes Can Be Changed through Persuasion:* Persuasion involves the use of a message to actively and consciously change an attitude. According to the elaboration likelihood model, persuasion through the central route (which involves careful thought about the message) produces stronger and more persistent attitude change than persuasion through the peripheral route (which relies on peripheral cues, such as the attractiveness of the person making the argument).

12.3 How Do Others Influence Us?

- *Groups Influence Individual Behavior:* The presence of others can improve performance (social facilitation) or result in decreased effort (social loafing). Loss of individuality and self-awareness (deindividuation) can occur in groups. Group decisions can become extreme (group polarization), and poor decisions may be made to preserve group harmony (groupthink).

- *We Conform to Others:* Conformity occurs when we alter our behavior or opinions to match the behaviors, opinions, or expectations of others. Conformity increases when we are in a large group and the group demonstrates unanimity.

- *We Are Compliant:* Compliance occurs when we agree to the requests of others. Compliance increases when we are in a good mood or are subjected to tactics such as the foot-in-the-door, door-in-the-face, and low-balling techniques.

- *We Are Obedient to Authority:* Obedience occurs when we follow the orders of an authority. As demonstrated by Milgram's famous study, people may inflict harm on others if ordered to do so by an authority. Individuals who are concerned about others' perceptions of them are more likely to be obedient. Obedience decreases with greater distance from the authority.

12.4 When Do We Harm or Help Others?

- *Many Factors Can Influence Aggression:* Aggression is influenced by biological, situational, and sociocultural factors. The amygdala and the neurotransmitter serotonin have been implicated in aggressive behavior. Situations that elicit negative emotions—including frustration—increase the likelihood of aggression. In societies that advocate a culture of honor, people are more likely to exhibit violence.

- *Steroids May Play a Role in Some Violent Behavior:* Research has demonstrated a modest correlation between testosterone and aggression. Steroids may promote aggressive behavior, at least in some users.

- *Many Factors Can Influence Helping Behavior:* Prosocial behaviors maintain social relations. Altruism toward kin members increases the likelihood of passing on common genes. Altruism toward nonrelatives increases the likelihood that others will reciprocate help when we need it.

- *Some Situations Lead to Bystander Apathy:* The bystander intervention effect occurs when we fail to help others in need. This effect is most likely to occur when other bystanders are present and we experience diffusion of responsibility; when a situation is unclear and we fear making social blunders; when we are anonymous; and when we perceive greater risk than benefit to helping others.

12.5 What Determines the Quality of Relationships?

- *Situational and Personal Factors Influence Friendships:* People are attracted to individuals that they have frequent contact with, with whom they share similar attributes, who possess admirable characteristics, and who are physically attractive.
- *Love Is an Important Component of Romantic Relationships:* Passionate love is characterized by intense longing and sexual desire. Companionate love is characterized by commitment and support. In successful romantic relationships, passionate love tends to evolve into companionate love.
- *Love Is Fostered by Idealization:* Romantic relationships may be more resilient when partners view each other in unrealistically positive terms.
- *Staying in Love Can Require Work:* How a couple deals with conflict influences the stability of their relationship. Being overly critical, holding a partner in contempt, being defensive, and mentally withdrawing are maladaptive strategies for coping with interpersonal conflict. Couples that attribute positive outcomes to each other and negative outcomes to situational factors and make partner-enhancing attributions report higher levels of marital happiness.

PUTTING IT ALL TOGETHER

Answer these questions to check your knowledge of the material in this chapter.

1. Due to the relocation of a manufacturing plant, there has been an influx of Muslim individuals into a rural, mostly Christian community. This change in the population has resulted in expressions of anti-Muslim prejudice in local schools. What strategies should the school administrators use to inhibit stereotypes and encourage acceptance of differences between groups?

2. Describe some television commercials or Internet advertisements that emphasize either the central route

or the peripheral route of communication of the elaboration likelihood model. Identify factors such as source, content, receiver, and one- versus two-sided arguments.

3. Give three modern-day examples of obedience to authority. In each instance, what factors contributed to this behavior? What situational factors could be, or could have been, changed to alter it?

4. A man goes to see a movie alone and suffers a heart attack in the theater. Identify four factors that will influence whether other patrons will choose to help him.

5. You have just gone out on a date with the person of your dreams—your "soulmate." Use the principles of romantic relationships to identify SPECIFIC things you can do to improve the odds that this relationship will last.

ANSWER KEY FOR REINFORCE QUESTIONS

Section 12.1

1.	b	p. 517
2.	a	p. 517
3.	b	p. 517
4.	b	p. 518
5.	b	p. 514
6.	a	p. 518
7.	c	p. 518
8.	c	p. 520
9	a	p. 522
10.	c	p. 525

Section 12.2

1.	a	p. 528
2.	c	p. 528
3.	a	p. 529
4.	c	p. 529
5.	b	p. 529
6.	d	p. 530
7.	c	p. 533
8.	b	p. 532
9.	c	p. 532
10.	c	p. 531

Section 12.3

1.	c	p.537
2.	d	p. 537
3.	a	p. 537
4.	c	p. 538
5.	d	p. 538
6.	b	p. 540

7. d p. 543
8. b p. 543
9. a p. 544
10. a p. 544

Section 12.4

1. b p. 547
2. d p. 552
3. b p. 547
4. a p. 550
5. c p. 548
6. b p. 548
7. c p. 548
8. b p. 552
9. d p. 552
10. a pp. 553–554

Section 12.5

1. c p. 556
2. b p. 557
3. a p. 558
4. b p. 558
5. c p. 562
6. b pp. 559–561
7. a pp. 560–562
8. b p. 559
9. d p. 562
10. a p. 559

HINTS FOR PUTTING IT ALL TOGETHER QUESTIONS

1. Strategies should include presenting the groups with positive information about the members of the negatively stereotyped group and requiring the members of the different groups to work cooperatively toward superordinate goals.

2. Answers should address how the central route of persuasion is used when people are motivated to listen, consider all the information, and use rational cognitive processes. The peripheral route of persuasion is used when people minimally process the message. In this case, impulsive decisions are made for superficial reasons, such as the attractiveness of the celebrity endorser. Issues of source, content, receiver, and one- versus two-sided arguments should be addressed within this context.

3. Contributing factors for the examples could include deindividuation, social facilitation, inappropriate norms, and conformity. Possible means of altering obedience include reducing the status of the authority figure, humanizing the victim, and changing characteristics of the situation to give more responsibility to the participant.

4. Answers for the possible bystander intervention effect should include the number of individuals present, the fear of making social blunders, the anonymity of the movie crowd and whether helpers could remain anonymous, and a cost/benefit analysis.

5. Answers should include the six factors listed by Gottman: show interest in your partner, be affectionate, show you care, spend quality time together, maintain loyalty and fidelity, and learn how to handle conflict.

KEY TERMS EXERCISES

First, fill in your own definition and example for each term. Then check each term against the textbook's definition. These exercises can also be cut out and used as flash cards.

aggression

Your Definition:
Your Example:
Textbook Definition:

bystander intervention effect

Your Definition:
Your Example:
Textbook Definition:

altruism

Your Definition:
Your Example:
Textbook Definition:

cognitive dissonance

Your Definition:
Your Example:
Textbook Definition:

attitudes

Your Definition:
Your Example:
Textbook Definition:

compliance

Your Definition:
Your Example:
Textbook Definition:

attributions

Your Definition:
Your Example:
Textbook Definition:

conformity

Your Definition:
Your Example:
Textbook Definition:

deindividuation

Your Definition:
Your Example:
Textbook Definition:

frustration-aggression hypothesis

Your Definition:
Your Example:
Textbook Definition:

discrimination

Your Definition:
Your Example:
Textbook Definition:

fundamental attribution error

Your Definition:
Your Example:
Textbook Definition:

elaboration likelihood model

Your Definition:
Your Example:
Textbook Definition:

implicit attitudes

Your Definition:
Your Example:
Textbook Definition:

explicit attitudes

Your Definition:
Your Example:
Textbook Definition:

ingroup favoritism

Your Definition:
Your Example:
Textbook Definition:

nonverbal behavior

Your Definition:
Your Example:
Textbook Definition:

prosocial

Your Definition:
Your Example:
Textbook Definition:

personal attributions

Your Definition:
Your Example:
Textbook Definition:

self-fulfilling prophecy

Your Definition:
Your Example:
Textbook Definition:

persuasion

Your Definition:
Your Example:
Textbook Definition:

situational attributions

Your Definition:
Your Example:
Textbook Definition:

prejudice

Your Definition:
Your Example:
Textbook Definition:

social facilitation

Your Definition:
Your Example:
Textbook Definition:

social loafing

Your Definition:
Your Example:
Textbook Definition:

social norms

Your Definition:
Your Example:
Textbook Definition:

CHAPTER 13 | Personality

CHAPTER OVERVIEW

Why do you act the way you do? How do you describe your personality? In this chapter, you'll read more about some of the most famous figures who have influenced how we understand psychological functioning. You'll also learn about how personality is assessed. Will your personality remain the same from situation to situation? Will your personality remain the same throughout your life? Finally, how accurate are we in understanding ourselves and our abilities?

13.1 How Have Psychologists Studied Personality?

How has psychologists' understanding of personality evolved over the past century? As you read more about Freud, Skinner, Rogers, and other psychologists who have studied personality, consider which theory best fits your understanding of how people's personalities develop.

At the beginning of each section in the Study Guide, there will be guiding questions. Before you read the chapter in your textbook, read through these questions and maybe even attempt to answer them based on either what you've already read or what you think the answer should be. Then as you study the chapter, you can use them to help guide your reading.

13.1 Guiding Questions

To guide your reading of the text, review the following questions. Then, as you read the chapter, look for the answers to these questions. You may want to note in your textbook where you find these answers.

1. Describe the major approaches to the study of personality.

2. Identify theorists associated with the major approaches to the study of personality.

3. Define key terms associated with the major approaches to the study of personality.

NOW READ Section 13.1 "How Have Psychologists Studied Personality?" keeping these questions in mind.

REVIEW: Now that you've read this section, go back to the 13.1 Guiding Questions and see if you can answer them based on what you've read. This is a check on your reading. If you can't answer a question, you need to go back to the text to reread that section.

VISUAL SUMMARY: Below is a summary of the major concepts in this section. To check your comprehension of the chapter, read the summary and ask yourself if you understand the concepts. If the concepts seem unfamiliar to you, you may want to go back to the book and reread those sections. This text is taken from the Visual Summaries on StudySpace at wwnorton.com/studyspace.

I. Personality Consists of Characteristic Thoughts, Emotional Responses, and Behaviors That Are Relatively Stable in Individual over Time and across Circumstances

II. Personality Trait Is Enduring Tendency to Act in Particular Way over Time and across Circumstances

III. Psychodynamic Theories Emphasize Unconscious and Dynamic Processes
   A. According to Freud:

i. unconscious forces and conflicts determine behavior.
ii. personality structure:
   a. id (seeks pleasure and avoids pain).
   b. superego (internalizes standards of conduct).
   c. ego (mediates between id and superego).
iii. defense mechanisms: unconscious mental strategies designed to neutralize distress associated with conflict between id and superego.
iv. psychosexual stages:
   a. oral.
   b. anal.
   c. phallic.
   d. latency.
   e. genital.
B. Neo-Freudians:
   i. focus less on sexual forces and more on social interactions between parent and child.

IV. Humanistic Approaches Emphasize Integrated Personal Experience
A. We seek to fulfill personal potential through greater self-understanding:
   i. Maslow emphasized self-actualization.
   ii. Rogers emphasized unconditional positive regard.

V. Personality Reflects Learning and Cognition
A. Cognitive-social theories emphasize how personal beliefs, expectancies, and interpretations of social situations shape behavior and personality.

VI. Trait Approaches Describe Behavioral Dispositions
A. Personality types: discrete categories of people based on personality characteristics.
B. Trait approach: focuses on individuals' differences in personality traits.
C. Five-factor theory (OCEAN):
   i. openness to experience
   ii. conscientiousness
   iii. extraversion
   iv. agreeableness
   v. neuroticism

REINFORCE: Are you ready to check your knowledge of this section? Answer the following multiple-choice questions with your textbook closed.

1. Which of the following factors did Gordon Allport NOT emphasize in his definition of personality?
   a. a changing, dynamic structure
   b. a psychophysical basis
   c. a coherent organization
   d. an id, an ego, and a superego

2. A personality trait:
   a. tends to be unstable
   b. is a tendency to behave in a certain way across various circumstances
   c. is the intention that naive observers agree characterizes a person
   d. is a temporary disposition to behave in a certain way

3. In Freud's model, consciousness:
   a. is divided into three zones or levels
   b. is more important than the unconscious
   c. is the domain within which the libido operates
   d. is closely related to id processes

4. During the phallic stage, children develop hostility toward the same-sex parent because they desire an exclusive relationship with the opposite-sex parent. Freud argued that this conflict is typically resolved by:
   a. the child's taking on many of the same-sexed parent's values and ideals
   b. the child's rationalizing the hostility in terms of the characteristics of the same-sex parent
   c. the id, which attempts to rein in the sexual urges
   d. the time the child turns 4

5. In Freud's structural model of personality:
   a. the superego dominates other structures in determining behavior
   b. the ego operates according to the reality principle
   c. the ego eventually becomes unresponsive to the id because of mental habituation
   d. the superego is the realistic, rational portion of the mind

6. Marta is the last person in her family to go to college. Her older siblings have encouraged her to be a doctor or a lawyer, but she feels that to be an artist would be her ultimate goal. Which of these theorists would most clearly be in favor of Marta's following her dream of becoming an artist?
   a. Shinobu Kitayama
   b. Sigmund Freud
   c. Walter Mischel
   d. Abraham Maslow

7. If you were a parent who embraced Carl Rogers's person-centered approach to personality, how would you treat your child?
   a. You would withhold treats and gifts to reinforce your rules.
   b. You would emphasize the child's responsibility for his or her failures.
   c. You would express love and support for the child no matter how she or he behaved.

d. You would surround the child with positive peers, because parents do not actually have much influence on children's behavior.

8. The five-factor theory has _____ factors and is _____ widely accepted than Eysenck's theory.
   a. more; more
   b. fewer; less
   c. more; less
   d. fewer; more

9. Researchers have found that the trait of conscientiousness predicts _____ and openness to experience predicts _____.
   a. friendliness; extraversion
   b. intelligence; impulsivity
   c. college grades; standardized test scores
   d. shyness; extraversion

10. Bandura's cognitive-social theory of personality sees _____ as an important determinant of behavior.
    a. one's beliefs concerning self-efficacy
    b. stereotypes
    c. attributional style
    d. biological predispositions

WHAT DID YOU MISS? Check your answers against the Answer Key at the end of this chapter of the Study Guide. The Answer Key also lists the page(s) in your text where each question is explained. If you missed any questions, go to the pages indicated in the Answer Key, reread those sections, go back to the questions, and see if you can answer them correctly this time.

ANOTHER OPPORTUNITY TO REVIEW: Answer these questions without your textbook. As a rule of thumb, if you can write only a few words about these questions, you probably need to go back and review.

1. Describe the major approaches to the study of personality.

   _____

   _____

2. Identify theorists associated with the major approaches to the study of personality. _____

   _____

   _____

3. Define key terms associated with the major approaches to the study of personality. _____

   _____

   _____

WHAT DO I NEED TO KNOW? Based on what you've discovered above, what are the areas where you need to focus your studying? Which objectives do you need to spend more time mastering? Write this information down in your own words.

1. _____

2. _____

3. _____

4. _____

5. _____

6. _____

13.2 How Is Personality Assessed, and What Does It Predict about People?

Who is better at understanding your personality and predicting your behavior—you or a good friend? Is your personality constant, or does it change from situation to situation? How have your culture and your gender influenced your personality?

13.2 Guiding Questions

To guide your reading of the text, review the following questions. Then, as you read the chapter, look for the answers to these questions. You may want to note in your textbook where you find these answers.

1. Distinguish between idiographic and nomothetic approaches to the study of personality.

2. Distinguish between projective and objective measures of personality.

3. Discuss the accuracy of observers' personality judgments.

4. Define situationism and interactionism.

5. Distinguish between strong situations and weak situations.

6. Discuss cultural and sex differences in personality.

NOW READ Section 13.2 "How Is Personality Assessed, and What Does It Predict about People?" keeping these questions in mind.

REVIEW: Now that you've read this section, go back to the 13.2 Guiding Questions and see if you can answer them based on what you've read. This is a check on your reading. If you can't answer a question, you need to go back to the text to reread that section.

VISUAL SUMMARY: Below is a summary of the major concepts in this section. To check your comprehension of the chapter, read the summary and ask yourself if you understand the concepts. If the concepts seem unfamiliar to you, you may want to go back to the book and reread those sections. This text is taken from the Visual Summaries on StudySpace at wwnorton.com/studyspace.

VII. Personality Refers to Both Unique and Common Characteristics
   A. Idiographic approaches: focus on the integration of characteristics in individual's lives.
   B. Nomothetic approaches: focus on how common characteristics vary from person to person.

VIII. Researchers Use Projective and Objective Methods to Assess Personality
   A. Projective measures examine unconscious processes by having people interpret ambiguous stimuli.
   B. Objective measures directly assess personality, usually through self-report questionnaires or observer ratings.

IX. Observers Show Accuracy in Trait Judgments
   A. Close friends may be more accurate in predicting our behavior than we are.

X. People Sometimes Are Inconsistent
   A. According to situationists, behavior:
      i. is determined more by situations than by personality.
      ii. cannot be reliably predicted without understanding the situation.

XI. Behavior Is Influenced by the Interaction of Personality and Situations
   A. According to interactionists, behavior is determined jointly by:
      i. situations.
      ii. personality traits.

XII. There Are Cultural and Gender Differences in Personality
   A. The Big Five personality traits are cross-cultural.
   B. Cross-cultural personality differences do not necessarily match cultural stereotypes.
   C. Differences between men and women:
      i. largely support cultural stereotypes.
      ii. are greater in individualistic societies.

REINFORCE: Are you ready to check your knowledge of this section? Answer the following multiple-choice questions with your textbook closed.

1. How do the idiographic and nomothetic approaches to studying personality differ?
   a. The first focuses on the characteristics specific to given people, whereas the latter looks at similarities across people.
   b. The first uses projective reports, whereas the latter employs case reports.
   c. The first uses research methods, whereas the latter employs psychobiography.
   d. They employ essentially the same methods, but make different assumptions about personality dynamics.

2. Broadly speaking, your textbook divides personality assessment procedures into _____ measures.
   a. self-report and physiological
   b. descriptive and projective
   c. projective and objective
   d. psychodynamic and humanistic

3. According to research on the Rorschach inkblot test, the test:
   a. does an excellent job of identifying specific psychological disorders
   b. identifies many adults and children as psychologically disturbed when in fact they are not
   c. is the most reliable of the many personality tests in use
   d. is well-validated and reliable

4. The objective measures of personality described in your textbook:
   a. are able to reveal information about a person that the person may not wish revealed
   b. enable people to project their emotional conflicts onto neutral stimuli
   c. do not allow for the assessment of specific traits
   d. assess what respondents report believing or observing

5. When Janelle was asked to describe her friends' personalities, she did so quickly and accurately. When asked to describe her own personality, it took her a while to organize her thoughts and respond. Her difficulty in responding to questions about her own personality provides evidence for which research finding?

a. People tend to lie about their characters to fit others' preconceptions.
b. People have limited knowledge of their own behaviors because they often pay attention to others' behaviors.
c. People like to appear thoughtful when asked questions about themselves.
d. People try to mask their excessive self-interest by appearing uninterested in their own behaviors.

6. In observing a given situation, who would give the most accurate description of a particular woman's personality?
a. a stranger, who might be more objective than her friends and family
b. a coworker who has known her for 2 years
c. her adult children, who have lived with her for decades
d. a professional who knows her; for example, her doctor or teacher

7. According to your textbook, most contemporary trait theorists:
a. strongly emphasize unconscious processes
b. emphasize the impact of both situations and personality in determining behavior
c. emphasize specific rather than general personality traits
d. have failed to respond to Mischel's critique of trait theory generally

8. One response to Mischel's situationism critique of trait theory is to argue that:
a. traits are more predictive of behavior if they are central rather than peripheral or secondary
b. some people may be more consistent than others
c. when behaviors are averaged across many situations, traits are better predictors of behavior
d. all of the above

9. Mischel has argued that trait theories have difficulty predicting behavior because:
a. the typical trait measures have low reliability
b. our behavior is more responsive to situational variables than such theories assume
c. the traits thus far identified relate to conscious rather than unconscious motives
d. they depend on self-report rather than on objective measures of traits

10. In terms of gender differences in personality:
a. women and men are most similar in personality in industrialized countries, such as the United States
b. women tend to be more agreeable and more neurotic
c. women tend to be more extraverted and more open to experience
d. more data have been collected on men, so it is difficult to compare personalities across genders

WHAT DID YOU MISS? Check your answers against the Answer Key at the end of this chapter of the Study Guide. The Answer Key also lists the page(s) in your text where each question is explained. If you missed any questions, go to the pages indicated in the Answer Key, reread those sections, go back to the questions, and see if you can answer them correctly this time.

ANOTHER OPPORTUNITY TO REVIEW: Answer these questions without your textbook. As a rule of thumb, if you can write only a few words about these questions, you probably need to go back and review.

1. Distinguish between idiographic and nomothetic approaches to the study of personality. _____
_____
_____

2. Distinguish between projective and objective measures of personality. _____
_____
_____

3. Discuss the accuracy of observers' personality judgments.
_____
_____

4. Define situationism and interactionism. _____
_____
_____

5. Distinguish between strong situations and weak situations.
_____
_____

6. Discuss cultural and sex differences in personality. _____
_____
_____

WHAT DO I NEED TO KNOW? Based on what you've discovered above, what are the areas where you need to focus your studying? Which objectives do you need to spend more time mastering? Write this information down in your own words.

1. _____

2. _____

3. _____

4. _____

5. _____

6. _____

13.3 What Are the Biological Bases of Personality?

Like many of the psychological factors you've been studying in this class, personality is affected by genetics and environment. Each of us is born with particular temperamental styles, which are the precursors to our adult personalities. Does the resulting personality change over time, or do aspects of it remain the same?

13.3 Guiding Questions

To guide your reading of the text, review the following questions. Then, as you read the chapter, look for the answers to these questions. You may want to note in your textbook where you find these answers.

1. Review research assessing personality traits among nonhuman animals.

2. Summarize the results of twin studies and adoption studies as those results pertain to personality.

3. Identify the genetic basis of novelty seeking, neuroticism, and agreeableness.

4. Identify distinct temperaments.

5. Discuss the neurobiological basis of extraversion/introversion.

6. Summarize the results of research on personality stability across time.

NOW READ Section 13.3 "What Are the Biological Bases of Personality?" keeping these questions in mind.

REVIEW: Now that you've read this section, go back to the 13.3 Guiding Questions and see if you can answer them based on what you've read. This is a check on your reading. If you can't answer a question, you need to go back to the text to reread that section.

VISUAL SUMMARY: Below is a summary of the major concepts in this section. To check your comprehension of the chapter, read the summary and ask yourself if you understand the concepts. If the concepts seem unfamiliar to you, you may want to go back to the book and reread those sections. This text is taken from the Visual Summaries on StudySpace at wwnorton.com/studyspace.

XIII. Genetic Makeup
    A. May predispose people to have particular traits.
    B. Its expression may be determined by environment.

XIV. Animals Have Personalities
    A. Extraversion, neuroticism, and ageeableness exist in most species.

XV. Personality Is Rooted in Genetics
    A. Genetics accounts for 40 percent to 60 percent of differences between individuals in personality traits.
    B. Personalities of adopted children are not significantly similar to personalities of their adoptive parents.

XVI. Temperaments Are Evident in Infancy
    A. Temperament:
        i. biologically based tendency to feel or act in ways that can predict adult personality.
        ii. activity level, emotionality, and sociability are temperaments that can be linked to personality traits.

XVII. Personality Is Linked to Specific Neurophysiological Mechanisms
    A. Behavioral approach system ("go"): brain structures lead organisms to pursue rewards.
    B. Behavioral inhibition system ("stop"): brain structures lead organisms to avoid potentially dangerous or pain-promoting behavior.

XVIII. Personality Is Adaptive
    A. The Big Five personality traits provide information in mate selection.

XIX. Personality Traits Are Stable over Time
    A. Personality traits:
        i. remain stable.
        ii. may be expressed differently in different situations.

REINFORCE: Are you ready to check your knowledge of this section? Answer the following multiple-choice questions with your textbook closed.

1. A science teacher tells her students that, like humans, monkeys have different personalities. The students think it is ridiculous to think that animals have "personality." Who is correct?
    a. The students are right; humans have personality and animals do not.
    b. The students are mostly right; people may "perceive" that animals have personality, but in fact

humans only "project" personality characteristics onto animals.

c. The teacher is right; but monkeys only show their personality differences in basic survival behaviors, such as eating and sleeping.

d. The teacher is right; monkeys show differences on basic human personality dimensions, such as extraversion and agreeableness.

2. Imagine that on your college or university campus, a number of dogs roam freely. If you test whether students have similar views of the dogs' "personalities," research suggests that:

a. students will project their own personality traits onto the dogs

b. most students will agree that the dogs have individual personalities, but there will be big differences in the traits attributed to them

c. owners of the dogs will rate the dogs' personalities as less positive than will nonowners

d. there will be a very high level of agreement regarding the personality traits displayed by the dogs

3. Which of the following statements represents one of the earliest pieces of evidence that personality has a genetic component?

a. Adopted children in the same family are not very similar in personality.

b. Identical twins are more similar in personality than fraternal twins.

c. People in the same culture, who apparently share similar genes, are similar in personality.

d. Men are more similar to other men in personality, and women are more similar to other women.

4. Although specific genes seem to be involved in personality, the effects of these genes on behavior are small. Why?

a. Environmental factors, such as culture, typically override genetic effects.

b. Free will is more important in determining behavior because it stems from personality and character.

c. Multiple genes interact independently with environment to produce general personality styles.

d. Genetic effects weaken over time.

5. According to recent psychological research, parenting style has how much influence on the personality of children?

a. less than had been previously assumed

b. more than psychologists had previously believed

c. strongest during the identity development stage of adolescence

d. strong in collectivistic cultures but weak in individualistic cultures

6. Which of the following characteristics have Buss and Plomin identified as basic traits or temperaments in infants?

a. novelty seeking, shyness, and activation

b. inhibition, extraversion, and sociability

c. activity level, emotionality, and sociability

d. shyness, sensation seeking, and agreeableness

7. In extraverts, the _____ is more active; in introverts, the _____ is more active.

a. BIS; BAS

b. BAS; BIS

c. prefrontal cortex; amygdala

d. amygdala; prefrontal cortex

8. Some evolutionary psychologists, such as David Buss, believe that:

a. the five-factor theory does not account for normal personality variation

b. Eysenck's personality model best describes the characteristics needed for human survival

c. the five-factor theory describes the personality characteristics that are important in mate selection

d. most personality theories cannot describe personality in a way that fits well with evolutionary theory

9. How are personality stability and age related?

a. Children are more stable in their traits than are older adults.

b. There is some stability at any age but particularly after age 50.

c. Age and personality stability are basically unrelated.

d. Stability in personality traits is constant across development.

10. Across cultures, as people age, they become _____ neurotic and extraverted and _____ conscientious.

a. less; more

b. less; less

c. more; less

d. more; more

WHAT DID YOU MISS? Check your answers against the Answer Key at the end of this chapter of the Study Guide. The Answer Key also lists the page(s) in your text where each question is explained. If you missed any questions, go to the pages indicated in the Answer Key, reread those sections, go back to the questions, and see if you can answer them correctly this time.

ANOTHER OPPORTUNITY TO REVIEW: Answer these questions without your textbook. As a rule of thumb, if you can write only a few words about these questions, you probably need to go back and review.

1. Review research assessing personality traits among nonhuman animals. _____

    _____

    _____

2. Summarize the results of twin studies and adoption studies as those results pertain to personality. _____

    _____

    _____

3. Identify the genetic basis of novelty seeking, neuroticism, and agreeableness. _____

    _____

    _____

4. Identify distinct temperaments. _____

    _____

    _____

5. Discuss the neurobiological basis of extraversion/ introversion. _____

    _____

    _____

6. Summarize the results of research on personality stability across time. _____

    _____

    _____

WHAT DO I NEED TO KNOW? Based on what you've discovered above, what are the areas where you need to focus your studying? Which objectives do you need to spend more time mastering? Write this information down in your own words.

1. _____

2. _____

3. _____

4. _____

5. _____

6. _____

13.4 How Do We Know Our Own Personalities?

Sue-Lyn is asked to lead a major project at work. How accurate will her perceptions of her ability to handle the job be? Most people have techniques to help them maintain a positive sense of self. How willing you are to make decisions independently or to look for guidance from family and friends may depend on your cultural background.

13.4 Guiding Questions

To guide your reading of the text, review the following questions. Then, as you read the chapter, look for the answers to these questions. You may want to note in your textbook where you find these answers.

1. Differentiate between self-awareness, self-schema, the working self-concept, and self-esteem.

2. Review theories of self-esteem.

3. Discuss research findings regarding the association between self-esteem and life outcomes.

4. Identify strategies people use to maintain positive self-views.

5. Discuss cultural differences in the self-concept and the use of self-serving biases.

NOW READ Section 13.4 "How Do We Know Our Own Personalities?" keeping these questions in mind.

REVIEW: Now that you've read this section, go back to the 13.4 Guiding Questions and see if you can answer them based on what you've read. This is a check on your reading. If you can't answer a question, you need to go back to the text to reread that section.

VISUAL SUMMARY: Below is a summary of the major concepts in this section. To check your comprehension of the chapter, read the summary and ask yourself if you understand the concepts. If the concepts seem unfamiliar to you, you may want to go back to the book and reread those sections. This text is taken from the Visual Summaries on StudySpace at wwnorton.com/studyspace.

XX. Our Self-Concepts Consist of Self-Knowledge
   A. Self-awareness: the self as object of attention.
   B. Self-schemas help in the perception, organization, interpretation, and use of information about the self.
   C. Working self-concept consists of personal information relevant to current situation.

XXI. Perceived Social Regard Influences Self-Esteem
  A. Self-esteem:
    i. is part of the self-concept.
    ii. evaluates personal worth.
    iii. may buffer against difficulties.
    iv. has little relationship to success in life.
  B. Sociometer: internal monitor of social acceptance or rejection.

XXII. We Use Mental Strategies to Maintain Our Views of Self
  A. Most people:
    i. overestimate their abilities.
    ii. overestimate their control over events.
    iii. are unrealistically optimistic about their futures.
  B. Strategies to maintain positive sense of self:
    i. self-evaluative maintenance
    ii. social comparisons
    iii. self-serving bias

XXIII. There Are Cultural Differences in the Self
  A. People in collectivist cultures tend to have interdependent self-construals.
  B. People in individualistic cultures tend to have independent self-construals.
  C. Universal desire for self-enhancement is stronger in individualistic cultures.

REINFORCE: Are you ready to check your knowledge of this section? Answer the following multiple-choice questions with your textbook closed.

1. Tory was asked, "Do you consider yourself smart?" Tory immediately answered, "I think I am just as smart as anyone else." Tory's ability to answer effortlessly and automatically, without having to think much about the question, shows that:
   a. she has low self-esteem and is providing a reactive answer
   b. she is unconsciously differentiating between the "I" and the "me" in her answer
   c. her self-schema contains information about her level of intelligence
   d. she probably does not value intelligence

2. According to your textbook, when an important figure rejects, demeans, or devalues a person, which of the following constructs is most likely to be affected?
   a. self-schema
   b. self-esteem
   c. self-concept
   d. self-knowledge

3. Shariah has noticed that people in her social group have been avoiding her. They no longer call her or ask her to go out with them. Shariah used to have high self-esteem, but now she is experiencing low self-esteem. What theory would predict this change in her self-esteem?
   a. social conformity theory
   b. self-other comparison theory
   c. sociometer theory
   d. self-appraisal theory

4. Terror management theory predicts that people will experience the highest self-esteem when:
   a. other people evaluate them positively
   b. they behave in self-consistent ways
   c. they are reminded of sickness and death
   d. others around them have low self-esteem

5. Ahmed states that he has high self-esteem and is happy with his life. Based on this information, it is possible to predict:
   a. that he has a high level of achievement in other areas of his life
   b. that he has a moderate level of achievement in other areas of his life
   c. that he has a low level of achievement in other areas of his life
   d. very little about other areas of his life

6. The "better-than-average effect" describes:
   a. almost no one
   b. about 10 percent of the population
   c. about 30 percent of the population
   d. most of the population

7. When George, who is the star of his high school basketball team, mentions many times that his cousin is a famous professional basketball star, he is "basking in the glow of reflected glory." This tendency:
   a. results in lower self-esteem for those listening to George
   b. results in lower self-esteem for George
   c. is called social esteem
   d. is a self-evaluation maintenance strategy

8. Making downward comparisons has been shown to:
   a. increase self-esteem
   b. decrease self-esteem
   c. have little effect on self-esteem
   d. have a negative effect on the people to whom one is being compared

9. After failing a test, Troy explained his poor performance by saying, "I planned to study really hard for this exam, but I was feeling sick, so I did poorly." During a previous exam, when Troy did well, he said that he studied for many hours and that all his hard work had paid off. Troy is showing evidence of:
   a. self-schema rearrangement
   b. a self-serving bias

c. a positive illusion

d. self-deprecation

10. One current view on self-enhancement suggests that:
    a. Easterners tend to self-enhance more than Westerners
    b. Westerners tend to self-enhance more than Easterners
    c. Easterners and Westerners tend to differ in how they self-enhance
    d. Easterners and Westerners both tend to self-enhance about equally and do so in similar ways

WHAT DID YOU MISS? Check your answers against the Answer Key at the end of this chapter of the Study Guide. The Answer Key also lists the page(s) in your text where each question is explained. If you missed any questions, go to the pages indicated in the Answer Key, reread those sections, go back to the questions, and see if you can answer them correctly this time.

ANOTHER OPPORTUNITY TO REVIEW: Answer these questions without your textbook. As a rule of thumb, if you can write only a few words about these questions, you probably need to go back and review.

1. Differentiate between self-awareness, self-schema, the working self-concept, and self-esteem. _____

   _____

   _____

2. Review theories of self-esteem. _____

   _____

   _____

3. Discuss research findings regarding the association between self-esteem and life outcomes. _____

   _____

   _____

4. Identify strategies people use to maintain positive self-views. _____

   _____

   _____

5. Discuss cultural differences in the self-concept and the use of self-serving biases. _____

   _____

   _____

WHAT DO I NEED TO KNOW? Based on what you've discovered above, what are the areas where you need to focus your studying? Which objectives do you need to spend more time mastering? Write this information down in your own words.

1. _____

2. _____

3. _____

4. _____

5. _____

6. _____

WHAT MATTERS TO ME: What facts in this chapter are personally relevant to you?

_____

_____

_____

CHAPTER SUMMARY

13.1 How Have Psychologists Studied Personality?

- *Psychodynamic Theories Emphasize Unconscious and Dynamic Processes:* Freud believed that unconscious forces determine behavior. He argued that personality consists of three structures: the id, the superego, and the ego. The ego mediates between the id and the superego, using defense mechanisms to reduce anxiety due to conflicts between the id and the superego. Freud proposed that we pass through five stages of psychosexual development and that these stages shape our personalities. In contrast to Freud, neo-Freudians have focused on relationships—in particular, children's emotional attachments to their parents.

- *Humanistic Approaches Emphasize Integrated Personal Experience:* Humanistic theories emphasize our experiences, beliefs, and inherent goodness. According to these theories, we strive to realize our full potential. Rogers's person-centered approach suggests that unconditional positive regard in childhood enables people to become fully functioning.

- *Personality Reflects Learning and Cognition:* Through interaction with the environment, people learn patterns of responding that are guided by their personal constructs, expectancies, and values. Self-efficacy, the extent to which people believe they can achieve specific outcomes, is an important determinant of behavior. The cognitive-affective personality system (CAPS) emphasizes self-regulatory capacities—that is, people's ability to set personal goals, evaluate their progress, and adjust their behavior accordingly.

- *Trait Approaches Describe Behavioral Dispositions:* Personality type theories focus more on description than on explanation. Trait theorists assume that personality is a collection of traits or behavioral dispositions. According to Eysenck's model of personality, there are three biologically based higher-order personality traits: introversion/extraversion, emotional stability, psychoticism. Each of these traits encompasses a number of lower-order traits. Five-factor theory maintains that there are five higher-order personality traits: openness to experience, conscientiousness, extraversion, agreeableness, and neuroticism.

13.2 How Is Personality Assessed, and What Does It Predict about People?

- *Personality Refers to Both Unique and Common Characteristics:* Idiographic approaches are person-centered. They focus on individual lives and each person's unique characteristics. Nomothetic approaches assess individual variation in characteristics that are common among all people.
- *Researchers Use Projective and Objective Methods to Assess Personality:* Projective measures assess unconscious processes by having people interpret ambiguous stimuli. Objective measures are relatively direct measures of personality, typically involving the use of self-report questionnaires or observer ratings.
- *Observers Show Accuracy in Trait Judgments:* Close acquaintances may better predict a person's behavior than the person can. Acquaintances are particularly accurate when judging traits that are readily observable and meaningful.
- *People Sometimes Are Inconsistent:* Mischel proposed the notion of situationism. According to this theory, situations are more important than traits in predicting behavior.
- *Behavior Is Influenced by the Interaction of Personality and Situations:* Interactionism maintains that behavior is determined by both situations and our dispositions. Strong situations mask differences in personality, whereas weak situations reveal differences in personality. Most trait theories adopt an interactionist view.
- *There Are Cultural and Sex Differences in Personality:* Cross-cultural research suggests that the Big Five personality factors are universal among humans. Sex differences in personality are consistent with common sex

stereotypes. For example, women report being more empathic than men, and men report being more assertive than women.

13.3 What Are the Biological Bases of Personality?

- *Animals Have Personalities:* Research on a wide variety of animal species has shown that animals have distinct personality traits that correspond roughly to the Big Five in humans.
- *Personality Is Rooted in Genetics:* The results of twin studies and adoption studies suggest that 40 percent to 60 percent of personality variation is the product of genetic variation. Personality characteristics are influenced by multiple genes. These genes interact with the environment to produce general dispositions. Novelty seeking has been linked to a gene associated with dopamine levels, and neuroticism and agreeableness have been linked to a gene associated with serotonin levels.
- *Temperaments Are Evident in Infancy:* Temperaments are biologically based personality tendencies. They are evident in early childhood and have long-term implications for adult behavior. Researchers have identified activity level, emotionality, and sociability as temperaments.
- *Personality Is Linked to Specific Neurophysiological Mechanisms:* Extraversion/introversion has been linked to differences in cortical arousal. Cortical arousal is regulated by the ascending reticular activating system. Extraversion/introversion has also been linked to the strength of our behavioral approach and inhibition systems. These systems are sensitive to reward and punishment, respectively.
- *Personality Is Adaptive:* Personality traits that facilitate survival and reproduction have been favored through natural selection and sexual selection. Individual differences result in diverse skills within a group and are advantageous to the group's survival.
- *Personality Traits Are Stable over Time:* With increasing age, scores on neuroticism, extraversion, and openness decrease. Scores on agreeableness and conscientiousness increase. Relative rankings on the Big Five personality traits remain stable, particularly in adulthood.

13.4 How Do We Know Our Own Personalities?

- *Our Self-Concepts Consist of Self-Knowledge:* Self-awareness is characterized by the experience of the self as an object. The self-schema is the cognitive aspect of the self-concept. The working self-concept is the immediate experience of the self at any given time.
- *Perceived Social Regard Influences Self-Esteem:* Self-esteem is the evaluative component of the self-concept.

TRY IT

The Best Part of Yourself

If you're like many people who've read a chapter on personality, you've have begun to think about your own personality. In that exploration, you've probably come to realize (again!) that there are things about yourself that you like and things that you don't like. So, what's the next step? For a variety of reasons, when we attempt to change situations or ourselves, we tend to focus on the aspects of a situation or ourselves that we don't like. Focusing on the negative can result in positive behavior change, so we feel better about ourselves, but it can also lead only to self-criticism. How about another approach?

Again, if you're like most people, your positive personality traits outweigh your negative traits, at least in the eyes of most people except for possibly yourself. Take a moment to focus on the parts of your personality that you like. If you can't think of anything about yourself, talk to friends or family members and ask them what they think are your positive personality traits. Maybe people will say you're faithful, have a good sense of humor, are kind, or are forgiving. If you too see those particular traits in your personality, they may be your "signature strengths." Positive psychology researchers have found that when people choose to use their signature strengths as often as possible, maybe every day, they feel better about themselves. Whatever the trait that you and others see as signature for you, make a real effort to use that trait every day in whatever interactions it seems appropriate. Try this for a couple of weeks, again as an experiment, and see what changes you note in yourself.

According to sociometer theory, our need to belong influences self-esteem. According to terror management theory, death anxiety influences self-esteem. Self-esteem is associated with happiness. Self-esteem is only weakly correlated with objective life outcomes, however.

• *We Use Mental Strategies to Maintain Our Views of Self:* Positive illusions of self are common. We employ numerous unconscious strategies to maintain positive views of ourselves, including self-evaluative maintenance, social comparisons, and self-serving biases.

• *There Are Cultural Differences in the Self:* People from collectivist cultures (e.g., Asian and African countries) tend to have interdependent self-concepts. People from individualist cultures (e.g., the United States, Canada) tend to have independent self-concepts. The tendency to engage in self-serving biases may be less common among collectivists than individualists, or they may differ on which dimensions they are biased against.

PUTTING IT ALL TOGETHER

Answer these questions to check your knowledge of the material in this chapter.

1. Choose a celebrity who is currently in the news (preferably for some outrageous behaviors). Try to understand that individual using the four approaches to personality highlighted in the text.

2. You are a legal consultant in a murder trial. The prosecution has portrayed your client as dangerous and unstable, presenting the results of the California Q-Sort, NEO Personality, Rorschach inkblot test, and Thematic Apperception Test. Use your knowledge of personality assessment to help refute this argument.

3. Your friend is in a stormy relationship. His girlfriend has admitted to cheating on him, but vows she is motivated to change. Use your knowledge of personality stability to give advice.

4. Give three examples of the mental strategies you use to maintain a positive view of yourself. Relate these strategies to your culture.

ANSWER KEY FOR REINFORCE QUESTIONS

Section 13.1

1. d	p. 569
2. b	p. 569
3. a	p. 570
4. a	p. 572
5. b	p. 571
6. d	p. 573
7. c	p. 574
8. a	p. 576
9. c	p. 578
10. a	p. 574

Section 13.2

1. a	p. 579
2. c	p. 580
3. b	p. 581
4. d	p. 581
5. b	p. 582
6. c	p. 582
7. b	p. 585
8. d	p. 584

9. b   p. 584
10. b   p. 586

Section 13.3

1. d   p. 589
2. d   p. 590
3. b   p. 590
4. c   p. 592
5. a   p. 591
6. c   p. 593
7. b   p. 595
8. c   p. 596
9. b   p. 597
10. a   p. 598

Section 13.4

1. c   p. 602
2. b   p. 604
3. c   p. 604
4. c   p. 604
5. d   p. 605
6. d   p. 606
7. d   p. 607
8. a   p. 608
9. b   p. 609
10. c   p. 612

HINTS FOR PUTTING IT ALL TOGETHER QUESTIONS

1. Answers should address your understanding of behavior and motivation from the psychodynamic, humanistic, learning/cognition, and trait approaches to personality.

2. Answers should address the specific limitations of each assessment method. In addition, a general critique of the reliability/validity of projective methods is in order. Also, predictive validity is reduced by the fact that people are sometimes inconsistent, behavior is influenced by the interaction of personality and situations, there are cultural and sex differences in personality, and these tests were not designed to measure dangerousness and instability.

3. Although there are rare exceptions (i.e., quantum change), personality and the associated behaviors are very stable over time. Answers should draw on the material in the section "Personality Traits Are Stable over Time" in Section 13.3.

4. Answers should address the unconscious strategies of self-evaluative maintenance, social comparisons, and self-serving biases. In addition, answers should address whether the strategies reflect living in an individualist or a collectivist culture (most likely individualist).

KEY TERMS EXERCISES

First, fill in your own definition and example for each term. Then check each term against the textbook's definition. These exercises can also be cut out and used as flash cards.

behavioral approach system (BAS)

Your Definition:
Your Example:
Textbook Definition:

five-factor theory

Your Definition:
Your Example:
Textbook Definition:

behavioral inhibition system (BIS)

Your Definition:
Your Example:
Textbook Definition:

humanistic approaches

Your Definition:
Your Example:
Textbook Definition:

defense mechanisms

Your Definition:
Your Example:
Textbook Definition:

id

Your Definition:
Your Example:
Textbook Definition:

ego

Your Definition:
Your Example:
Textbook Definition:

idiographic approaches

Your Definition:
Your Example:
Textbook Definition:

interactionists

| Your Definition: |
| Your Example: |
| Textbook Definition: |

nomothetic approaches

| Your Definition: |
| Your Example: |
| Textbook Definition: |

objective measures

| Your Definition: |
| Your Example: |
| Textbook Definition: |

personality

| Your Definition: |
| Your Example: |
| Textbook Definition: |

personality trait

| Your Definition: |
| Your Example: |
| Textbook Definition: |

personality types

| Your Definition: |
| Your Example: |
| Textbook Definition: |

projective measures

| Your Definition: |
| Your Example: |
| Textbook Definition: |

psychodynamic theory

| Your Definition: |
| Your Example: |
| Textbook Definition: |

psychosexual stages

Your Definition:
Your Example:
Textbook Definition:

superego

Your Definition:
Your Example:
Textbook Definition:

self-serving bias

Your Definition:
Your Example:
Textbook Definition:

temperaments

Your Definition:
Your Example:
Textbook Definition:

situationism

Your Definition:
Your Example:
Textbook Definition:

trait approach

Your Definition:
Your Example:
Textbook Definition:

sociometer

Your Definition:
Your Example:
Textbook Definition:

CHAPTER 14 | Psychological Disorders

CHAPTER OVERVIEW

It's hard to watch television, read a magazine, or check the news on the Web without hearing about someone's struggle with a psychological problem. In this chapter, you will find out just how common psychological disorders are. How do we determine if someone has a psychological disorder? What are the most common psychological disorders? Some disorders, such as depression and anxiety, seem pretty straightforward. Other disorders are sources of controversy—about which symptoms define them, but also about how many people suffer from them.

14.1 How Are Psychological Disorders Conceptualized and Classified?

How do psychologists determine whether an individual has a psychological disorder? Psychological disorders usually develop in the context of a predisposition (diathesis) and a stressor (environment). There are cognitive, biological, environmental, and psychological contributors to psychological disorders. Gender and cultural background may also play a role in whether one develops a psychological disorder and how one copes with it.

At the beginning of each section in the Study Guide, there will be guiding questions. Before you read the chapter in your textbook, read through these questions and maybe even attempt to answer them based on either what you've already read or what you think the answer should be. Then as you study the chapter, you can use them to help guide your reading.

14.1 Guiding Questions

To guide your reading of the text, review the following questions. Then, as you read the chapter, look for the answers to these questions. You may want to note in your textbook where you find these answers.

1. Describe the multiaxial classification system of the *Diagnostic and Statistical Manual of Mental Disorders.*

2. Identify assessment methods for psychological disorders.

3. Describe the diathesis-stress model.

4. Identify biological, psychological, and cognitive-behavioral causes of psychological disorders.

5. Discuss sex differences and cultural differences in psychological disorders.

NOW READ Section 14.1 "How Are Psychological Disorders Conceptualized and Classified?" keeping these questions in mind.

REVIEW: Now that you've read this section, go back to the 14.1 Guiding Questions and see if you can answer them based on what you've read. This is a check on your reading. If you can't answer a question, you need to go back to the text to reread that section.

VISUAL SUMMARY: Below is a summary of the major concepts in this section. To check your comprehension of the chapter, read the summary and ask yourself if you understand the concepts. If the concepts seem unfamiliar to you, you may want to go back to the book and reread those sections. This text is taken from the Visual Summaries on StudySpace at wwnorton.com/studyspace.

I. Psychopathology Means Sickness or Disorder of the Mind

II. Psychopathology Is Different from Everyday Problems
   A. Disorders are distinguishable from normal low points in life by:
      i. severity.
      ii. duration.
   B. Abnormal behavior:
      i. deviates from cultural norms.
      ii. is maladaptive.
      iii. causes the person or others distress.

III. Psychological Disorders Are Classified into Categories
   A. Etiology: factors that contribute to development of disorder.
   B. *Diagnostic and Statistical Manual of Mental Disorders (DSM)* is a:
      i. method for categorizing mental disorders.
      ii. multiaxial system that evaluates five dimensions of psychosocial functioning.
      iii. categorical approach that does not place disorders on a continuum of severity.

IV. Psychological Disorders Must Be Assessed
   A. Assessment:
      i. is mental health practitioner's examination of patient's mental state to diagnose possible disorders.
      ii. may continue throughout treatment process.
      iii. may involve structured or unstructured interviews, observations, self-report questionnaires, or other tests.
      iv. may be evidence-based.

V. Psychological Disorders Have Many Causes
   A. According to diathesis-stress model of diagnosis, disorder may develop when underlying vulnerability is coupled with precipitating environmental event.
   B. Biological factors:
      i. toxins
      ii. genetics
      iii. maternal illness
      iv. malnutrition
      v. neurological dysfunction
   C. Psychological factors:
      i. thoughts
      ii. emotions
   D. Family systems model: problems in individual indicate problems in family.
   E. Sociocultural model: psychopathology results from interaction between individual and culture.

   F. Cognitive-behavioral approach: psychopathology results from learned, maladaptive thoughts and beliefs.
   G. Internalizing disorders are more common in females, whereas externalizing disorders are more common in males.
   H. Culture-bound syndromes: specific to particular cultures.

REINFORCE: Are you ready to check your knowledge of this section? Answer the following multiple-choice questions with your textbook closed.

1. In determining whether a behavior indicates psychopathology, which of the following criteria is NOT important?
   a. Does the person recognize that he or she has a disorder?
   b. Does the behavior deviate from cultural norms?
   c. Does the behavior cause the person distress?
   d. Is the behavior maladaptive?

2. The first categorization of mental disorders developed out of:
   a. Kraepelin's realization that not all people with abnormal behavior have similar symptoms
   b. the statistical finding that mental disorders involve separate traits and behaviors
   c. behaviorist treatments that applied to a few, not all, categories of disorder
   d. brain imaging studies that revealed that disorders had unique biological correlates

3. To bring about accurate diagnoses, the *Diagnostic and Statistical Manual*:
   a. requires a five-component assessment of a patient's mental health status
   b. groups disorders into neurotic and psychotic disorders
   c. groups disorders by which theorist discovered them
   d. groups disorders first by gender, then by age, then by culture, then by severity

4. Dawn is a nurse on the psychiatric ward of a hospital. When a patient is first admitted to the hospital, Dawn evaluates how well the patient is able to recall recent events, hold a logical and understandable conversation, and follow simple directions. Dawn, therefore, uses the _____ to initially evaluate her patients' need for treatment.
   a. Minnesota Multiphasic Personality Inventory
   b. Thematic Apperception Evaluation
   c. Multidimensional Assessment Tool
   d. mental status exam

5. Jaleesa thinks she may be depressed, so she visits a psychologist. The psychologist asks her a series of

questions in response to the information Jaleesa provides. The psychologist is using a(n) _____ approach to interviewing.
   a. neuropsychological
   b. validity testing
   c. structured
   d. unstructured

6. What is the most frequently used questionnaire for psychological assessment?
   a. brain scan
   b. Minnesota Multiphasic Personality Inventory
   c. Thematic Apperception Evaluation
   d. Beck Depression Inventory

7. The diathesis-stress model of mental illness takes the view that:
   a. certain biological or environmental factors make us vulnerable to mental illness, but do not directly cause it
   b. if stress is sufficiently intense, anyone can become mentally ill
   c. mental illness is common in families experiencing a high level of stress
   d. an individual's ability to cope with stress is the best predictor of mental illness

8. Which of the following statements is accurate regarding biological factors in the development of mental illness?
   a. Maternal malnutrition, ingestion of toxins, and other prenatal factors influence whether offspring develop mental illness.
   b. Fraternal twins are twice as likely as identical twins to have the same mental illness.
   c. Brain scans using computerized tomography (CT) show functional deficits in almost all brain regions in people with mental illness.
   d. About 75 percent of people who have a family member with a mental illness will develop the same mental illness at some point in their lives.

9. Alan entered therapy because he was becoming very depressed. Alan's psychotherapist suggested that Alan pay attention to his thoughts and beliefs and analyze them for irrational assumptions and unrealistic expectations that might contribute to his depressed mood. In helping Alan, the psychotherapist was using a _____ perspective.
   a. psychodynamic
   b. humanistic
   c. cognitive-behavioral
   d. sociocultural

10. Based on what you know about internalizing and externalizing disorders, you would expect suicide attempts to be higher in _____ and drug problems to be higher in _____.
   a. Westerners; Easterners
   b. younger generations; older generations
   c. people from a higher social class; people from a lower social class
   d. females; males

WHAT DID YOU MISS? Check your answers against the Answer Key at the end of this chapter of the Study Guide. The Answer Key also lists the page(s) in your text where each question is explained. If you missed any questions, go to the pages indicated in the Answer Key, reread those sections, go back to the questions, and see if you can answer them correctly this time.

ANOTHER OPPORTUNITY TO REVIEW: Answer these questions without your textbook. As a rule of thumb, if you can write only a few words about these questions, you probably need to go back and review.

1. Describe the multiaxial classification system of the *Diagnostic and Statistical Manual of Mental Disorders.*

   _____

   _____

2. Identify assessment methods for psychological disorders.

   _____

   _____

3. Describe the diathesis-stress model. _____

   _____

   _____

4. Identify biological, psychological, and cognitive-behavioral causes of psychological disorders. _____

   _____

   _____

5. Discuss sex differences and cultural differences in psychological disorders. _____

   _____

   _____

WHAT DO I NEED TO KNOW? Based on what you've discovered above, what are the areas where you need to focus your studying? Which objectives do you need to spend more time mastering? Write this information down in your own words.

1. _____

2. _____

3. _____

4. _____

5. _____

6. _____

14.2 Can Anxiety Be the Root of Seemingly Different Disorders?

Excessive worry in the absence of true danger is the definition of anxiety disorders. These disorders range from being anxious about specific situations (phobias) to being anxious about everything (general anxiety disorder). There are characteristic cognitive, situational, and biological factors that seem to predict whether a person will have an anxiety disorder.

14.2 Guiding Questions

To guide your reading of the text, review the following questions. Then, as you read the chapter, look for the answers to these questions. You may want to note in your textbook where you find these answers.

1. Distinguish between anxiety disorders.

2. Identify cognitive, situational, and biological factors that contribute to anxiety disorders.

NOW READ Section 14.2 "Can Anxiety Be the Root of Seemingly Different Disorders?" keeping these questions in mind.

REVIEW: Now that you've read this section, go back to the 14.2 Guiding Questions and see if you can answer them based on what you've read. This is a check on your reading. If you can't answer a question, you need to go back to the text to reread that section.

VISUAL SUMMARY: Below is a summary of the major concepts in this section. To check your comprehension of the chapter, read the summary and ask yourself if you understand the concepts. If the concepts seem unfamiliar to you, you may want to go back to the book and reread those sections. This text is taken from the Visual Summaries on StudySpace at wwnorton.com/studyspace.

   VI. Anxiety Disorders Are Characterized by Excessive Anxiety in Absence of True Danger

  VII. There Are Different Types of Anxiety Disorders
- A. Phobic disorders: fears of specific objects or situations.
- B. Generalized anxiety disorder: diffuse, constant anxiety not associated with specific object or event.
- C. Posttraumatic stress disorder: involves nightmares, intrusive thoughts, and flashbacks to earlier trauma.
- D. Panic disorder: sudden, overwhelming attacks of terror.
- E. Agoraphobia: fear of situations from which escape may be difficult.
- F. Obsessive-compulsive disorder (OCD): characterized by frequent intrusive thoughts and compulsive actions.

VIII. Anxiety Disorders Have Cognitive, Situational, and Biological Components
- A. Cognitive: anxious individuals perceive ambiguous or neutral situations as more threatening than do nonanxious individuals.
- B. Situational: anxious responses may develop when another person's anxious response is observed and then generalized to other situations.
- C. Biological: anxious individuals have differences in their brains that predispose them to develop anxiety disorders.
- D. OCD:
  - i. may result from causes that interact.
  - ii. may develop from classical conditioning.
  - iii. is partly genetic (brain differences).
  - iv. may be due to environmental factors (streptococcal infection).

REINFORCE: Are you ready to check your knowledge of this section? Answer the following multiple-choice questions with your textbook closed.

1. The central characteristic of anxiety disorders is:
   - a. the feeling of excessive anxiety in the absence of any real threat
   - b. fluctuating moods that are not related to events in the environment
   - c. the feeling of being anxious without the physical symptoms of anxiety
   - d. that the parasympathetic nervous system is in a state of chronic arousal

2. Arianna is a nervous and shy adult, is often afraid of making mistakes in public, and is worried about being judged by others. Arianna probably:
   - a. was inhibited as a child
   - b. had overly strict parents
   - c. has perfectionistic personality disorder
   - d. will develop paranoid personality disorder at some point in her life

3. Tommy has obsessions about cleanliness and is a compulsive hand-washer. Which of the following pieces of evidence would support the view that his obsessive-compulsive disorder is related to classical conditioning?
   a. Tommy has been rewarded by his parents for hand-washing many times, so he continues to engage in the behavior.
   b. Tommy sees his brother engage in compulsive hand-washing, so he also engages in the behavior.
   c. Tommy experiences a large reduction in anxiety whenever he washes his hands, so he continues the behavior whenever he becomes anxious.
   d. Tommy believes that hand-washing will prevent him from becoming sick.

4. Which of the following statements is NOT accurate regarding the biological correlates of obsessive-compulsive disorder (OCD)?
   a. People with a disease affecting the caudate nucleus sometimes have symptoms of OCD.
   b. Electrical stimulation of brain areas involved in OCD can relieve OCD symptoms.
   c. Infections affecting the cerebellum are widespread in people who have OCD.
   d. A severe streptococcal infection can cause symptoms of OCD.

5. What brain region is damaged when a person is under chronic stress?
   a. the cerebellum
   b. the hippocampus
   c. the amygdala
   d. the prefrontal cortex

6. A woman is sweating profusely, is short of breath, has numbness in her feet and hands, and feels as though she is dying. She is likely suffering from:
   a. generalized anxiety disorder
   b. a panic attack
   c. a panic disorder
   d. obsessive-compulsive disorder

7. You and your roommate leave your room to go to the library, but he walks back to the door several times to make sure it is locked. He cleans the room frequently even when it isn't dirty. Your roommate may be suffering from:
   a. generalized anxiety disorder
   b. agoraphobia
   c. obsessive-compulsive disorder
   d. panic disorder

8. If you experience intense, uncontrollable fear when you encounter or think about a specific object, you are likely to be diagnosed with:
   a. a panic disorder
   b. obsessive-compulsive disorder
   c. generalized anxiety disorder
   d. phobic disorder

9. Which of the following symptoms does NOT characterize a panic attack?
   a. sweating
   b. high heart rate
   c. feelings of going crazy or dying
   d. heightened anxiety lasting for days

10. Someone with panic disorder is likely to develop
    _____.
    a. attention deficit hyperactivity disorder
    b. agoraphobia
    c. obsessive-compulsive disorder
    d. bipolar disorder

WHAT DID YOU MISS? Check your answers against the Answer Key at the end of this chapter of the Study Guide. The Answer Key also lists the page(s) in your text where each question is explained. If you missed any questions, go to the pages indicated in the Answer Key, reread those sections, go back to the questions, and see if you can answer them correctly this time.

ANOTHER OPPORTUNITY TO REVIEW: Answer these questions without your textbook. As a rule of thumb, if you can write only a few words about these questions, you probably need to go back and review.

1. Distinguish between anxiety disorders. _____
   _____
   _____

2. Identify cognitive, situational, and biological factors that contribute to anxiety disorders. _____
   _____
   _____

WHAT DO I NEED TO KNOW? Based on what you've discovered above, what are the areas where you need to focus your studying? Which objectives do you need to spend more time mastering? Write this information down in your own words.

1. _____

2. _____

3. _____

4. _____

5. _____

6. _____

14.3 Are Mood Disorders Extreme Manifestations of Normal Moods?

Depression and bipolar disorder are two of the most common psychological disorders. The milder form of depression is called dysthymia, and the milder form of bipolar disorder is called hypomania. Culture and gender may play roles in whether we develop these disorders and how well we cope with the ones we develop.

14.3 Guiding Questions

To guide your reading of the text, review the following questions. Then, as you read the chapter, look for the answers to these questions. You may want to note in your textbook where you find these answers.

1. Distinguish between major depression and bipolar disorder.

2. Discuss cultural and sex differences in depression.

NOW READ Section 14.3 "Are Mood Disorders Extreme Manifestations of Normal Moods?" keeping these questions in mind.

REVIEW: Now that you've read this section, go back to the 14.3 Guiding Questions and see if you can answer them based on what you've read. This is a check on your reading. If you can't answer a question, you need to go back to the text to reread that section.

VISUAL SUMMARY: Below is a summary of the major concepts in this section. To check your comprehension of the chapter, read the summary and ask yourself if you understand the concepts. If the concepts seem unfamiliar to you, you may want to go back to the book and reread those sections. This text is taken from the Visual Summaries on StudySpace at wwnorton.com/studyspace.

IX. There Are Two Categories of Mood Disorders
    A. Major depression: characterized by severe negative moods or lack of interest in normally pleasurable activities.
        i. dysthymia: a depressive disorder not severe enough to be diagnosed as a major depression.
    B. Bipolar disorder: alternating periods of depression and mania.

X. Mood Disorders Have Biological, Situational, and Cognitive Components
    A. Biological: genes play role in inception.
    B. Situational: stressors play role in development.
    C. Cognitive: cognitive triad and learned helplessness play roles in development of mood disorders.

REINFORCE: Are you ready to check your knowledge of this section? Answer the following multiple-choice questions with your textbook closed.

1. People who suffer from depression are affected primarily by _____; people who suffer from bipolar disorder are affected primarily by _____.
    a. both mania and low mood; either mania or low mood
    b. low mood; mania
    c. low mood; low mood and mania
    d. low mood; hallucinations and delusions

2. Aliyah has difficulty falling asleep and tosses and turns all night. Her insomnia may be a symptom of:
    a. mania
    b. depression
    c. either depression or mania
    d. neither depression nor mania

3. Gender and depression:
    a. are unrelated, contrary to popular opinion
    b. are related, such that sometimes men have higher rates of depression and sometimes women have higher rates
    c. are related, with women showing higher rates of depression
    d. are related, in that women show higher rates of depression because their roles as mothers, wives, and workers have no redeeming value and thus make them depressed

4. If you display negative moods, sleep disturbances, difficulty concentrating, and suicidal thoughts that persist at least two weeks, you are likely to be diagnosed with:
    a. anxiety disorder
    b. major depression
    c. hypomania
    d. bipolar disorder

5. What distinguishes dysthymia from major depression?
    a. There is a difference in the intensity of the symptoms.
    b. The former is short in duration, whereas the latter can last for years.
    c. Dysthymia is a milder form of bipolar disorder.
    d. They are unrelated disorders.

6. According to the cognitive triad proposed by Aaron Beck, the thinking of people suffering from depression involves:

a. a negative view of the self and the situation with a positive view of the future

b. a negative view of the self, a negative view of the situation, and a negative view of the future

c. a negative view of the self with a positive view of the situation and the future

d. a positive view of the self, the situation, and the future

7. According to the learned helplessness model of depression, people with depression tend to attribute negative outcomes to _____ and attribute positive outcomes to luck.

a. others

b. personal shortcomings

c. unrealistic role models

d. errors in logic

8. Dillon experiences low mood, crying, and sleep disturbance. He has a hard time getting excited about anything. He would probably benefit from a drug that increased activity in which neurotransmitter system?

a. monoamine system

b. glutamate system

c. peptide system

d. purine system

9. Sarah, a high school student, just received a grade of B on a paper. She is very ashamed that she did not perform according to her high standards. She tells herself, "Sarah, you are a really bad student—you need to study harder. This is simply unacceptable!" She believes that she may not get into college because she is a lazy and unmotivated person and that her future is doomed. According to the _____ model, Sarah is highly likely to develop _____.

a. cognitive triad; generalized anxiety disorder

b. learned helplessness; generalized anxiety disorder

c. cognitive triad; major depression

d. pessimism prototype; depression

10. Tara has had many negative experiences over which she had little control. For example, her parents were divorced, her brother became a drug user, and her husband of 10 years left her for another woman. At this point, Tara has given up trying to make her life better because she believes she can do nothing to change her life for the better. Tara's attitude may lead her to develop:

a. panic disorder

b. major depression

c. generalized anxiety disorder

d. borderline personality disorder

WHAT DID YOU MISS? Check your answers against the Answer Key at the end of this chapter of the Study Guide. The Answer Key also lists the page(s) in your text where each question is explained. If you missed any questions, go to the pages indicated in the Answer Key, reread those sections, go back to the questions, and see if you can answer them correctly this time.

ANOTHER OPPORTUNITY TO REVIEW: Answer these questions without your textbook. As a rule of thumb, if you can write only a few words about these questions, you probably need to go back and review.

1. Distinguish between major depression and bipolar disorder.

_____

_____

2. Discuss cultural and sex differences in depression. _____

_____

_____

WHAT DO I NEED TO KNOW? Based on what you've discovered above, what are the areas where you need to focus your studying? Which objectives do you need to spend more time mastering? Write this information down in your own words.

1. _____

2. _____

3. _____

4. _____

5. _____

6. _____

14.4 What Are Dissociative Disorders?

What if you woke up one day and didn't know who you were or where you were? What if you believed that two or more distinctly different identities existed within you? Dissociative disorders are rare and controversial.

14.4 Guiding Questions

To guide your reading of the text, review the following questions. Then, as you read the chapter, look for the answers to these questions. You may want to note in your textbook where you find these answers.

1. Describe dissociative amnesia, dissociative fugue, and dissociative identity disorder.

2. Identify possible causes of dissociative identity disorder.

3. Discuss the current controversy regarding dissociative identity disorder.

NOW READ Section 14.4 "What Are Dissociative Disorders?" keeping these questions in mind.

REVIEW: Now that you've read this section, go back to the 14.4 Guiding Questions and see if you can answer them based on what you've read. This is a check on your reading. If you can't answer a question, you need to go back to the text to reread that section.

VISUAL SUMMARY: Below is a summary of the major concepts in this section. To check your comprehension of the chapter, read the summary and ask yourself if you understand the concepts. If the concepts seem unfamiliar to you, you may want to go back to the book and reread those sections. This text is taken from the Visual Summaries on StudySpace at wwnorton.com/studyspace.

XI. These Mental disorders Involve Disruptions of Identity, of Memory, or of Conscious Awareness

XII. Dissociative Amnesia and Fugue Involve Loss of Memory
   A. Dissociative amnesia: forgetting that an event happened or losing awareness of blocks of time.
   B. Dissociative fugue: loss of identity coupled with travel to another location.

XIII. Dissociative Identity Disorder (DID) Is a Controversial Diagnosis
   A. DID:
      i. is occurrence of two or more distinct identities in individual.
      ii. was formerly called multiple personality disorder.
   B. Dramatic fluctuations in rates of diagnosing call its validity into question.

REINFORCE: Are you ready to check your knowledge of this section? Answer the following multiple-choice questions with your textbook closed.

1. There is evidence that a diagnosis of dissociative identity disorder may be invalid, at least in some cases. As discussed in your textbook, which of the following statements does NOT support this claim?
   a. The frequency of this diagnosis has increased dramatically since it first came to psychologists' attention.
   b. The diagnosis frequently occurs after someone has committed a crime.
   c. While older cases involved only one or two "extra" personalities, the current cases frequently involve many extra personalities.
   d. Many therapists have claimed responsibility for causing dissociative identity disorder.

2. Cases of dissociative identity disorder:
   a. are much more common in males
   b. are caused by faking on the part of the patient
   c. have no known causes or antecedents
   d. have increased dramatically in the past 30 years

3. One explanation offered in the textbook for the rapid recent increase in the diagnosis of dissociative disorders is that:
   a. more men, the group in which dissociative disorders are most prevalent, are seeing therapists
   b. more therapists believe these disorders are real and elicit reports from their patients that confirm this belief
   c. more criminals are receiving psychiatric screening, and dissociative disorders are particularly prevalent in this group
   d. dissociative disorders are caused by an environmental toxin that is now more widespread

4. What evidence suggests that people who appear to have dissociative identity disorder may be faking symptoms of the disorder?
   a. People started developing the disorder after a highly visible court case in 2001.
   b. Therapists often encourage patients to report symptoms of dissociative identity disorder to win court cases.
   c. The number of personalities that people with dissociative identity disorder report having has steadily increased over time as the disorder has become better known.
   d. Most people who report having the disorder had easy and unproblematic childhoods, and such a background makes developing the disorder highly unlikely.

5. Karen claims that multiple "people" with different personalities live inside her body; they take over her experience and express themselves at unexpected times. Each of these personalities has a different voice, a different age, and a different set of interests. Which of the following groups of people would be most likely to believe that Karen is suffering from a valid psychological condition?
   a. lawyers
   b. judges
   c. psychotherapists
   d. personality researchers

6. Dissociative identity disorder is an example of:
   a. a serious psychological condition that claims many more victims than most people realize
   b. an invalid psychological diagnosis
   c. a genetically invariant disorder
   d. a diagnosis that has been affected by societal forces

WHAT DID YOU MISS? Check your answers against the Answer Key at the end of this chapter of the Study Guide. The Answer Key also lists the page(s) in your text where each question is explained. If you missed any questions, go to the pages indicated in the Answer Key, reread those sections, go back to the questions, and see if you can answer them correctly this time.

ANOTHER OPPORTUNITY TO REVIEW: Answer these questions without your textbook. As a rule of thumb, if you can write only a few words about these questions, you probably need to go back and review.

1. Describe dissociative amnesia, dissociative fugue, and dissociative identity disorder. _____
   _____
   _____

2. Identify possible causes of dissociative identity disorder.
   _____
   _____

3. Discuss the current controversy regarding dissociative identity disorder. _____
   _____
   _____

WHAT DO I NEED TO KNOW? Based on what you've discovered above, what are the areas where you need to focus your studying? Which objectives do you need to spend more time mastering? Write this information down in your own words.

1. _____
2. _____
3. _____
4. _____
5. _____
6. _____

14.5 What Is Schizophrenia?

A rare diagnosis, schizophrenia is strongly affected by genetics. Environmental conditions, however, can worsen the lives of people with schizophrenia.

14.5 Guiding Questions

To guide your reading of the text, review the following questions. Then, as you read the chapter, look for the answers to these questions. You may want to note in your textbook where you find these answers.

1. Distinguish between positive and negative symptoms of schizophrenia.

2. Identify biological and environmental factors that contribute to schizophrenia.

NOW READ Section 14.5 "What Is Schizophrenia?" keeping these questions in mind.

REVIEW: Now that you've read this section, go back to the 14.5 Guiding Questions and see if you can answer them based on what you've read. This is a check on your reading. If you can't answer a question, you need to go back to the text to reread that section.

VISUAL SUMMARY: Below is a summary of the major concepts in this section. To check your comprehension of the chapter, read the summary and ask yourself if you understand the concepts. If the concepts seem unfamiliar to you, you may want to go back to the book and reread those sections. This text is taken from the Visual Summaries on StudySpace at wwnorton.com/studyspace.

XIV. Schizophrenia
   A. Schizophrenia: characterized by split between thought and emotion.
   B. Involves alterations in thought, in perceptions, or in consciousness.
   C. Has multiple subtypes.

XV. Schizophrenia Has Positive and Negative Symptoms
   A. Positive symptoms are excesses in functioning:
      i. delusions (false beliefs based on incorrect inferences about reality)
      ii. hallucinations (false sensory perceptions experienced without external source)
      iii. loosening of associations (speech pattern in which thoughts are disorganized or meaningless)
      iv. disorganized behavior (acting in strange or unusual ways or exhibiting inadequate self-care)

B. Negative symptoms are deficits in functioning:
  i. apathy
  ii. lack of emotion
  iii. slowed speech
  iv. slowed movement
C. Positive symptoms are usually treated more effectively with medication than negative symptoms are.

XVI. Schizophrenia Is Primarily a Brain Disorder
  A. Schizophrenia:
    i. is characterized by brain differences.
    ii. occurs in individuals who are genetically predisposed to develop it.

XVII. Environmental Factors Influence Schizophrenia
  A. In the genetically vulnerable individual, this disorder may be triggered by environmental stress:
    i. dysfunctional family
    ii. urban environment
    iii. possibly viruses

REINFORCE: Are you ready to check your knowledge of this section? Answer the following multiple-choice questions with your textbook closed.

1. Positive symptoms of schizophrenia are _____, whereas negative symptoms are _____.
   a. perceived by the person with schizophrenia as positive; perceived by others as negative
   b. excesses of abnormal behaviors; deficits of normal behaviors
   c. positive in terms of their impact on the person with schizophrenia; negative in terms of their impact on the person with schizophrenia
   d. comorbid with at least one other disorder; a singular feature of schizophrenia

2. The symptoms most commonly associated with schizophrenia are:
   a. showing evidence of one or more distinct personalities and fluctuating moods
   b. delusions and hallucinations
   c. rapidly alternating periods of anxiety and depression
   d. extreme impulsiveness and sensation seeking

3. Neuroimaging studies have shown that in the brains of people with schizophrenia:
   a. brain activity is centered on the amygdala and hippocampus
   b. decreased volume and functioning occur in various brain regions
   c. increased volume is visible in the frontal lobes

d. regions that affect people with bipolar disorder are also overactive in people with schizophrenia

4. Compared to people who develop mood or substance use disorders in adulthood, people who develop schizophrenia:
   a. show more odd or difficult behavior as children
   b. seek treatment at an earlier age
   c. are more likely to take their medications
   d. tend to be higher functioning intellectually as children

5. Speech in people with schizophrenia:
   a. is similar to the language of people with dissociative disorders
   b. is usually very simple, employing the language of a 4-year-old
   c. can shift rapidly between topics with no apparent logic
   d. is typically delayed in its development by about 5 years

6. The frequency of schizophrenia across cultures is:
   a. very similar, afflicting about 10 percent of adults
   b. very dissimilar, afflicting between 1 percent to 10 percent of adults, depending on culture
   c. very similar, afflicting about 1 percent of the population
   d. largely unknown because many cultures do not recognize symptoms of schizophrenia as problematic

7. What are the odds that Jamie will develop schizophrenia if both of his parents have the disorder?
   a. There is only a slight chance because the disorder tends not to run in families.
   b. It is almost certain because he has inherited the genes associated with the disorder from both parents.
   c. The odds are approximately 50 percent.
   d. It is difficult to estimate because researchers are still determining what causes the disorder.

8. One of your roommates comes from a small rural town and the other one from a large city. Does this difference affect their probability of ever experiencing a schizophrenic episode?
   a. No; genetic factors tend to override environmental factors in schizophrenia.
   b. Maybe; it depends entirely on the stress level of each environment.
   c. Yes; the roommate from the urban area is at higher risk.
   d. Yes; the roommate from the rural area is at higher risk.

9. The theory that schizophrenia may be related to environmental causes:
   a. is outdated
   b. finds some support in studies of the influenza immunization patterns of pregnant women and of urban stress
   c. is supported by cross-cultural adoption studies
   d. demonstrates a misuse of the biopsychosocial model

WHAT DID YOU MISS? Check your answers against the Answer Key at the end of this chapter of the Study Guide. The Answer Key also lists the page(s) in your text where each question is explained. If you missed any questions, go to the pages indicated in the Answer Key, reread those sections, go back to the questions, and see if you can answer them correctly this time.

ANOTHER OPPORTUNITY TO REVIEW: Answer these questions without your textbook. As a rule of thumb, if you can write only a few words about these questions, you probably need to go back and review.

1. Distinguish between positive and negative symptoms of schizophrenia. _____
   _____
   _____

2. Identify biological and environmental factors that contribute to schizophrenia. _____
   _____
   _____

WHAT DO I NEED TO KNOW? Based on what you've discovered above, what are the areas where you need to focus your studying? Which objectives do you need to spend more time mastering? Write this information down in your own words.

1. _____
2. _____
3. _____
4. _____
5. _____
6. _____

14.6 Are Personality Disorders Truly Mental Disorders?

A personality disorder exists when elements of an individual's personality are so extreme that they cause distress to the person or others. Two of the most well-known personality disorders are borderline personality disorder and antisocial personality disorder.

14.6 Guiding Questions

To guide your reading of the text, review the following questions. Then, as you read the chapter, look for the answers to these questions. You may want to note in your textbook where you find these answers.

1. Distinguish between personality disorders.

2. Identify the symptoms and possible causes of borderline personality disorder and antisocial personality disorder.

NOW READ Section 14.6 "Are Personality Disorders Truly Mental Disorders?" keeping these questions in mind.

REVIEW: Now that you've read this section, go back to the 14.6 Guiding Questions and see if you can answer them based on what you've read. This is a check on your reading. If you can't answer a question, you need to go back to the text to reread that section.

VISUAL SUMMARY: Below is a summary of the major concepts in this section. To check your comprehension of the chapter, read the summary and ask yourself if you understand the concepts. If the concepts seem unfamiliar to you, you may want to go back to the book and reread those sections. This text is taken from the Visual Summaries on StudySpace at wwnorton.com/studyspace.

XVIII. Personality Disorders Are Maladaptive Ways of Relating to the World
    A. Symptoms occur in clusters:
        i. "odd" cluster (paranoid, schizoid, schizotypal)
        ii. "anxious" cluster (avoidant, dependent, obsessive-compulsive)
        iii. "dramatic" cluster (histrionic, narcissistic, borderline, antisocial)

XIX. Borderline Personality Disorder (BPD) Is Associated with Poor Self-Control
    A. BPD:
        i. is characterized by disturbances in identity, in emotion, and in impulse control.
        ii. is often precipitated by history of trauma and of abuse.

XX. Antisocial Personality Disorder (APD) Is Associated with a Lack of Empathy
   A. APD:
      i. is characterized by lack of empathy and of remorse.
      ii. occurs in individuals with differences in brain functioning.
      iii. is influenced by genetics and negative environmental factors.

REINFORCE: Are you ready to check your knowledge of this section? Answer the following multiple-choice questions with your textbook closed.

1. Tom has often been in trouble with the justice system, appearing in court more than 20 times for instigating fights, stealing cars, or robbery. Tom seems to have no empathy for his victims and has even laughed when talking about stealing from or hurting them. Tom would likely be diagnosed with:
   a. multiple identity disorder
   b. amoral apathy syndrome
   c. antisocial personality disorder
   d. narcissistic personality disorder

2. Which of the following items does NOT characterize borderline personality disorder?
   a. social phobia
   b. weak sense of self
   c. self-mutilation
   d. emotional instability

3. Which of the following behavioral characteristics would suggest that a person is suffering from antisocial personality disorder rather than some other personality disorder?
   a. He or she has a weak sense of self and does not like to be alone.
   b. He or she shifts rapidly from one mood or emotion to another without any obvious reason.
   c. He or she is consistently uncaring toward others.
   d. He or she engages in self-mutilation and is very manipulative of others.

4. A large adoption study discussed in your textbook found that antisocial behavior in adopted males:
   a. is strongly related to their same-sex siblings' behavior
   b. is more closely related to the antisocial behaviors of their adoptive fathers than of their biological fathers
   c. is more closely related to the antisocial behavior of their biological fathers than of their adoptive fathers
   d. is related to cognitive and motivational factors and mostly unrelated to genetic factors

5. Personality disorders are classified along with _____ in the *Diagnostic and Statistical Manual* because they _____.

   a. mood disorders; involve extreme moods
   b. anxiety disorders; involve fear in relationships
   c. multiple personality disorder; involve dysfunction in personality expression
   d. mental retardation; are typically long-lasting

6. Floyd has always tended to have "love/hate" relationships with people who are close to him. He constantly worries about whether people will leave him so he smothers them with affection only to feel rejected and disappointed when they back away from this behavior. He has threatened to commit suicide a number of times, and most people view him as very emotionally unstable. Floyd would probably be diagnosed with:
   a. narcissistic personality disorder
   b. obsessive-compulsive personality disorder
   c. bipolar disorder
   d. borderline personality disorder

7. A clear influencing factor in the lives of people with borderline personality disorder is:
   a. a history of violence or abuse
   b. the traumatic breakup of their parents' marriage
   c. an adolescent peer group that encouraged impulsive, selfish behavior
   d. the role modeling of a sibling with the same personality disorder

8. A clear biological mechanism for the development and maintenance of antisocial behavior, demonstrated by David Lykken and colleagues, is:
   a. an enlarged amygdala
   b. overactive frontal lobes
   c. reduced overall arousal of the sympathetic nervous system
   d. overproduction of serotonin and dopamine

WHAT DID YOU MISS? Check your answers against the Answer Key at the end of this chapter of the Study Guide. The Answer Key also lists the page(s) in your text where each question is explained. If you missed any questions, go to the pages indicated in the Answer Key, reread those sections, go back to the questions, and see if you can answer them correctly this time.

ANOTHER OPPORTUNITY TO REVIEW: Answer these questions without your textbook. As a rule of thumb, if you can write only a few words about these questions, you probably need to go back and review.

1. Distinguish between personality disorders. _____

_____

_____

2. Identify the symptoms and possible causes of borderline personality disorder and antisocial personality disorder.

_____

_____

WHAT DO I NEED TO KNOW? Based on what you've discovered above, what are the areas where you need to focus your studying? Which objectives do you need to spend more time mastering? Write this information down in your own words.

1. _____

2. _____

3. _____

4. _____

5. _____

6. _____

14.7 Should Childhood Disorders Be Considered a Unique Category?

Two of the most common psychological disorders in childhood are autism and attention deficit hyperactivity disorder. These disorders have the potential to interfere with many aspects of children's lives.

14.7 Guiding Question

To guide your reading of the text, review the following question. Then, as you read the chapter, look for the answers to this question. You may want to note in your textbook where you find these answers.

1. Identify the symptoms and possible causes of autism and attention deficit hyperactivity disorder.

NOW READ Section 14.7 "Should Childhood Disorders Be Considered a Unique Category?" keeping this question in mind.

REVIEW: Now that you've read this section, go back to the 14.7 Guiding Question and see if you can answer it based on what you've read. This is a check on your reading. If you can't answer the question, you need to go back to the text to reread that section.

VISUAL SUMMARY: Below is a summary of the major concepts in this section. To check your comprehension of the chapter, read the summary and ask yourself if you understand the concepts. If the concepts seem unfamiliar to you, you may want to go back to the book and reread those sections. This text is taken from the Visual Summaries on StudySpace at wwnorton.com/studyspace.

XXI. Some Childhood Disorders, such as Attention Deficit Hyperactivity Disorder (ADHD), Improve over Time, whereas Others, such as Autism, Do Not

XXII. Autistic Disorder Involves Social Deficits
    A. Autism:
        i. is a developmental disorder characterized by deficits in social interaction, by impaired communication, and by restricted interests.
        ii. has genetic component.
        iii. is related to brain differences.

XXIII. ADHD Is a Disruptive Impulse Control Disorder
    A. ADHD:
        i. is characterized by restlessness, inattentiveness, and impulsivity.
        ii. has genetic component.
        iii. may be caused by an interaction among brain differences, poor parenting, and social disadvantages.

REINFORCE: Are you ready to check your knowledge of this section? Answer the following multiple-choice questions with your textbook closed.

1. Rates of autism have recently:
    a. decreased, which means there are many children with autism who are undiagnosed
    b. decreased because physicians are reluctant to label a child negatively
    c. increased because the disorder has passed from child to child
    d. increased, which is probably due to the recent recognition and diagnosis of milder forms of autism

2. Which of the following disorders involves deficits in social interaction, impaired communication, and limited interests?
    a. attention deficit hyperactivity disorder
    b. obsessive-compulsive disorder diagnosed in childhood
    c. autism
    d. borderline personality disorder

3. Jacob has clear symptoms of attention deficit hyperactivity disorder: difficulty paying attention and lack of behavioral control. Jacob's behavior resembles that of people with damage to which of the following brain areas?

a. the amygdala
b. the hippocampus
c. the hypothalamus
d. the frontal lobes

4. Tom is a 32-year-old chemical engineer. He was diagnosed with attention deficit hyperactivity disorder (ADHD) as a child. Compared to his friends, who have not been diagnosed with ADHD, Tom is more likely to:
a. also have an Axis III disorder
b. have struggled to be successful in his career
c. have children with a number of different women
d. have more problems with depression

5. Asperger's syndrome is:
a. a form of autism that involves severe intellectual impairment
b. the childhood precursor to obsessive-compulsive disorder in adults
c. a form of high-functioning autism
d. a form of autism characterized by hyperactivity

6. Symptoms of autism:
a. appear around 6 years of age
b. can be seen in limited form in some infants
c. vary greatly, depending on the sex of the child
d. include a pronounced interest in social stimuli

7. Which of the following characteristics is NOT a primary symptom of autism?
a. difficulties with verbal communication
b. lack of awareness of others, even caregivers
c. restricted activities and interests
d. mental retardation

8. According to your textbook, in recent decades there has been a dramatic increase in the number of children diagnosed as having autism. This increase is thought to stem primarily from:
a. greater awareness of the symptoms of this disorder
b. an increase in susceptibility to the disorder
c. changes in the levels of environmental toxins linked to the disease
d. viral factors not yet identified

WHAT DID YOU MISS? Check your answers against the Answer Key at the end of this chapter of the Study Guide. The Answer Key also lists the page(s) in your text where each question is explained. If you missed any questions, go to the pages indicated in the Answer Key, reread those sections, go back to the questions, and see if you can answer them correctly this time.

ANOTHER OPPORTUNITY TO REVIEW: Answer this question without your textbook. As a rule of thumb, if you can write only a few words about this question, you probably need to go back and review.

1. Identify the symptoms and possible causes of autism and attention deficit hyperactivity disorder. _____

WHAT DO I NEED TO KNOW? Based on what you've discovered above, what are the areas where you need to focus your studying? Which objectives do you need to spend more time mastering? Write this information down in your own words.

1. _____
2. _____
3. _____
4. _____
5. _____
6. _____

WHAT MATTERS TO ME: What facts in this chapter are personally relevant to you?

CHAPTER SUMMARY

14.1 How Are Psychological Disorders Conceptualized and Classified?

- *Psychopathology Is Different from Everyday Problems:* Psychological disorders are common in all societies. Psychological disorders differ from everyday problems. Individuals with psychological disorders behave in ways that deviate from cultural norms and that are maladaptive.
- *Psychological Disorders Are Classified into Categories:* The *Diagnostic and Statistical Manual of Mental Disorders* is a multiaxial system for diagnosing psychological disorders. The five axes used for the evaluation of mental health are major clinical disorders, mental retardation and personality disorders, medical conditions, psychosocial problems, and global assessment.
- *Psychological Disorders Must Be Assessed:* Assessment is the process of examining a person's mental functions and psychological health to make a diagnosis.

Assessment is accomplished through interviews, behavioral observations, psychological testing, and neuropsychological testing.

- *Psychological Disorders Have Many Causes:* The diathesis-stress model suggests that mental health problems arise from a vulnerability coupled with a stressful precipitating event. Psychological disorders may arise from biological factors, psychological factors, or cognitive behavioral factors. Females are more likely than males to exhibit internalizing disorders (such as major depression and generalized anxiety disorder). Males are more likely than females to exhibit externalizing disorders (such as alcoholism and conduct disorders). Most mental disorders show some universal symptoms, but the *DSM* recognizes a number of culture-bound mental health problems.

14.2 Can Anxiety Be the Root of Seemingly Different Disorders?

- *There Are Different Types of Anxiety Disorders:* Phobias are exaggerated fears of specific stimuli. Generalized anxiety disorder is diffuse and omnipresent. Posttraumatic stress disorder involves frequent and recurring nightmares, intrusive thoughts, and flashbacks related to an earlier trauma. Panic attacks cause sudden overwhelming terror and may lead to agoraphobia. Obsessive-compulsive disorder involves frequent intrusive thoughts and compulsive behaviors.
- *Anxiety Disorders Have Cognitive, Situational, and Biological Components:* Cognitive, situational, and biological factors contribute to the onset of anxiety disorders. This is well illustrated by obsessive-compulsive disorder, which is influenced by conditioning and genetics and may be induced in children exposed to a streptococcal infection that causes autoimmune damage to the brain.

14.3 Are Mood Disorders Extreme Manifestations of Normal Moods?

- *There Are Two Categories of Mood Disorders:* Mood disorders include major depression and bipolar disorder. Major depression is characterized by a number of symptoms, including depressed mood and a loss of interest in pleasurable activities. Depression is more common in females than in males and is most common among women in developing countries. Bipolar disorder is characterized by depression and manic episodes— that is, episodes of increased activity and euphoria.
- *Mood Disorders Have Biological, Situational, and Cognitive Components:* Both depression and bipolar disorder are, in part, genetically determined. The biological factors implicated in depression are neurotransmitter (MAO, serotonin) levels, frontal lobe functioning,

and biological rhythms. Poor interpersonal relations and maladaptive cognitions—including the cognitive triad and learned helplessness—also contribute to depression.

14.4 What Are Dissociative Disorders?

- *Dissociative Amnesia and Fugue Involve Loss of Memory:* Dissociative amnesia involves forgetting that an event happened or losing awareness of a substantial block of time. Dissociative fugue is a type of dissociative amnesia that involves a loss of identity.
- *Dissociative Identity Disorder Is a Controversial Diagnosis:* Also called multiple personality disorder, dissociative identity disorder involves two or more identities within one person. It is believed to result from severe abuse—through dissociation, individuals develop distinct identities to cope with different traumas. Dissociative identity disorder is a controversial diagnosis. Skeptics note that the condition is often diagnosed after someone has been accused of a crime and may reflect the faking of symptoms. Also, in recent years, there has been a sharp rise in reported cases, possibly as a consequence of therapists suggesting symptoms of dissociative identity disorder to their patients.

14.5 What Is Schizophrenia?

- *Schizophrenia Has Positive and Negative Symptoms:* Positive symptoms include excesses, such as delusions and hallucinations. Negative symptoms are deficits in functioning, such as apathy and lack of emotion.
- *Schizophrenia Is Primarily a Brain Disorder:* The brains of people with schizophrenia have larger ventricles and less brain mass, with reduced frontal and temporal lobe activation. A variety of neural structural and neurochemical abnormalities exist as well.
- *Environmental Factors Influence Schizophrenia:* The stress of dysfunctional family dynamics and urban environments may trigger the onset of schizophrenia. Exposure to pathogens may also contribute to the development of this disorder.

14.6 Are Personality Disorders Truly Mental Disorders?

- *Personality Disorders Are Maladaptive Ways of Relating to the World:* The *DSM* identifies 10 personality disorders clustered in three groups. Paranoid, schizoid, and schizotypal comprise the odd and eccentric cluster; avoidant, dependent, and obsessive-compulsive comprise the anxious and fearful cluster; histrionic, narcissistic, borderline, and antisocial comprise the dramatic, emotional, and erratic cluster.
- *Borderline Personality Disorder Is Associated with Poor Self-Control:* Borderline personality disorder involves

disturbances in identity, in affect, and in impulse control. Borderline personality disorder is associated with reduced frontal lobe capacity, low levels of serotonin, and a history of trauma and abuse.

- *Antisocial Personality Disorder Is Associated with a Lack of Empathy:* Antisocial personality disorder is characterized by socially undesirable behavior, hedonism, sensation seeking, and a lack of remorse. Antisocial personality disorder is associated with lower levels of arousal, a smaller amygdala, and deficits in frontal lobe functioning. Both genetics and environment seem to contribute to the development of this condition.

14.7 Should Childhood Disorders Be Considered a Unique Category?

- *Autistic Disorder Involves Social Deficits:* Autism emerges in infancy and is marked by impaired social functioning and communication and restricted interests. Autism is heritable and may result from genetic mutations. Autism has been linked to abnormal brain growth, exposure to antibodies in utero, faulty brain wiring, and mirror neuron impairment.
- *Attention Deficit Hyperactivity Disorder Is a Disruptive Impulse Control Disorder:* Children with ADHD are restless, inattentive, and impulsive. The causes of ADHD may include environmental factors such as poor parenting and social disadvantages; genetic factors; and brain abnormalities, particularly with regard to activation of the frontal lobes, limbic system, and basal ganglia. ADHD continues into adulthood, presenting challenges to academic work and to career pursuits.

PUTTING IT ALL TOGETHER

Answer these questions to check your knowledge of the material in this chapter.

1. A close friend describes feeling down and not being as happy as she has in the past. What characteristics would you look for to determine whether your friend suffers from a psychological disorder?

2. Do you know someone who suffers from an anxiety disorder? If not, might you ask around within your social group to find a person who suffers from one? Once you have found a person who doesn't mind talking about his or her anxiety disorder, ask to interview the person sufficiently to identify the cognitive, situational, and biological factors that contribute to her or his behavior. Write about how these factors relate to both the nature and nurture aspects of the disorder.

3. Your friend with the depressed mood decides to seek psychotherapy. On what bases might her therapist diagnose your friend as suffering from major depression, dysthymic disorder, or bipolar disorder?

4. You are hired as a legal consultant. The case revolves around an individual who claims to suffer from dissociative identity disorder. Summarize the evidence both pro and con that this is a legitimate diagnosis.

5. A man and woman are deciding whether to have a child. The man has suffered periodic bouts of schizophrenia his entire life. They know that schizophrenia is primarily a brain disorder with a genetic component, and they do not want to pass this disorder on to their child. Summarize for them the genetic and environmental contributors and estimate the likelihood that their child will develop schizophrenia.

6. In the same couple, the woman has been diagnosed with antisocial personality disorder. Again, summarize for them the genetic and environmental contributors for the disorder and the likelihood that their child will develop it.

7. Another couple has a 2-year-old who has been diagnosed with autism. Summarize for the parents the core symptoms of autism.

ANSWER KEY FOR REINFORCE QUESTIONS

Section 14.1

1. a   p. 620
2. a   p. 621
3. a   p. 621
4. d   p. 623
5. d   p. 624
6. b   p. 624
7. a   p. 626
8. a   p. 626
9. c   p. 628
10. d   p. 628

Section 14.2

1. a   p. 631
2. a   p. 635
3. c   p. 636
4. c   p. 637
5. b   p. 632
6. b   p. 634
7. c   p. 635
8. d   p. 632

9. d   p. 634
10. b   p. 634

Section 14.3

1. c   pp. 639–640
2. c   pp. 639–640
3. c   p. 640
4. b   p. 639
5. a   p. 639
6. b   p. 643
7. b   p. 643
8. a   p. 642
9. c   p. 643
10. b   p. 642

Section 14.4

1. d   p. 648
2. d   p. 648
3. b   p. 649
4. c   p. 648
5. c   p. 649
6. d   p. 648

Section 14.5

1 b   p. 650
2. b   p. 651
3. b   p. 653
4. a   p. 653
5. c   p. 652
6. c   p. 650
7. c   p. 653
8. c   p. 654
9. b   p. 654

Section 14.6

1. c   p. 660
2. a   p. 659
3. c   p. 660
4. c   p. 662
5. d   p. 657
6. d   p. 659
7. a   p. 660
8. c   p. 662

Section 14.7

1. d   p. 664
2. c   p. 664
3. d   p. 668
4. b   p. 668
5. c   p. 665

TRY IT

An Ounce of Prevention Is Worth a Pound of Cure

As you've studied this chapter on psychological disorders, you might have thought about people you've known who've had psychological problems. Perhaps you wondered if you have a psychological problem. As you will discover in Chapter 15, psychological and medical science have developed many techniques for improving the lives of people with most psychological disorders, but preventing a disorder before it develops is probably a better strategy. Through the course of this book, you have read about many techniques for preventing or reducing the impact of depression and anxiety, two of the most common psychological disorders. Have you tried these techniques through the semester? Have you included one or more of them in your daily routine or as part of, say, your weekly stress management routine? If you haven't thought about these techniques in a while, revisit the previous chapters and give them a try. Especially with the end of the semester approaching and with the stress you may be feeling, preventing anxiety and depression from getting out of hand is a good goal. Keep looking for techniques that work for you.

---

6. b   p. 665
7. d   p. 665
8. a   p. 664

HINTS FOR PUTTING IT ALL TOGETHER QUESTIONS

1. The symptoms of psychological disorders vary widely, but the symptoms of all psychological disorders share these characteristics: They vary from cultural norms, are maladaptive, may be self-destructive, and may cause distress to others. Answers should address these characteristics.

2. Answers should address possible contributing cognitive, situational, and biological factors as identified.

3. Answers should focus on the symptoms and course of major depression, dysthymic disorder, or bipolar disorder.

4. On the pro side: DID seems to emerge in response to repeated abuse—through repeated dissociation, different identities develop to cope with different traumas. There is evidence from handwriting and other physiological

measures that indicates different functioning for the different identities. On the con side: This condition is often diagnosed AFTER someone has been convicted of a crime, and there has been a sharp rise in cases that correspond to media portrayals of the diagnosis.

5. Answers should note that schizophrenia is largely a biological disorder. However, recent research suggests that environmental factors play a role. In particular, environmental stressors such as dysfunctional family relationship, urban stress, and exposure to pathogens play a role in the development of schizophrenic behavior.

6. Answers should note that APD is associated with lower levels of arousal, a smaller amygdala, and deficits in frontal lobe functioning. Twin and adoption studies suggest that genes play a role in APD. However, environmental factors such as low socioeconomic status, dysfunctional families, abuse, and malnutrition also contribute to the development of this disorder.

7. Answers should note that autism is characterized by impairments in social interaction, deficits in communication, and restricted interests.

KEY TERMS EXERCISES

First, fill in your own definition and example for each term. Then check each term against the textbook's definition. These exercises can also be cut out and used as flash cards.

agoraphobia

Your Definition:
Your Example:
Textbook Definition:

autistic disorder

Your Definition:
Your Example:
Textbook Definition:

antisocial personality disorder (APD)

Your Definition:
Your Example:
Textbook Definition:

bipolar disorder

Your Definition:
Your Example:
Textbook Definition:

assessment

Your Definition:
Your Example:
Textbook Definition:

borderline personality disorder

Your Definition:
Your Example:
Textbook Definition:

attention deficit hyperactivity disorder (ADHD)

Your Definition:
Your Example:
Textbook Definition:

cognitive-behavioral approach

Your Definition:
Your Example:
Textbook Definition:

delusions

Your Definition:
Your Example:
Textbook Definition:

dissociative identity disorder (DID)

Your Definition:
Your Example:
Textbook Definition:

diathesis-stress model

Your Definition:
Your Example:
Textbook Definition:

dysthymia

Your Definition:
Your Example:
Textbook Definition:

disorganized behavior

Your Definition:
Your Example:
Textbook Definition:

etiology

Your Definition:
Your Example:
Textbook Definition:

dissociative disorders

Your Definition:
Your Example:
Textbook Definition:

family systems model

Your Definition:
Your Example:
Textbook Definition:

generalized anxiety disorder (GAD)

Your Definition:
Your Example:
Textbook Definition:

major depression

Your Definition:
Your Example:
Textbook Definition:

hallucinations

Your Definition:
Your Example:
Textbook Definition:

multiaxial system

Your Definition:
Your Example:
Textbook Definition:

learned helplessness

Your Definition:
Your Example:
Textbook Definition:

negative symptoms

Your Definition:
Your Example:
Textbook Definition:

loosening of associations

Your Definition:
Your Example:
Textbook Definition:

obsessive-compulsive disorder (OCD)

Your Definition:
Your Example:
Textbook Definition:

panic disorder

Your Definition:
Your Example:
Textbook Definition:

psychopathology

Your Definition:
Your Example:
Textbook Definition:

positive symptoms

Your Definition:
Your Example:
Textbook Definition:

schizophrenia

Your Definition:
Your Example:
Textbook Definition:

posttraumatic stress disorder (PTSD)

Your Definition:
Your Example:
Textbook Definition:

sociocultural model

Your Definition:
Your Example:
Textbook Definition:

CHAPTER 15 | Treatment of Psychological Disorders

CHAPTER OVERVIEW

The development of psychotherapy is responsible, in part, for the growth of the field of clinical and counseling psychology. Psychological researchers have developed a number of specific types of psychotherapies designed to treat a wide range of psychological disorders. In conjunction with psychiatrists, psychologists have also developed treatment approaches that involve the use of both psychotherapy and pharmacological treatments.

15.1 How Are Psychological Disorders Treated?

Psychological disorders can be treated with either biological or psychological techniques or a combination of the two. Psychotherapies based on cognitive-behavioral, psychodynamic, or humanistic perspectives have been developed. A wide variety of mental health practitioners can assist individuals in coping with psychological disorders.

At the beginning of each section in the Study Guide, there will be guiding questions. Before you read the chapter in your textbook, read through these questions and maybe even attempt to answer them based on either what you've already read or what you think the answer should be. Then, as you study the chapter, you can use them to help guide your reading.

15.1 Guiding Questions

To guide your reading of the text, review the following questions. Then, as you read the chapter, look for the answers to these questions. You may want to note in your textbook where you find these answers.

1. Distinguish between forms of psychotherapy.

2. Describe the major categories of psychotropic drugs.

3. Identify alternative biological treatments for mental disorders.

4. Distinguish between specialized mental health practitioners.

NOW READ Section 15.1 "How Are Psychological Disorders Treated?" keeping these questions in mind.

REVIEW: Now that you've read this section, go back to the 15.1 Guiding Questions and see if you can answer them based on what you've read. This is a check on your reading. If you can't answer a question, you need to go back to the text to reread that section.

VISUAL SUMMARY: Below is a summary of the major concepts in this section. To check your comprehension of the chapter, read the summary and ask yourself if you understand the concepts. If the concepts seem unfamiliar to you, you may want to go back to the book and reread those sections. This text is taken from the Visual Summaries on StudySpace at wwnorton.com/studyspace.

I. Psychotherapy Is the Generic Term for Formal Psychological Treatment

II. Biological Therapies Are Based on Medical Approaches to Illness and to Disease

III. Psychotherapy Is Based on Psychological Principles

A. Psychotherapy is aimed at changing patterns of thought or of behavior.

B. Most therapists use eclectic approaches, but all psychotherapies depend on:
   i. client expectations.
   ii. therapist-client relationships.

C. To help the patient gain insight into his or her psychological processes, psychoanalysis uses:
   i. free association.
   ii. dream analysis.

D. Features of contemporary psychodynamic therapy include:
   i. exploring distressing thoughts.
   ii. looking for recurring themes.
   iii. focusing on the therapist-patient relationship.

E. Talking about or writing about emotions can lead to positive physical and psychological changes.

F. Humanistic therapies encourage people to fulfill their potential through self-understanding.

G. Behavioral therapies are based on these ideas:
   i. behavior is learned.
   ii. behavior can be unlearned through classical and operant conditioning.

H. Cognitive therapy is based on these ideas:
   i. distorted thoughts produce maladaptive behaviors and emotions.
   ii. distorted thoughts can be modified.

I. Cognitive-behavioral therapy incorporates techniques from cognitive and behavior therapy to:
   i. correct faulty thinking.
   ii. change maladaptive behaviors.

J. Group therapy offers the opportunity to improve by hearing another's experiences.

K. Family therapy offers the opportunity to change attitudes and behaviors that are disruptive to the family.

IV. Culture Can Affect the Therapeutic Process
   A. Culture plays a critical role in determining whether various cultural or ethnic groups will find psychotherapy available and will use it.

V. Medication Is Effective for Certain Disorders
   A. Psychotropic medication affects mental processes.
   B. Anti-anxiety drugs decrease anxiety by increasing activity of GABA.
   C. Antidepressants decrease depression by increasing availability of serotonin and other neurotransmitters.
   D. Antipsychotic drugs reduce psychotic symptoms by blocking effects of dopamine.

VI. Alternative Biological Treatments Are Used in Extreme Cases
   A. Electroconvulsive therapy (ECT): strong electrical current is delivered to the brain, aiming to reduce depression.
   B. Transcranial magnetic stimulation (TMS): electrical pulses are used to disrupt neural activity, aiming to reduce depression.
   C. Deep brain stimulation (DBS): electrical stimulation is delivered from electrodes implanted in the brain, aiming to alleviate depression and obsessive-compulsive symptoms.

VII. Therapies Not Supported by Scientific Evidence Can Be Dangerous
   A. Research helps guarantee the safety and effectiveness of treatment methods.

VIII. A Variety of Providers Can Assist in Treatment for Psychological Disorders
   A. Clinical psychologist:
      i. has a Ph.D. or Psy.D.
      ii. is skilled in working with individuals with mental illness.
   B. Psychiatrist:
      i. has an MD.
      ii. can prescribe psychotropic drugs.
   C. Counseling psychologist:
      i. has a Ph.D.
      ii. deals with adjustment problems that do not involve mental illness.
   D. Psychiatric social worker:
      i. has a master's degree in social work (MSW).
      ii. deals with issues of psychiatrically ill patients and their families.
   E. Psychiatric nurse:
      i. has a bachelor's degree and usually a master's degree, both in nursing.
      ii. works in a hospital or residential program that specializes in serious mental illness.
   F. Paraprofessional:
      i. has limited advanced training.
      ii. assists individuals with mental illness.

REINFORCE: Are you ready to check your knowledge of this section? Answer the following multiple-choice questions with your textbook closed.

1. The two basic approaches to treating mental illness are:
   a. psychological and biological
   b. psychopharmacology and behavior therapy
   c. Freudian therapy and client-centered therapy
   d. behavior modification and cognitive therapy

2. The goal of Freud's psychodynamic approach to therapy was to:
   a. have patients acknowledge their abuse history
   b. have clients acknowledge the mismatch between their ideal and actual selves
   c. uncover the unconscious feelings and motives that were creating problems for the patient
   d. retrain maladaptive behaviors through techniques such as classical conditioning

3. You are seeing a therapist who doesn't pass judgment on your behavior, encourages you to talk about your subjective experiences, and frequently attempts to paraphrase, or say back to you, what you have just said. Your therapist is probably using:
   a. behavioral modification
   b. a variant of the psychodynamic approach
   c. cognitive-behavioral therapy
   d. client-centered therapy

4. You undergo therapy for a fear of snakes. The therapist first asks you to think about snakes, then shows you pictures of them, and finally, several sessions later, gives you the opportunity to pick up a snake. Your therapist is using:
   a. overload techniques
   b. exposure techniques
   c. distraction
   d. modeling

5. Group therapy increased in use after World War II because:
   a. it was particularly effective in dealing with anxiety and depression related to combat situations
   b. the number of people needing therapy far exceeded the number of available therapists
   c. group therapy best mimicked an organized military context
   d. it was found to be the best empirically validated treatment available at that time

6. Brendon believes that he is worthless, that other people do not like him, and that he will never have satisfying interpersonal relationships. To counteract this belief, Brendon's therapist helps him to change his negative thoughts about himself to more realistic thoughts and then encourages him to rehearse those thoughts in place of the negative thoughts. The therapist is using:
   a. behavioral rationalization
   b. rational creativity
   c. cognitive restructuring
   d. emotive analysis

7. Selective serotonin reuptake inhibitors work by:
   a. allowing serotonin to remain in the synapse
   b. facilitating the reuptake of serotonin into the presynaptic neuron
   c. blocking serotonin's effects on the postsynaptic receptors
   d. converting serotonin to another chemical form

8. Antipsychotic medications would not be effective if they did not:
   a. block serotonin
   b. block dopamine
   c. enhance dopamine
   d. enhance serotonin

9. If you have an advanced degree in clinical psychology, which of the following can you NOT do in most states?
   a. have a private practice
   b. conduct long-term psychotherapy
   c. prescribe drugs for mental health problems
   d. work in a hospital setting

10. Which of the following factors is most important in choosing a therapist?
    a. the type of therapy the therapist uses
    b. the therapist's previous success in treating the disorder the client is suffering from
    c. whether the therapist can prescribe drugs
    d. the therapist's degree

WHAT DID YOU MISS? Check your answers against the Answer Key at the end of this chapter of the Study Guide. The Answer Key also lists the page(s) in your text where each question is explained. If you missed any questions, go to the pages indicated in the Answer Key, reread those sections, go back to the questions, and see if you can answer them correctly this time.

ANOTHER OPPORTUNITY TO REVIEW: Answer these questions without your textbook. As a rule of thumb, if you can write only a few words about these questions, you probably need to go back and review.

1. Distinguish between forms of psychotherapy. _____

2. Describe the major categories of psychotropic drugs. __

3. Identify alternative biological treatments for mental disorders. _____

4. Distinguish between specialized mental health practitioners. _____

_____

_____

WHAT DO I NEED TO KNOW? Based on what you've discovered above, what are the areas where you need to focus your studying? Which objectives do you need to spend more time mastering? Write this information down in your own words.

1. _____

2. _____

3. _____

4. _____

5. _____.

6. _____

15.2 What Are the Most Effective Treatments?

Rather than being a "one size fits all" approach, psychotherapies have been developed to treat specific psychological disorders. For some disorders, psychotherapy alone is helpful. For many others, a combination of pharmacotherapy (medication) and psychotherapy leads to the best outcome.

15.2 Guiding Question

To guide your reading of the text, review the following question. Then, as you read the chapter, look for the answers to this question. You may want to note in your textbook where you find these answers.

1. Identify the treatments that are most effective for specific psychological disorders.

NOW READ Section 15.2 "What Are the Most Effective Treatments?" keeping this question in mind.

REVIEW: Now that you've read this section, go back to the 15.2 Guiding Question and see if you can answer it based on what you've read. This is a check on your reading. If you can't answer the question, you need to go back to the text to reread that section.

VISUAL SUMMARY: Below is a summary of the major concepts in this section. To check your comprehension of the chapter, read the summary and ask yourself if you understand the concepts. If the concepts seem unfamiliar to you, you may want to go back to the book and reread those sections. This text is taken from the Visual Summaries on StudySpace at wwnorton.com/studyspace.

IX. Effectiveness of Treatment Is Determined by Empirical Evidence
   A. Psychological disorders are best treated by techniques demonstrated through scientific research to be most effective.

X. Treatments That Focus on Behavior and on Cognition Are Superior for Anxiety Disorders
   A. Phobias: best treated through systematic desensitization.
   B. Panic disorder: best treated with cognitive-behavioral therapy.
   C. Obsessive-compulsive disorder: best treated with cognitive-behavioral therapy or exposure with response prevention.

XI. Many Effective Treatments Are Available for Depression
   A. Treatment options:
      i. pharmacological therapy (MAOI, SSRI)
      ii. cognitive-behavioral therapy
      iii. alternative therapies (ECT, TMS, DBS)
   B. The placebo effect needs to be considered in judging effectiveness of medication.
   C. There are differences in the rates of depression in men and in women.

XII. Lithium Is Most Effective for Bipolar Disorder
   A. Lithium is an "anti-manic" drug.
   B. Bipolar disorder is often treated with both lithium and antidepressants.

XIII. Pharmacological Treatments Are Superior for Schizophrenia
   A. Typical antipsychotics (e.g., Haldol) and atypical ones (e.g., Risperdal):
      i. are the best treatment for schizophrenia.
      ii. may have side effects.
   B. Social skills training can be a useful adjunct to pharmacological treatment.
   C. Most individuals with schizophrenia improve over time.

REINFORCE: Are you ready to check your knowledge of this section? Answer the following multiple-choice questions with your textbook closed.

1. Barlow, among many other clinical and research psychologists, has argued that:

a. psychologists should make greater use of evidence-based treatments
b. the research community should be more open to alternative treatments, even if the treatments have little validation
c. treatment techniques should be developed in the "real" world rather than in the psychological laboratory
d. psychological theory is the most important aspect of developing new treatments

2. The best approach for treating anxiety disorders is:
a. psychoanalytic therapy
b. the use of psychoactive drugs
c. cognitive-behavioral therapy
d. deep brain stimulation

3. A friend reports that he is constructing a fear hierarchy regarding his fear of heights for use in his next therapy session. He is suffering from:
a. hallucinations related to schizophrenia
b. obsessive-compulsive disorder
c. depression
d. a phobia

4. One of the most effective treatments for panic disorder is _____ because it helps people _____.
a. cognitive therapy; correctly estimate the danger involved in a panic attack
b. rational-emotive therapy; challenge their sense of low self-control
c. transcranial magnetic stimulation; pair panic experiences with relaxation
d. shock therapy; compare their own mildly distressing symptoms to strong and persistent physical discomfort

5. Lee-Joon is participating in a research study. The researchers are comparing brain changes in people receiving different types of treatment for obsessive-compulsive disorder. Lee-Joon recently completed cognitive behavioral therapy and now will have his brain scanned. Compared to people receiving other kinds of therapy, Lee-Joon's brain:
a. will show little change, because cognitive behavioral therapy is not a biological treatment
b. will show the same brain changes as people receiving drug therapy
c. will show increased brain changes but not in the same areas as people receiving drug therapy
d. will show changes in brain function, whereas those receiving drug therapy will not

6. In a study in which treatment with the drug clomipramine was compared with exposure and ritual prevention for obsessive-compulsive disorder, it was found that:
a. exposure and response prevention was more effective

b. the drug was the superior treatment
c. neither worked better than a placebo
d. both forms of treatment were equally effective

7. Tyresia is experiencing a depressive episode and undergoes cognitive therapy to treat her symptoms. If she were in therapy with Aaron Beck, she would most likely be asked to challenge her negative thoughts about:
a. herself and her upbringing
b. herself, her situation, and the future
c. her future as a successful human being
d. her skills and assets

8. _____ is best treated with medication. This treatment can be a problem because _____.
a. Depression; people with depression are often too apathetic to take their medication
b. Depression; there are few good pharmacological treatments available
c. Bipolar disorder; the drugs are so expensive almost no one can afford them
d. Bipolar disorder; aspects of the disorder are considered pleasurable and attractive, so there is an incentive to stop taking the medication

9. Clozapine was an improvement over previous antipsychotic medications because it:
a. acted specifically on the dopamine neurotransmitter system
b. reduced the negative as well as the positive symptoms of schizophrenia
c. had only moderate Parkinsonian effects
d. also worked for disorders such as bipolar disorder

10. Odelia has schizophrenia and has been successfully treated with medication; her visual and auditory hallucinations have decreased, and she no longer believes that her great aunt speaks to her through the television. However, Odelia still has some odd behaviors, and others view her as a little strange. Odelia's doctor will most likely recommend that she receive:
a. social skills training
b. emotion management training
c. assertiveness training
d. dialectical behavior training

WHAT DID YOU MISS? Check your answers against the Answer Key at the end of this chapter of the Study Guide. The Answer Key also lists the page(s) in your text where each question is explained. If you missed any questions, go to the pages indicated in the Answer Key, reread those sections, go back to the questions, and see if you can answer them correctly this time.

ANOTHER OPPORTUNITY TO REVIEW: Answer this question without your textbook. As a rule of thumb, if you can write only a few words about this question, you probably need to go back and review.

1. Identify the treatments that are most effective for specific psychological disorders. _____

_____

_____

WHAT DO I NEED TO KNOW? Based on what you've discovered above, what are the areas where you need to focus your studying? Which objectives do you need to spend more time mastering? Write this information down in your own words.

1. _____

2. _____

3. _____

4. _____

5. _____

6. _____

15.3 Can Personality Disorders Be Treated?

Personality disorders can be distressing to the people with the disorders or to the people in their lives, and they are often difficult to treat. However, effective treatments have been developed for both antisocial and borderline personality disorders.

15.3 Guiding Question

To guide your reading of the text, review the following question. Then, as you read the chapter, look for the answers to this question. You may want to note in your textbook where you find these answers.

1. Discuss therapeutic approaches for borderline personality disorder and antisocial personality disorder.

NOW READ Section 15.3 "Can Personality Disorders Be Treated?" keeping this question in mind.

REVIEW: Now that you've read this section, go back to the 15.3 Guiding Question and see if you can answer it based on what you've read. This is a check on your reading. If you can't answer the question, you need to go back to the text to reread that section.

VISUAL SUMMARY: Below is a summary of the major concepts in this section. To check your comprehension of the chapter, read the summary and ask yourself if you understand the concepts. If the concepts seem unfamiliar to you, you may want to go back to the book and reread those sections. This text is taken from the Visual Summaries on StudySpace at wwnorton.com/studyspace.

XIV. Individuals with Personality Disorders May Not Respond to Treatment because They Often See the Environment Rather Than Their Own Behavior as the Cause of Their Problems

XV. Dialectical Behavior Therapy Is Most Successful for Borderline Personality Disorder (BPD)
  A. Dialectical behavior therapy: changing cognitions, behaviors, and developing emotion regulation skills through the use of mindfulness.
  B. Patients with BPD who show long-term improvement are those who receive intensive treatment.

XVI. Antisocial Personality Disorder Is Extremely Difficult to Treat
  A. Treatment is made difficult by patients':
    i. lack of concern for rights of others.
    ii. lack of concern for the consequences of their own actions.
    iii. tendency to lie.
  B. Prognosis is poor, but behavioral and cognitive approaches have demonstrated greatest effectiveness.

REINFORCE: Are you ready to check your knowledge of this section? Answer the following multiple-choice questions with your textbook closed.

1. People with borderline personality disorder (BPD) would be easier to treat if:
   a. there were beneficial treatments available
   b. a simple version of behavior therapy could be tailored to BPD behaviors
   c. the patients saw their behavior as problematic
   d. drugs were available to treat BPD cognitive distortions

2. Shanaia has recently been treated with antidepressants and is engaging in intensive, long-term therapy in an inpatient setting. The best form of therapy for her disorder includes elements of behavioral and cognitive therapy along with mindfulness meditation. Shanaia has:
   a. severe depression
   b. bipolar disorder
   c. borderline personality disorder
   d. obsessive-compulsive disorder

3. About personality disorders, we can say that:

a. we know a great deal about their causes and effective treatments

b. effective treatments have been devised in the absence of understanding their causes

c. compared to other forms of mental difficulty, they are relatively easy to treat

d. individuals suffering such disorders are seldom motivated to seek treatment

4. Most therapists agree that personality disorders, such as borderline personality disorder and antisocial personality disorder:

a. are difficult to treat

b. respond to drugs such as selective serotonin reuptake inhibitors

c. are well understood in terms of their causes

d. tend to go away on their own

5. The individuals with borderline personality disorder who have the best prognosis are:

a. those who have received drug interventions

b. those treated on an outpatient rather than an inpatient basis

c. individuals from high socioeconomic conditions who have received intensive treatment

d. those who have received cognitive therapy

6. Individuals with antisocial personality disorder are difficult to treat because they:

a. are so focused on the future that they lose sight of their present difficulties

b. care little about how others feel about their behavior

c. have excessively low self-esteem and feel therapists will not want to treat them

d. view their problems as too overwhelming to treat

7. Currently, the best approach to treating borderline personality disorder is:

a. traditional psychotherapy

b. dialectical behavioral therapy

c. behavior modification

d. antipsychotic drugs

8. Therapy for antisocial personality disorder appears to work best:

a. if it is done on an inpatient basis or in a correctional facility

b. the patient has control over when the therapy sessions are held

c. if therapy is done on an individual rather than a group basis

d. if antipsychotic drugs are used as part of the treatment

9. Individuals with antisocial personality disorder:

a. are very responsive to treatment

b. are responsive to treatment if it is used before age 40

TRY IT

You Are What You Think

As you have seen throughout this chapter, the cognitive-behavioral model consistently comes out on top as the psychotherapy treatment of choice. This model is practical and useful whether you have a psychological disorder or you are dealing with some of the negative moods that can occur for most of us. Again, to review, the model is based on the idea that how we talk to ourselves, how we explain the events in our lives to ourselves, determines whether we feel dysthymic (in a bad mood) or euthymic (in a good mood). According to one of the techniques in this model, you can change your mood by changing your negative thinking to more realistic thinking. Here's a simple version of the technique.

When you feel dysthymic (upset, anxious, etc.), stop and ask yourself, "How do I feel?" and "What am I saying to myself?" If you find yourself replying, "I am a failure," "I'm not handling my relationships well," or something negative like that, write down what you are saying and then ask yourself, "Is this always true?" "Am I always like this?" Chances are, what you have been saying is not always true or completely true. Then ask yourself, "What would I tell a good friend who was describing this situation to me?" You probably would not tell your good friend, "Yeah, that's true. You *are* a failure." You would probably say something like, "Sometimes you may be unsuccessful, but other times you're very successful." Now, practice saying that modified and more realistic statement to yourself. According to the cognitive-behavioral model and documented by a large amount of research supporting this model, if you consistently change your pattern of thinking in this way (and in ways like this!), you will change your mood.

---

c. tend to improve after age 40 without therapeutic intervention

d. respond best to relationship-based psychotherapies, such as client-centered therapy

10. Tommy has a 20-year history of stealing, armed robbery, physical violence, and lying and cheating to get out of trouble. These behaviors started in grade school. Based on what is known about the origins and treatment of this kind of disorder, which of the following statements would best represent a knowledgeable psychiatrist's opinion on Tommy's treatment options?

a. "Tommy, I wish that someone had intervened with you when you were younger. I think you could have been helped more effectively then."

b. "Tommy, given the outstanding history of deviance you have had, hospitalization is your best option."

c. "Tommy, the best treatment for you currently is deep brain stimulation, which might remove some of your impulsive and aggressive tendencies."

d. "Tommy, the most promising treatment option for you right now is heavy medication, including lithium and perhaps an antipsychotic."

WHAT DID YOU MISS? Check your answers against the Answer Key at the end of this chapter of the Study Guide. The Answer Key also lists the page(s) in your text where each question is explained. If you missed any questions, go to the pages indicated in the Answer Key, reread those sections, go back to the questions, and see if you can answer them correctly this time.

ANOTHER OPPORTUNITY TO REVIEW: Answer this question without your textbook. As a rule of thumb, if you can write only a few words about this question, you probably need to go back and review.

1. Discuss therapeutic approaches for borderline personality disorder and antisocial personality disorder. _____

_____

_____

WHAT DO I NEED TO KNOW? Based on what you've discovered above, what are the areas where you need to focus your studying? Which objectives do you need to spend more time mastering? Write this information down in your own words.

1. _____

2. _____

3. _____

4. _____

5. _____

6. _____

15.4 How Should Childhood Disorders and Adolescent Disorders Be Treated?

What is the best treatment for children and adolescents with depression? Are there any risks for adolescents in using anti-depressant medication? Is medication alone the best way to help children with autism or ADHD?

15.4 Guiding Questions

To guide your reading of the text, review the following questions. Then, as you read the chapter, look for the answers to these questions. You may want to note in your textbook where you find these answers.

1. Discuss the current controversy regarding the use of drugs to treat depression among adolescents.

2. Identify drugs and behavioral treatments for ADHD.

3. Describe applied behavioral analysis.

4. Discuss the use of oxytocin in the treatment of autism.

NOW READ Section 15.4 "How Should Childhood Disorders and Adolescent Disorders Be Treated?" keeping these questions in mind.

REVIEW: Now that you've read this section, go back to the 15.4 Guiding Questions and see if you can answer them based on what you've read. This is a check on your reading. If you can't answer a question, you need to go back to the text to reread that section.

VISUAL SUMMARY: Below is a summary of the major concepts in this section. To check your comprehension of the chapter, read the summary and ask yourself if you understand the concepts. If the concepts seem unfamiliar to you, you may want to go back to the book and reread those sections. This text is taken from the Visual Summaries on StudySpace at wwnorton.com/studyspace.

XVII. The Use of Medication to Treat Adolescent Depression Is Controversial
 A. Combining antidepressant drugs with cognitive-behaviorial therapy provides the best outcomes.
 B. Some adolescents who take antidepressants experience suicidal thoughts, but:
  i. this happens rarely.
  ii. the benefits from the drugs seem to outweigh the risks.

XVIII. Children with ADHD Can Benefit from Various Approaches
 A. Children with ADHD respond best to stimulant medication combined with behavioral therapy.

XIX. Children with Autism Benefit from Structured Behavioral Treatment

A. Understanding behavioral analysis is an intensive treatment for autism based on operant conditioning.

B. Traditional psychotropic medications do not seem effective, but oxytocin seems to improve social contact and relatedness.

C. Early diagnosis is most helpful, but individuals with severe autism are less likely to improve, even with treatment.

REINFORCE: Are you ready to check your knowledge of this section? Answer the following multiple-choice questions with your textbook closed.

1. All other variables being equal, which of the following adolescents would be most likely to experience suicidal thinking during treatment?
   a. Tammy, who is taking a tricyclic
   b. Jahangir, who is in cognitive-behavioral therapy
   c. Juan, who is taking Prozac
   d. Lee, who is taking a placebo

2. Dr. Ramos, a psychiatrist, treats many adolescent patients who suffer from depression. She often treats these patients with selective serotonin reuptake inhibitors, such as Prozac. If she would like to add a treatment component that has been shown to improve outcomes for adolescents, she should recommend both Prozac and:
   a. dialectical behavior therapy
   b. client-centered group therapy
   c. exposure and response prevention
   d. cognitive-behavioral therapy

3. Both _____ and _____ have proven effective in the treatment of adolescent depression; these results indicate that _____.
   a. Prozac; tricyclics; chemical interventions may be most appropriate for adolescent depression
   b. Prozac; Ritalin; adolescent depression is multifaceted and complex
   c. long-term cognitive behavioral therapy; short-term psychodynamic therapy; adolescents need to find a treatment approach that works for them
   d. cognitive-behavioral therapy; interpersonal therapy; psychological treatments may be the best treatment option if adolescents will comply with them

4. The drug Ritalin is a _____ that leads to _____ in children with attention deficit hyperactivity disorder.
   a. peripheral nervous system depressant; decreased motor activity
   b. peripheral nervous system stimulant; increased motor control

   c. central nervous system depressant; decreased brain activity
   d. central nervous system stimulant; increased attention

5. The major benefit of _____ for treating attention deficit hyperactivity disorder is _____.
   a. client-centered group therapy; social support
   b. Ritalin; improvement that is incremental and increases over time
   c. behavior therapy; more long-lasting outcomes than medication alone
   d. cognitive therapy; greater academic success

6. Based on what is known about the characteristics of autism, which of the following therapy techniques would be most effective in encouraging a child with autism to make appropriate eye contact with a therapist?
   a. play therapy, where the child with autism could first see eye contact modeled with dolls
   b. behavioral modeling, where the child with autism could watch as an adult and a child without autism modeled eye contact
   c. reinforcement with food, where a therapist could give a small food reward each time the child with autism made appropriate eye contact
   d. drug therapy, where the child with autism would be put on a GABA agonist medication to reduce self-stimulatory behaviors; reducing inappropriate behaviors can lead to the expression of more-appropriate behaviors, such as making eye contact

7. Which of the following is a likely outcome for a child with autism in applied behavior analysis treatment for 2 years or more?
   a. Intelligence, as assessed by an IQ test, will increase so that the child will probably be able to enter regular kindergarten.
   b. Social skills will be excellent.
   c. Inappropriate behaviors will have decreased or be totally eliminated.
   d. Subjective well-being or happiness will be the same as that of other children.

8. How do SSRIs affect children with autism?
   a. The drugs reduce repetitive, self-stimulating behaviors.
   b. The drugs improve mood and make behavioral treatments easier to implement.
   c. The drugs increase social bonding.
   d. The drugs do not produce effects in children with autism, even though they work effectively on other disorders, such as depression and obsessive-compulsive disorder.

9. When the drug Ritalin is given to children with attention deficit hyperactivity disorder, it:
   a. dramatically increases positive behaviors while slightly reducing negative ones
   b. increases positive behaviors while leaving negative ones relatively unaffected
   c. slightly increases positive behaviors while dramatically reducing negative ones
   d. reduces arousal and hyperactivity, but has little effect on specific, overt behaviors

10. According to your textbook, the prognosis for a child with autism is:
    a. often poor because most treatments are difficult to maintain or have not shown promise
    b. poor if the child is treated with behavioral modification
    c. excellent if biological treatments are used
    d. good if the disease appears later in life

WHAT DID YOU MISS? Check your answers against the Answer Key at the end of this chapter of the Study Guide. The Answer Key also lists the page(s) in your text where each question is explained. If you missed any questions, go to the pages indicated in the Answer Key, reread those sections, go back to the questions, and see if you can answer them correctly this time.

ANOTHER OPPORTUNITY TO REVIEW: Answer these questions without your textbook. As a rule of thumb, if you can write only a few words about these questions, you probably need to go back and review.

1. Discuss the current controversy regarding the use of drugs to treat depression among adolescents. _____

2. Identify drugs and behavioral treatments for ADHD. ____

3. Describe applied behavioral analysis. _____

4. Discuss the use of oxytocin in the treatment of autism.

WHAT DO I NEED TO KNOW? Based on what you've discovered above, what are the areas where you need to focus your studying? Which objectives do you need to spend more time mastering? Write this information down in your own words.

1. _____
2. _____
3. _____
4. _____
5. _____
6. _____

WHAT MATTERS TO ME: What facts in this chapter are personally relevant to you?

_____
_____
_____
_____

CHAPTER SUMMARY

15.1 How Are Psychological Disorders Treated?

- *Psychotherapy Is Based on Psychological Principles:* Psychotherapy is the generic name for formal psychological treatment. Psychodynamic treatment focuses on insight and uncovering unconscious conflicts. Humanistic approaches focus on the person as a whole, encouraging personal growth through self-understanding. Behavioral approaches focus on modifying maladaptive behaviors. Cognitive approaches restructure thinking. Group therapy is cost-effective, improves social skills, and provides support. Family therapy adopts a systems approach, seeing the individual as part of a larger context.
- *Culture Can Affect the Therapeutic Process:* Culture influences the expression of psychological disorders, recovery from psychological disorders, and willingness to seek psychotherapy. In some cultures, mental health problems and psychotherapy are highly stigmatized, preventing people from seeking help. Psychologists must be prepared to provide culturally sensitive assistance to people from different cultural backgrounds with different belief systems.
- *Medication Is Effective for Certain Disorders:* Psychotropic medications change neurochemistry. Anti-anxiety drugs increase GABA activity. Antidepressants affect serotonin availability. Antipsychotics block the effects of dopamine, reducing positive symptoms.
- *Alternative Biological Treatments Are Used in Extreme Cases:* When traditional treatments are not successful, alternative treatments are used. These include psychosurgery, electroconvulsive therapy, transcranial magnetic stimulation, and deep brain stimulation.

• *Therapies Not Supported by Scientific Evidence Can Be Dangerous:* Increasingly, psychologists are turning to evidence-based practices. Some treatment approaches that have no credible evidence to support their use have proved detrimental, and all may prevent or delay a patient from receiving effective evidence-based therapy.

• *A Variety of Providers Can Assist in Treatment for Psychological Disorders:* A variety of specialized mental health practitioners exist. These specialists include clinical psychologists, psychiatrists, counseling psychologists, psychiatric social workers, psychiatric nurses, and paraprofessionals. The providers differ in their training and work in diverse settings.

15.2 What Are the Most Effective Treatments?

• *Effectiveness of Treatment Is Determined by Empirical Evidence:* Randomized clinical trials should be used to assess the effectiveness of treatments for psychological disorders. Psychological treatments vary according to the particular disorder being addressed, are based on techniques developed in the lab by psychologists, and are not guided by a single, overall grand theory.

• *Treatments That Focus on Behavior and on Cognition Are Superior for Anxiety Disorders:* Behavioral methods—in particular, systematic desensitization and exposure—alleviate specific phobias. Cognitive restructuring, coupled with exposure, is effective in treating panic disorder. Obsessive-compulsive disorder (OCD) responds to medications that block serotonin reuptake and to exposure and response prevention. Deep brain stimulation holds promise for the treatment of severe cases of OCD.

• *Many Effective Treatments Are Available for Depression:* Pharmacological treatments include MAO inhibitors, tricyclics, and SSRIs. Cognitive behavioral treatments target distorted cognitions—in particular, the cognitive triad. Alternative therapies include exercise, electroconvulsive therapy, transcranial magnetic stimulation, and deep brain stimulation. Sex differences in rates of depression have resulted in the development of specific guidelines for treatment.

• *Lithium Is Most Effective for Bipolar Disorder:* Lithium has been found to be most effective in stabilizing mood among bipolar patients. This drug has considerable side effects, however. Psychological therapy can help support compliance with drug treatment.

• *Pharmacological Treatments Are Superior for Schizophrenia:* First-generation antipsychotic medications are most effective for reducing the positive symptoms of schizophrenia. Tardive dyskinesia and other side effects are common with these older antipsychotic drugs. Clozapine acts specifically on neurotransmitter receptors and reduces positive and negative symptoms, with fewer side effects. Drug therapy is most effective when com-

bined with psychosocial treatment. The prognosis for patients depends on factors such as age of onset, gender, and culture.

15.3 Can Personality Disorders Be Treated?

• *Dialectical Behavior Therapy Is Most Successful for Borderline Personality Disorder:* DBT combines elements of behavioral, cognitive, and psychodynamic therapy. Therapy proceeds in three stages. First, the most extreme behaviors are targeted and replaced with more appropriate behaviors. Next, the therapist explores past traumatic events. Finally, the therapist helps the patient develop self-respect and independence.

• *Antisocial Personality Disorder Is Extremely Difficult to Treat:* Psychotherapeutic approaches have not proved effective for treating antisocial personality disorder. Behavioral and cognitive approaches have been more effective, primarily in a controlled residential treatment environment. Generally, the prognosis is poor. Focusing on prevention by addressing conduct disorder in childhood may be the best strategy.

15.4 How Should Childhood Disorders and Adolescent Disorders Be Treated?

• *The Use of Medication to Treat Adolescent Depression Is Controversial:* The use of SSRIs, such as Prozac, in the treatment of depression in adolescents is increasingly common. SSRIs may lead to increased suicidality, but the available evidence indicates that such medications may have more benefits than costs. Cognitive-behavioral treatment is also effective in the treatment of depression, particularly when combined with drug treatment.

• *Children with ADHD Can Benefit from Various Approaches:* Ritalin, despite its side effects, is an effective pharmacological treatment for ADHD. Research has provided support for the effectiveness of behavioral therapy in the treatment of ADHD, with behavioral therapy resulting in better long-term outcomes than medication therapy.

• *Children with Autism Benefit from Structured Behavioral Treatment:* Structured behavioral treatment has proved effective in improving the symptoms of autism. Applied behavioral analysis—an intensive treatment based on the principles of operant conditioning—has been used successfully in the treatment of autism. A biological treatment for autism has not been identified, but treatment with oxytocin holds promise.

PUTTING IT ALL TOGETHER

Answer these questions to check your knowledge of the material in this chapter.

1. A friend of yours has been suffering symptoms of depression, lacking energy and finding himself unable to concentrate. As you are taking a course in psychology, he asks you what you know about psychotherapy and how to find a psychotherapist. Summarize for him the types of specialized practitioners who treat psychological disorders and what to look for in choosing a psychotherapist.

2. You friend with depression comes back to see you. His therapist has suggested that he engage in exercise to help alleviate his depression, and he wants to know what you think. What can you tell him about the most effective treatments for depression?

3. A member of your family is constantly in trouble. He has engaged in numerous sociopathic activities (e.g., lying with little remorse, theft, fraud) and would qualify for the diagnosis of antisocial personality disorder (APD). Your family is considering sending the person in trouble to a treatment center that focuses on behavior and cognition. Summarize the research on treatment for APD and make recommendations to the family.

4. Your school-age nephew has received a diagnosis of ADHD from a licensed psychologist, but his classroom teacher says that all he needs is a little "structure." Based on research findings, make recommendations to your nephew's parents about what to do.

ANSWER KEY FOR REINFORCE QUESTIONS

Section 15.1

1. a p. 675
2. c p. 676
3. d p. 678
4. b p. 680
5. b p. 680
6. c p. 679
7. a p. 683
8. b p. 684
9. c p. 687
10. b p. 689

Section 15.2

1. a p. 693
2. c p. 693
3. d p. 694
4. a p. 695
5. b p. 696
6. a p. 696
7. b p. 701
8. d p. 705
9. b p. 706
10. a p. 707

Section 15.3

1. c p. 709
2. c p. 710
3. d p. 709
4. a p. 709
5. c p. 710
6. b p. 711
7. b p. 710
8. a p. 711
9. c p. 712
10. a p. 712

Section 15.4

1. c p. 714
2. d p. 714
3. d p. 716
4. d p. 717
5. c p. 719
6. c p. 719
7. a p. 719
8. a p. 720
9. c p. 717
10. a p. 721

HINTS FOR PUTTING IT ALL TOGETHER QUESTIONS

1. Answers should discuss the practitioners mentioned in the text, including clinical psychologists, psychiatrists, counseling psychologists, psychiatric social workers, psychiatric nurses, and paraprofessionals. The friend needs to find someone he can trust and with whom he can establish a productive therapeutic relationship.

2. Answers should summarize some of the effective treatments for depression, including antidepressants, cognitive-behavioral therapy, exercise, ECT, transcranial magnetic stimulation, and deep brain stimulation. Answers might also mention gender differences in the treatment of depression.

3. Answers should address the issue that behavioral and cognitive approaches are sometimes used to treat antisocial personality disorder; however, no approach appears to be particularly effective. Some individuals reduce their antisocial behavior after age 40.

4. Answers should note that medications such as Ritalin can be quite effective in treating children with ADHD. In the long term, however, behavioral therapy may be more effective than the use of psychotropic drugs. Many practitioners will combine these approaches.

KEY TERMS EXERCISES

First, fill in your own definition and example for each term. Then check each term against the textbook's definition. These exercises can also be cut out and used as flash cards.

anti-anxiety drugs

Your Definition:
Your Example:
Textbook Definition:

behavior therapy

Your Definition:
Your Example:
Textbook Definition:

antidepressants

Your Definition:
Your Example:
Textbook Definition:

biological therapies

Your Definition:
Your Example:
Textbook Definition:

antipsychotics

Your Definition:
Your Example:
Textbook Definition:

client-centered therapy

Your Definition:
Your Example:
Textbook Definition:

applied behavioral analysis (ABA)

Your Definition:
Your Example:
Textbook Definition:

cognitive-behavioral therapy (CBT)

Your Definition:
Your Example:
Textbook Definition:

cognitive restructuring

Your Definition:

Your Example:

Textbook Definition:

expressed emotion

Your Definition:

Your Example:

Textbook Definition:

cognitive therapy

Your Definition:

Your Example:

Textbook Definition:

insight

Your Definition:

Your Example:

Textbook Definition:

dialectical behavior therapy (DBT)

Your Definition:

Your Example:

Textbook Definition:

psychotherapy

Your Definition:

Your Example:

Textbook Definition:

electroconvulsive therapy (ECT)

Your Definition:

Your Example:

Textbook Definition:

psychotropic medications

Your Definition:

Your Example:

Textbook Definition:

exposure

Your Definition:

Your Example:

Textbook Definition:

3